The Daily Telegraph
HOW WE SAW IT

First published in Great Britain
in 2004
1 3 5 7 9 10 8 6 4 2

First published by Ebury Press
Random House, 20 Vauxhall Bridge
Road, London SW1V 2SA

Random House Australia (Pty) Limited
20 Alfred Street, Milsons Point, Sydney,
New South Wales 2061, Australia
Random House New Zealand Limited
18 Poland Road, Glenfield,
Auckland 10,
New Zealand
Random House South Africa
(Pty) Limited
Endulini, 5A Jubilee Road,
Parktown 2193, South Africa
The Random House Group Limited
Reg. No. 954009

www.randomhouse.co.uk

A CIP catalogue record for this book
is available from the British Library.
ISBN 0 091 89463 8

Papers used by Ebury Press are
natural, recyclable products
made from wood grown in
sustainable forests.

Reproduction by Telegraph Imaging.
Printed and bound
in Singapore by Tien Wah.

Body type set in Janson.
Headlines set in Telegraph Light,
cut by Monotype, based on the
Telegraph headline face designed
by Walter Tracy, Victor Clarke
and Shelley Winters.

*Top right: the old Daily Telegraph
device and motto – 'Was, Is & Will Be'
– which appeared above the paper's
leader column. It was designed by
the College of Arms*

THE DAILY TELEGRAPH

HOW WE SAW IT

1855–2005

Christopher Howse

Christopher Howse

EBURY
PRESS

LUDGATE HILL & CIRCUS FROM FLEET STREET. 4523.

L.S.&P.Co.

Looking east from the Telegraph in 1897, down Fleet Street, full of horse buses advertising soap and milk, with an engine of the London Chatham and Dover Railway crossing the viaduct demolished only in 1990

Foreword
W.F. Deedes

Where there is hope in these catastrophes

There are so many ways of reading the last 150 years of this country's history, on which these pages dwell. Those of a certain disposition might conclude we spent the first half of them grabbing an empire and the second half dissolving it. Others will see it as an epoch in which we built up great strength and wealth, only to dissipate much of it by fighting two world wars.

It has been a time in which a cynic might observe that the long political struggle to win universal suffrage created an electorate so bored by politics that many omitted to use their vote. The radical will see it as a time in which the class distinctions, privilege and degree of the Victorian age were slowly translated into a more equal society. An older generation, turning their mind to what they have read about men like Peel, Palmerston, Gladstone, Disraeli and Salisbury, might conclude – wrongly in my view – that we are today governed by pygmies.

However you choose to read them, the 150 years of the life of this newspaper were momentous years. For almost half of them, starting in 1931 as a reporter, I have had a view of events from the stalls. This second slice of years has been shaped to an extent few appreciate by the First World War, the greatest catastrophe of modern times.

The Victorian years were not half as peaceful as we suppose. The Crimean War, breaking into two mid-Victorian decades of roaring prosperity and quiet politics, was a national disgrace, marked by the incompetence of our higher command. We have the word of Florence Nightingale that 16,000 lives – more than half the total of dead – were lost by bad administration. The Indian Mutiny of 1857 was a revolt of troops rather than population; but it reflected unease in the great mass of Indian opinion at the pace Westernisation was proceeding. The second Boer War 1899–1902, in which my father fought and which brings us into Churchill's time, was also marked, before Roberts and Kitchener, by pretty indifferent generalship.

But when we come to the assassination of the Austrian archduke at Sarajevo in 1914 and what came after it, Tennyson's lines ring true:

Far other is this battle in the west,
Whereto we move, than when we strove in youth,
And brake the petty kings.

This is not the place to rehearse the history of either World War; but the second half of this narrative is easier to understand if we accept the extent to which the Great War enfeebled us, led indirectly to the Second World War of 1939–45, accelerated the end of Empire, transformed European thinking and reverberates beyond the close of the 20th century.

There are other themes which this panorama displays. It is mistaken to view the Victorian age as stuffy, sexually repressed and buttoned up. There were people like Galsworthy's Soames Forsyte, but there were also the powerful influences of John Bright, W.E. Forster, Charles Darwin and John Stuart Mill and others, which many followed. By the standards of today, the living conditions of the poorer three-quarters of the country were deplorable; but as with all human progress, such conditions provoked action.

The last two decades of the century, sometimes known as "municipal socialism", produced baths, wash-houses, museums, public libraries, parks, gardens, open spaces and allotments, all of them on the rates. There was a great awakening of voluntary effort, settlements such as Toynbee Hall in the East End of London were established, the Salvation Army came to life, the Fabians under the Sidney Webbs entered the field and trade union activity expanded. Silently, the Industrial Revolution began to obliterate old distinctions of rank and creed.

A view of events from the stalls: William Deedes in characteristic pose (above, right) at the leader-writers' desk at the Telegraph. He set off (left) in 1935 to report from Abyssinia, where he was to meet Evelyn Waugh and help to inspire his novel 'Scoop'. (Extracts from W.F. Deedes's despatches from the depressed areas of Britain in 1937 feature on page 170.) He won an MC in 1944. He was elected MP in 1950 while continuing his career with the Telegraph, and joined the Cabinet in 1962. He edited The Daily Telegraph from 1974 to 1986, in which year he was created a peer, but he continued to write frequent leading articles and features

'However you choose to read them, the 150 years of the life of this newspaper were momentous years'

The days of *The Daily Telegraph* began a decade after the Irish famine of 1845–46, which led to wholesale emigration to the United States of America. For some years the ordeal left Ireland prostrate and incapable of agitation; but eventually the Fenian Movement arose as a reminder of the legacy left by that famine, a legacy with us to this day. Gladstone was the first politician to take the conciliation of Ireland seriously. His pursuit of Home Rule or self-government for Ireland, which it had lost in 1800, twice caused the fall of his governments. When Home Rule came after the First World War, it divided the island between a Roman Catholic majority and a Protestant minority; and it so remains. The toils of Ireland extend throughout the lifetime of *The Daily Telegraph*.

Wars accelerate invention, mainly though not exclusively of military weapons. The Victorian age did relatively little to strengthen the arm of its military. In the last three-quarters of a century, man has developed a capacity for destruction which is awesome. The choice open to him now lies between harnessing his more dazzling inventions such as nuclear power towards improving the human condition or laying his world to waste. We enter an era in which choice becomes paramount.

Some will declare that the greatest change wrought in Britain in the last century and a half lies in the composition of our population. At the turn of the century we were welcoming refugees to these shores. The coming of the steamboat diminished our insularity. Both world wars, particularly the second, led to pressure on our gates. But it was the wave of Commonwealth immigration in the 1950s which began radically to alter some of our neighbourhoods.

Travelling with a parliamentary committee through the sub-continent and the Caribbean twice during the 1970s, I learned something about the source of this huge spring, which in recent years has broadened. A great part of the world now sees Britain as a desirable country of residence. When the steamship replaced the sail, a door was pushed ajar. When aeroplanes took to the skies the door was pushed wide open. Every country has a digestive capacity in this respect; and that is for government to judge. Experience suggests that on this judgment good race relations heavily depend.

In the course of this narrative Christopher Howse notes some of the tensions within the Established Church. Today the changed composition of our population has led to differences not simply within the Church of England but between the world's faiths. This part of our story lies in the years ahead.

My own hopes spring from experience in reporting for this newspaper catastrophes overseas such as earthquakes, famines and wars, which bring from all quarters of the earth helping hands to whom religious differences are of no account. When you have watched aid workers of Christian and Muslim and other faiths and of no religious faith at all, working together to shield women and children from death, united for humanity's sake, you have caught a glimpse of what is possible. You have seen a sign in the sky.

Introduction
Christopher Howse

A very surprising navigation with no chart to go by

Christopher Howse

> ❝I have rummaged happily through volumes bound in crumbly leather, covering myself with dust and wondering how people could have managed with such small type ❞

Opposite: Mafeking relieved – big news in a 14-page Saturday edition in 1900. The newsboys themselves folded the large sheets into papers

The dominant emotion in looking at the world through the eyes of *The Daily Telegraph* of the past 150 years is surprise. It is a surprise that Victorians in the 1880s wanted to read so much about sexual immorality that they happily devoured 170,000 words on the trial of W.T. Stead, who kidnapped – or bought – a 13-year-old girl. That is a greater wordage than the whole of this book.

It is a surprise that Colt revolvers were advertised freely for sale on the front page; that the custody of an elephant should be determined in the High Court of Chancery; that Queen Victoria should have attempted personally to revive an old man drowned when her yacht cut his schooner in two; that thousands rioted in Hyde Park when pub opening hours on Sundays were curtailed; that opium should in a leading article be praised over ganja; that mobs should be allowed to cause disturbance inside a church every Sunday for a year; that a building 600ft long stood opposite Westminster Abbey full of performing animals and women on trapezes; that milk was sold in the Mall from cows in St James's Park.

A century ago some things were surprisingly similar to those that we complain about today. "A state of terror exists," an inner-city magistrate said in 1898, "which is appalling in a civilised country." He was talking about lawless young thugs given the name "Hooligans", who were swearing, barging and robbing people in the street. "Where are the police?" asked readers repeatedly in the 19th century when they had been burgled or terrified on a railway journey.

It wasn't just law and order that showed recognisable traits. Trains crashed in the 1860s and 1950s, and no one would take the blame. Some days it was hotter than ever before; some days the Thames froze. Fashion exercised its iron law of absurdity – making women wear stuffed birds on their heads or corset themselves so tightly they could not sit down; and for men, if Oscar Wilde's advice in the *Telegraph* was to be heeded, it was goodbye to trousers in favour of silk stockings. Indeed Prince Albert, decades earlier, had himself painted sitting next to Victoria with no trousers on, but what were then known as "tights", combined with Puss-in-Boots turnover footwear (page 11).

And how energetic people were under Victoria. They would bicycle off 200 miles to York at midnight, or swim the Channel fortified by brandy and hot coffee. (Though, in 1926, the first woman to swim the Channel even managed to consume slices of pineapple as she went.) They dug up all London for sewers and Undergrounds and new roads.

Then, how vividly Bennet Burleigh, a correspondent who covered 24 wars, conveyed what it is like to be attacked in battle from all sides by warriors with sword and spears. Eyewitness accounts fill in vivid details that television cameras now miss.

There was the very moment in 1861 when the 270 feet of Chichester Cathedral's spire collapsed: "At 1.30pm the tower opened its mouth – separating on both sides – and the spire gradually sank down within it, absorbed as though an earthquake had dug its grave." There was the terrible ruin of houses in Clerkenwell, blown up by Fenian explosives in 1867. The rough sharpness, reforming zeal and jollity of

---

1855-2005
Some dates in the life of The Daily Telegraph

1855 Friday June 29 The *Daily Telegraph and Courier* first published
1855 June 30 Saturday afternoon special issue for death of Lord Raglan in the Crimea
1855 September 8 The words *"and Courier"* dropped from title on Leader page
1855 September 17 Price cut

from twopence to a penny
1855 December 31 first editor, Alfred Bate Richards, resigns
1860 *Telegraph* moves from The Strand to 135 Fleet Street
1861 Circulation rises to 141,000, almost as many as all other London dailies combined
1862 *Telegraph* appeal raises £6,000 (worth about £400,000 in today's prices) for starving cotton workers in Lancashire
1863 Supplement for wedding of Prince of Wales and Princess

Alexandra sells 200,000
1873 Edwin Arnold become "a chief editor" on the death of Thornton Leigh Hunt
1873 *Telegraph* sponsors George Smith's excavation of ancient tablets recounting Deluge story in what is today Iraq
1874 *Telegraph* sponsors H.M. Stanley's journey of exploration across Africa
1876 *Telegraph* carries daily boast: LARGEST CIRCULATION IN THE WORLD

1881 *Telegraph* pioneers artist's impression to catch Lefroy, the Railway Murderer
1882 New offices with pillared hall opened at 135 Fleet Street
1882 *Telegraph* campaigns to save London Zoo's elephant Jumbo from sale to America
1884 *Telegraph* sponsors the exploration of Kilimanjaro by Harry Johnston
1887 June 22 *Telegraph* gives party in Hyde Park for 30,000 schoolchildren, visited by Queen Victoria celebrating

her Golden Jubilee
1895 *Telegraph* raises fund of 100,000 shillings as testimonial for W.G. Grace
1896 Edwin Arnold, editor of the *Telegraph*, is disappointed not to be made Poet Laureate in succession to Tennyson
1897 Winston Churchill reports for the *Telegraph* from North-West Frontier
1899 April 9 *The Sunday Daily Telegraph* first published; it lasts seven weeks
1899 Appeal for Widows' and

the Victorians did not disappear in the 50 years up to the accession of Elizabeth in 1952. In 1856 they had fantastic pantomime special effects at Christmas; in 1935 the dancing images came through television. Kipling wrote as well from the front in 1915 as had the 22-year-old Churchill from the North-West Frontier in 1897. The wireless telegraph caught Crippen in 1910, when in 1881 it had been the first newspaper artist's impression that caught Lefroy the railway murderer. The Victorians were moved by the image of homelessness of Luke Fildes's painting *Applicants for Admission to a Casual Ward* in 1874; the Georgians of 1937 were moved to give Christmas presents in their thousand to the children of the unemployed.

The same surprising changes and similarities are found in the past 50 years – it is just that we thought we knew about the recent past. But we have forgotten how strangely different the tone of voice, the very appearance of people was when we were very young.

It has not been by accident that some themes in the later part of the book parallel or contrast with those in the earlier. My general principle for inclusion has been the opposite of that in *1066 and All That*, which was composed of all the history you can remember. I have taken most of that as read. There is no Battle of the Somme; no sinking of the *Titanic*; no hunger marchers; no Hiroshima; no moon landing; no assassination of

Kennedy; not even the fall of the World Trade Centre.

The huge, heavy bound volumes of *The Daily Telegraph* are a mine still full of treasure. I have rummaged happily through their crumbly leather binding, covering myself with dust and wondering how people could have managed with such small type. There has been an element of fortune. The volumes covering the American Civil War had been damaged by a tempest. There is no index to the tens of millions of words through the decades, and historians of the past century and a half have often gone to *The Times*, because it is indexed after a fashion. They have missed a lot. I should like to stay in those mines for years.

Anyway, this is not a history of *The Daily Telegraph*, but a slice of something of far wider interest: what buyers of a mass-appeal newspaper have wanted to know about. It is the very stuff of their daily lives. I haven't drawn on the files of *The Morning Post*, that cranky vehicle founded in 1772 and amalgamated with the *Telegraph* in 1937. There is a fashion item (page 117) from the short-lived *Sunday Daily Telegraph* in 1899, but I have not explored the files of the real *Sunday Telegraph*, a spectacular success since its foundation in 1961. It is not their anniversaries in 2005.

The Daily Telegraph itself has been making news in the past year. But newspapers have an editorial life of their own, and under Charles Moore and his successor Martin Newland, journalists have gone about their ceaseless, painstaking, stopgap task with confidence, because *The Daily Telegraph* is defined by its readers. It is the readers' world that is represented in this book, and it is vastly entertaining.

Orphans' Fund raises unheard-of sum of £255,275
1903 Sir Edward Levy-Lawson, the proprietor, created 1st Baron Burnham
1910 Exclusive reports from Atlantic by wireless telegraph of arrest of Crippen
1915 Rudyard Kipling reports from the front
1920 Statue of Edith Cavell unveiled by Queen Alexandra in London thanks to the *Telegraph*'s Nurse Cavell Memorial Fund

1924 Arthur Watson editor (until 1950).
1925 First daily crossword in a British newspaper
1928 January 18 *The Daily Telegraph* acquired by the Berry family
1930 Exclusive report on plans to arrest Gandhi
1930 Splendid new Art Deco building opened at 135 Fleet Street
1930 Price cut again from twopence to a penny, and circulation soars

1934 *Telegraph* banned in Nazi Germany
1935 World's first television column
1937 October 1 *The Morning Post* (founded November 2, 1772) amalgamates with *The Daily Telegraph*
1937 *Telegraph* launches fund to buy Christmas presents for children of unemployed
1939 April 25 News replaces small ads on front page
1947 April Daily sales exceed a million

1950 Colin Coote editor.
1964 Maurice Green editor
1964 September colour supplement appears each Friday
1974 W.F. Deedes editor
1980 Circulation rises to 1,439,000
1985 Conrad Black acquires control of *Telegraph*
1986 Max Hastings editor
1987 *Telegraph* leaves Fleet Street for the Isle of Dogs
1994 *The Electronic Telegraph* launched as the first British

daily on the internet
1995 Charles Moore editor
2000 An edition printed daily in Spain
2001 Christmas charity appeal raises £1.3 million
2003 Martin Newland becomes editor
2004 Lord Black resigns as chairman
2004 Sir Frederick and Sir David Barclay buy *Telegraph*
2005 June 29 *The Daily Telegraph* celebrates its 150th anniversary

PART 1
Victorian variety
1855–1901

The young Queen Victoria, with a little help from Albert, was happy to see part of her life as a sporting idyll, as depicted by Edwin Landseer, one of her favourite painters, in 'Windsor Castle in Modern Times' (1845)

1855 A hectic year to be

A volatile population in London was prepared to riot when Sunday drinking was
governing authority in the balance when a disgruntled army officer decided to start

HYDE PARK RIOTS

Demonstrations turn violent over Sunday drinking

When police tried to control thousands of
protesters and locked up dozens, the
Telegraph joined those who cried foul

There were riots in Hyde Park on Sunday
July 1, 1855, two days after *The Daily
Telegraph* was launched. The crowds felt
animosity towards two pieces of
legislation. One was the Sale of Beer
Act, which had just come into effect. It prohibited
public houses from serving liquor on Sundays
between 2pm and 6pm, or after 10pm.

The other piece of legislation that the crowds
disliked had not yet become law. It was the Sunday
Trading Bill, sponsored by Lord Robert Grosvenor.
He aimed, he said, at "obtaining an entire holiday
for the over-worked labouring portion of the
population". But it was the intended closure of
places to which working people could resort on a
Sunday that annoyed them, and for some it was a
threat to their livelihoods. The Bill also antagonised
political opponents of sabbatarianism.

From the first, the *Telegraph* declared its sympathies
with working people deprived of their Sunday beer.
The paper adopted a populist, anti-aristocratic, anti-
sabbatarian stance. In its second issue, on June 30, it
reported that a London solicitor was planning to
prosecute some of the gentlemen's clubs if they did
not comply with the Beer Act.

"A domiciliary visit from Scotland-yard to White's
or Boodle's," the paper commented, "would be, to
say the least, exceedingly amusing."

Not so amusing were some of the events of
Sunday July 1 when, as expected, "a vast concourse"
gathered in Hyde Park. The Sunday before, there
had been two or three hours of unruliness, with
carriages being stopped. About 120 police were
present, but no arrests were made. The Chief
Commissioner of the Metropolitan Police, Sir
Richard Mayne, was told, presumably by the Home
Secretary, Sir George Grey, that he "had not taken
sufficient means to put down the disturbance". So
on Sunday July 1, police notices were put up on
gates into the park prohibiting meetings to discuss
the Sunday Trading Bill.

The full story of what happened that afternoon
came out over the next four weeks. On Monday
July 2 the *Telegraph*'s 600-word report gave few
hints of police brutality. Sir Richard Mayne made his
headquarters at Emboro's Dairy Farm, near the
Serpentine lake. "The constables had laid themselves
on the grass, and were amusing themselves under
the shade of the trees, some reading, and others
eating cold meat and bread they had brought for
their dinners."

By 3pm, 20,000 people were said to be gathered on
the north bank of the Serpentine. "A stray vehicle
or equestrian now began to appear, and immediately
the mob commenced with groans, hisses, cries of
'Go to church' and a variety of indescribable noises,
to overwhelm the luckless individual, whose
frightened animal started, and became unmanageable,
going off at a furious rate. At this point, some of the
mob managed to get an enormous eel out of the
Serpentine, and they commenced throwing it over
the heads of the people, and, at last, at the police."
The eel was to figure prominently in investigations
into what went wrong that day.

By this time, the paper estimated, the crowd
immediately north of the Serpentine numbered
40,000. The police now received orders to clear the
carriage roads. "The constables accordingly charged
the mob with drawn truncheons, the people

INBRIEF

SEPTEMBER 17, 1855

News from the Great Salt Lake
City to the 1st of June has
come to hand. The grasshoppers
had destroyed the third crop
of grain, and starvation or an
abandonment of the settlements
were the alternatives presented
to the Mormons.

born

threatened, and war was going badly in the Crimea. Britain was a country with its
a radical newspaper. He called it the Daily Telegraph & Courier

*Policemen still wore tall
hats, not helmets, in
1855. The Telegraph
accused them of making
brutal use of their
truncheons in Hyde Park.
'We would rather be
subject to a Police Force
armed with swords rather
than staves,' it declared*

retreated in disorder, women and children were
knocked down and trampled on, several people were
forced into the Serpentine, and about forty of the
ringleaders of the mob captured." Still the crowd
increased, and carriages were told of the danger by
constables at the park gates. Eventually, "the
populace, having nothing to hoot at, gradually
dispersed". There were 104 arrests.

In a leading article, the paper called sabbatarian
legislation "the unwise interference of a few
over-sensitive religionists" but concluded that it
could not "approve of the conduct of the Hyde Park
assemblages". In its own, longer, report that day the
Times put the numbers in the Park at nearly 150,000
in all. It reported two inflammatory speeches by

unnamed orators, on the subject of Lord Robert
Grosvenor's Bill.

An immediate result of the riot was Lord Robert
Grosvenor's withdrawal of the Sunday Trading
Bill in the Commons. (Lord Robert could sit
in the Commons, since he held only a courtesy
title.) "It was not agreeable to be bullied,"
the *Telegraph* reported him telling the House.
"He repudiated the imputation that the present
Bill was intended to enforce a more stringent
observation of the Sabbath."

By the Tuesday, the *Telegraph* had adopted a
strong line against the police. "On Sunday
well-dressed females were not exempted from the
truncheon argument," it said in a leading article. As

for the police, "their long habit of dealing with 'unfortunate women' has steeled them against the common sympathies of men". It was no use Englishmen congratulating themselves that their police used only truncheons. "We would rather be subject to a Police Force armed with swords rather than staves. A truncheon aimed by a practised hand at the back of the neck, after rabbit-killing fashion, is about as deadly an accolade as an unoffending citizen can receive."

On the day after the riot, a "dense mob of persons, the majority of a very low class", some throwing stones, gathered outside Marlborough Street magistrates' court, where those arrested were to be tried. Meanwhile dozens of the accused sweltered in the summer heat in crowded cells.

The magistrate, Mr Hardwick, heard evidence from Superintendent Hughes, who was to figure largely in future proceedings. He sketched the police action to control the crowd, and in cross-examination said he "believed that all the tumult arose from Lord Robert Grosvenor's Bill, and because people wanted to eat, drink and shave on a Sunday. (Laughter)". Similar remarks about shaving, a shaft at Sunday trading restrictions under which some barbers had been charged, were to draw laughter several times in the coming weeks.

There was more laughter when a lawyer acting for many of the accused said that "among the prisoners was the son of a Member of Parliament whom the police had locked up, supposing him to be a common person". With the concurrence of the Government attorney, the magistrate allowed most of those held to be released under their own recognisances, to appear again the next day.

The next day there was no doubt about the political dimension of the trials. The Government attorney, putting Sunday's crowd at between 50,000 and 100,000, suggested that their numbers were "alone calculated to produce terror to the public". On the contrary, Mr Ballantine, the defence lawyer, urged the right of "every Englishman to meet in a public place".

The magistrate said that the law stated that any large meeting of people was likely to excite terror, but "when the large assemblage meets together for some specific object, as in the present case, to manifest dissatisfaction with some measure passing through Parliament – when it meets to coerce or deter the Legislature from passing a particular measure, the law holds the meeting to be of a tumultuous nature". He then discharged 10 men held for acting in a riotous manner, with the words, "It will be better for you if you do not again form any portion of tumultuous meetings."

The next batch to be tried were those accused of throwing stones or assaulting the police. The magistrate refused to discount the oath of a constable just because he was a constable. Any complaint against the police, he said, should be lodged with the Police Commissioners, who would refer it to a magistrate if it was well founded.

Of those accused of throwing stones, two were

jailed for a month; eight were fined 20 shillings or 14 days' prison; 14 were fined 10 shillings or seven days'; and four were discharged.

From police, rioters and the press came the frequently repeated opinion that unfair or vicious behaviour was "un-English". The *Telegraph* noted that "it was generally remarked the great number of Irishmen in the A Division [of the police], and the difficulty of understanding them correctly, or getting from them a direct answer when required to give evidence against the parties in custody". Later evidence from the police force discounted this prejudice.

On Thursday the *Telegraph* returned to the fray: "If Miss Nightingale haply returned to England," its leader said, "she might have been laid prostrate by a brutal upper-cut from a truncheon." The Home Secretary assured the Commons on Thursday that there would be a full inquiry into the previous Sunday's events.

Next Sunday, July 8, there was more public

'Battle of the Hyde Park,' 'Punch' captioned this cartoon in July 1855, continuing satirically: 'Gallant and daring act of Private Lobbs (of the Crushers), who, by himself, stormed an old tree, and very nearly captured three small boys.' In the background police can be seen raising their truncheons against part of the crowd while some lounge on the grass

JULY 13, 1855
THE AZTECS AND EARTH MEN AT LEICESTER SQUARE
We were favoured yesterday by the obliging manager of this exhibition to a private view of the Aztecs and their equally interesting little companions, the Earth Men. The interest attached to the former has in no wise abated since their first introduction to the public. The mystery of their origin and the conjecture that they are the last remnants of the race once venerated in Central America as the gods of Iximaya cause an unabated desire to visit these little creatures.

The Earth Men, a diminutive people from the desert of the great Orange River, in Southern Africa, are also a peculiarly interesting race of pygmies. Their form is perfect and no marble statue ever developed finer lines or more correct symmetrical proportions. The boy, although 16, is but the size of a child of four years of age; and the girl, Flora, is a miniature of female development on the most minute scale.

disorder. A crowd gathered in Hyde Park, but, as the *Telegraph* reported next day, the atmosphere was good humoured: "One could have fancied it to be Greenwich Fair transplanted." The crowd "laughed heartily as they saw a dustman mounted upon a broken-down coach-horse imitating with droll gravity the demeanour of Sir Richard Mayne. Nuts and oranges and those little luxuries which Lord Robert Grosvenor pretends he would not withhold from the people, were freely selling." There were cries of "No bishops", "No Beer Bill", and "Down with the Sabbatarians." Shrubs and railings were pulled up and a policeman in plain clothes who was recognised was smothered in cow dung.

At about 5pm a portion of the crowd led by boys broke off and went to Belgrave Square, south of the Park and broke windows. "The most absurd part of such demonstrations," the *Telegraph* said, "is that the mob do not display the slightest judgment or knowledge either of friend or foe." They broke the windows of the Duke of Wellington's house. They frightened Lady Somerset, in her eighties. "They tried to set fire to the straw outside a house where a lady lay ill: it is to be hoped they did not know the meaning of its being placed there." Straw in those days was laid outside houses of the sick to deaden the noise of hooves and iron-rimmed wheels, and to signify that noise should be avoided.

Window-breaking continued along several streets, including one where tradesmen lived, until detachments of police arrived. A constable tried to arrest a man who denied throwing a stone that had hit a policeman in the face, but the crowd fought back, with blows and sticks and stones. The police had to relinquish their prisoner, an inspector remarking, "We are not among Englishmen, or they would not treat us so."

The crowd then stopped carriages passing along the street, but the second vehicle along held Lord Cardigan, the hero of Balaclava, and so the people cheered him, and off he went, bowing from time to time in acknowledgment. Some of the crowd went on breaking windows, including those of the workhouse in Mount Street, Mayfair.

The gentlemen's clubs in Pall Mall expected attack. A great crush developed outside the Army & Navy Club. One member said to the people nearest that an attack on their club would be most ungrateful since most of the members "were now laying down their lives for the honour of the country in the Crimea".

On Tuesday July 10 a case of perjury against the police was due to be heard. It was brought by Mr Francis Mair, who had been arrested during the riots of July 1. Mair's case was later to be the most fully investigated and reported, but for the time being, he decided not to press charges, since he had heard that there was to be an official inquiry into the whole affair. Mr Hardwick, the magistrate, acknowledged that was no stain on Mair's character, but he added that it would be prudent for respectable people like him to refrain from joining crowds that could turn into tumultuous assemblies.

Investigating the Sunday Beer Act

On July 10, 1855, the same day that Mr Hardwick, the Marlborough Street magistrate, heard Francis Mair's complaints about his treatment in Hyde Park, a Commons select committee was sitting to examine the Beer Act and its restrictions on Sunday opening hours. Mr Hardwick found time to give evidence. He said that he favoured the opening of public houses from 1pm to midnight on Sundays. He thought drunkenness had decreased in London over the past few years, which he attributed to the "education and improved manners of the people". He did not favour the opening of theatres on Sundays, but he thought the opening of places of amusement would draw people away from public houses. He did not think the opening of the Crystal Palace on Sundays would "shock the religious feelings of the great mass of the community".

Sir Richard Mayne, the Chief Commissioner of the Metropolitan Police, gave figures to the same committee on "persons who had been in the hands of police for drunkenness". Two periods were compared: January to June 1854 and January to June 1855. The area covered was within a radius of 16 miles from Charing Cross, excluding the City of London; the population was more than two and a half million. In 1854 the total taken in for drunkenness was 13,814, and in 1855 12,333. In the Covent Garden area there was a notable decline from a total of 1,922 to 1,370. One of his superintendents considered this diminution a consequence of the Beer Act.

Sir Richard said that the number of people inconvenienced by being unable to buy a drink after 10pm on a Sunday was 3,000 at the South-Western Railway station (Waterloo) alone. In rural districts he thought more inconvenience came from public houses being closed on Sundays from 2pm to 6pm. He thought there were more cons than pros in closing public houses from two till six, and that they might safely be open from 1pm to 11pm. In his 26 years' experience there had been an improvement in the conduct of the people.

The Government pressed on with a new Beer Bill to replace the unpopular Beer Act. The new law came into effect on Sunday August 19. The hours in which public houses could open would be 1–3pm and 5–11pm on Sundays, Christmas Day, Good Friday and "any fast or thanksgiving day" (as declared from time to time). The houses were not to re-open until 4am the next day.

INQUIRY INTO THE RIOTS

Cries of: 'Who stole the rabbit pie?'

The harshness and humour of life were revealed by a prompt and thorough inquiry into the Hyde Park disturbances

Vivid eye-witness accounts of the Hyde Park riots began to be published when the Royal Commission into events of July 1 started its hearings on July 17. The commission had been promised by the Home Secretary on July 5. The Commissioners sat at the Court of Exchequer in the great ancient space of Westminster Hall, but such was public interest that the court was often crowded "to excess". The commission was made up of three judges: J.A. Stuart Wortley MP, the Recorder of London, as president; Gilbert Henderson, Recorder of Liverpool; and Robert Baynes Armstrong, Recorder of Manchester.

On a typical day evidence was heard from an army cap maker, an upholsterer, an engineer, a barrister, a bookbinder, a licensed victualler, a flour-factor, a solicitor's clerk, a linen-draper, a hosier and glover, a waiter in a public house, a member of the Stock Exchange and "a native of Schleswig Holstein".

Several witnesses spoke of stone-throwing. Boys, ruffians, "roughs" and "the lowest rabble" were blamed for causing trouble. Several witnesses saw women and children hit with truncheons. Members of the crowd were reported to have called out "Shame" at violent behaviour by the police, especially towards women and children.

The case of Francis Henry Mair, the man who had initiated an action against the police, stood out among those considered by the commission. One witness, a tailor, said he saw Mair attacked by three policemen at the east end of the Serpentine. They "were treating Mr Mair with very great and unnecessary violence". Mair was "a tall gentleman in delicate health, and I thought his appearance might have protected him from such violence". There was some excitement in the crowd, and people said, "What a shame!" The witness said Mair parried the police attack with "a light stick".

Mair himself was then called. He was the picture of respectability, living at 44 Charlwood Street, Pimlico, and working as an "ecclesiastical estate agent". In the park at about four o'clock he was "suddenly pushed forward by two policemen to whom he never spoke". He stopped against the corner post of some railings. He saw police advance on the people with their truncheons and tell them to get back, but they could not, and the police "struck them with their truncheons indiscriminately, right and left".

Mair's evidence was that he had said to policeman 370A: " 'What are you going to do, fellow – are you going to kill us all?' He said they are our orders; but I did not know whether he meant to imply that his orders were to kill us." Mair said, "D—n such orders!" The policeman struck at him, and missed. "Afterwards he rushed through the posts, and struck at him again. Witness parried the blow with a stick, the point of which touched the policeman on the groin. Witness said immediately, 'I beg your pardon, I did not mean to assault you.' Several policemen then collared him, and dragged him on the road about one hundred and twenty yards. Witness did not attempt to resist, as it would have been worse than folly to have done so."

Mair told the commission that he had said, "Who will see fair play?" thereby "hoping that some gentleman would follow". A barrister called Downing Bruce did so. Mair was taken to Vine Street police station in a cab and charged with assault and riotous behaviour; Downing Bruce offered to become bail, but the inspector said he could not take bail for an hour or two. Mair was put in a cell 10ft long and 7ft wide with "two drunk and disorderlies who had been there from Saturday night. There was a privy – not a water closet – in the cell, and the smell was very offensive, as the night was very hot. Three other persons were afterwards put in the cell, and there were six of them there all night." Mair "suffered very much during the night, and the perspiration ran off his fingers' ends". He said he "lay down on the leaden floor on his back as the air was purer there than higher up".

The next day Mair's solicitor succeeded in seeing him, though policeman 370A and a sergeant sat between them. Policeman 370A had said that "directly he heard Mr Mair speak he knew he was a gentleman, and he was determined to take a gentleman as a warning to the rest". At 6pm Mr Mair was taken off to Marlborough Street magistrates' court nearby, and his case was dismissed. The magistrate, Mr Hardwick, said that "there was no charge against or imputation upon him".

On July 26 the commission heard from police constable 413A, John Winter, aged 28, who had been with the police four and a half years, before that having been with the Irish constabulary for six. He said that at 4.30 that Sunday afternoon orders were given to clear the carriageway. With constable 370A he began to do so, striking the railings and telling the people to stand back. "Mr Mair was near and refused to go back when requested to do so. The other constable said, 'I am only obeying my orders,' to which Mr Mair replied, 'D—n your orders. I shall not stand back.' When he called on the other people near him not to do so, 370A went up to Mr Mair, who pushed that constable in the chest with a stick."

Constable Winter said: "I can swear that 370A did

INBRIEF

JULY 6, 1855

SHAVING UPON THE SABBATH
In the police court, at Boston, Lincolnshire, on Friday morning, Justice Russell delivered the opinion of the court in the case of E.C. Deming, barber. In this case the defendant was charged, first, with doing work on the Lord's day, shaving other persons than himself, the same not being a work of necessity or charity; second, with keeping open his workhouse for the same purpose.

The first point was whether shaving was a work of necessity or charity. On this point the justices of the court were all agreed that it was. If shaving by a barber or another person on the Sabbath is not a work of necessity or charity, then is a person who shaves himself liable, and even the cooking of food upon that day illegal? The exchange of ministers, the celebration of the marriage-rite, or the performance of the funeral ceremony, might be held as an infringement of the Sabbath. The defendant was ordered to be discharged.

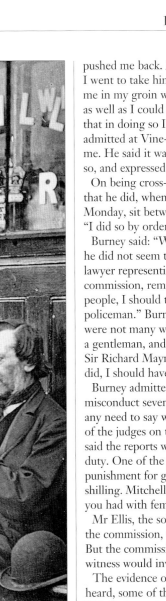

The men sitting outside a pub, in John Thomson's photograph from his series 'London Street Life', made a precarious living from placing advertisements on public walls. Such men were typical of the urban working class who wanted the freedom to spend their Sunday leisure in licensed premises

not strike Mr Mair on his head with his staff." He also swore that "during the whole of that day I did not strike a single person with my truncheon". Winter showed the commission a hole in his helmet made by a stone, a "great many" of which were being thrown.

Constable 370A was called. He was Robert Burney, aged 35. He had been with the police 12 years. When ordered to clear the railings by the pathway, "I did so by knocking my staff on the railings by way of caution to the people to stand back. Mr Mair refused to stand back. I then told him I was only acting by my orders in requesting the people to stand back. Mr Mair said, 'D— you and — your orders.' I went up to Mr Mair and he

pushed me back. Mr Mair had a stick in his hand. I went to take him by the collar when he thrust at me in my groin with the stick. I warded off the blow as well as I could with the truncheon. I cannot say that in doing so I struck Mr Mair. Mr Mair admitted at Vine-street station that he had assaulted me. He said it was not the act of a gentleman to do so, and expressed his regret."

On being cross-examined, Constable Burney said that he did, when at the police station on the Monday, sit between Mr Mair and his solicitor. "I did so by order of my superiors."

Burney said: "When I took Mr Mair into custody he did not seem to like my grasp." Mr Mitchell, the lawyer representing the complaining parties at the commission, remarked to Burney: "Very few people, I should think, do like the grasp of a policeman." Burney replied: "I should think there were not many who did. I told Mr Mair that he was a gentleman, and would act courteously with him. If Sir Richard Mayne had done the same as Mr Mair did, I should have taken him into custody."

Burney admitted that he had been reported for misconduct seven times. He did not think there was any need to say what for. But, on being told by one of the judges on the commission that he must, he said the reports were trivial, for "gossiping" while on duty. One of the judges asked what was the punishment for gossiping, and Burney said a fine of a shilling. Mitchell asked: "Was any of the gossiping you had with females?" Burney admitted it was.

Mr Ellis, the solicitor acting for the police before the commission, wanted to recall Mair as a witness. But the commission ruled that recalling each witness would involve great difficulties and time.

The evidence of many other complainants were heard, some of them not entirely coherent. J.M. Parker, a bookbinder of Park-street, Westminster, had gone to the park out of curiosity and heard some of the people address the police as "sanguinary crushers". (Laughter.) The conduct of those he saw reminded him more of what he had read of "Wild Indians" than "civilised beings". (Hisses.) He saw a number of persons exciting the mob, whom he considered were foreigners from their "moustachios, and cadaverous and seedy appearance". (Laughter.)

George Weller, a beer retailer from East-lane, Walworth, said Superintendent Hughes had been struck by a clod of mud thrown at him, accompanied with coarse expressions. The police, Weller said, had used no violence whatever in clearing the way. He considered they exercised great forbearance. He heard "epitaphs" applied to the police (laughter) – such as, "Who stole the rabbit pie?" This, he explained, alluded to a policeman who had been in trouble about a rabbit pie. (Renewed laughter.)

William Stephens, a hairdresser of Great Marylebone Street gave evidence of what happened outside the park. He had conducted a friend of his wife's to a house in Park Street (a prosperous neighbourhood), near Grosvenor Square. There was a crowd of 200 or 300 in the street (outside the house of Lord Robert Grosvenor, the sponsor of the Sunday trading legislation).

Stephens received a blow in the back and when he turned round "received a heavy blow in the mouth from the fist of a policeman. A series of blows followed, and at length he was felled into the road by a truncheon. His eye was blackened, his mouth cut, and his lower row of teeth loosened. His coat was torn to shreds. There were four or five policemen upon him."

Stephens told the commission that "a gentleman in a balcony called out, 'Take their numbers.' On endeavouring to do so, he received a blow from a truncheon on the back of his head." The next thing he knew he was in a cab, but not in custody. He went to Marylebone Lane police station and made a complaint. He had been under medical treatment ever since.

Elizabeth Bloxham, a servant in a coffee-house, gave evidence that bore on Stephens's. She went into the park every Sunday and she had seen the police rush upon the people near the Serpentine. A policemen told her that if she did not go away he would "rough" her. After seeing "a policeman cut a man's head open with a truncheon" she did go away. It was then she saw the police attack Stephens.

"One hit him and he staggered. As he was recovering, four or five others came up and struck him to the ground. One policeman said to another, 'Break his d—d head' – or 'back'. She did not know which. Mr Stephens's hat fell off. One of the policemen kicked it and stamped upon it. Mr Stephens said, 'What are you going to do with me?' When policeman 80– (she did not know what letter) said, 'D—n you, that is what I'll do with you,' and struck him a violent blow on his mouth with his fist." She helped Stephens to a cab and accompanied him to the police station.

William Humphreys a "boot-closer" of Marylebone Court, gave evidence that agreed with Elizabeth Bloxham's. John Hughes, a commercial traveller, of Park Street, was on his balcony and gave precisely similar evidence. Edward Nightingale, an apprentice of Pratt Street, Lambeth, corroborated it.

On July 20 the *Telegraph* reported the evidence about the behaviour of Superintendent Hughes that Sunday. "A reporter of the press", Charles Utting, aged 30, of Pimlico, had identified a police officer on a bay horse as Hughes. He saw him "back the horse round, stand up in his stirrups, and strike right and left with a long riding whip. His conduct was like that of a madman. He saw him strike two or three respectable women." At this there was a "sensation" in the crowded court. Mr Utting said he had been on Kennington Common and other places during the Chartist riots of 1848 but "never saw anything equal to that of the police in Hyde Park".

A commercial traveller, James Bowstead, of Farringdon Road, said he had been arrested and at Vine Street police station was put in a cell "like a pig sty but perfectly dark with fourteen persons who had not room to sit down". His own clothes had

been torn in his arrest and most of those detained with him took off "a great portion of their dress", presumably because of the heat. They were allowed "as much refreshments as they were pleased to pay for". Bowstead had been refused bail.

Several witnesses identified a dozen or so constables by their numbers. But the Recorder of Manchester agreed with those who said the numbers were indistinct because of the scrollwork round the figures. One witness had reported a constable 155, but when the man with that number appeared before the commission, his superior officer explained that he was employed by the Inland Revenue checking omnibus numbers, and that last time he had worn his uniform was at the Duke of Wellington's funeral in 1852.

A police inspector called McIntosh, aged 38, gave evidence about the eel. It was dead, and thrown at the police, striking two sergeants in the face. "The eel was afterwards thrown into the Serpentine. About a quarter of an hour after, the eel made a mysterious reappearance, and was again thrown at the police. I ordered 480M to take it away, who, in doing so, was mobbed by a party of 200 or 300 men who wished to get the eel. I then sent a couple of policemen to the succour of 480M."

In answer to questions, he said he did not think the police irritated the people. "It was right taking away the eel, however much the crowd might have thought it a 'slippery trick'. The eel was at last conveyed to the barracks. I am certain it has not been stuffed and taken to Scotland-yard." Inspector McIntosh said that the crowd frightened horses by drumming on the tops of their hats. After speaking with Superintendent Hughes he ordered his men to draw their truncheons, but only to flourish them above the heads of the people.

There was more about the eel from James Henbery, a park-keeper, who was in the Dairy Lodge at the heart of the disturbances. He gave evidence about a man who was pulled from the Serpentine and arrested, and according to some beaten by the police. Henbery said that the man taken from the Serpentine was violent and had to be brought to the house by four men, where, at his suggestion, he was handcuffed. "I did not see the policeman strike the man. I am blind in one eye. (Laughter.) The crowd surrounded my place and I was afraid they would have pushed the fencing down. It was the dead eel that set them all to work. (Laughter.) The man taken from the Serpentine had only a pair of trousers on when he was put into a cab and taken off."

On Saturday July 28 the commission briskly heard the evidence of two dozen policemen, questioned by the lawyers and the commissioners. None of the policemen admitted to hitting out, except when arrest was being resisted. When he was called to give evidence, Sir Richard Mayne, the Chief Commissioner of Police, told the commission that he never received any written orders from the Government, although he "made the Secretary of State acquainted with my instructions for the Sunday". Superintendent Hughes was, he said, in

Several witnesses to the inquiry into the Hyde Park riots said that the identifying numbers on policemen's collars were hard to read. 'Punch' came up with its own 'proposed new uniform for the police, with letters and numbers properly marked'

charge and he had been 25 years in the force and "was always found to be competent". Sir Richard explained he had given written orders to Hughes at 4.30pm that said: "Now act vigorously in compelling all rioters to move up the road." At 5pm he wrote: "All persons shouting at the carriages to be removed from the railings." Sir Richard listed the police casualties as "45 assaulted, seven kicked, 25 struck with stones and 13 with sticks". As for granting bail, he had sent a memorandum to Vine Street at 10pm: "Bail is not to be taken for persons charged with rioting unless the bail is sufficient for the appearance of the prisoner next day."

When asked questions about the cells he answered: "I am not responsible for them. There is not much room in Vine-street station. I attribute the mixing of the Hyde Park prisoners with thieves and drunken persons in the cells to the fact of the place being overcrowded."

In a second day of evidence, Sir Richard gave figures for the years in which police had joined the force. Out of 5,707, more than a sixth, 967, had joined only in 1854. But in their first year of service there had been 822 resignations "from their not liking the severity of the duty, and other causes". Of the whole Metropolitan force, "4,416 were English, 370 Irish and 145 Scotch".

One of the Commissioners said he was "glad to hear of it, because an anonymous letter had been sent to the commission, stating the force to a large extent was composed of Irish". Another Commissioner, Mr Stuart Wortley, said that the letter was signed "An English Gentleman", but it was not couched in terms one would expect from an English gentleman. He begged to say "once and for all that the commission could take no notice of such communications". The commission hearings wound up on August 2.

The *Telegraph* sometimes forgot how seriously it viewed the Hyde Park disturbances. In a leading article at the end of August it proposed jocularly that a memorial be erected "To the Hyde Park Martyrs". It should be inscribed: "To those citizens who nobly bled in defence of beer drinking between the hours of three and eleven on a Sunday."

The Royal Commission on the riot on July 1 reported in November. The *Telegraph* thought the commissioners had a leaning towards the police, but "their partiality has not, as far as we can discern, led them to conclusions in direct contradiction to evidence". The commissioners "report misconduct upon the part of several constables as well as Superintendent Hughes, but they are themselves forced to admit that these constables form but a small portion of those who were guilty of the outrages complained of".

The commission had found that Hughes "was not justified in giving his men orders to use their staves; that he did not show sufficient consideration for the safety of unoffending individuals; that he did not exercise proper control over his subordinates; and that, by a more calm and forbearing demeanour on his part, much angry excitement at the time and afterwards would have been prevented". The paper

declared that both Hughes and Sir Richard Mayne should resign.

"But how does our twaddling Home Secretary deal with this case?" the *Telegraph* asked. He "dilates, in a dozen paragraphs also, upon the importance of judgment, temper, and coolness, in an officer placed in command of a body of men commissioned to preserve public order, and then concludes by saying that it would be harsh and uncalled for to dismiss a man who had offended most grossly against every one of the rules just laid down with such emphasis".

The paper also blamed Sir Richard Mayne for the gross overcrowding of the police cells crammed with those arrested and for letting the crowd get out of control in the first place. In short, the Royal Commission only followed what was "the system now-a-days. The subordinates who but obey directions are heavily punished, whilst the chief who should be responsible for their proceedings, and who is the real criminal, escapes with, at the utmost, a little animadversion."

By the time the commission reported there had been several autumn Sundays on which crowds demonstrated in Hyde Park again. This time it was over the price of bread. But the police had managed things more tactfully.

There were to be more riots in Hyde Park (in 1866 the railings were torn out when police locked the gates against a crowd). But the events of July 1855 had indicated that a Metropolitan police force must adjust to new ways of responding to disorder. The subsequent Royal Commission showed that Victorian authorities were at least ready to examine their own behaviour in public.

From the Telegraph

Where are the police?

November 20, 1855

To the Editor of The Daily Telegraph.

Sir – It is my business every evening to cross the Green Park, being the nearest way to Piccadilly from Westminster. I am constantly annoyed by prostitutes, who frequent the paths as soon as it becomes dusk; they will not let anybody pass without trying to detain them, and no sooner are you clear of one of these wretched women than you are assailed by another. On Thursday night (being very foggy) there was an unusual number, and no sooner did a person appear than he was assailed by them, and if he used a little violence, so as to escape, he was instantly set upon by numbers, and frightfully ill-treated, if not robbed. Now, Sir, I have complained to the Police till I am tired of doing so, the only answer I get being, "Then you should go another way".

A PEDESTRIAN,
WESTMINSTER, NOV 17

THE ELECTRIC TELEGRAPH

The speed of lightning and perfect secrecy

Telegraph wires brought the new paper instantaneous reports. But laying thousands of miles of cable was a brave task

The electric telegraph meant modernity and it meant power. In 1845 the Government had enacted a law requiring any new railway to provide telegraph wires along the track. The telegraph could win wars. During the Crimean war, in May 1855, a month before *The Daily Telegraph* first appeared, a line 301 miles long had been laid to the Crimea from Varna in Turkey, Britain's ally. Via existing cables across Europe and the Channel, the French and English commanders in the Crimea were put into instant contact with Paris and the War Office and Admiralty in London.

"Thus the great officers at either end of this vast space could communicate direct, with the speed of lightning and perfect secrecy," as a contemporary put it. The cyphered messages were printed in dots and strokes by a ribbon on to a revolving paper cylinder. With the electric telegraph, news of the war came first to London whereas, before, it had come via the enemy metropolis of St Petersburg.

So it was a shrewd choice to invoke the electric telegraph in the new newspaper's name, or the first half of it. It appeared as the *Daily Telegraph & Courier* because, as explained in its first leading article on June 29, 1855, "the former name we trust appropriate from the sources of our special information, and the latter as an evidence of our means of dissemination and circulation". The word *Courier* was dropped little by little, already put in smaller print from August 20, and removed from the top of the leader column from September 8. At the top of the front page, *The Daily Telegraph*, in quaint large gothic type, much like today's, remained.

There had long been telegraphs signalling visually from hilltop to hilltop; hence the common place-name Telegraph Hill. What made the difference was electricity travelling hundreds of miles through cables. Victorian imaginations were fired by the idea of messages conveyed at astonishing speed. The twin powers of electric telegraph and the steam railway were annihilating all barriers, social as well as geographical. A fan was John Francis, who at the early date of 1851 published the confidently titled

A History of the English Railway, Its Social Relations and Revelations.

The telegraph benefited the highest and the lowest, he wrote. "It purchases; it sells; it equalises prices; it destroys monopolies; it places the poorest tradesman on a level with the wealthiest speculator; it renders commerce healthier; and it possesses that which it has been said distinguishes most modern discoveries, it is as free to the peasant as to the prince; as open to the mean as to the mighty; it is controlled and controllable by all. It communicates between London and Scotland in the three hundred and fiftieth part of a second; it stops runaway trains; it prevents accidents; it surprises gentlemen who pay second-class fares and ride in first-class carriages with a demand for extra money; it is a worker of social miracles as difficult properly to appreciate as it is easy to operate with."

That year, 1851, the industrious year of the Great Exhibition, had seen the laying of the first commercially successful cable across the Channel, from Dover to Sangatte. It was insulated with gutta-percha, the Victorians' plastic, derived, like rubber, from latex gathered from Malayan trees. Everything from golf balls to picture-frames were made from it. None of the subsequent undersea cables would have been possible without it.

Serious attention was already being paid to the vast challenge of laying a cable across the Atlantic.

Brunel beneath a huge paddle-wheel of his 32,000-ton iron steam ship, 'Great Eastern', built on the Isle of Dogs and launched in 1858. She could carry 2,000 miles or more of waterproof telegraph cable, and laid five trans-Atlantic cables before being taken out of service in 1874

A year after *The Daily Telegraph* first came out, the Atlantic Telegraph Company was registered. The manufacture of an insulated cable hundreds of miles long was completed in June 1857, and within six weeks it was coiled up in the American warship *Niagara* and the British ship *Agamemnon*, lent by governments keen to benefit from the venture.

The *Niagara* began to lay her half from Valentia, off the coast of Kerry, the most westerly part of Europe, on August 5. On August 11, when 380 miles had been laid, the cable snapped. Both ships returned to Plymouth with the remaining cable.

On June 10, 1858 the same ships left Plymouth to rendezvous in mid-ocean. A great storm delayed their rendezvous until June 25. On June 26, having spliced together the ends of the cable on board, they began to sail away from each other. The cable broke almost immediately. Another splice was made, and after 40 miles had been laid the cable broke again. The third time, a break occurred after the *Agamemnon* had paid out 146 miles.

When the ships had returned to harbour, it was found that enough cable remained to connect the British and American shores. The ships set sail and started to pay out cable again from mid ocean on July 29. On August 5 the *Niagara* made land with her cable at Trinity Bay, Newfoundland, and on the same day the *Agamemnon* reached Valentia.

There was now an electrical connection between the two sides of the Atlantic. But a disastrous error was made by the chief electrician of the project who attempted to use high-potential currents. On August 16 communication was at last established by using weak currents, the method devised by Sir William Thomson (later Lord Kelvin). But the cable insulation had been ruined by the earlier attempts and the signals failed after October 20.

The whole enterprise had to begin again. It took until 1865 to raise the money. The plan was to use a single ship, and Brunel's 32,000-ton iron steamer, the *Great Eastern*, launched in 1858, was chosen. She sailed from Ireland with 7,000 tons of cable and 500 crew. During July the cable failed repeatedly. But by August 2, 1,200 miles had been paid out. Suddenly there was a break, and despite all efforts it proved impossible to pick up the dropped cable.

In 1866 the company was reconstituted as the Anglo-American Telegraph Company, and on July 13 the *Great Eastern* sailed from Ireland with 1,990 miles of cable. She reached Trinity Bay a fortnight later. The Atlantic had been bridged.

By the end of her cable-laying career in 1874, the *Great Eastern* had laid five trans-Atlantic cables. The next year she was taken out of service, and in 1888 was sent to the breakers'. By 1870 Britain was linked to India. By 1887 107,000 miles of submarine cable had been laid. By Victoria's Diamond Jubilee, 10 years later, the total was 162,000 miles. Britain had invested £30 million of the £40 million capital behind it, and most of the cable had been manufactured on the banks of the Thames, where the *Telegraph* was drawing its news telegrams from the end of the earth.

From the Telegraph

Sailing with 150 miles of cable stowed aboard, all in one piece

August 7, 1855

The Mediterranean Electric Telegraph Company is on the point of despatching their cable, which is shortly to complete telegraphic communication between London and Algiers.

The communication being now complete from London to Cagliari, in the south of Sardinia, and the line from Algiers to Cape Bonan, on the African coast, having been opened last January, nothing is now wanted to complete the work than a submarine cable from Cape Spartivento, adjoining Cagliari, to Bonan. This is the cable now lying coiled in the hold of the ship *Result*, 1,700 tons register.

The cable is the largest and heaviest, besides being the longest, ever laid down. It is 150 miles long, each mile weighing eight tons, and the whole cable weighing 1,200 tons. This is exclusive of twelve miles of lighter cable sent with it to avoid all chance of deficiency. This cable is the manufacture of Messrs. W. Keeper and Co, of Leadenhall Street. Its stowage demands the greatest care, owing both to the enormous weight, and to the circumstance that it is all in one piece.

Seventy-one miles of it have been put in the lower hold, forty-two miles on the orlop deck, thirty miles in 'tween decks, seven miles in the after-hold, and the twelve miles of what is called small cable, although it weighs 5 tons to the mile, is also on 'tween decks. It is expected that the present cable will be laid down in four days.

The Mediterranean Telegraph Company anticipate that in two years and a half they will have a direct communication with Bombay, and from thence by telegraphs already at work in the presidencies, to Calcutta; and they consider this line they are just about to complete as only the preliminary steps to this result.

Their proposed line, joining the one at present open to Cagliari at Cape Spartivento, will first be taken to Malta, and thence direct under the Mediterranean to Alexandria. This will be an immense distance – 984 miles of submarine cable, without a station; from Alexandria to Suez, by land, 248 miles; another submarine cable under the Red Sea to Aden, with two stations, Cosiri and Liddah, 1,552 miles, and from Aden to Bombay, with stations at the Kooria Moorta Islands and Ras-al-had, 1,907 miles.

When this undertaking is complete the communication with Calcutta, which now takes on an average 36 days, will be reduced to a few minutes.

Professor Faraday, about two years ago, called the attention of telegraphic companies to the fact that there was great difficulty in sending any communication through a greater length of wire than 300 miles; but since that time Mr Brett has been experimenting, with a view to overcome this difficulty, and has perfectly succeeded in doing so. By connecting each individual wire in this coil of six, and also those belonging to another cable intended for an American company he was enabled to experiment on a length of 1,250 miles with perfect success.

Paying out tons of continuous cable

THE CRIMEA

Crisis in the war: the death of Lord Raglan

After a winter when soldiers starved in the mud, the Commander-in-Chief died on the second day of the Telegraph's existence

The Crimea campaign "engrossed the attention of all classes to the exclusion of every other topic" at the beginning of 1855, according to the *Annual Register*, which reported with none of the clouding of hindsight that succeeding events tend to supply. After nine months of war, "public sympathy and indignation were roused to the utmost by the conviction that the soldiers of the finest army Great Britain had ever sent forth were ingloriously perishing of disease, overtasked and underfed, from the absence of the most ordinary foresight".

It was an unprecedented venture to maintain an army at war over winter at such a distance. The consequences were painful. At home a dozen departments were responsible for meeting requirements, and were slow, understaffed and short of money. In the field, full ships and warehouses sat within a few unbridgeable miles of dying men for want of organised transport. A balmy winter climate had been expected; rain, then freezing weather set in for men lightly clothed with no sufficient tents or even firewood, and nowhere to lie but the mud. They ate meat raw for the lack of a fire. Coffee was sent out green to men without the means to roast it. Dysentery swept the camps and hospitals. Sick men had to suck on hard biscuit; shortage of lime juice led to scurvy. Starving horses gnawed each other's tails and fell dead from hunger. Men and beast lacked the strength to reach the harbour; it could take 12 hours to struggle without food or shelter through the mud to fetch supplies.

As news of the frozen misery of the soldiers reached Britain, those at home experienced feelings of impotent frustration. Lord John Russell resigned

Sailing ships full of supplies reached the harbour at Balaclava (in a photograph, below, by Roger Fenton), but freezing and hungry men at the front lacked the strength to fetch them. These bearded Scots Fusilier Guards (right), Privates Reynolds and Temple and Corporal Judd, survived to show off their medals and be photographed at Aldershot in 1856 by Joseph Cundall and Robert Howlett for the Photographic Institution's series 'Crimean Heroes'

as Leader of the House of Commons in February after a speech in which he said: "If you had been told, as a reason against the expedition to the Crimea last year, that your troops would be seven miles from a secure port, which at that time, in contemplation of the expedition, we hardly hoped to possess, and that at seven miles' distance they should be in want of food, of clothes, and of shelter, to such a degree that they should perish at the rate of from 90 to 100 a day, I should have considered such a prediction as utterly preposterous." An inquiry was instituted, which attracted preconceived political opposition and straightforward evidence.

The founder of *The Daily Telegraph* shared the widespread discontent with the way the Government was running the war, and hoped in his new paper to do something about it. The launching of the paper at the end of June could hardly have been at a more critical moment. That month the allies had made a resolute effort to end the siege of Sebastopol by a great bombardment. But on June 18 the Russians, scarcely harmed, it seemed, by the hours of gunfire, repelled an Anglo-French assault, inflicting hundreds of casualties on the besiegers. "I never before witnessed such a continued and heavy fire of grape combined with musketry from the enemy's works," Lord Raglan declared in a melancholy despatch.

It seemed that no end to the war was in sight, that another winter would redouble the ghastly effects of the one gone by, and that the Government had no idea how to improve matters. On June 29, the *Telegraph*'s first day of publication, two thirds of the front page carried advertisements, but the other third carried news, in the form of lists of casualties from the days before the attack on Sebastopol. In its first editorial comment, the new paper made two main points about the war. One was to urge the restoration of the Polish Empire, to challenge Russia and deprive it of a useful recruiting ground. The other was to criticise Lord Raglan "in granting a truce in the very pause of combat, when probably a success awaited our arms, which would have led to the immediate capture of Sebastopol and the saving of thousands of British and French lives".

Under a headline IMPORTANT RUMOUR, that first issue carried a report that Lord Raglan had resigned through ill health. The truth was even more newsworthy, for the next day, unexpectedly, came tidings of Raglan's death at 8.35pm on June 28.

The *Telegraph* got the news into a second edition at half past two on the afternoon of Saturday June 30. "The event has plunged the whole army into the most profound grief," Lord Panmure, Secretary of State for War, had announced that morning to the editor of *The Daily Telegraph & Courier* (along with the editors of every other paper that received despatches from the War Office).

If the loss of the Commander-in-Chief dampened spirits, it also removed a scapegoat. In the *Telegraph*'s judgment, he was a man whose "deeds more properly belonged to a past generation, and

who ought to have been left to pass the winter of his days in comparative tranquillity and comfort at home, rather than to face the horrors of a Russian winter, and sustain the fatigues of a monster campaign with impaired faculties".

A newspaper knows the future no better than anyone else. In August 1855 the Russians made a determined effort to raise the siege of Sebastopol. The *Telegraph*, appealing to presumed radical sympathies, published readers' letters asserting in revolutionary language that the Government of Britain found itself "as far off from humbling and crumpling up Russia as at the beginning of the struggle".

But on Tuesday, September 11, the fall of Sebastopol was confirmed and "the lingering doubts with which the sceptical portion of the public retired to bed on Monday night, as to the authenticity of the news announcing the evacuation of south Sebastopol by the Russians, were dissipated at an early hour by the echoes of a *feu de joie* of 61 guns, fired from the Tower of London."

On September 13 the *Telegraph* listed the 70 officers of the 2,000 British men killed in the storming of Sebastopol. Although the paper sided with those who had advocated peace with Russia earlier in the year, it allowed a "kind of stern satisfaction" at allied successes. Russia retreated, and sank her ships. When Austria threatened to join in against Russia, she accepted peace terms on February 1, 1856.

'The Roll Call' (above), showing exhausted Grenadier Guards after an engagement in the Crimea, was the sensation of the Royal Academy exhibition in 1874. The Commander-in-Chief of the Army, the Duke of Cambridge, was astonished that the artist, Elizabeth Thompson, later famous as Lady Butler, should have 'grasped the speciality of soldiers'. The buyer of the picture gave it up to Queen Victoria, who wanted to buy it, for the £126 that he had paid for it

From the Telegraph

Let the working classes agitate to bring an end to the war

August 2, 1855

To the Editor of The Telegraph & Courier.

Sir – I rejoice to see that the working classes have energetically taken up the vital question of Peace or War, believing it to be a question which at present agitates society, and which only wants vent to declare itself. The sons of toil are not the only class sickened at the dilly-dallying manner in which this war has been conducted – not the only party alive to its manifold bunglings for, I am informed, the middle, and even the upper classes, are beginning to view the whole affair in a very sorry light.

It has been reserved, however, for the working classes – invariably the first in all great movements of reform – to agitate the subject, and may they honourably fulfil that duty. Let us hope, too, that the middle and upper classes will "follow in their wake". What better moment could there be for an agitation over the whole country, one universal cry being raised from Land's End to John O'Groats for a speedy termination of the war.

Winter approaches. The season for effective operations in the Baltic, according to Admiral Sir Chas. Napier, is well-nigh gone. That leviathan fleet is again on the eve of returning home, having accomplished still less than its "fettered" predecessor, although expected to do far more. One of those dreary Crimean winters which decimated our soldiers last year again awaits them. Cholera spreads its ravages in the camp – sparing neither high nor low.

Every Gazette reveals an appalling list of killed and wounded, although the same despatch that bears the dead-list conveys the stereotyped intelligence that "The army is healthy; nothing of importance has taken place." Alas! when the impression – the thrill of horror – which the reading of the first list of killed and wounded created in the public mind is contrasted with the *sang froid* with which such lists are now received, surely the growing unpopularity of the war must be readily conceded?

The people have trusted to their rulers either to vigorously prosecute the war or abandon it. Their voice has overthrown one Government and set up another in its stead, from whom great things were expected; still they find that they are as far off from humbling and crumpling up Russia as at the beginning of the struggle. Russia is now better prepared to withstand us than when first she launched her armies on the Danube. Instead of our trade flourishing in war times, the very reverse has proved to be the case. Work is scarce and provisions dear; and, therefore, they are now resolved to put their faith no longer in Governments, but to take the matter into their own hands. The agitation once fully commenced, there is no fear of the result.

Trusting, then, that this righteous agitation will spread far and wide, and that your daily bringing the question of peace before the public, may impress them with a strong sense of its importance, I remain, yours truly,

AN HONEST REFORMER,
LONDON

VICTORIA IN FRANCE

The Paris crowds shout: 'Vive la reine'

The first visit to Paris in centuries by an English monarch proved a sunny triumph, except for the Queen's sense of fashion

At 20 minutes to two on a hot August Saturday in 1855, accompanied by a squadron of men at war, the new royal steam yacht *Victoria and Albert*, "a perfect model of marine beauty, gliding noiselessly over the surface of the water at an average speed exceeding that of a parliamentary train", brought a healthy, happy-looking Queen into harbour at Boulogne four and a half hours after she left her house at Osborne on the Isle of Wight.

The report of her arrival filled a quarter of the four-page *Daily Telegraph & Courier* of Monday August 20. That little joke about the parliamentary train referred to the slow and uncomfortable services that the railway companies had been obliged to provide at restricted fares in return for the Acts of Parliament that allowed them to lay their lines over compulsorily purchased land.

Queen Victoria's own territorial claims still theoretically extended to France, according to the titles recited at her coronation. She was the first English monarch to visit Paris since Henry VI had been proclaimed king there as a child in 1431. Elements of the French character alarmed Victoria, notably the tendency to revolution and despotism punctuated by democracy. But France was now a monarchy, indeed an empire in the eyes of its ruler Napoleon III, and an ally of Britain in the Crimean war – though God forbid that Napoleon should go through with his plan to take military command.

The Queen's eight-day visit to Paris was a return for the Emperor's visit to Windsor earlier in the year, during which she had reminded him that they had met in 1848 at a breakfast raising funds for a public wash-house in the Fulham Road. Victoria was suspicious of this man who had proclaimed himself Emperor after a coup in 1851 after years spent in exile in England. During that time she had never formally received him at court. He was to die, having lost his throne, in exile in Chislehurst in 1873. In the meantime she meant to get on with him as well as circumstances permitted. It helped that she understood and spoke French perfectly well.

In her journal of the days in Paris, published years later, Victoria was to note his great qualities – indomitable courage and self-reliance – his belief in omens that was "almost romantic", his calmness,

Boulogne was en fête in August 1855 when the bright new royal steam yacht 'Victoria and Albert' docked and, with thrones of states standing ready in a 'Kiosque', Napoleon III was able to welcome the Queen for her visit, as pictured here by the painter Louis Armand

gentleness and power of fascination. Victoria was 36; he was 47. Fulke Greville in his own diaries, to be published amid some scandal in time for Victoria's Golden Jubilee, opined that Napoleon had simply made love to the Queen, and "as his attentions tickled her vanity without shocking or alarming her modesty, and the novelty of it made it very pleasant, his success was complete". Napoleon also very sensibly praised Albert, whose inspection of the Exhibition of Industry and Fine Arts in Paris (an imitation of London's Great Exhibition of 1851) was a great motive for the visit.

The French went out of their way to prepare a welcome. At Boulogne crowds shouted "*Vive la reine!*", military bands played *God Save the Queen*, officials ushered the party to a "Kiosque" decked in scarlet and gold. Unknown to the Queen, and the readers back in England until the story came to light a week later, the Emperor had narrowly escaped death that morning when he rode his horse up on to the cliffs to see the royal yacht approach. The horse bolted, and the Emperor dropped his telescope, but retained a hold on the bridle. He succeeded in pulling up his mount on the verge of the precipice. Despite the excitement, he managed to return to the Kiosque to take his seat in one of the thrones of state in time to greet the royal party.

From the Kiosque a carriage procession set off for the station. There the Nord railway company had spent 100,000 francs (£4,000) erecting a 70ft triumphal arch amid flowery parterres, decked with allegorical figures and "Civilisation" spelled out in large letters, lest the allegory be missed. In a

marquee draped with Gobelin tapestries and stuffed with white sofas the carpet declared, "Welcome to France". The nine-carriage train puffed out of the station at half past two and the Queen was in Paris by twenty past seven.

Even the Parisians showed "respectful enthusiasm", as hawkers moved among the crowds selling bronze medals of Victoria and Albert at "very moderate" prices, although the cost of seats in the boulevards "rose to an enormous extent". The "immense quantity of human beings" must have impressed the Queen, a *Telegraph* correspondent thought, even more than the illuminations, inscriptions and triumphal arches woven with "the colours of England and France" and the initials VA.

The Queen was to stay at the Palace of St Cloud, and during the carriage ride of "14 kilometres" there from the station, "at each step she could hear expressions of welcome" made with a measure of decorum even by the numerous working class.

On the Sunday, the Queen, a little fatigued, remained in her pleasant rooms at St Cloud, decorated according to the tastes of Marie Antoinette. It was reported, though not in the *Telegraph*, that a lady-in-waiting insisted on having the legs of one of Marie Antoinette's tables sawn down because it was would be too high for Victoria.

The Queen was delighted. "My sitting-room and drawing-room (quite lovely) and two more rooms," she confided to her journal, "all look out on the garden, with its fountains and beautiful long avenues of beech trees, orange trees and brilliant flowers." A little bathroom and dressing-room had splendid views. "While I was dressing, stopped to look at the Cent Gardes, magnificent men of six feet and upward, ride by, and then, hearing a charming sort of fanfare, went to another window and saw a body of Zouaves marching by."

That Sunday, the Queen ducked divine service at the British embassy in Paris, the *Telegraph* noted, although it did not add that the embassy chaplain came to her armed with a sermon on *The Pharisee and the Publican*, which he delivered during a short service in a specially prepared room.

The next day Victoria plunged into sight-seeing, beginning with the Exhibition of Fine Arts and the Sainte-Chapelle. People threw open their windows to see her carriage pass, although many were disappointed to find her face obscured beneath a parasol. "A common-looking woman in a cap and blue apron, standing on her doorstep, I overheard saying to her neighbour, '*Avez-vous vu la petite Princesse? Est-elle gentille et gracieuse!*'" wrote one of the *Telegraph* correspondents.

The French papers reported little of the visit, even though everyone from the deepest-dyed Orleanists to the fiercest republican greeted the Queen enthusiastically. When the Queen unexpectedly visited Notre Dame, "the respectful attention shown to the august visitor by the Archbishop and his coadjutors" was, in the opinion of a *Telegraph* correspondent, "an event meriting special note in these days of religious intolerance".

The contemporary delight in declamatory hangings was taken to a fine pitch at the Maison Dorée, where the Queen on her way to the opera could read an inscription in Latin: "Victoria, Queen of England, with your appearance, with the aid of God, may victory, so much desired, also arrive."

Albert duly made a detailed examination of the Exhibition of Industry and bought several items. The Queen reviewed 50,000 men in the Champ de Mars, rode a horse through the woods of St Germain and even visited the tomb of Napoleon, which caused a sensation. Another curious outing was to see the tomb of James II, deposed in 1688; Victoria had paid for its restoration privately.

Each day of the visit the sun beat down on the people thronging to see the Queen. Two hundred thousand applied for invitations to the grand ball at the Hôtel de Ville. Their Majesties opened it with a quadrille, the orchestra being conducted by Strauss. Some mysterious "Arab chiefs" were then presented to the Queen.

For all this, *The Daily Telegraph* was not cheered, and dismissed the visit in in its leader columns as "stiff, courtly and hollow civility". France under Napoleon III remained "an absolute despotism". Yet the next day, the paper carried a leader praising Napoleon III ("There is something about the Napoleon family that one cannot fail to admire") and looking forward to "a happy future of amity and good will" between the two nations. Presumably the task of writing the leader had fallen to someone different from the man the night before; the paper's opinions were by no means stable in 1855. In any

case, the *Telegraph* did not hesitate to carry an even longer leader the next day mocking a leading article in *The Times*, which it pretended was the work of "Jeames" – the archetypal foolish domestic retainer. "For 400 years no reigning sovereign of England has seen, or could see, the beautiful metropolis of France," *The Times* had written. "Why not?" asked the *Telegraph*; there was no reason why Henry VIII might not have taken a trip to Paris from the Field of the Cloth of Gold, or Victoria herself in earlier years. "Everybody in this kingdom with a dozen sovereigns in his pocket and as many ideas in his head has seen Paris," *The Times* had written, "but not the first gentleman in this country." To this the *Telegraph* responded by suggesting that "lady" not "gentleman" was the word Jeames was looking for.

The *Telegraph*'s Paris correspondent bore witness to the eagerness of the crowds and the satisfaction of the Queen as she left for her return journey, having had "many occasions to convince herself of the kindly and enthusiastic feelings of the French towards her" and leaving 25,000 francs (£1,000) to be distributed among the poor.

If the Queen wondered about the ambivalent attitude of *The Daily Telegraph*, she would have been mortified to discover that some Parisians thought her appearance during the visit rather vulgar. During her time at Windsor that year, the Empress Eugenie has changed the fashions of England by introducing the crinoline. Victoria's impact was different. An unlikely reflection of fashionable French opinion was General Canrobert, who had recently been replaced as French Commander-in-Chief in the Crimea.

"Despite the great heat," he remembered years later, "she had on a heavy bonnet of white silk with streamers behind and a plume of stork's feathers on top. Her countenance seemed friendly enough. She had a white, flounced dress, but her mantle and

INBRIEF

NOVEMBER 22, 1855

Sir – There is nothing that demands a reform so much as those public omnibuses, the principal objects of the present proprietors being, as it would appear, to try how much they can cramp their passengers, and disgust them with their want of conveyance. Indeed, I have noticed that some of the recently constructed omnibuses are actually built smaller than ever, the object evidently being to save a few pounds' worth of wood. Messrs Wilson and MacNamara, having lately paid a visit to Paris, I trust will take a hint from the Parisian carriages, which are delightful to ride in, each person being separated from his neighbour in a kind of armchair with a nicely stuffed back, quite as comfortable as riding in a private carriage.
Your obedient servant,
A Daily Rider
Islington, Nov 20

Victoria, photographed in an informal pose by Roger Fenton in 1854, the year before her visit to Paris, was in her thirties when Napoleon III was said to have tickled her vanity by 'making love' to her

sunshade was of a raw green that I did not think went with the rest of her outfit. My attention was fixed by a voluminous object that she carried on her arm – a vast handbag, like those our grandmothers used to carry, of white satin or silk, on which was embroidered in gold a fat poodle."

That evening Canrobert sat next to the Queen at dinner and noticed how the rings on every finger, and even her thumbs, one bearing a huge blood-red ruby, made it difficult for her to use a knife and fork. The general spoke to the Queen amiably, made her laugh and discussed the war. Despite his criticism of her dress, he detected in her an air of dignity, even of greatness.

Unaware of any of the Canrobert's considered judgments, the Queen hurried home happily. As the royal train steamed towards Boulogne, crowds waved from the platforms of the stations it passed; at Amiens a 21-gun salute was fired when the train pulled in, and elegantly dressed ladies looked down from balconies as the Queen made her way across the platform between the guard of Cuirassiers to a saloon specially prepared for her. Her arrival at Boulogne was marked by 101 guns and a grand dinner at the Hotel du Pavillion Imperiale. The Emperor accompanied her aboard the *Victoria and Albert*, leaving after midnight. By nine o'clock the next morning the Queen was back at Osborne.

Brick tunnels for the vast Crossness sewage pumping works. At its opening in 1865 the Prince of Wales and the Archbishop of Canterbury joined a lunch for 700 beside a 'great sea of sewage', according to The Daily Telegraph

DIGGING UP LONDON
Unblocking the streets and sewers

The discovery that dirty water caused cholera spurred the energetic Victorians to build a huge new network of sewers

Sewers and streets were two crying needs in the London of 1855. The population was an estimated 2.5 million, up by 200,000 from 1851 when the last census had been taken, and 600,000 more than the numbers for 1841.

In 1848 the new Consolidated Commission for Sewers set about flushing out London's 369 sewers and trying to do away with the capital's 200,000 cess pits. But the commission was disbanded in 1855 to be replaced by the Metropolitan Board of Works – or "of Perks" as cynical satirists called it – which, under new laws that year, gained control of 117 square miles of London. Before it was set up, the paving of London's streets and the management of the drains beneath came under parish councils. The Strand, for example, came under seven different vestry boards. Traffic became jammed, pedestrians fell beneath wheels, the streets wallowed in mess, the river stank and people died, notably in cholera outbreaks.

A hero of the fight against cholera was John Snow, the pioneering anaesthetist who had administered chloroform to Queen Victoria at the birth of Prince Leopold in 1853. Snow had observed that the flushing of the sewers into the Thames in 1848 had been followed by a bad epidemic of cholera in 1849. He suspected that cholera was water-borne and that the Thames, turned into a sewer, was a reservoir of infection. During a cholera outbreak in 1854 Snow observed the connection between infection and use of a public pump in Broad Street (now Broadwick Street), Soho, near which a sewer ran. When the pump was put out of action, the outbreak declined.

Despite further epidemiological work by Snow, not everyone was convinced of the link betwen dirty water and cholera by the time Snow died, aged 45, in 1858.

But Sir Benjamin Hall, the man who in 1855 brought in the Act establishing the Board of Works, was clear in his aims. "I was determined on the merciful abatement of the epidemic that ravaged the Metropolis," he declared. It is often said that the "Great Stink" of 1858, which made Parliament gasp at the noisome effluent outside its windows, spurred reform. But work was in hand a decade before, and the *Telegraph* from its earliest numbers pressed the need to clean up the river.

"In spite of warnings without end, in contempt of past experience, we still continue to inhale a poison-laden atmosphere and to drink water the multitudinous organic and inorganic impurities of which almost defy the combined labours of the chemist and microscopist to describe," the paper warned in a leading article in July 1855. "We still do our best to pollute and convert into a common sewer that noble stream which should bring to us health as well as wealth."

The *Telegraph* blamed commercial greed and

From the Telegraph
Sir Joseph Paxton's glass-covered ring-road

July 9, 1855

The Thames is the first thing which should engage our attention. This naturally magnificent river is, as everyone knows, turned into a huge rushing filthy sewer, according to the present system. Its banks present a more dingy, dirty, confused, and hideous appearance than those of any river in the world running through a great commercial city. There are no quays such as we see everywhere else, no proper steamboat pier accommodation, and wharves worthy of Lethe, rather than of the busiest and most enterprising Metropolis in the world.

Now that we are going to have a river terrace from the new Houses of Parliament to Chelsea, it would be a great opportunity to complete the work. The only objection will be the increased rapidity of the stream; but artificial means may remedy this to a greater extent, and iron piles would allow the water to keep nearly its own channel. If, however, the force of the stream be increased, it will be beneficial, considering the present state of the sewers. When, with relation to these, will our agriculturists plead for the use of that which now disfigures London with its impurity?

Another great question is the grand convergent junction underground of our railways. The expense of carrying out such a plan is nothing compared with Sir

Joseph Paxton's scheme for covered galleries over London. Imagine the noise and inconvenience attending this. We have had enough of the glasshouse fancy – an excellent thing at Sydenham – if the people might only visit it on Sundays. We do not want to raise our citizens under forcing frames and grow Aldermen like cucumbers. We must protest against being disturbed in our slumbers by a whistle and a roar overhead, as if the powers of darkness were engaged in a tournament.

The same objection does not apply to a chance visit to the cellar, when a train shall be heard flying, like the *soupçon* of an earthquake, some dozen feet below the Roman pavement under our feet. Thus the Thames Tunnel may yet come into play, and Mr Brunel's memory be made much of. Of the practicability of the whole plan we have ample proof. Look at the Lime-Street Tunnel in Liverpool. In this manner, we may hope to see, ere long, three or four main lines, passing under London, with divergent and connecting lines, and the idea of the writer of the charming fiction of Heliondé may, at no distant period, be carried out in the more sober planet of Rhea.

We are quite in earnest in saying that no scope has yet been given to the invention and vast mechanical talent of our engineers. We should like to see London purified, tunnelled and fortified, and the Thames embanked with grand and uniform quays; and then, if not a beautiful city – as none can be where every man adopts his own style, and generally bad style, of architecture – our Metropolis would become the most distinguished for use, comfort, and scientific appliances in the world.

Joseph Paxton

Elaborate ironwork at Crossness, where the sewage pumps were loyally named after the Royal Family

public apathy for the noxious state of London's river. "The Thames bears upon its buoyant tide riches for the merchant whilst its waters are swollen with the feculence of the myriads of living beings that dwell upon its banks and with the waste of every manufacture that is too foul for utilisation. What matter? The merchant is served, and the population is spared the trouble of constructing a cloaca maxima."

The importance of carrying a Bill like Hall's through Parliament was urged by a letter to which the paper gave a whole column of space: "Sewers upon sewers, bearing the refuse of gas-works, of thousands of noisome factories, of chemical and dye works innumerable, with the feculence and excrement of the inhabitants of hundreds of thousands of houses pour down from London alone into the Thames," wrote Mr Francis of Richmond upon Thames. "Wandsworth, Kew, Brentford, Isleworth, Richmond, Twickenham, Teddington, Kingston, Ditton, and so on to Hampton Court, all contribute a full measure of their corruptions to the water we drink – one might almost say eat."

Lord Palmerston was much to blame for "despotic and uncalled-for interference" wrote Francis,

echoing the radical persona adopted by the *Telegraph* in its early days. "The evils which may arise from two or three years' delay, and two or three years' consequent pestilence and misery, are at his door, and at no one else's."

But before the end of the year, the Metropolis Local Management Act had been passed, giving the Board of Works power over sewers and roads. Now it had to decide on which ingenious schemes should be supported and how they could be funded. One extraordinary plan had already been hatched by the endlessly energetic Joseph Paxton, the architect of the Crystal Place, who in 1855 had been newly elected to Parliament. Having despatched an army of navvies to build a railway in the Crimea, he turned his attention to London's own transport problems and came up with the "Great Victorian Way" (*pictured below*).

Paxton's proposals were ready by the second week of June, a fortnight or so before the first issue of *The Daily Telegraph*. There was, he hoped, to be a 10-mile girdle of glass and iron around London, encasing a continuous street, 72ft wide, with shops and houses, and, elevated above it by 26ft, a double-track railway. Warm, safe and commercially

'Glasshouse fancy': Paxton's scheme for the Great Victorian Way, a covered ring-road round London, with elevated railways at each side

buoyant, the Great Victorian Way, curving from the City, south of the river, and west to Kensington Gardens, then back east via Islington, could be completed for £34 million.

"Imagine the noise and the inconvenience," said the *Telegraph* in a leading article. "We have had enough of the glasshouse fancy." The Board of Works was not convinced either, and instead encouraged a joint scheme for transport and sewerage devised by the man it appointed as its own engineer, Joseph Bazalgette.

Bazalgette's plan incorporated a mid-level interceptory sewer running beneath Oxford Street, and a low-level sewer running east under a new embankment to the Thames. An underground railway was to follow the same course. In the meantime the Board set 22,000 men to work constructing new sewers, one of which ran beneath the Strand, blocking traffic for weeks.

In 1858, when the Embankment scheme lay in the balance, Paxton succeeded in setting up a parliamentary committee on the project, with himself as chairman. Though his own crystal way was never to be adopted, he was determined to support Bazalgette's plans for 100 miles of interceptory sewers, collecting all that came their way and sending it down river. At last in 1862, Acts of Parliament gave the go-ahead for the Victoria Embankment north of the Thames, the Albert Embankment on the south side, and the sewers that went with them.

Paxton, who died in 1865, was not to see the completion of Bazalgette's great work. Far in east London, beyond the river Lea, the Abbey Mills pumping station was constructed with its great beam engines raising the contents of the low-level sewer 36 feet to meet the waters of the high-level and middle-level sewers and send them on their way to treatment works at Beckton (conceived in a style described as "Medieval with Byzantine and Norman Features").

South of the river, Crossness pumping station had four huge steam-driven pumps, employing 52-ton fly-wheels, built to Bazalgette's specifications. The pumps were named Victoria, Prince Consort, Albert Edward (the Prince of Wales) and Alexandra (the Princess of Wales). No irony was intended, and in 1865 the Prince of Wales himself, with the Archbishops of Canterbury and York in the party, opened the Norman-style building with its 208ft chimney.

The Daily Telegraph devoted a 4,000-word report to the event (finding room on the same page for a 2,000-word leading article calling for the demolition of Newgate prison, which was not pulled down until 1902). The opening of the Crossness station was "unprecedented in its

Joseph Bazalgette, the engineer behind the construction of 100 miles of interceptory sewers that are still in use today, and of the Thames Embankment, where his monument declares: 'Flumini vincula posuit' *– He chained the river*

magnitude, tremendous in its import, unexampled in its celebration".

The paper regretted the lack of ladies at the grand opening, for although "everything was very nice and clean and pretty, it had been felt, somehow, that the ceremony was of too stern and downright a nature to be participated in by the fair sex". During the speeches and subsequent luncheon, "the great sea of sewage was all around and beneath, pent up and bridled in, that the Lords and Commons might have their holiday, but chafing and striving and panting to leap out like a black panther, at the turning of a handle, at the loosening of a trap, at the drawing of a bolt."

Lunch for six or seven hundred noblemen and gentlemen was enjoyed to the accompaniment of the Marine band. The only two toasts were "the Queen" and "Prosperity to the Main Drainage as a national undertaking", given by the Prince himself and greeted with a storm of enthusiasm.

Abbey Mills in its own Venetian Gothic glory was finished in 1868. That year, too, saw the opening of the embankment from Westminster to the Temple, sadly cramping the fine river frontage of Somerset House, but speeding horse traffic to the City.

Before the end of the century, ugly new streets, Victoria Street (begun in 1851), Queen Victoria Street and Farringdon Street (1871), Northumberland Avenue (1873), Charing Cross Road and Shaftesbury Avenue (1884), were cut through slums and medieval houses.

Wren churches were demolished (St Benet Gracechurch in 1868, St Mary Somerset in 1869, St Dionis Backchurch in 1878, St Mary Magdalene, Old Fish Street, in 1887, St Olave Jewry in 1888) to speed the traffic.

In 1855 the *Telegraph* presciently advocated a network of underground railways beneath London. By 1863 a steam railway had been completed from Baker Street to Farringdon. By 1898 main roads were more congested than ever, and Sir Edward Bradford, the Commissioner of Metropolitan Police, noting "the manner in which heavy carts and wagons are driven along the centre of the streets, causing obstruction to all lighter traffic", issued instructions to the police "to direct all carmen and drivers of heavy vehicles to keep to the near side as much as possible".

It was a counsel of desperation. But in the same year a new electric railway 100 feet below London was cut from the Bank of England five miles to Shepherd's Bush, opening new possibilities to commuters.

Bazalgette's sewers are still in use today, and a bronze bust on the Victoria Embankment by Embankment Underground station honours his achievements.

From the **Telegraph**

A new railway one hundred feet below London

September 6, 1898

When, in June next, the Central London Railway is completed it will tap the traffic of the Metropolis at every important point from the very heart of the City to Shepherd's Bush. In the enterprise no less than three and a quarter millions sterling have been sunk, which includes the cost of the two six-mile tunnels for the up and down trains, 13 platforms and stations, railway carriages and electric locomotives numbering 196 and 28 respectively, and an enormous engine house, generating station, and sheds for storing trains.

From 6 o'clock on Monday morning till 10 o'clock on Saturday night 3,000 men have been constantly employed since the middle of 1896, when the operations were commenced. These men work in shifts of 12 hours on ordinary weekdays, with two hours off for meals, and for

The Greathead Shield, advancing under air pressure, left tons of earth to be dug out by hand

eight hours on Saturday. Down in the tunnels and borings they are supplied with barley water to an unlimited extent, but no beer or other alcoholic beverages are allowed.

At present the tunnelling is complete almost from Shepherd's Bush Station to the General Post Office, and only a small portion remains to be dug out between the latter station and the Bank. Even now it is possible to walk continuously for more than five-and-a-half miles, from Shepherd's Bush to the Bank, at a depth varying from 54ft to 100ft below the most crowded streets of London. But the depth is not too great to shut out the roar of our mighty traffic, and at every point there is an indistinct rumble to remind you that, even down in these clayey caverns, you are not so far from the madding crowd.

Since operations began about 600,000 cubic yards of clay and soil have been taken out. This represents in weight about a million tons of earth, which is brought up to the surface in hard, solid lumps that expand and crumble after a few hours exposure to the air. Most of it was dug out by a Greathead Shield. These work by pressure produced by air and water, and penetrate the earth, cutting circular masses as they advance, which are then dug out of the cylinder. No less than 90,000 tons of cast iron have been used in the construction of the two tunnels thus excavated and of the shafts leading down to them.

In the course of a conversation Mr Huddlestone, the chief engineer in charge of the construction of this new electrical railway, said that when the line is complete there will be a

two-and-a-half minute train service to and from the Bank and Shepherds Bush in the morning and evening. The whole journey will occupy 25 minutes.

"Have your carriages and engines been made in England?" — "All the carriages have been made in England. The engines – there is a separate locomotive for each train, not a motor at the ends of the first and last carriages – are, however, made in America. Owing to the engineers' strike of last year we have been compelled to get them and several other things from the United States."

"What are the carriages like?" — "After the style of Pullman cars, the seats being placed longitudinally, and the entrances at either end. Seven cars will constitute a train, and each car will accommodate 48 passengers."

"Are all the carriages of the same class?" — "No. There will be either two or three first class, as required, and the rest thirds. Several will be reserved for smokers. We have no seconds, and I think the first fare will be about two fifths more than the third. But what the fares will be I have, as yet, no idea. There is some talk of having a uniform fare – that is, a fixed charge for any distance on the line."

"But a passenger will not pay a through fare when he only wants to go from the Bank to Chancery Lane, for instance, a penny fare by bus?" — "Of course all that is undecided. The system of uniform fares works very well in New York and in Liverpool."

THE FIRST TELEGRAPH

Largest circulation in the world

The Daily Telegraph & Courier began as a twopenny newspaper with a fast, modern, radical image. It nearly failed

A strange figure called Colonel Arthur Burroughs Sleigh founded *The Daily Telegraph* in 1855 to highlight the scandalous way the Crimean War was being conducted, and in particular the shortcomings of the Duke of Cambridge.

Since almost everyone had his own idea of how the war was going wrong, and no one much cared about what the *Telegraph* thought of the Duke of Cambridge – who went on to become Commander-in-Chief of the Army – this was no clear selling point. Price was. In 1855 *The Times* and *The Morning Post* cost fivepence (5d; one must remember the obvious fact that there were 240 pence in a pound). Many who could not afford this would pay a penny an hour in a coffee house to read a paper; it could mean a long wait. But at the end of June 1855 the Government was to remove the remaining penny tax from newspapers; so the first issue of *The Daily Telegraph & Courier* on Friday, June 29, 1855 was well timed.

The price was twopence. This brought it within the reach of skilled workers. *The Times* immediately reduced its price to fourpence. In that first issue the *Telegraph* carried a letter signed E. Harrison, presumably a genuine would-be reader. "As I cannot afford more than sixpence per week," he wrote, "I intend, if the *Telegraph & Courier* is a really independent paper, to get a partner, and, instead of taking in a sixpenny weekly one, as I have been in the habit of doing, to take in, with him, your daily one."

What did Mr Harrison and his partner get for their daily twopence? There were four pages – the same depth as the modern paper but two inches wider. The front page was half advertising and half news; in that first issue, the front-page news was the official despatches from the Crimea, with lists of casualties, not only officers, but privates, too.

The paper on which this was printed strikes a modern reader as of fine quality, for it was made from pulverised rags, not from wood pulp. In August 1855, the *Telegraph* reported on some "very interesting" technology to make paper from wood.

The inside pages held reports from Parliament, the City, and the courts with long leading articles, news of royalty in the Court circular, short items from abroad sent by telegraph, and domestic news of fires, crime and weather. A staple was accidents: a boy fell 30 feet from scaffold; another drowned after a sudden cramp in the river Lea; a workman was pierced through the chest when machinery broke at Westminster Bridge; a carpenter fell to his death from a ladder in Shoe Lane; a soldier's pipe ignited some cartridges in his pocket, yet he lived; a clergyman caught his foot in the door of a Welsh pony-car and was dragged on his face, which he saved from fatal damage at the expense of two broken wrists.

There were plenty of murders and attempted murders. One day in August a publican was stabbed by a woman who had grabbed a knife from another selling sheep's trotters outside, and a clergyman in Dorset was shot in the street by a Captain.

Adopting the name *Telegraph* was to claim a modern, fast image. The first issue declared: "In the principles of *The Telegraph & Courier*, (the former name we trust appropriate from the sources of our special information, and the latter as an evidence of our means of dissemination and circulation), and in our conduct of this journal, we shall be guided by a high tone of independent action; we shall be bound to the fetters of no party; we will be fearlessly independent

The cover for a popular song (below, left), drawn by Alfred Concanen, shows two respectable women at tea, with a picture of the vestry clerk on the wall and a copy of The Daily Telegraph to hand. The first issue (right) sold for twopence, but Edward Levy-Lawson (below, in a Spy cartoon), as proprietor and presiding editor, later drew in a mass readership for the Telegraph as a penny paper, to achieve the largest circulation in the world

WRITTEN EXPRESSLY FOR THE COMING PANTOMIMES.

OH LOR, OH LOR! OH DEAR, OH DEAR!

A CYNICAL SONG BY
FRANK W. GREEN & OSWALD ALLAN.
MUSIC BY
EDMUND FORMAN.
LONDON: FRANCIS BROS & DAY, (BLENHEIM HOUSE,) 195, OXFORD ST W.
PUBLISHERS OF SMALLWOOD'S PIANOFORTE TUTOR, THE EASIEST TO LEARN & TO TEACH FROM.

Telegraph & Courier.

No. 1.]   LONDON, FRIDAY, JUNE 29, 1855.   [TWOPENCE.

– not the independence of unchecked and thoughtless attack, but the independence of the utterance befitting reflecting Englishmen; we shall be ever thoroughly loyal and constitutional in our sentiments, in the objects of our labour, and in the advice of our fellow-subjects – purely patriotic in our motive – and as Christians our reliance upon, and our motto shall be – *Dieu et mon Droit.*"

The front-page title *Daily Telegraph & Courier* appeared without a "The". From the first it was set in a funny gothic type, complete with a decorated full stop at the end. From August 20, "*& Courier*" was reduced to much smaller type under a big single line proclaiming *The Daily Telegraph.* It then looked much as it was to remain until 2003, when some fiddly bits within the letters were done away with.

There might only have been four pages, but the tiny type used for reporting Parliament and court cases accommodated 2,000 words per column, and there were six columns to a page. Little space was wasted on headlines, which seldom had a line to themselves, instead running straight on to the news, thus: "STATISTICS OF DRUNKENNESS – The following report was presented at the last meeting of the Edinburgh Police Commission."

Above the leaders, from September 4, were an engraved lion and unicorn, couchant, flanking the royal arms, very obscurely printed. Then came the announcements of plays at the Royal Opera, Drury Lane; the Theatre Royal, Haymarket; the Royal Lyceum Theatre and Astley's Royal Amphitheatre, Lambeth ("This evening Mazeppa and the Wild Horse; after which les Grands Caracles, or Equestrian Acts in the Circle").

There was less to read in the *Telegraph* than in *The Times.* In truth the early news-gathering was haphazard and the opinions radical and inconsistent. The first editor was Alfred Bate Richards (1820-76), whose name has not before figured in histories of the *Telegraph.* He lasted six months. Sleigh presumably met him when Richards was editor of *The British Army Despatch.* His real enthusiasm was for volunteer rifle corps, and in this he was spectacularly more successful than in editing the *Telegraph.* By the end of the century rifle volunteers numbered more than 300,000, before they were absorbed into the territorial army.

For the new-born *Telegraph*, a niche was being sought among educated or self-educated working people. "If Artisan and Peer," the paper suggested, "can alike peruse daily the same wholesome literary matter, produced by first-class writers, the general tone of society must benefit." By presumption the buyers were men, not women, although another reader's letter from the early days welcomed the prospect of the *Telegraph* "furnishing every citizen's breakfast table with a paper of his own, which he can leave for the whole family to peruse at their leisure when he goes to his office or business".

The paper opposed the power of the Church, the Lords and the Crown; it stood for the working man and "democracy", a word that carried different connotations in those days. To many it meant mob

TELEGRAPH EDITORS OF THE 19TH CENTURY
Editorial control of The Daily Telegraph remained principally in the hands of Edward Levy-Lawson, the 1st Lord Burnham, but the three men below edited the paper from day to day, writing hundreds of leading articles and shaping its news

Thornton Leigh Hunt (1810–73): radical family

Edwin Arnold (1832–1904): wrote on Buddha

J.M. Le Sage (1837–1926): wiser than his looks

rule. "She cannot and will not be the Queen of a democratic monarchy," Victoria wrote of herself in 1880. "And those who have spoken and agitated in a very radical sense must look for another monarch; and she doubts they will find one."

Edmund Yates, a popular journalist and colleague for some years of the *Telegraph*'s ebullient George Augustus Sala, characterised the typical *Telegraph* reader as "the man on the knifeboard of the omnibus" (on the open top of the bus, that is). But the paper did not expect to do without a higher class of reader. In July 1855 it devoted half a column on the front page to annual prizes for boys at King's College School. On August 15 it listed gentlemen who had leased shooting on the grouse moors.

It wrote of England and the English, not of Britain. This was a cast of mind, not a policy. The Queen visited France in 1855 as Queen of England, in both English and French eyes. Scotland came into it when the Queen went to Balmoral; Wales was forgotten; Ireland made itself felt in times of trouble. Despite a gradual increase in news from abroad and the provinces, the *Telegraph*, like other London papers, focused on the metropolis, as it would for the rest of the century.

Sales of daily papers in London were small – in the 1840s the 10 titles sold only 49,000 between them. The newcomer floundered, and by September 1855 the *Telegraph*'s circulation had fallen to two or three hundred a day. But Sleigh boldly took sole control of ownership and cut the price to a penny. New research by George Newkey-Burden, an expert on the paper's early history, suggests that Arthur Sleigh retained ownership of the *Telegraph* for longer than had previously been thought.

The unprecedented price-cut to a penny from September 17 sent the circulation bouncing back into the thousands. Though in its early existence the *Telegraph* found it hard to make its way via established distributors, Sleigh recruited an army of ragged boys to sell the paper. Their success convinced wholesalers to distribute it after all, and by the beginning of 1856 it was selling 20,000 or 30,000 a day. But Sleigh had overstretched himself financially and accepted an offer from the printer Joseph Moses Levy to buy the enterprise.

J.M. Levy (1812–88) delegated the running of the paper to his son Edward, and he was to be its *de facto* editor until 1903. Under Edward Levy (who took the additional name of Lawson in 1879, and was created Lord Burnham in 1903) the chief editor was Thornton Leigh Hunt (1810–73), son of the radical newspaper editor and man of letters, Leigh Hunt.

For the rest of the 19th century, proprietor, editors and writers leant towards bohemianism, if not penniless bohemianism. (J.M. Levy's brother built the Gaiety Theatre in the Strand, near the *Telegraph*'s first offices. Edward Levy-Lawson married the daughter of the foremost character actor of his day. Thornton Hunt, though married with a large family, remained "irregular in his domestic relations" according to a contemporary

biographer.) But Edward Levy meant business. Among office "Rules and Regulations" in the 1860s was the stipulation: "The Editor cannot be seen by anyone; all communication with him must be by letter, to which no answer can be guaranteed."

Politically the Levy-Lawson family were Liberals till they broke with Gladstone, through whose friendship they had in 1860 hastened the abolition of duty on paper (not newspapers, but newsprint). New premises, at 135 Fleet Street, were acquired that year thanks to increased profits, and the circulation was rising too. By 1861 it was 141,000, almost equal to all the other London papers' together. For the wedding of the Prince of Wales to Princess Alexandra in 1863, it sold 205,884.

By 1870 circulation was 196,000; by 1877 242,000. Readers got 10 pages of close print each day, 12 on Saturdays. By then the paper was boasting daily: LARGEST CIRCULATION IN THE WORLD.

An omnibus from Holloway, Mr Pooter's home, proclaims the Telegraph's offices in Fleet Street (top), rebuilt in 1882 with a grand pillared hall

Victorians at home

The English found in the Telegraph a mirror that reflected their own inexhaustible low drama. It was nothing at all like the staid caricature of Victorian life invented by

SEXUAL MORALS

Eliza Armstrong, a 13-year-old girl bought for £5

When W.T. Stead exposed the evils of under-age prostitution, Telegraph readers learnt every detail of a sensational case

'OFFENSIVE PUBLICATIONS" was the headline in the *Telegraph*'s small type on an item of parliamentary reporting four inches long in the issue of Wednesday July 8, 1885. George Cavendish Bentinck had asked the Home Secretary "whether his attention has been directed to publications relating to objectionable subjects which have been printed and extensively circulated throughout the metropolis by the proprietors of the newspaper called the *Pall Mall Gazette*". He also asked whether he was "aware that both yesterday and today the sale of the *Pall Mall Gazette* has been suspended at the railway stations and the principal bookstalls – (Cheers) – and has only been carried on by individuals in the streets, many of them under age, who exhibited placards of an objectionable description. (General cheering)".

Sir Richard Cross, the Home Secretary, answered only that "the publication of obscene matter is a misdemeanour at common law" and was punishable by fine or imprisonment. "The question as to whether any particular writing is obscene is one for a jury."

What were *Telegraph* readers expected to make of that snippet amid that day's 12,000 words of parliamentary reporting? If they lived in London might they be tempted to rush out and buy, whether or not from an under-age newsboy, a copy

of the *Pall Mall Gazette*? It is very likely they would have known already that the reference concerned sexual intercourse with girls under the age of consent – that is, below 13. The *Pall Mall Gazette*, a daily evening paper, had run a "tease" in its issue the Saturday before, warning readers that in its Monday issue it would address "those phases of sexual criminality" that the Criminal Law Amendment Bill should oppose. "All those who are squeamish, and all those who are prudish and all those who live in a fool's paradise of imaginary innocence and purity, selfishly oblivious of the horrible realities which torment those whose lives are passed in the London Inferno, *will do well not to read the Pall Mall Gazette of Monday*."

The *Pall Mall Gazette*'s controversial investigations did not come out of the blue. The man behind them was W.T. Stead, one of those astonishingly energetic Victorians who, as a radical journalist, delighted in living in a blaze of publicity – and who was one day even to succeed in attracting headlines for his manner of death. He was among those who went down with the *Titanic* in 1912. But for now he was on the brink of telling the world how he had bought a girl of 13.

On that scandalous Monday of 1885 Stead had just celebrated his 36th birthday. The son of a nonconformist clergyman, he had made his name by contributing to the newly-founded liberal paper, the *Northern Echo*, and without ever having set foot in a newspaper office was appointed its editor in 1871. In 1880 he became assistant editor of the *Pall Mall Gazette*, edited by John Morley, the future biographer of Gladstone. In 1883 Morley became an MP and Stead replaced him, initiating what Matthew Arnold called "the new journalism" – vivid, campaigning, even rabble-rousing. There was something of the same flavour about the *Telegraph*'s first years. It was thanks to a campaign by Stead that in 1884 Gordon had been despatched to Khartoum and his death.

White slavery was the banner for 1885 – more particularly under-age prostitution. It was something Parliament had been half-heartedly addressing since 1881. In both 1883 and 1884 a Criminal Law Amendment Bill, seeking to raise the age of consent to 16, had been dropped. Parliament was busy with other things, in 1884 electoral reform. In 1885 a new attempt looked likely to fail,

'The Pall Mall Gazette' made its campaign of 1885 the raising of the age of consent to 16. The whole country followed the trial of its editor W.T. Stead (right), who, to draw attention to vice in London, claimed to have bought a young girl. His dubious methods earnt him a jail sentence, which he proudly marked each year by donning his prison uniform

energies – pantomimes and railway smashes, cycling and skating, high fashion and the succeeding generations

because of the fall of Gladstone's administration and the makeshift status of its replacement under Salisbury. Ireland was causing chaos and on the same day that the *Pall Mall Gazette* launched its new campaign – under the heading THE MAIDEN TRIBUTE OF MODERN BABYLON – the House of Commons was also busy voting, by 263 to 219, to prohibit yet again Charles Bradlaugh, the campaigning atheist, from taking the oath as an MP.

A regular reader of the *Telegraph* would be quite familiar with all this. He – or she – might not wish to read the *Pall Mall Gazette*, for its reports were indeed shocking. There were salacious digressions on the sexual ill-treatment of women. But the *Telegraph* reader might still be interested to know what Parliament and the law were going to do about child prostitution and its exposure.

It was not as if *Telegraph* readers were unaware of sexual offences against children. On the same day as the short report of George Cavendish Bentinck's question there were two briefs items in the "Police Intelligence" column. Under the small headline DISGRACEFUL CONDUCT came the sentencing at Clerkenwell magistrates' court of Henry Richard, 26, of Camden Town to three months' hard labour for "indecent conduct" in Finsbury Park towards five schoolgirls aged between 10 and 13. At Lambeth, the magistrate sentenced a "filthy fellow", Joseph Foster, a milkman, to two months' hard labour for feloniously assaulting several young girls. This was nothing like organised child prostitution, but day after day the *Telegraph*'s court

reports detailed the most extraordinary violent and sexual assaults. The proportion of offences against girls reported must have been higher than the share of cases that they represented – among the thefts of watches and endangering of railway trains – presumably because they made better copy under their eye-catching little headings: SHOCKING; ASSAULT ON A CHILD; SERIOUS CHARGE.

The newspaper reader would also know of Stead's politics. "The future belongs to the combined forces of Democracy and Socialism, which when united are irresistible," he wrote at the beginning of his Maiden Tribute campaign. He blamed "princes and dukes, and ministers and judges, and the rich of all classes" for the evils he was exposing.

But even those who opposed Socialism might side with Stead to fight the evil of child prostitution. Josephine Butler, a redoubtable campaigner against state inspection of prostitutes, was among them. Another ally directly involved with the Maiden Tribute campaign was Bramwell Booth, the son of the founder of the Salvation Army. Stead had set up a "Special Commission" of investigation, and he gained support from Cardinal Manning, the Earl of Shaftesbury, and Frederick Temple, the future Archbishop of Canterbury, at that time Bishop of London.

It was in this complicated pattern of alliances and enmities that *The Daily Telegraph* reported, opposite the account of Cavendish Bentinck's question, the introduction in the House of Lords by the Bishop of Gloucester of the question of "juvenile immorality". The Bishop urged speed in debating the Criminal Law Amendment Bill if it was ever to become law. The bishops of Peterborough and Oxford seconded his resolution, and the Archbishop of Canterbury commended it. Stead's campaign was gaining political momentum.

The next Monday, the *Telegraph* carried a mysterious paragraph in its "Police Intelligence" column. A woman had applied to the magistrate at Marylebone, about her daughter, who had left home on Derby Day for a situation in domestic employment. She had promised to write, but no word had come. The woman broke down and wept and said in broken sentences that the girl was only 13 and "after having read what had recently been published in an evening newspaper" she greatly feared some harm had befallen her. The magistrate remarked it was negligent of the mother to let her daughter go off with strangers, and he directed the case should be further inquired into.

This was the first wind of Stead's extraordinary exercise in actually buying a girl, to show how easily it could be done. In the first instalment of the *Pall Mall Gazette* series, Stead had written of "a child of 13 bought for £5", and he called her "Lily". It was left unclear who had been doing the buying. But it had been Stead, who on June 3 had purchased a girl called Eliza Armstrong from her mother (who had now complained to the magistrate). The person who actually made the deal was Rebecca Jarrett, a Salvation Army worker who had once been a prostitute, brothel-keeper and drunk. Mrs Jarrett was quite clear that the mother, Elizabeth Armstrong, knew what fate might await the child. Eliza herself did not.

The exercise had then taken a strange turn. Eliza was taken to a midwife and known abortionist, who attested to her virginity. The midwife sold Stead a bottle of chloroform. Poor Eliza was then taken to what she took for a hotel, but was a brothel, and actually given a whiff of chloroform. Stead came into the room when she was awake, alarming her, and he left at once. The next day the girl was passed on to Bramwell Booth, and was to be taken to France and settled in a respectable position.

When Mrs Armstrong began making a row before the magistrate, Stead remained so fired by his crusading zeal that he did not see that he had wrong-footed himself. Such crimes were already strongly penalised. Nevertheless religious bodies backed Stead's main campaign, and he received the support of *The Christian*, *The Church Review*, *The Methodist Times* and *The Tablet*, the Catholic weekly.

By now the police had caught up with Stead. He failed to convince Mrs Armstrong that her daughter Eliza would be better off in a new life, and on August 24 he returned the girl to her mother. He and five others now faced trial on charges concerned with Eliza's abduction. The first to appear was Mrs Jarrett, on September 2, tried at Bow Street magistrates' court with abduction, indecent assault and administering "a certain noxious thing". No longer did the *Telegraph* report the events through

hints and small paragraphs. Under the heading THE CASE OF ELIZA ARMSTRONG, whose name everyone knew by now, it devoted two columns, more than 3,000 words, to the first day's hearing at Bow Street.

"The prisoner did not wear the characteristic dress of the Salvation Army, though her plainly cut dress was not dissimilar. Her bonnet was of the shape affected by Salvation Army 'lasses'. Her age is apparently between 35 and forty, and her height is given at 5ft 8in. In complexion she is dark, and her almost black hair, cut short on the forehead, is worn with a fringe. The expression of her countenance, as she stood in the dock motionless and silent, was not very prepossessing. Whilst taking a keen interest in the proceedings, she did not betray much anxiety."

The prosecuting counsel gave an outline of the case – the child's disappearance and eventual recovery; the administration of the chloroform. A charge of indecent assault had also been brought against the French woman who kept the house the girl was taken to. In the report of the initial day's hearing her name was given as Madame Bovary – Flaubert's exciting heroine; on the second day it was adjusted to Mourey; she spelled her own name Mourez. The case was adjourned for five days, and Stead hurried back from a holiday in Switzerland.

The Bow Street hearing against the six accused occupied five days in September. It was given huge coverage by the *Telegraph* – 14,000 words the first day, 10,000 on each of the next four. That wordage would occupy more than 150 pages of a novel-sized book. Hundreds of people crowded outside the court hoping to hear the evidence. Among friends of the accused who gained admittance was Josephine Butler.

The paper said that Mrs Jarrett's antecedents were "admittedly bad". She had been held in prison and had to stand in the dock, but her five co-defendants were allowed to stand, then sit, beside it. There was Bramwell Booth, wearing Salvation Army uniform and using an ear-trumpet, and Stead, who took "copious notes" and chose to defend himself, though a barrister was at hand to give advice and assistance. At Stead's side was Sampson Jacques, a journalist who had helped him in the investigation, and was said now to look amused. By them were Madame Louise Mourez and Mrs Elizabeth Combe, a diminutive woman in Salvation Army uniform, who "kept a cheerful demeanour". The prosecuting counsel opened with a speech two hours long, ending: "Mr Stead must indeed be a very credulous man if he believes there is an English mother in the country who would sell her child for prostitution and give a receipt for it." Sampson Jacques cried out: "Oh, oh."

Eliza Armstrong herself then gave evidence. In answer to questions, she said that she had turned 13 in April and had been living in Lisson Grove. Mrs Jarrett, giving her name as Mrs Sullivan, had asked her mother to let her go into service. Her elder sister, aged 17, was already away in service. Mrs Jarrett took her to buy a pair of boots and new frock, hat, necktie, scarf and other things. They went by

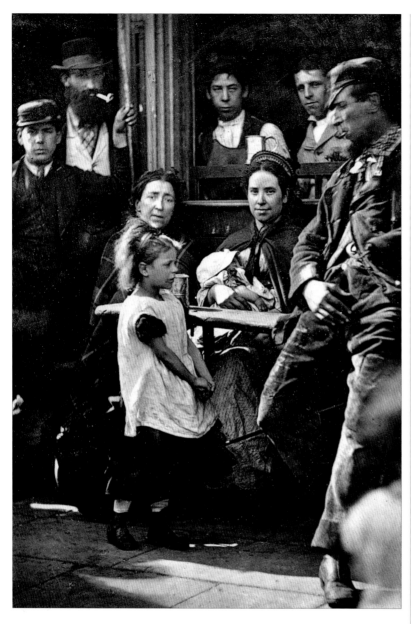

During Stead's trial a neighbour of Eliza Armstrong said she saw the girl coming out of a public house where her parents were drinking at lunchtime after money was said to have been paid for her. The photographer John Thomson showed just what such a pub would have looked like (above) in his series 'London Street Life'

omnibus to Albany Street in Marylebone and had tea in a house, and Mr Stead came in. After tea Mrs Jarrett went with her to buy underclothing.

Mrs Jarrett took her by Hansom cab to Milton Street, near Dorset Square. There was a French gentleman in the house. Mrs Jarrett asked for "Madame".

Eliza: The defendant Mourez is the person. She came into the room. I could tell she was French, because she could hardly speak English a little bit.

Counsel: What took place? — Madame took me into another little room.

When in the room with madame what took place? — She examined me indecently.

Where were you when she did this? — I was standing up by the side of her.

What did you do when she did this to you? — I tried to get away.

Did you say anything? — No.

What did she do when you tried to get away? — She let go of me.

Did she say anything to you before she did this? — No.

Was the door of the room open or shut? — Open.

Did you call out at all? — No.

Did she hurt you? — No. She then took me out of the room into the next room where Jarrett was.

What did she say? — She sat there till the gentleman came in.

Did you say anything to Jarrett as to what had happened? — Yes, I said to Jarrett, "She is a dirty woman." Jarrett made no reply.

Mrs Jarrett took her by cab to Poland Street, Soho, and the cab stopped by a ham and beef shop. Two men went into a house next to it, went upstairs, and they followed. The men went to a back room on the first floor. Eliza was taken to the front room, a bedroom. One of the men was Mr Jacques.

Mrs Jarrett told Eliza to look at a picture book. She then told her to go to bed. Eliza undressed and went to bed. Mrs Jarrett after a time lay down on the bed, clothed.

Counsel: Did she do anything to you? — She put something on a handkerchief.

Could you see what it was? — No.

What did she do? — She put it up to my nose.

Could you smell anything? — It was a funny smell.

Did she say anything when she gave it you? — She said it was scent, and told me to give a good sniff up.

What did you do? — I did sniff, and then I threw the handkerchief to the side of the bed.

While this took place, did you hear anything? — She got up then, and I heard somebody at the door. The door was open.

Did you see anyone come in? — There were curtains all round the bed. But I heard someone come in. I could hear his voice. It was a man's voice, and I screamed out, "There is a man in the room." I then heard the man go out. Jarrett came in and said, "What's the matter?" I said, "There is a man in the room." She pulled the curtains of the bed up, and said, "There is no man in the room."

Mrs Jarrett went out of the room and returned shortly and said, "Get up and dress yourself because there are too many men in the house." They left in a four-wheel cab that was waiting outside the house.

The man Eliza had not seen to recognise in the house got up on the box of the cab while she was inside, and it went off, travelling for a long time. It stopped at a large house into which the man went, and the cab stood there about an hour. Mrs Jarrett took her to a bedroom and said they would sleep there that night; it was after midnight, Eliza said.

At breakfast she met Mrs Combe, and Mr Stead was there. That day she was taken by train and boat to Paris, and lived at the Salvation Army headquarters there. Her remark that she sold the *War Cry* there provoked laughter in court. After some weeks she was taken to live with a family in the country, near Drôme, helping to look after the baby and carry out work in the house. She was brought back and reunited with her mother after 11 weeks away.

Eliza had been in the witness box for several hours, both before and after lunch. In the time left that day, her mother, Elizabeth Armstrong, gave evidence. She said that Mrs Jarrett, under the name Sullivan, had arranged with her to take the child into service, but had not given a farthing to herself, apart from a present of a shilling for her baby. After a few days, when reports in the *Pall Mall Gazette* had been brought to her attention, she had gone to the local magistrate at Marylebone.

At the end of the day's proceedings, bail was granted to all the defendants, including Mrs Jarrett, who, the defence counsel said, had been in charge of a refuge for women with which Mrs Josephine Butler was connected. As they left, the defendants were hissed, especially Stead and Mrs Jarrett.

The next day police had to hold back the crowd outside the court. Cross-examined, Eliza Armstrong explained that her father, a chimney-sweep, rented one room and the whole family, with five children, lived there (one girl being away in service). The house was let into five rooms, with about 15 people living there. She admitted she would not have been sorry to get away from home, that her father had a hard time of it, and that when she was living in France she became healthier and stronger.

She said that her mother's statement to the court – that her father did not know she was to go away – was untrue. She was disappointed that her mother, who said she had gone over to a nearby school, did not come back to see her off.

When her mother's turn came to answer questions, she became agitated on several occasions, exclaiming: "You are not going to baffle me. You are not going to cross-question me the way you did my child."

The thrust of the questioning attempted to show that Mrs Armstrong was a drunkard and spent the money she had received for her daughter on drink.

Counsel: Have you been fined for using obscene language in the streets? — Oh, I often swear.

On the very day that the child left your home – on June 3 – were you taken up drunk in the streets with a child in your arms? — No, I was not.

Were you fined the next day? — Yes, I was, through my husband's ill-using me, which is proved. He ill used me for allowing the child to go. It's nothing to do with the case. [To the magistrate] Am I bound to answer the questions?

Magistrate: Yes, you are. Were you drunk on June 3? — They said I was.

Counsel: What magistrate did you come before? — Mr Cooke.

Had you an infant in your arms at the time? — I might have had.

Do you say you were so drunk you can't recollect? — I was not "so drunk" at all.

Were you kept in custody all night? — No, I was not; I was bailed out.

By your husband? — No, a gentleman who belonged to the public house. He was not there. He sent someone to bail me out.

And then you were fined next morning five shillings? — Yes.

Later she shouted at Mrs Jarrett, fiercely shaking her fist: "I should like to get hold of you for a few

INBRIEF

AUGUST 2, 1855

On Saturday last, a public demonstration of the very interesting process of Messrs. Wait and Burgess, the patentees for the manufacture of pulp from wood fibre, took place at the temporary works, Victoria Wharf, Augustus Street, Regent's Park Basin, in the presence of many persons interested in the manufacture of paper. Among those present were Lord Stanley, Sir Henry Webb, two of Lord Palmerston's secretaries and several of the leading paper makers and publishers of the metropolis.

Messrs. Wait and Burgess have been engaged for more than a year and a half in experiments on a large scale for the conversion of wood fibre into pulp, the main difficulty to be overcome being, not so much the reduction of the fibre, as to affect this process with a certainty and rapidity which should ensure a constant supply of pure, white pulp. It is obvious that if this object can be accomplished by the employment of a cheap and inexhaustible material like wood, the advantage over the comparatively dear and increasingly expensive materials of rags will be immense.

minutes, you beauty. You have joined the Salvation Army! I'd like to get at you."

The next witness was Ann Broughton, a neighbour, whose most notable claim was that, just before Mrs Jarrett took Eliza away at three in the afternoon, Mrs Broughton had seen the child coming out of the Black Man public house, and the girl had said her mother and father were inside. Mrs Armstrong's story to the last was that she had missed Eliza's departure by going on an errand to a school, and that she had not seen her husband in the middle of the day.

At the end of the day's hearing, outside the court, Mr Booth, recognisable by his uniform, was followed towards Drury Lane by a hostile crowd and "bonneted" and maltreated. Mrs Combe had to be led to a place of safety by the police.

The next day, it was Stead's turn to cross-examine Mrs Armstrong. "Supposing Jarrett's house was a gay house?" he asked. "Then," Mrs Armstrong replied, "I should not have let the girl go."

Mr Armstrong, Eliza's father, then gave evidence. He admitted he had "knocked down" his wife after having words with her about letting Eliza go without his leave. He said it was he who got the landlord of the Black Man to bail his wife out after she was arrested that night. He denied he had been at home during the day, or that he had gone then to the public house with his wife.

The last day of the magistrates' court hearing was set for 12 days' time, September 26. It was expected to take an hour. As it turned out it was to end only after more than five hours' wrangling. Stead wanted to read a statement. The magistrate explained that his own task was to see if there was a *prima facie* case to answer, and that he could not allow a statement of motive to be read.

Stead was allowed to give a reason for the use of chloroform. He said it was to shield Eliza "from knowledge even that a man had entered her room". But she had flung the handkerchief aside, and though Mrs Jarrett had told him she was asleep, when he came into the room, he found she was not.

When Stead said that the girl "far from resenting the examination from one of her own sex, never mentioned it to anyone, even to her mother, until she was put up to it by the police", the magistrate stopped him and said: "The child did resent it, because she said she tried to get away from the woman. She said she was frightened and tried to call out. You are placing an entirely wrong complexion on the facts of the case."

Again the magistrate stopped him when he called Mrs Armstrong "a drunken woman" who had been fined three times. "There are a great many persons in other classes of life," the magistrate remarked, "who ought to be taken to the police-court and fined for drunkenness, perhaps on more occasions than Mrs Armstrong." (Applause.)

At last the hearing ended and the magistrate committed the defendants for trial before a jury at the Central Criminal Court at the Old Bailey.

With appetites whetted, readers fed on new

From the **Telegraph**

Not a fit paper for her sister to read

July 13, 1885

WANDSWORTH – SERIOUS CHARGE –
Henry Bauman, a dealer in flowers, of High
Street, Clapham, was accused of criminally
assaulting Mary Jane Evans, aged 13.

The complainant said her father was a
bricklayer, living in Bromell's Road. She had
no mother. She had known the prisoner about
two months, and had been living with him
as a general servant. On Wednesday, she
went upstairs to clean the back room. Bauman
followed, threw her on the floor, and
assaulted her.

Mr Partridge, the Magistrate: Did you try to
resist? — Witness: Yes.

Mr Partridge: Did you call out? — Witness: I
called out to him to leave me alone.

Mr Partridge: Loud? — Witness: Not very
loud. I had one glass of beer at dinner. He gave
it to me. He and his man dined with me.
Mistress, with her little girl, left home on
Tuesday for Hastings. He made me drink three
other glasses of beer, and I was "tight". I
became bad and he took me to my bedroom.
I don't remember anything afterwards. I awoke
at half past eight and he brought me up some
tea. On Thursday, he pulled me into his room
but I got away and went downstairs.

The witness further stated that she
communicated what had happened to her sister.

The defendant declared that the charge was
not true. There were men downstairs who
could have heard if she had called out.

Mr W. Soper, surgeon, of Clapham Road,
gave medical evidence, showing that it was not
an isolated case.

The complainant's married sister deposed
that the prisoner's wife requested her to sleep
with the girls. She slept there on Tuesday
night. The next morning, the accused brought
in the *Pall Mall Gazette*. She saw her sister
reading it, and she took it from her. Witness
carried it to the prisoner and said it was not a
fit paper for her sister to read. He said he
would put it away and not let her see it.
Witness left, but returned at night, but she
could not get in, as the door was locked. The
next day, she questioned her sister, and asked
her if anything had happened. She then told
her. Witness informed the prisoner that she
intended to take her sister to the police station.
He said he had not done her any harm, but if
the doctor proved anything, he must submit to
what he had done.

INBRIEF

SEPTEMBER 1, 1885

Today, so stern authority has
decreed, the time-honoured
cows and the historical
milk-stool are to disappear from
the Mall in St James's Park. The
institution was no doubt
quaintly incongruous, but
somehow it has become very
popular, and if the Ranger could
see his way to reprieving those
cows and the cans of milk the
public would be glad.

It may be that those who sell
the harmless beverage – and
they hold their queer stall by
such a right as a century's
permission gives a family – have
exceeded their vested
privileges, and, by enlarging the
sphere of their commercial
operations, have made the
corner at the Spring-gardens
entrance too much like a booth
at a fair to claim the favour so
long extended to their kith and
kin. But with this the public does
not concern itself.

A great many besides the
children and the nursery maids
will be sorry to see the historical
cows driven away from the old
corner. "A can of milk, ladies!
A can of red cow's milk, ladies!"
is no longer heard, but the
temptation of the pure rich
draught is still as eloquently
addressed to passers-by as
ever, and, from the guardsmen
to the baby, all will be sorry
when the horned favourites
have gone.

sensations during the Old Bailey trial. The coverage
was vast – more than 100,000 words in all (the
length of a substantial novel this time) – during the
12 days the court sat between October 24 and
November 10. The verdict was reported on the
same day that Gladstone set off from Hawarden on
what was to become his celebrated Midlothian
campaign in the general election. It would have to
be something to compete with "The Armstrong
case" – this headline was all that was thought
necessary each day to attract the reader's attention.

At the Old Bailey trial Stead insisted on
conducting his own defence. He was also anxious to
maximise publicity. The judge, Mr Justice Lopes,
was not hostile to Stead, and only reined him in
when he went beyond the legal proprieties.

A recently enacted law enabled defendants to give
evidence in trials for crimes classed as
misdemeanours, though not in trials for the more
serious felonies. Before this, defendants had been
obliged to remain silent. The Attorney General told
the court that the charges now brought,
misdemeanours, were chosen precisely to allow the
defendants to have their say.

Stead, Jacques, Booth, Jarrett, Combe and Mourez
were arraigned for abduction; Mourez was also
charged with assault on the girl. There was some
delay while the judge directed Booth to be allowed
his ear-trumpet.

The Attorney General, Sir R.E. Webster, outlined
the case against the defendants, and it was this that
stood, by the end of the trial, despite many loose ends.

At the magistrates' court, the defence counsel had
tried to show that Mrs Armstrong had gone to a
pub with no intention of seeing the girl off. Now,
the counsel for the prosecution did not mention
that Mrs Broughton had said in the earlier hearing
that at three o'clock Eliza came out of a pub where
her parents were drinking. In any case when
Rebecca Jarrett left with the girl, the arrangement
with Mrs Armstrong was already completed.

The prosecution outline of the case ignored the
claims by the defence during the magistrates' court
hearing that Eliza's father knew of her planned
departure at lunch-time. "It appears," the Attorney
General continued, "that in the afternoon Mr
Armstrong came home, and, not having been
consulted about his daughter going away, he got
angry with his wife and knocked her down. I am
afraid that in consequence of this Mrs Armstrong
went out, and had more drink than she ought.
The result was that she was taken in charge by the
police. The quarrel, however, was made up
immediately, and there is no reason whatever to
doubt that both husband and wife thought their
daughter had gone to a situation."

The prosecution case depended on the sequence
of events described in the magistrates' hearing: that
Eliza was taken away, examined by Madame
Mourez, taken to a bedroom in Poland Street and
chloroformed, and then taken by cab to another
house, where she slept. "There can be no doubt," the
Attorney General stressed at the Old Bailey, "that in

"God, even my God, hath anointed me with oil of gladness above my fellows."

from
HOLLOWAY GAOL

this house chloroform was again administered, and in all probability she became insensible. There is no question that a doctor came to this house." Stead had earlier kept quiet about the doctor's involvement.

When it was Stead's turn to examine Mrs Armstrong, he began by asking her about her drunkenness after her daughter had left.

Stead: How were you as to drink then? — I did not have a drop until my husband struck me.

What time were you taken into custody? — About 10 at night.

The judge: What were you taken into custody for? — For having a few words with a person I know. (Laughter.)

Mr Russell: Were you charged with being drunk and disorderly? — Well, they put down disorderly. (Laughter.) I was bailed out.

On the Wednesday when your daughter left did you ask Mrs Broughton to lend you 6d? — No, I asked her if she could lend me 1d to get some sweets to keep the baby quiet. She was about to lend it me, but Jarrett produced a shilling instead, and gave it to me to get something for the baby. I bought a comb for Eliza and a pair of socks for the baby. There was only a farthing left.

Did you get drunk on that farthing? — Yes – (Laughter) – I suppose I did, according to the accounts you give of me.

The judge: You must answer the question seriously. Do you mean to say that you got drunk on that farthing? — No, my Lord.

Mr Stead: Did you spend any of the shilling on drink? — No.

But you bought drink that day? — I had a glass at night, after my husband had struck me.

Where did you get the money for the drink? — From my husband. It was housekeeping money. I am not a person who goes out drinking, although I have got that character from you.

Strangely enough, Stead himself admitted in court that he had been in a state of "intense excitement" while conducting his investigations, and, though a teetotaller and non-smoker, had drunk champagne in a brothel to pass for a man accustomed to the world of vice. The defendants had asserted that Eliza was sold for sexual purposes. But they could not prove this in court. At the same time, Stead had some explaining to do. Why had Eliza actually been chloroformed? What did he mean to achieve by having Louise Mourez, a known abortionist, examine her? If Eliza had not been a virgin, would that have undermined his story?

The trial ended on November 7 with Booth and Jacques being found not guilty, and the charges against Mrs Combe dropped. Poor Rebecca Jarrett, who had often spoken at random out of panic, was, like Mourez, jailed for six months for assault. Jacques got two months for aiding and abetting. Stead, guilty of abduction and aiding and abetting assault, was sentenced on November 10, after more formalities, to three months, served in Holloway.

He enjoyed his time there. "As I was taking my exercise this morning in the prison yard," he told John Morley when he came to visit him, "I asked myself who was the man of most importance alive. I could only find one answer – *the prisoner in this cell*."

In the meantime the Criminal Law Bill had been passed. It raised the age of consent to 16, allowed brothels to be searched for a missing girl after a complaint by anyone acting in her interest; and it provided for girls to be taken from immoral parents.

Not only Stead's *Pall Mall Gazette*, but all the press, had made the most of the scandalous case. The *Telegraph* was intended for respectable people, and yet its huge coverage of the case did not duck the sexual question at its heart, nor the realities of a family of seven living in one room.

Stead moved on to other campaigns, but on the anniversary of his imprisonment, he would dress in his convict uniform, with its identification number and broad arrows.

In memory of Nov 10th 1885.
William T. Stead.

From the **Telegraph**

Terrible, maddening ganja

July 9, 1885

A ganja eater is a criminal of which we have happily no counterpart in this country. He is an Asiatic monster. We hear, no doubt, of men being "mad with drink"; but their frenzy differs both in degree and kind from that which results from indulgence in the juice of the hemp. For ganja is a preparation of this herb, and, though its production is punishable by the laws in India, is unfortunately so easy to procure that crime from this cause is constantly occurring.

Thus in the latest Indian papers we find a case of a man, brutalised by its use, stabbing right and left in a Bombay bazaar and note that the magistrate, when passing sentence, deplored the increase in this "most dangerous class", the "ganja-eating people". Similar preparations – similar, at any rate, in effect – are lamentably widespread, and almost every savage tribe in the world has a "hashish" of its own.

Opium and ganja are the two narcotics best known in the East. In the West, fortunately, we have but little experience of either. The former steals away, albeit with consummate fascination, a man's intellectual energies, and, in consequence, therefore, his physical energies too. The latter makes a mad, wild beast of him, works him up suddenly into a frenzy of malignant purpose, reckless of his own life or others. The Indian government, therefore, draws a wide distinction between the two. Without actually encouraging, as it has been accused of doing, the consumption of the poppy juice in the Empire, it is content to restrict its use by limitations on the sales. In the case of ganja, however, it had positively forbidden the drug, and the sale or purchase of it is penal by law.

Nor is this distinction without some justification. The opium eater is an innocuous and harmless person. He injures no one but himself; he sins, perhaps, by omission, but not by commission. The ganja eater, on the other hand, is invariably a law-breaker. He becomes at once a criminal. The villainous decoction seems to have the strange power of bringing to the surface all that is vicious and bad in its most violent form. Of such men murderers and assassins are made.

In the Ghazi villages it is "ganja" or "bang", as the different preparations of hemp are called, which is used for the stimulation of the fanatics, who are then sent out into the world to "run amok" and "to kill or be killed", for the Faith. "Hashish" is another product of the same terrific plant, and is itself a root of the word "assassin". Drugged with this awful paste, the slaves of the Old Man of the Mountains went forth into camp and city, palace and cottage, to take the lives proscribed by the tyrant in the Vultures Nest on the peaks of Alumet. In eastern warfare captains have fortified their men, when courage seemed faltering or the undertaking desperate, with the maddening juice; and during the Indian mutiny of 1857 and 1858 the rebel Sepoys often met our troops when intoxicated and frantic with "bang". There are no such incidents in the records of the poppy drugs.

Opium, so says one who was an authority on the perilous subject, does not "intoxicate" nor produce any state of body at all resembling that which is produced by alcohol. The pleasure of wine is always rapidly mounting towards a crisis, and, that being reached, the pleasure has rapidly declined; while that of

'*Opium,*' opined the Telegraph, '*communicates serenity and equipoise*'

opium comes on at once, remains stationary for several hours, and then ceases abruptly. "The one is a flickering flame, the other a steady and equable glow." More than this, however, he averred that, whereas wine disorders the mental faculties, opium, on the contrary, introduces amongst them the most exact order and harmony. "Wine robs a man of his self possession;" opium sustains and reinforces it. The former unsettles the judgment and exaggerates the toper's sentiments both as to likes and dislikes, but the latter communicates serenity and equipoise to all the faculties. Both have a tendency to open men's hearts and make them benevolent towards those they consider friends; but men under the influence of alcohol become maudlin, shake hands, swear eternal friendship, shed tears, while under the influence of the drug they are only larger hearted, sensibly benign to all, and intelligently generous.

"In short, a man who is inebriated is, and feels that he is, in a condition which calls up into supremacy the merely human – too often the brutal – part of his nature; but the opium eater feels the diviner part of his nature is paramount – that is, the moral affections are in a state of cloudless serenity; and high over all is the great light of the majestic intellect."

Of course, a great deal depends here, as in every other argument, upon the precise meaning of "intoxication". It is a notorious fact that people in weak health can be made tipsy by green tea, and it is recorded of a medical man that he said a patient of his, in recovering from a very exhausting illness, had got drunk off a beef steak! So that in this, the very broadest translation of the word, opium does "intoxicate"; but in the ordinary sense, as meaning a hilarious exultation and proportionately grievous depression of the spirit, it cannot be said to do so nor, if we may believe De Quincy, are the immediate after effects of the drug such as are supposed, for he declares that for 10 years, during which he took opium at intervals, the day succeeding that upon which he indulged in the luxury was always one of usually good spirits. In the end, however, the narcotic told upon him, and after a severe struggle with the habit he overcame the craving, and shook off its fetters. Here, then, we have the characteristic of this drug, and can recognise the wide difference between it and the terrible maddening "ganja" of Arabia and India.

WE ARE WHAT WE BUY

Revolvers for sale; old artificial teeth bought

The small ads reflected all the urgent desires of Telegraph readers, from perfect skin to portable railway conveniences

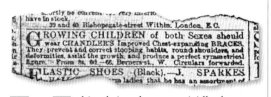

Nothing brings home so vividly the energy and the strangeness – to us – of life in Victorian London than the small advertisements that filled the columns of *The Daily Telegraph*. "Colt's Holster or Cavalry Revolver," announced an advertisement on the front page of its first number in 1855. "Great length of range, force and penetration. In case complete with Caps, Flask, Mould and Wrench, £7. Order through any Army and Navy Agent, or of the inventor and manufacturer, SAMUEL COLT, 14 Pall Mall London." A neighbouring column of news on that page listed dozens of killed and wounded ("Private William McCabe, severely; Private William Lewis, slightly…") in the Crimea.

Further down the page a tempting question was addressed to Ladies: "Why give such a high price for your Paris and other wove STAYS, when you can get any size you require, in German wove, for 3s 11d? W. CARTER, 22 Ludgate-street."

Railway accident insurance; genuine cocoa; a volume of *Surgical and Pathological Observations*; "Scotticisms corrected"; Money lent; "The *Telegraph & Courier* delivered by eight o'clock every morning in Town at one shilling a week"; "Avoid tight lacing"; "Slack's Nickel Silver is the hardest"; Keating's cough lozenges; Bedding; "Cole's Alga Marina – chronic rheumatism completely cured"; "Asthma – Dr Locock's Pulmonic Wafers give instant relief"; Gold Reviver, 1s 6d a bottle; Superior Hats! The crowd of small ads shouted for attention like the street cries of London.

Misfortune and sickness was bread and butter to the advertisers. "GROWING CHILDREN of both sexes should wear Chandler's improved chest-expanding BRACES. They prevent and correct stooping habits, round shoulders and deformities, assist growth and produce a perfect symmetrical figure. From 8s 6d."

INBRIEF

July 18, 1855

STRANGE INCIDENT

An American paper gives the following extract from a private letter from an officer in the Crimea, to a citizen of Buffalo:– "A curious thing occurred yesterday. A sapper was brought from the trenches with his jaw broken, and the doctor told me there was a piece of it sticking out an inch and a half from his face. The man said it was done by a round shot, which the doctor disbelieved, but the poor fellow insisted, and said, 'Yes, and it took off the head of the man next to me.' This was conclusive, and the surgeon proceeded to remove the bone; it came out quite easy, when the doctor said to the man, whose face appeared to preserve its form pretty well, 'Can you move your jaw?' 'Oh, yes, sir,' was the reply. The doctor then put his finger into the man's mouth, and found the teeth were there, and at length assured the soldier that it was no jaw of his that was broken, but that of his headless comrade, which had actually been driven into his face, inflicting a severe, but not dangerous wound. Upon this the man's visage, which had been rather lengthened, rounded up most beautifully."

Are you quite secure and content with your appearance? Perhaps this would attract your attention: "ALEX ROSS's ENAMEL (as used by Madame Vestris). All imperfections of the skin are hidden by its use and a transcendent beauty produced. Price 10s 6d." Half a guinea for transcendent beauty was value indeed.

There was hope for less tractable troubles. "OSTEO EIDON WHAT IS IT? See Patent, March 1, 1862. No. 560 – GABRIEL'S SELF-ADHESIVE MINERAL TEETH & FLEXIBLE GUMS, without palates, springs or wires, and without operation; warranted for mastication and articulation."

"JOZEAU'S SYRUP AND PATE OF LACTUCINE (active principal of lettuce). Possess all the soothing properties of opium without its dangers. Highly recommended by the medical profession in colds, asthma and all chest infections."

A hardy perennial of the advertisement columns became familiar through its expansive claims under the biblical quotation "FOR THE BLOOD IS THE LIFE". This was "Clarke's World-famed Blood mixture. Trademark – 'Blood Mixture'. For Cleansing and Clearing the Blood from all impurities. Cannot be too highly recommended. For Scrofula, Scurvy, Skin Diseases, and Sores of all kinds, it is a never-failing and permanent cure. It: Cures Old Sores, Cures Ulcerated Sores On The Neck, Cures Ulcerated Sore Legs, Cures Blackheads Or Pimples On The Face, Cures Scurvy Sores, Cures Cancerous Ulcers, Cures Blood And Skin Diseases, Cures Glandular Swellings, Clears The Blood From All Impure Matter, From whatever cause arising. As this Mixture is pleasant to the taste, and warranted free from anything injurious to the most delicate constitution of either sex, the proprietor solicits sufferers to give it a trial to test its value."

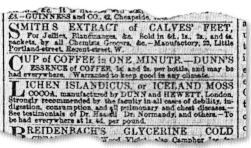

The small ads sometimes spoke with the more discreet voice of a confidential friend: "WALTER'S RAILWAY CONVENIENCE. May be obtained at 16, Moorgate Street, near Bank, London. No lady should travel without one. Female attendant at the private entrance."

There were desirable goods for everyday purposes: "CUP OF COFFEE IN ONE MINUTE – Dunn's essence of coffee"; "FIVE HOURS LIGHT FOR A PENNY guaranteed by burning the PENNY CANDLE SOLIDIFIED GAS (registered). Magnificent transparent candles".

If it was good enough for Queen Victoria, what more could you want than "Glenfield Starch, exclusively used in the Royal Laundry, and pronounced by her Majesty's Laundress to be the finest starch she ever used. Sold in packets only by all grocers." Or "ORTON'S SURREY SAUCE – this delicious condiment (as used in the Royal Kitchen at Windsor) may be obtained from any sauce vendor. one shilling per bottle"; "RECKETT'S PARIS BLUE IN SQUARES, Used In THE PRINCE OF WALES'S LAUNDRY."

The columns were an employment exchange: What might catch the eye of the job-seeker could turn out to be leisure: "WORK, BOYS, WORK AND BE CONTENTED. This serio-comic song, by Harry Clifton (the celebrated comic singer) is the best song ever written. Everyone should have it. Free for 18 stamps. – Hopwood and Crew, 42, New Bond Street."

Or there might be an opening for a personal trainer: "SWORD EXERCISE – WANTED, A TEACHER of the sword exercise – address AZ, Julian's Library, 84, Connaught-terrace, Hyde Park."

Sometimes the advertisers were in the weaker position: "MONEY, fourteen pounds – a Tradesman, unexpectedly requiring this amount for ten days, will deposit security at once convertible for £60, and pay £5 – appoint interview, J W, 7 Allen Street,

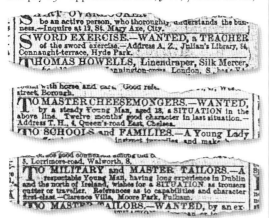

Goswell Street, EC." Or was there a catch?

As a last resort you could flee the metropolis: "THE EMIGRANT'S GUIDE TO IOWA AND NEBRASKA – issued free, or by post one penny – contains particulars of Prairy Farms and Good Lands for Sale at Low Prices, giving 10 years' credit. For rates of fare to Burlington, Iowa, Lincoln and Omaha, Nebraska, Western States, San Francisco, etc, for any other information, apply to the BURLINGTON AND MISSOURI RIVER RAILROAD COMPANY."

Paul Verlaine and Arthur Rimbaud (in a detail, right, from 'A Corner of the Table', 1872, by Ignace-Henri-Jean-Théodore Fantin-Latour) advertised French lessons in The Daily Telegraph *when they were living in Camden Town, in 1873. A fortnight later Verlaine shot Rimbaud*

French lessons from Rimbaud and Verlaine

Paul Verlaine (*above*, *left*) had fled his wife and was living with the 18-year-old Arthur Rimbaud (*right*) in Camden Town when on June 21, 1873 they placed a small advertisement in *The Daily Telegraph* among the columns of "Toothache", "Half Guinea Trousers", "Mourning for Widows", "Chocolat Menier", "Medical Electricity" and "Tolkien's Pianos (Secondhand)".

It is not known what takers the scandalous French poets had before the violent quarrel that led to the imprisonment of Verlaine and the eventual exile of Rimbaud in Africa. There had been a knife fight and on July 3 Verlaine wrote a letter dated "At sea" to Rimbaud in Great College Street, Camden Town, saying: "I really had to go, this violent life with all these scenes for no reason but your whim doesn't bloody suit me any more." Meanwhile, Rimbaud had begun a letter begging Verlaine to return, and promising to be better tempered. He delayed posting the letter since he didn't have a penny for the stamp, and so received Verlaine's from the ferry before adding to his own a postscript that he would stay in London but might have to sell Verlaine's clothes to live.

As it turned out, Rimbaud joined Verlaine in Brussels, where on July 10 Verlaine fired two revolver shots at him, hitting him in the wrist with one. Rimbaud was taken to hospital, Verlaine to the police station, paying for his moment of madness with a two-year prison sentence. It gave Rimbaud a chance to finish his prose poem *A Season in Hell*.

From the **Telegraph**

Three Blind Men
by 'One of the Crowd'

James Greenwood gained a wide following under the pen-name 'One of the Crowd' with his low-life tales of London published every Saturday

February 18, 1882

The fog was so dense that it really made no vast amount of difference whether one endeavoured to make his way along the street with his eyes open or shut; nevertheless, the spectacle of two blind men out in such weather without even a dog to guide them seemed to appeal to compassion more strongly even than if it had been broad daylight. They were shabby enough to be beggars, but they were not begging. They were walking lingeringly up and down before a pawnbroker's shop in the neighbourhood of Holborn.

There was a passage by the side of the shop, and now and again one of them would desist from stamping his feet and blowing his fingers and, approaching this narrow entry, incline his head as if listening. Presently there emerged from the passage a third blind man, and the other two, recognising the sound of his footsteps, eagerly made up to him, and one of them, as I could make out by the gleaming lamps outside the pawnbrokers window put out his hands, as though fully expecting something of bulk to be delivered into them. But he was disappointed.

"I ain't got it, Joe," remarked the last comer, angrily; "after all we're no better off than ever."

And then, the three laid their blind heads together, and the expression of their blank faces grew more dismal, and he who had emerged from the passage stood perking his head this way and that as though he would be grateful for someone with eyes to help him out of a difficulty. It occurred to me that they were anxious that someone should lead them across the road, and I volunteered to do them that small service. But I was mistaken. It wasn't that they wanted. The man who had been on an unsuccessful errand to the pawnbroker's held in his hand a dirty card and, guided by my voice, he held it towards me. "You can do us a kindness, howsoever," said he, "by telling us what it says on this pawn ticket."

I took the document in question, and informed him that it related to a concertina pledged a few days before for the sum of 18 pence.

"One and six was the sum," said the blind man, "for I pawned it myself, and a halfpenny is the interest. But now we want to take it out, sir, they want a penny more, the cheating wagabones, and what's that for, I wonder?"

I looked at the pawn ticket again, and discovered on it a minute marginal note, "Drawer one penny."

"There you are Tommy," remarked one of the others; "That accounts for it. You told them to put it in a drawer and they've charged for doing it."

"I don't recollect telling them," returned the other, turning his head aside as though his two companions could see the flush of guilt that rose to his face.

"Taint likely you would after you spent 18 pence in rum before you come home," said his friend, sharply. "You're a nice one, you are, for a partner;" an opinion which the third blind man mutteringly endorsed, adding aloud that it was pretty nigh time there was an alteration, and there'd have to be one too.

The delinquent looked abashed, but he had a spirit, and was quick tempered. "All right," said he, "if it is to be a break say the word, and don't make any more bones about it. Here's the ticket, get it out yourselves, and much good may it do the pair of you, who won't be able to get any more music out of it than though it was an old bellow. Shake hands at parting if you like; if you don't do the other thing. I don't care."

They were walking slowly away from the pawnbrokers through the fog, and they talked so loud that it was impossible for anyone near at hand not to overhear what was said.

"Oh no, you don't care, Tommy," remarked one of the two sarcastically; "I take the weary weskit off my back to raise the money to get the music back after you had wrongfully pawned it and you don't care. Taint likely!"

This, seemingly, was touching on a tender point, for Tommy's at no time melodious voice grew huskier and two living tears glistened in his dead eyes as he made answer, "I might be unfriendly, but I wouldn't be mean, if I was you Dick, knowing as you do the why and the wherefore, I'd agree to say no more about it on my promising to pay it back to you in instalments. Here you are – here is both the ticket, that for the weskit and for the concertina as well. And here –" and as he uttered the words he produced from a pocket a shilling and a sixpence, and was seemingly about to add, "and here's the money I raised on the waistcoat." But it possibly occurred to him that a little rum would be a comfort to him in his loneliness if he parted company with his old partners. He slipped the money back, and offered them the pawn ticket only. To this they not unreasonably demurred, and a row seemed rapidly brewing and was to be prevented if possible.

Though if it had come to fisticuffs, three blind men fighting it out in a fog would have been a novel spectacle – the other two would have had no chance against Tommy, even though they made a combined attack on him. They were much older than he, and mild speaking, wizened little men whereas he, though wasted and haggard looking, was still, as regards age, in the prime of life, and though his broad back was bowed he was big boned and muscular. His general aspect suggested that he had been at one time a miner, and had lost his sight in a coal pit accident.

I took the liberty of offering to settle the pecuniary difficulty, and further and by way of promoting perfect harmony, to pay for a breakfast for them, before they started on their day's business. I did not need telling what the latter was, for by this time I recognised them and probably should have done so before but for the wraps with which the lower parts of their faces were enveloped to keep out the fog. They were three wandering minstrels, who for many years past I had seen now and again perambulating the streets of London playing and singing as they plodded along in a row just off the pavement.

The two little men gratefully accepted my offer, but the other, when he found that the proposed treat was to take the mild form of coffee and bread and butter, asked to be excused, and earnestly requested that he might be permitted to have his "whack" of the sum I thought of expending to spend in rum. I told him that a substantial and sober breakfast would do him more good, to

'They were shabby enough to be beggars, but they were not begging.'
Gustave Doré caught the atmosphere of the world that Greenwood
described in his series of engravings, 'London: a Pilgrimage'

which he respectfully made answer that I might think so, but that
rum was what he chiefly lived on – that, and a crust of bread.

"That is a strange sort of diet," I remarked.

"Ah! But perhaps you don't happen to know that I am suffering
from a strange sort of complaint," returned the blind man, "and
that rum is the only physic that will touch it."

He laughed as he said it, as though it were merely a little joke,
but there was no corresponding humour in his face. On the
contrary, all of a sudden he appeared more haggard and anxious
than before. His words, too, seemed to convey to his two friends
a meaning they did not impart to me, and which caused them to
relent towards him.

"He's right in what he says, sir," one of them remarked, "and if
you would let him have his way it would oblige all three of us."

So, provided with the modest sum I dispensed, Tommy left us,
promising to return to the coffee shop in half an hour or so. I
felt curious for many reasons to learn something of the
partnership that existed between them, as well as of the "why and
the wherefore" that had led to the pawning of the concertina,
and of which the burly blind man who had temporarily taken his
departure spoke so mysteriously. Then again, what was the
"strange complaint" from which he was suffering, and for which
the only medicament was "rum and a crust of bread"?

They seemed to be aware that I was pondering this last
mentioned idiosyncrasy of their friend Tommy, for as soon as he
had demolished his first slice and swallowed his first saucer full
of hot coffee, one of the little old men remarked, "He would sell
his boots for it, sir – rum I am speaking of. We've known him to

sell 'em, and the cap off his head, and go about in consequence
in snowy weather with a hankisher tied round his head."

"That's true, Dick."

"We've known him do worse than that," returned the other; "I
can overlook a lot, but when it comes to taking the wittles out of
our mouths to put a quarter of rum into his own, I say, as I said
before, it is coming it a little too strong."

"Dick means pawning of the music," said the other little old
blind man, who seemed the kindlier disposed of the two. "Well,
well, that was a bit too bad. But you, see, sir," he continued,
feeling for my sleeve to find whether I was within whispering
distance of him, "Tommy is the only one that can play on it, and
our two voices is so worn with the weather that we're all gone in
our high notes unless they're eked out with the playing. Well,
Dick here and me get wet through and fall queer. Dick has a
touch of his old rheumatism, and I get such a shocking cold in
my head that I couldn't snuffle like a Christian, let alone sing; so
that you see we come to a dead block. Tommy was all right, but,
of course, he couldn't go out alone."

"Why not?" I asked.

"How could he touch his way along, and with both his hands
wanted for the music? So there was nothing doing for five mortal
days and nothing coming in 'cept the few odd bits of things we
could sell or pawn, and a share of the money raised that way
didn't go far, you may depend, to'rds buying Tommy his usual
dosage of physic. As he told you, sir, he lives on rum pretty
nearly, and can't live without it, he can't rest of nights without it,
and goes on in such a way that if you wasn't used to sleep with
him he would give you the creeps. Well he got that hunger on
him at last, that unbeknown to us, he sneaked out the music,
which was our only main-sail in a manner of speaking and he
went and pawned it for 18 pence, and melted every blessed penny
of it in rum. But, mind you, he was ashamed of it. We couldn't
make out what he was crying about when he came back, having
swallowed the three quarters right off, and then he up and told
us that."

"Bah! I say now, as I said before, it was a shabby action,"
interrupted the other blind man.

"So it was, from an 'ornary pint of view, Dickie, my boy,
but – there's the why and the wherefore. Always bear that in
mind, Dickie."

"You have alluded to a why and a wherefore several times
before," I ventured to observe. "May I ask what you mean by it?"

"Why, as to that," replied the kindly old blind man, after some
hesitation, "if Tommy were here himself he could tell you the
story a deal better than I can though I have heard it so often –
for he don't make any secret of it – that I can give it you almost
in Tommy's own words. It's about the way in which he lost his
precious eyesight, and come to be what he is. He wasn't like me
and Dickie here, one of us lost his sight by smallpox when we
were quite young, and the other was born blind. The man we're
speaking of, sir, had his sight as well as the rest, and was
according to his own account as strong and able a man as ever
walked. He was a coal whipper, and worked down at Shadwell
and, as a young man, was that strong at carrying heavy weights
there was no chap in his line could come nigh him. But he was a
drinker, and all his earnings went at the public house. Not
having ever seen his face, I can't say; but he says that in them
times he was a good looking fellow, and might have had his pick

of half a dozen handsome girls for a sweetheart, but there was only one he could bring his mind to take to, and she was a lighterman's daughter. But the father was a tee-totaller, and the girl was of the same persuasion, and though he took a strong liking for her and she liked him, she told him she could never marry a drunkard, and so they had a quarrel about it, and her father interfered and said things to Tommy – so he said himself – that raised the devil in him. But he kept it quiet: he couldn't forget the old man's taunting or the girl's disdainful way of treating him, and he swore to himself that she should marry a drunkard, though he played artful to get her to do it for a whole year. He pretended that what the girl's father had said to him when they quarrelled had sunk into his mind, and that he was resolved to give up the drink. After a talk the old lighterman he says, 'Very well, Tom, let it drop, let the matter rest 'til a month after Christmas' – it was then the end of October – 'and then perhaps, we'll speak of it again.'

"Well, sir, as Tommy tells the story, he never touched a drop the whole time, and though he was sometimes nearly mad with thirst for it, he kept his heart up by thinking how he would take it out of 'em all when he gained what he was fighting for. He did gain it. No one had seen him inside a public house, or the worse for liquor, right up to the time mentioned, and he begged so hard that the old man gave his consent and they was married on Valentine's Day in February. It was a precious shame, but he kept the promise he had all along been keeping his heart up with. Before the end of the week he went deliberate and got roaring drunk, and so came home to her, and jeered and laughed at her, and told her that that was how she might expect to see him every day of her life. He was furious drunk when her father came, and struck him and turned him out of the house. The father wanted his girl to leave her husband, and come home and live there again, but she was one of the pious sort, and told him she must bow to her fate, and keep with the man she had sworn to be true to at the altar, which was just what Tommy – I am giving you his own words for it – didn't bargain for. He made sure, when he had his spits out against her, that she would be glad to go back to her father, and so he would be rid of her. But that was where he made a mistake. She stuck to him for all his ways of trying to tire out her patience and make her give in. Half starving her wouldn't do it or beating her when he was in his drunken fits. The more cruel he was the more she clung to him, 'til, to use Tommy's own words, he used to hate the sight of her and the sound of her voice.

"Well, at last she had a child, a boy it was, and the very image of her. If it had been the image of him it might have been different, but, being so much like the woman he hated and yet was tied to, made him worse than ever, if that could be, and so she dragged on her miserable life for six years afterwards, having no more children; and then she died, leaving the boy for her husband to take care of. He was worse off than ever now. His wife use to earn enough to keep herself and the boy after a fashion, but now she was gone, he had to provide for his child and his self as well. This wasn't always an easy matter; for he had grown to be a regular drunkard and was gone all to the dogs, in a manner of speaking, and could get work only as an odd jobber. He talks freer about his wife than about the boy; but we've heard him, when he has had a very bad night, let out things that showed the poor little chap had an awful time of it.

"As Tommy himself tells the story the boy and him lived together for about three years, and then he made up his mind to turn him out to fish for himself as well he could. Tommy got so bad by that time that he couldn't get any work at all, and he resolved on going on tramp to seek it. So he ses to the boy – nine years old he was – 'I've had enough of you, and I daresay you've had enough of me. Now we're going to part – you one way and me another. And we're parting, mind you, for good and all, whatever happens. Wherefore you go you've got to say that your father and mother are both dead – you'll get on all the better for saying that you ain't got no relations in the world. If so be as we should meet no matter when or where, and you give anybody to understand by word or look that I'm your father don't you expect any mercy from me, because you won't get any.'

"So they parted. But Tommy's idea is that the boy was afraid to go right away from him, and followed him about at a distance everywhere he went, though where he stowed away of nights or how he picked up a bit of wittles to keep him alive, of course he couldn't say. Roaming about the country at the end of a couple of months – it was in the summertime – Tommy found himself at Kingston, and so hard up that he had to go to the workhouse to ask for a lodging. He had been there a week before, and there was some question about letting him in 'til somebody at the workhouse asked him his name, and when he told it ses 'e, 'That's the same name as that poor boy gave that we brought here last week. Come along 'ome my man,' he says. So he takes Tommy to the infirmary, and there, sure enough, was his boy all gone wrong, and just upon dying. But he knew his father, and, only that he was mortal afraid of those last words he had spoke to him, would have been precious glad, I daresay, to have made it up with him. But Tommy wouldn't own him. 'He's nothing to do with me,' he ses, 'ask him if he is.'

" 'Well he looks at you as if he knew you,' said they.

" 'I tell you I never set eyes on him before in my life,' Tommy says. 'Strike me blind if I ever did.' So they believed him at that, and let him go to his ward and in the morning he heard that the boy was dead. And here comes the strange part of it. He wasn't struck blind of a sudden but a sort of light settled in his eyes, and in less than a month he was stone blind and incurable. It isn't for me to say that it was a judgement on him but that's what he says it was, and he ought to know better than anyone he knows. Anyhow, it gave him a fright he hasn't got over yet and he has been joined with us these six years and more, and he was a long time a begging before that. He's all right in the day time and when he is in company, but unless he is well primed with rum he can't get a wink of sleep of nights. It's the boy's eyes that haunt him, and the look he gave him when he took that oath that he didn't know him. And in the nick of time," continued the little old blind man, pricking up his ears, "as just as I've done telling you all about him, here he comes."

And at that moment Tommy put his face in at the door, beaming with recently imbibed rum. He had not behaved unhandsomely, however. Out of the sixpence I gave him he had spared that other penny the pawnbroker had demanded over and above the 18 pence and halfpenny and now carried the precious concertina under his arm. The fog had abated somewhat at this time and a few minutes afterwards the music of the ransomed concertina was heard in the roadway, vigorously accompanying a spasmodic rendering of "Dear father, come home".

THE DUNMOW FLITCH

A medieval custom revived, or invented

Thanks to an historical novelist, from 1855 a side of bacon once more went to a couple who had not regretted they were married

The Dunmow Flitch is a side of bacon presented to a couple judged to have lived together for a year and a day without repenting of their marriage. The *Telegraph* was published in time to report on July 19, 1855 that "yesterday, this ancient ceremony, which has been for many years past in abeyance, was revived with great enthusiasm".

The man behind the revival was Harrison Ainsworth (1805–82), the bestselling author of historical novels such as *Guy Fawkes*, *Rookwood* and *The Tower of London*. He put up the money to present a flitch "according to the old custom" to a couple who:

*Never since the parish clerk said Amen
Have wished themselves unmarried again.*

In 1855 the *Telegraph* reported, "two parties claimed the flitch – a French literary gentleman and his wife, and a tradesman and his wife residing at Chipping Ongar. Large numbers of persons arrived in the country excursion train and a general holiday was observed."

"The proceedings commenced with a mock trial at the town hall, where the claimants made good their title to the flitch of bacon before a jury of maids and bachelors. Flitches having been awarded to both the French and English claimants, a procession, consisting of police constables, yeomen, ladies with garlands, a stud of horses, bands of music, banners, maids and bachelors of the jury, and flitches of bacon carried by eight yeomen, was formed, and moved through the town into an adjacent meadow.

"The claimants were brought unto the ground in triumphal chairs, and certain ponderous oaths having been administered, the flitches were presented with due solemnity amidst the hearty cheers of the spectators. Rural sports of every description followed, and a dinner was given, over which Mr Harrison Ainsworth presided." Money raised that day went to the rebuilding of Dunmow Town Hall.

Was the event a genuine tradition? In some ways it was reminiscent of that triumph of early Victorian romantic historicism, the Eglinton Tournament of 1839, when 100,000 thronged by means of canal boat and railway train to a medieval joust in Scotland only to be soaked and muddied by an August downpour.

Dunmow had its own excursion trains and medieval make-believe, but, whatever the spuriousness of detail, the event was based on historical fact. The presentation of the Flitch was claimed to have begun in 1111, and it was certainly about that time that Dunmow Priory, Essex, was established as a house of Augustinian Canons, an ancient religious order of priests. The Victorians referred to them indifferently as monks or friars, even though friars – who went begging from place to place – had not been invented at the beginning of the 12th century.

The first dated presentation of the bacon is in 1445. But Dunmow is already mentioned late in the 14th century, both by Chaucer's Wife of Bath and by William Langland, as the place where bacon is given to a happy couple.

It has been suggested that the custom arose from some kind of jocular tenure. This convention meant that some estate was held by a tenant as long as he kept up the payment of some silly item – a fish or strawberry – or performed some more or less risible act.

We read of 110 acres in Suffolk being held as long as the tenant each Christmas Day performed in front of the King "altogether and at once, a Leap, a Puff and a Fart" (*simul et semel unum Saltum, unum Sufflum et unum Bombulum*). For more examples see Thomas Blount's *Fragmenta Antiquitatis* (1679; enlarged 1815). In any case, at Dunmow the oldest documents promise a gammon – a leg – not a side of bacon.

After the dissolution of the monasteries, the custom devolved upon the lord of the manor, who regularly held a court under English law to rule on matters such as strayed animals and field boundaries. There is a discussion of the Dunmow Bacon ceremony in the original *Spectator*, in the issue for October 15, 1714. The last "legitimate instance" of the presentation was in 1751 to Thomas and Ann Shakeshaft.

That unlikely antiquary William Hone, a radical and hater of the Established Church, included the story of Dunmow in his vastly influential *Every-Day Book* (1826). But in 1851 the lord of the manor refused a gammon to a couple called Hurrell. It was after this that Harrison Ainsworth stepped in with his reinvention, and produced a narrative poem to justify it. By then a jury of six spinsters and six bachelors considered the arguments of a Counsel for the Flitch and a Counsel for the Claimants. After that it was all marquees, refreshments, bands, sideshows, coconut-shies, sunburn and general jollity.

The Flitch was awarded after 1855 in 1869, 1874 and 1890, then annually till 1906. In 1996 it was decided to present it, or at least to hold a trial, every four years, most recently in July 2004.

INBRIEF

AUGUST 3, 1855

ALARMING BALLOON ACCIDENT
On Monday evening, a large number of people assembled at the Adam and Eve Gardens, Old St Pancras Road, to witness the ascent of Mons. Gardonia, in a balloon. The balloon had only ascended a few feet when it came in contact with a newly erected orchestra in the gardens, which caused Mons. Gardonia to be thrown from his seat in the car.

Struggling, he caught hold of the wickerwork and hung suspended over its side. The balloon continued to ascend, 'til at length, when over St Giles's Cemetery, the aeronaut let go of his hold, and falling into the cemetery, his head came in contact with a monument. He received several severe contusions on the head, from which, however, no immediate danger is apprehended.

CHRISTMAS SPIRIT

Pantomimes and a pound of plum pudding

Plum pudding was essential to the richness of Christmas in 1856 – even when it was weighed out by the ounce in a workhouse

The Haymarket boasted 'Harlequin and the Three Bears' (above), even if the traditional harlequinade (below) was becoming overwhelmed by novelty scenes and special effects

Thirteen years after the publication of *A Christmas Carol*, an English Christmas had all the rich concentration of Dickens's story. The shopping was still largely done the day before, and not everyone had a holiday on December 25. *The Daily Telegraph* came out on both Christmas Day and Boxing Day.

In a celebratory mood the paper thought it worthwhile to write a leading article on Christmas fare. It pictured London as a cornucopia filled with good things from global trade. "What though there be a total failure of crops at Xante and Patres, or a political complication in Spain beyond the power of man to comprehend? We have the evidence of the grocers' 'emporiums' to demonstrate that in this overgrown metropolis there are currants and raisins enough for the consumption of all Christendom. Plum puddings and mince pies must be luxuries peculiarly British, or why do we monopolise all the 'candied peel' of more favoured climates?"

The railways brought in gifts of pheasant and hares from the country, "while, on the reciprocal principle, which is the basis of mutual friendship and kindly feeling, codfish, oysters, and Christmas hampers in countless numbers, form the metropolitan contribution destined to furnish the hospitable boards of country cousins and provincial friends – dainties which are tithed by the functionaries of the rail, if rumour belies them not".

"And the Union Workhouses," Scrooge had asked the gentlemen seeking his charitable donations. "Are they still in operation?" They were in 1843, and still were in 1856 and for decades to come. A "union" was an amalgamation of parishes, but some London parishes were big enough to support a workhouse each.

The Daily Telegraph filled columns of tiny print on December 26 with reports from the workhouses of London, on the grounds that "those who contribute the funds should be made acquainted, at least once a year, with the number of the poor, and other local statistics in their parishes". The statistics included the allowance of food for Christmas dinner.

St Marylebone's 1,931 workhouse inmates (including 482 children) were each allowed half a pound of plum pudding, half a pound of roast beef, one pint of porter, one ounce of tea, four ounces of sugar, one ounce of butter.

At St Pancras, 1,433 were given one pound of plum pudding and half a pound of roast beef, free from bone; tea, sugar, and tobacco, and snuff for those who desired it; and apples, oranges, nuts, and sweetmeats for the children. St Pancras was a parish the management of whose workhouse, the paper noted, "has been challenged, and consequently subject to Poor law interference. It turns out, however, that the charges were rather the result of electioneering tactics, than of any real ground of complaint."

At the West London Union, with 504 adults and nearly 200 children, the ration was only "seven ounces roast beef, eight ounces plum pudding, 12 ounces potato, and one pint of porter". And so it went on.

For those with the ticket money, the London theatres staged bright and inventive pantomimes from Christmas night onwards. Tradition was tempered with innovation. The traditional harlequinade was now becoming almost subordinate to introductory scenes, the paper judged. "Now the introduction is everything, and the managers vie with each other in the magnificence with which they decorate this part of the entertainment, to which the so-called 'comic business' (ie the harlequinade) comes in as a sort of supplement."

The variety was extraordinary. There was *See Saw Margery Daw, or Harlequin Holiday and The Island of Ups and Downs* at Drury Lane; *The Babes in the Wood, or Harlequin and the Cruel Uncle* at the Haymarket; *Conrad and Medora, or Harlequin Corsair and The Little Fairy at the Bottom of the Sea*, with a *William Tell* play thrown in, at the Lyceum.

The Adelphi was keen to meet "the demand for a class of pantomime rejecting the grosser vagaries of our theatrical ancestors and distinguished by the more refined sprightliness of

modern travesty", and this year staged *Mother Shipton; or Harlequin Night of Love* written by Mark Lemon, the founding editor of *Punch*.

Astley's was renowned for equestrian displays and its pantomime was no exception. "We are glad to welcome, in *Paul Pry on Horseback, or Harlequin and the Magic Horseshoe*, a number of clever feats performed by the noble animal, useful to man, and introduced with considerable ingenuity," the *Telegraph*'s man at Astley's wrote. "There is a fire horse in the introduction, who plays an important part in the transactions which take place, and there are Phoebus and Aurora in a chariot of fire; then there is a scene, in which Paul Pry's horse steals a purse of gold from a wicked old man, Mr Criball, whose soul, of course, migrates into Pantaloon; and finally, after the inquisitive hero has worked out his mission – that is, has pryed into the tricks and frauds of all knaves – there is a splendid transformation scene, in which Mr William Cooke, as Mars, willing to defend Truth and Honour, drives a war chariot, to which are attached ten gold footed steeds."

The lessee of the Surrey Theatre in Lambeth had "for months before the holly of Christmas has burst into blossom, been busy with his inventive faculties and his dextrous workmen, devising means of enjoyment" for the pantomime. "*Harlequin and the Summer Queen, or, King Winter and the Fairies of the Silver Willows* is full of the brilliant scenic effects and graceful and novel devices for which the Surrey realms of pantomime have achieved a well deserved fame". That was the modern trend for pantomime.

The weekly riots at the dockland church of St George-in-the-East spilled over to engulf the parish's mission house at Wellclose Square (above)

From the Telegraph

Christmas Eve shopping: all bustle, hurry and geese

December 25, 1856

Yesterday was a busy day in the metropolis – all bustle and hurry. The day was wet, muddy, and uncomfortable; still it did not damp the ardour of the wayfarers, and, as of old, men and women were to be seen trudging home laden with geese, turkeys, beef, mutton, and pork, not forgetful of a little drop of the "creature comfort" to wash the good fare down; whilst the juvenile portion of the community struggled along, loaded with bunches of holly, mistletoe, and evergreens of all varieties.

The quantity and quality of poultry exhibited at Leadenhall and Newgate market has not been exceeded for some years, all the continental markets having been brought into requisition to supply the demand. Prices were somewhat high, but the goods were decidedly "prime". Geese brought from 6s 6d to 10s; turkeys, from 5s to 25s.

The meat markets were well stocked with some of the primest sort. Prime beef brought as high as 11d per lb. At Billingsgate there was a large supply of the finny tribe; cod, which looked beautiful, was in great request. Vegetables and fruit were also abundant. The ingredients for plum puddings, however, being in great demand, a stiffish price was obtained. Raisins brought from 6d to 8d per lb, and currants from 8d to 10d.

RITUAL VIOLENCE

A year of riots in a dockland parish church

Catcalls, pea-shooters and fireworks met the reforming rector who introduced worship that smacked of Romanism

There can be few rivals, by way of violence and protraction, to the wrangles inside the church of St George-in-the-East in 1859 and 1860. It was a strange parish to start with. The beautiful Hawksmoor church, big enough to hold 2,000, was surrounded by crazily packed slums, with 30,000 living within the parish boundary. The London docks at the height of their activity were nearby, and a jumble of spars, ropes, barrels, waggons, cranes, planks, beer houses and rum shops, drunken sailors and prostitutes filled the muddy thoroughfares.

Here, Dickens wrote in 1864, the "accumulated scum of humanity seemed to be washed from higher grounds, like so much moral sewage, and to be pausing until its own weight forced it over the bank and sunk it in the river". In the 733 houses lining the four streets round the church, there were 154 brothels. In this teeming chaos, two energetic slum priests made it their business to bring the Christian life to all those that the Church of England could count as its parishioners. The Rector, Bryan King, was joined by a curate, Charles Lowder. Both were intent on the reshaping of church services instigated by the Oxford Movement.

Today it is hard to believe that the placing of a cross on the altar, the lighting of candles in the daytime or the singing of parts of the service could tar clergy with the hated smear of papistry. At George's it meant week after week of riots, in the church itself, as hostile parishioners, and more vocally people from outside the parish, disrupted services that smelt to them of Romanism.

The church wardens became enemies of the rector, and the church wardens had the power to appoint a Sunday lecturer. They chose the Rev Hugh Allen, who had no sympathy with Puseyite fripperies. The battle lines were drawn when Mr Allen's lecture, or sermon, ended at a time when the Rev Bryan King, dressed in coloured vestments, and his choristers were preparing to come to the altar for the Litany service (which is found in the Book of Common Prayer).

For 11 months, except for a six-week break when the church was closed by the Bishop, gangs of roughs came in order to cat-call, light matches, throw filth, spit, use pea-shooters on the choirboys, bleat at bearded clergymen, hiss, groan, stamp, slam pew doors, clap, sing, shout and threaten violence in the name of the Establishment, without a blush at the sacrilege of turning the house of God into worse than a den of thieves. For many who came it was better than a music-hall, and free.

"St George's-in-the-East is becoming a standard pest and nuisance," remarked the *Telegraph* on August 24, 1859. The day before, "the afternoon lecture ended, and the church warden proceeded to clear the church, in order that preparations might be made for the four o'clock service. These preparations appeared to include crosses, coloured candles, and altar cloths of the approved Romanistic pattern; and of such habitual decoration the public appeared to have obtained an inkling, for when the doors were thrown open at five minutes to four o'clock, an excited and riotous mob rushed in shrieking and howling towards the altar. It must be further observed, that a body of about 100 persons had previously refused to leave the church at the termination of the lecture, and had remained crowded round the altar.

"A clergyman came out of the vestry – one might almost call it the stage door – accompanied by a knot of choristers habited in white robes. The priest himself is stated to have been attired in an Oxford master's hood, with the red all turned outwards, and on the scarf at the back of his neck was woven a cross.

"He wore likewise a large black beard and moustaches; so that this Stepneian Puseyite must have looked something between Archbishop Laud and Mother Shipton."

When the clergyman and choristers went through

Nicholas Hawksmoor's chaste masterpiece, St George-in-the-East, was filled for a year with violence and clamour

"their usual bowings and prostrations at the foot of the altar" there came from the mob a "most hideous din and uproar, accompanied by responses not to be found in the Book of Common Prayer, and not often heard in a church, or indeed anywhere out of a beer garden or Billingsgate. One set of people jeered the clergyman by imitating the ba'aing of a goat; while another vociferated and hissed." After the priest had finished the service, one man incited the crowd to tear down the altar, while another pursued the retreating clergyman into the churchyards, until with "hooting, yelling, catcalling, and other Protestant diversions the proceedings terminated. One might imagine that London was carried back to the days of Lord George Gordon and the 'No Popery' riots. The inquiry that must naturally suggest itself to the mind of the reader on perusing the account of this scandalous disturbance is, 'Where were the police?'"

The *Telegraph* had no fear of being accused of Puseyite sympathies, for it had repeatedly "denounced the most miserable mummeries of the vain and besotted men; their dancing masters' postures and genuflections; their Covent-Garden bouquets, and property-room candlesticks; their sham farces and feasts; their prurient confessional parlours, their schools, where they birch the little boys and girls; their whole semi-theatrical, semi-superstitious ritual and discipline". But setting the Puseyites packing did not excuse "desecrating a church with violence and clamour".

On September 2, the paper reported, the Vestry Clerk of St George's wrote to the Bishop of London, concluding: "This lamentable state of things has now continued for some months, and will probably still continue, so long as the services are conducted by the Rev Bryan King and those appointed by him, in the objectionable way complained of."

A fortnight later the Bishop directed that the church should close while he tried to mediate. He persuaded Mr King to do without his vestments, and the times of service were adjusted to avoid a clash. But when the church opened again on November 6, the *Telegraph* reported that "unhappily the mediation has ended in nothing, except, indeed, in inducing a fiercer and more outrageous display of passion on the part of the parishioners than has hitherto been experienced".

At the morning service, "Mr King turned his back to the congregation, and turning to the altar said, 'In the name of the Father, the Son, and the Holy Ghost,' instead of the ordinary passages. This was followed by hisses, stamping of feet, and the slamming of pew doors. Mr King, unmoved by this display of feeling, proceeded to the delivery of his sermon.

"However long he might be permitted to continue the rector of that parish, he said, he should never enter the walls of that church without a feeling of shame on account of the gross outrages which had been committed there. Their services henceforward would be performed without those Eucharistic vestments which were peculiar to them. He could never again put on those beautiful robes, and henceforth therefore they must worship God in this holy sacrifice in the garb of humiliation."

When he returned to church for the afternoon Litany, he was "hissed, hooted, and yelled at during the whole of the service". The rector cancelled the 7pm service out of considerations of safety.

So it went on, week after week. On April 29, 1860 the service was again drowned out by hecklers. "During the hymn which was sung after prayers a gentleman ascended the pulpit who had a moustache and a huge beard. He was received with a shout of derisive laughter, loud cries of 'nanny' and imitation of the cry of a goat. The reverend gentleman appeared to be astonished at this strange reception, and evidently did not understand it." He was not experienced in the St George's mob's customary greeting for bearded clergy, being the visiting Canon of Cape Town Cathedral.

"The Rev Bryan King pronounced the benediction from the altar, and was mocked and hissed in a most disgraceful manner. The evening hymn, which was sung prior to the blessing, was parodied by 'Hot Codlins' and similar pieces of profanity. The police had the usual obstructions in clearing the church; but Inspector Alison, who is not a man to be tampered with, having issued the word of command to his men, the mob fled before them, and the doors of St George's were once more closed."

Mr King was blamed for enrolling a bodyguard of gentlemen, including the amateur boxer Tom Hughes to protect him. He said that if the police would not protect him someone must. The matter was debated in the Lords, where Bishop Philpotts of Exeter, then aged 82, asserted that the vestments that King had been forced to leave off were within the law.

From June 1860, a body of policemen were in attendance at St George's every Sunday. King was persuaded to take a holiday, and three years later he took a country living. Rows over ritual continued, despite attempts in 1874 to regulate them by statute. Clergymen were prosecuted. But vestments and candles, even incense, became more widely accepted.

According to a guide published by the English Church Union (a High Church group formed in 1860), if there were 336 churches that used vestments in 1882, there were 2,158 by 1901; in 1882 581 had candles on the altar, and by 1901 there were 4,765.

As for St George-in-the-East, one night in May 1941 incendiary bombs gutted it entirely. Only Hawksmoor's robust outer walls and towers survived. Today a 1960s church nestles within the monumental shell, and, inside, a mosaic behind the altar shows Christ on the cross, flanked by the Apostle John and the Virgin Mary, and in the nave votive candles burn before an icon of the risen Christ.

INBRIEF

JANUARY 22, 1874

It was telegraphed yesterday from Philadelphia that Chang and Eng died on Saturday last at the age of sixty-three years, at their home in North Carolina. They had long since enjoyed all the advantages of American citizenship, and assumed the characteristic surname of Bunker.

They were, according to report, decent, unobtrusive men; and, strange to relate, they were married, and each of them had numerous children. As Chang and Eng, two quiet Chinamen – for it is extremely dubious whether they came from Siam – who spent the autumn of their lives as tobacco-planters in a remote part of the United States, they may speedily fade away from public recollection as the Siamese Twins.

The remains of the poor creatures thus mercifully freed from a bondage worse than death will undoubtedly be dissected. Chang, it is stated, lived two hours longer than Eng. For years past, the morbid fascination of American marvel-mongers has been exercised in conjuring up hypotheses of the horrible results which must accrue if one of the Twins permanently survived his brother.

SAVE JUMBO!

Americans buy the elephant London loved

In 1882 Americans wanted to buy London's favourite zoo animal, but he certainly wasn't going to go without a struggle

The Zoological Society of London at Regent's Park decided in 1882 to sell Jumbo the elephant to Barnum and Bailey's in America. He had reached 21, the age of mature adulthood, and they feared his temper would put at risk the children that were regularly given rides on his back. In any case he cost a good deal to feed, and their funds were limited. A deal for $10,000 was struck.

"Jumbo is certainly the largest of his race in Europe," the *Telegraph* reported. "His height is 11 feet to his withers, and he is able, with uplifted head and trunk, to take a nut or pin from a ledge 25 feet above the ground." He had come from Abyssinia by an indirect route to the zoological gardens when he was only the size of a Shetland pony. As for his condition, "the regular feeding and exercise, the careful tending, the abundance of oil carefully bestowed upon his skin, the shelter of a substantial roof and the comfort of a clean floor, may all be set off against the influence of a native climate and the strengthening effect of natural wanderings in search of food".

On February 20 *The Daily Telegraph* reported an attempt to get the creature into a travelling box. When a chain was fastened around him, the elephant began to trumpet, his calls becoming the louder when they were answered by Alice his "little wife" in a nearby cell of the elephant house. William Newman, the trainer known as "Elephant Bill", sent by Barnum's, calmed him and fed him biscuits, which he conveyed to his mouth with his trunk one by one. But still Jumbo refused to enter the travelling box. The next plan was to lead him on foot to the docks five miles away. But he became uneasy at the unfamiliar surroundings and had to be returned to the waiting Alice.

In the meantime, readers of *The Daily Telegraph* were wondering why he had to be sold to America at all. "Who can read the account of the sufferings of poor Jumbo on his attempted removal," wrote one lady, "without being deeply moved? Is it not a stain upon our national vaunted regard for the dumb creatures?"

4907   L.S.

Jumbo – 'the largest of his race in Europe' – with his keeper, Matthew Scott. Children who had enjoyed rides on the elephant's back sent in pocket money to save him from exile

Children wrote too: "I am sure that all his little friends here would be only too glad to subscribe out of their pocket money," wrote Alice, from West Hampstead. And a "Child of Eight" wrote: "Please do not let Jumbo go to America. I have had many beautiful rides on him."

The *Telegraph* realised it was on to a winner as far as the sympathy of its readers went. Thanks to one of the paper's star reporters, Godfrey Turner, (though he always wrote anonymously), news of Jumbo dominated the pages for more than a month, though there were plenty of other things happening – "terrible outrages" in Russia, a bold solo crossing of the Channel by balloon, an attempt on Queen Victoria's life by a madman with a revolver.

A telegram came from America to Barnum's agent in London: "Elephant to be shipped as soon as possible; spare no expense." William Newman was not a man to be thwarted. The next morning he tried to get the elephant accustomed to wearing chains about his feet, while by the afternoon the zoo was crowded with children eager to see Jumbo as he paced about the grounds. Enough buns to fill a village bakery were fed to him, and by the day's end 1,343 people had visited Jumbo.

"If it be true that he has lost his wits, or is likely to lose them," Godfrey Turner, wrote, "then it must be allowed he is a consummate actor." But some at the zoo remembered elephants before that had run mad – Chuny, an Indian elephant, had killed his keeper and was shot by a squad of Grenadiers.

The *Telegraph* continued to carry excerpts from dozens of letters, many from children, some in tears, many offering to send pocket-money, one school of 600 boys prepared to send a penny each.

The secretary of the Zoological Society felt obliged to send a letter for publication explaining that "the risk of an outbreak on the part of so huge and powerful an animal" should not be lightly run. At the least Jumbo might then have to be destroyed. And in any case Barnum's had 20 elephants, well cared for and had bred two in captivity, "an occurrence hitherto unprecedented".

The paper of February 24 brought P.T. Barnum's "Message to England". "Fifty millions of American citizens anxiously awaiting Jumbo's arrival," he cabled. "My forty years' practice of exhibiting best that money could procure makes Jumbo's presence here imperative. Hundred thousand pounds would be no inducement to cancel purchase."

Meanwhile the travelling box for Jumbo's removal was constructed more strongly by Pickford's coach-builders, and the restraining chains were covered with leather by the Queen's harness-makers.

Saturday March 4 brought the startling news of a writ from the High Court of Chancery served on

From the **Telegraph**

Stuffed birds on the head – a barbarous form of decoration

April 3, 1888

There is, apparently, a good time coming for the little birds, who are now shot by millions to adorn ladies bonnets and hats. Fashion is generally an inexorable goddess, but in the present instance it seems that even her decrees are about to be altered to suit the requirements of the more merciful of her followers.

This custom of trimming ladies' head-gear with stuffed birds, principally humming-birds and birds of Paradise – although our prettiest native songsters have by no means been spared – has gone on for a long time, and the natural and inevitable consequence has been that the supply of birds shows serious signs of being exhausted. It would certainly be wise if the ladies, for their own sakes, were to eschew this rather barbarous form of decoration for a period, because with the increasing rarity of the birds will come a corresponding rise of price, and they will thus reap a double advantage from decreeing a truce to the mission of these lovely feathered creatures.

As regards the merciful side of the questions, protests have constantly been heard against the prevailing taste; but, as might naturally have been expected, the caprice and thoughtlessness of tyrannous fashion carried the day, and ladies who liked to combine a tasteful "get up" with humanitarianism either experienced the pain and grief of being "out of the fashion" or had to run counter to the pitiful impulses of their hearts.

Some women do, no doubt, robe themselves in costumes to which collective society has not given its unmistakable "cache" out of sheer principle; others, again, do so from mere ignorance that they are offending, and mental failure to keep up with the times. Some women are born unfashionable; others have unfashionability thrust upon them, sorely against their will, and usually for some reason connected with their personal exchequer.

When, however, a person of the gentler sex knows what is tasteful and becoming and fashionable, and elects not to wear that something, the preliminary struggle involved is too painful to bear thinking about. It is a horrible 19th-century martyrdom, worse than being burnt at the stake, because it does not – like the latter form of torture – end in a brief space of time. An animated torch must burn out sooner or later; whereas a lady who condemns herself to the diurnal donning of outworn and socially discarded habiliments bears her burden about with her all day long throughout a whole season, and even for many successive seasons.

In Florentine frescos the saint who was once unfortunate enough to be grilled alive is represented as always carrying his gridiron at his side or on his back; and a modern English lady who abstains from donning a sealskin mantel, or a hat ornamented with the slaughtered darlings of tropical forests, might with equal justice be depicted on canvas accompanied by the material evidences of her heroism – for example, the bonnet of an unfashionable type which, for conscience sake, and the little birds' sake, she has compelled herself to wear. Such excellent females are now rewarded. Fashion has come, or is coming, to their aid. What they have long condemned, everybody is going to condemn and the plumage which now adorns innumerable bonnets will be cast on one side like broken gods.

the superintendent of the zoo, forbidding him from allowing the elephant to leave the zoo. The action was brought by some Fellows of the Zoological Society who argued that its Council had no right to dispose of this beast without consulting them.

As Jumbo waited in chains, the Court of Chancery under Mr Justice Chitty decided his fate. It was admitted that the zoo had previously sold lions, tigers, pumas, eagles, parrots and, to Baron James Rothschild, horn-eyed tragopans, which are pheasants that "have the power of instantaneously inflating their striped and parti-coloured wattles". The court ruled in favour of the right to sell Jumbo.

It was "what might have been expected from English equity", the *Telegraph* remarked in a leading article. "No collection of animals could be maintained with judgment unless a power to sell was lodged in the hands of the managers."

"If the worst comes to the worst, and Jumbo must go, his innumerable friends and admirers can only 'drop some natural tears, and wipe them soon'. He will be well treated; he will make thousands of new little acquaintances; millions of negroes will welcome their compatriot; and if he returns, Young London will have a Restoration Day in Regent's Park, perhaps as worthy of commemoration as the entry of King Charles II into London on the 29th of May, more than two centuries ago. Then, made wise by travel and fearless by adventures, Jumbo will placidly survey Old England again, and recount to Alice a long list of travellers' tales, perhaps as thrilling and marvellous as those which Othello related to Desdemona."

By Saturday March 11, Jumbo had been persuaded by his old keeper, Matthew Scott, to "walk quietly in and out of his box". Crowds flocked to the zoo before he left. Monday saw 24,007 visitors, compared with 1,701 on the corresponding Monday a year before. A concourse of 10,000 accompanied the elephant as he walked back that afternoon to his quarters.

"The number of letters and edible presents daily sent to him increases," the paper reported on March 16, "and not a few of them are indicative of mental weakness on the part of the senders." A woman sent a piece of wedding cake. A man sent six dozen oysters. The *Telegraph* wondered if Jumbo might not moralise on the marvellous unreasonableness of mankind. The guinea that bought the oysters might "rescue more than one poor family from hunger and brooding desperation". Pumpkins, however, the elephant enjoyed.

During the next week, Jumbo was allowed to grow accustomed to his travelling box. On Wednesday March 22, amid sleet and snow, a new attempt was made to remove him from the zoo and deliver him to the

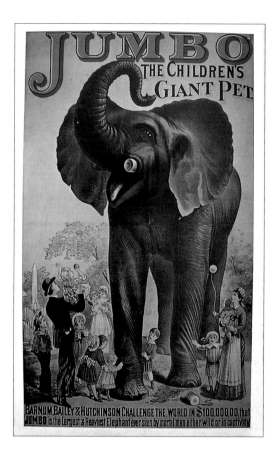

Barnum, Bailey and Hutchinson were proud to show off the world's biggest elephant. 'My forty years' invariable practice of exhibiting best that money could procure makes Jumbo's presence here imperative,' cabled P.T. Barnum

docks for the voyage to America. He had spent the night in his box, chained by his forefeet to an oak baulk in front. The idea was now to attach a hobble chain to his hind feet. Jumbo exerted all his ingenuity to resist this. To raise one foot, a gang of 12 men would pull at a rope attached to a tree. But Jumbo trod on the end they tried to get round his foot, or kicked it away; one rope snapped with a sound "like the report of a gun". The elephant knelt with his hind legs, and seemed ready to somersault from his box.

"Elephant Bill" Newman had no cruel intentions, and among hundreds of worried spectators was a superintendent from the Royal Society for the Prevention of Cruelty to Animals. Jumbo was calmed, and as the morning wore on, took wisps of hay from the bale in front of him, or examined the workmen's tools with the end of his trunk.

Ten cart-horses were harnessed to the great box, and at first its 11-ton weight made it sink to its axles in the ground. It took three hours to haul it onto the road outside the zoo. Slowly Jumbo began his journey, seemingly untroubled by the motion. The crowd shouted insults at the representatives of his new owners, who had fixed up a notice on the vehicle "Barnum, Bailey and Hutchinson, New York". His escorts, Newman and Scott, patted his trunk soothingly, and at intervals Jumbo explored with its end the horses and their harnesses in front of him. His demeanour was described as subdued but not cowed. He trumpeted occasionally.

His route to Millwall Dock took him via Camden Town, Gray's Inn Road, past the Clerkenwell House of Detention (mended since the Fenian explosion, see page 72) down Old Street and the Minories to St Katharine's Dock, where the Thames Steam Tug Company was to take over from Pickford's. As the creaking van ran down the hill towards the quay, friction made a wheel smoulder, and fire was quenched only with several buckets of water. A crane deposited his box in the barge for Millwall, and he began restlessly "rocking it to and fro as a boy rocks a boat".

On the three-mile journey from St Katharine's to Millwall by barge Jumbo consumed a gallon and a half of ale. He remained in good temper all day, despite having cut his head by butting the front of his box. Next day he was transferred into the steamer *Assyrian Monarch* for the Atlantic voyage.

As it moved down river, Jumbo's trumpetings "were heard with curious astonishment by the Russian Jewish refugees" who made up most of the passengers. They had attracted much sympathy in England for their sufferings in Russia. Near the open sea, Lady Burdett-Coutts, the philanthropist, came aboard with a parcel of buns, which Jumbo obligingly consumed. She also gave the emigrant children sweets, and their parents "pressed forward to kiss the hands of the Baroness, as well as, in Eastern fashion, the hem of her garment".

Before the ship got under way "the American flag was hoisted and a bottle of whisky was presented to the big African passenger, who, having allowed the full contents to be poured into his proboscis, closed the valve tightly, carried the draught to his mouth without spilling a drop, and made his customary sign of desiring more". Even so, his behaviour on board proved "all that could be wished".

But at 6.30 next morning the wind got up and by nine the gale had turned into a hurricane. (Nineteen were drowned in the Le Havre lifeboat.) The ship began to roll in the heavy seas. The captain decided to let go the anchor and they weathered the storm as best they could, the emigrants assembling in their "ritualistic scarves" and Jumbo standing sturdily in his strong-box, proving his qualities as sailor.

On Easter Monday, April 10, a telegram from New York told of Jumbo's safe arrival in New York. During the voyage the elephant had been slightly sea-sick for the first few days, but soon recovered. The passengers had formed a Jumbo Club.

So he began his tour of the country in a 10-ton car 40 ft long, pulled by a team of 16 horses. "The behaviour of Jumbo has been excellent," the *Telegraph* reported from New York.

There was to be no return to revisit Alice, as envisaged by the *Telegraph* leader-writer. Three years later Jumbo was fatally struck by a goods train at St Thomas, Ontario. He reached out his trunk to Matthew Scott as he breathed his last.

Barnum's had him stuffed, and he was displayed at Tufts University, Massachusetts, until fire struck in 1975. A jar of his ashes is still used as a good-luck charm by the college athletics team. Scott took to caring for smaller animals at Barnum and Bailey's winter headquarters at Bridgeport, Connecticut, and died in the city's almshouse in 1914.

From the Telegraph

Forty Arabs, 10 bears and some monkeys in one loft

July 1, 1885

It is not often that a single stable holds 40 Arabs, 10 bears and "some" monkeys. Yet, in Liverpool, so we are assured by the proceedings of the City Police Court, this extraordinary congregation of tenants has actually been discovered under one roof, and the sanitary authorities have taken objection to it.

But, we are tempted to ask, why the sanitary authorities? If the bears had objected, or the monkeys, or even the Arabs, we could have understood it; but what could it matter to the Health Inspector? He said it was calculated to cause fever. Now, whoever heard of a bear that had fever, "and especially", so the report professes, "typhoid fever"? There was no ventilation, we are told. Well, neither monkeys nor Arabs care for ventilation, and, as for bears, it is a notorious fact that they bung themselves into caves for several months together for the express, special and very particular reason that there shall be no sort of ventilation whatsoever; and they find it very comfortable, or they would not do it year after year.

For the Arab no one can speak. When he is on the desert he cannot help being in draughts. The desert is a very draughty place. Nor when he is inside what he calls his house is the ventilation less complete, for an Arab differs from almost all other people in preferring an abode that is all holes. The Bedouin tent is a mere scarecrow of one, and when he "settles down" as he would call it, in some unconsidered knuckle-end of a town, he erects a habitation that is quite unique. Having got together as much matting as he can procure he obtains some flexible sticks of green wood or bamboos, and, having bent them into curves, stretches the matting over them.

The bamboos, however, start, give-way, and fly up out of the ground. The result is that the matting is all at angles, in rags, and generally absurd. Yet the householder does not repair his tenement. Half his roof may be off; the frontage has gaps in it, of which every vagabond goat, dog and cat takes advantage; but he does not seem to care. So long as the wind can blow through he is certain of a measure of relief from the heat.

When, however, he comes to Liverpool, the Arab finds the conditions of life considerably altered. He is in a country where, contrary to all his previous experiences, it is the one, only and most cherished ambition of the native to boast that he lives in a house without a single draught. Every aperture is carefully plugged up, lest the wind should get in. Doors of wood, windows of glass, framed in the same material, defend every point that the elements might assault. Nor is he slow to discover the appropriateness of such arrangements. The winds of Europe, of Liverpool, are not those of the desert. The barelegged man is at a disadvantage in Lancashire. Our breezes are neither Sirocco nor Simoom, Khamsin nor Harmattan – such as frizzle the date flowers upon their boughs, and kill "the bud of the mimosa", the turtle dove upon her nest – but more temperate zephyrs are suggestive of coal fires, greatcoats and cordials "hot with".

So the poor Arab, landing in a brisk north-easterly wind, has a natural tendency to huddle. His camels do it, when the night strikes sharp in the sandy solitudes of the Soudan, or the bitter, bleak passes of El-Hejaz. It is his first idea to pack up as close as possible. His bears do the same. They have long ago learned that one living body communicates warmth to another by contact. Their first question, therefore, when seeking lodgings, is, "How many can get in?" Other people might ask, "How many rooms are there?", not so the Arab. His only idea is to crowd as many persons as possible into the smallest practicable space.

In the Liverpool stable, therefore, he was altogether at his ease. The temperature of the loft was raised by the number of persons crowded within to comfortable warmth. That there were bears and monkeys among them did not matter. They all contributed to the general stock of heat. It is true the loft was only 45ft by 15ft; but after all there were only 40 Arabs, 10 bears and "some" monkeys. It might have been much worse.

CRIME WAVE: GAROTTING

Strangled from behind: the new street terror

London was swept by an outbreak of garotting by robbers that spread fear and provoked magistrates to stern measures

Playing on the fashion for wide crinolines, 'Punch' proposed an anti-garotting device that would save citizens from sudden attack from behind

Garotting was the great excitement of 1862. There had been incidents before of street robbers crushing a victim's windpipe from behind and rifling his pockets, but this year such crimes were being done in broad daylight, or in frequented streets, with police close at hand.

People were shocked by the suddenness and savagery of the attacks. "Frequently, when the garotter had throttled his victim into unconsciousness," said a contemporary report, "the confederate struck the poor man crushing blows with a 'life-preserver', and after robbing him without a struggle, left him bleeding and mangled on the pavement, disfigured and perhaps injured for life."

The outrages spread "terror" throughout London; everyone was alarmed. A jeweller was attacked in Kingsland Road at 11pm one day in January and died of crushing injuries to his throat a week later. Not all the attacks were garottings alone; a gunmaker who was attacked in the Commercial Road in March had his arm so injured that it had to be amputated, and he died later of complications.

On a summer night in a well-lit place, James Pilkington, the MP for Blackburn, was attacked on his way home from Parliament after midnight. The *Telegraph* remarked rather heartlessly in its leading article that the perpetrators had at last found a use for the unadmired Guards' Memorial, in the shadows of which they had hidden. The bulky granite and bronze sculpture, with its piles of cannon and Crimean veterans in bearskins, still stands unsoftened by time, in the same spot at the bottom of Regent Street today, or almost the same spot. It was in fact moved 30 feet to allow room for a statue of Florence Nightingale.

A similarly cynical comment came from the *Annual Register*: "It has been said that the way to draw attention to railway mismanagement is to smash a bishop. An assault upon a Member of Parliament compelled the attention of the Home

Secretary to the state of the streets." *The Daily Telegraph*'s robust suggestion was that people should go about with "life-preservers", cudgels of their own, or even daggers, and kill the attackers.

More police were recruited during the year, some arrests were made and some perpetrators jailed. The *Telegraph* mentioned among the criminals "ticket of leave men", those on parole from jail, and this was not mere prejudice, for it was found that some of those later convicted had been sentenced three or even four times to "penal servitude for terms of years, and had been released before the expiration of their sentences 'for good conduct' ".

Garotting was a word to strike fear into the heart. *Punch* said it was also familiarly known as "putting on the hug", but this was as much of a euphemism as "mugging" was to be a century later. The crimes grew more frequent as the dark evenings of autumn returned. People bought all sorts of devices for self-protection, seldom to much avail.

In October two men, Roberts and Anderson, were charged with a savage attack on a medical student called Ryk Le Sueur in Bloomsbury Street at 6pm. Another man had taken part of the attack but was jailed for a separate crime. "One of them struck Le Sueur such a fearful blow with a 'knuckle-duster' – an American invention, being a kind of solid brass glove, of great weight – that one side of his face was smashed in, his front teeth were knocked in, and many teeth in both the upper and lower jaw were broken – his face and cheek dreadfully cut. He was in short disfigured for life."

Roberts and Anderson came to trial at the Old Bailey before Mr Baron Bramwell. After their conviction they were taken to Newgate and brought back for sentence on another day at the same time as a group of others who were convicted of similar crimes. The judge was clearly determined to make an example. But he only allowed medical evidence to be given after the jury had played their part, lest it sway the verdict, "because strictly it had nothing to do with the specific charges". When the surgeon gave evidence of the victim's injuries it "created great sensation on the court". Anderson got penal servitude for life; Roberts for 20 years.

In all, about two dozen were sentenced in these sessions. "Though a few daring outrages of the same kind were perpetrated during the winter," the *Annual Register* reported, "the reign of terror was at an end, and the inhabitants of the metropolis once more traversed their streets without starting at every footstep or turning pale at every shadow."

The Garotting Terror also left its mark on literature. Anthony Trollope put more than one such incident into his novels. The first echoed the experience of James Pilkington, who was attacked before a fellow MP could aid him. But in *Phineas Finn*, Trollope has the hero, a young MP, come to the help of an older MP called Kennedy, in Park Street, Mayfair, on a rainy night. Phineas saw two men following Kennedy and "one of the men had followed him up quickly and had thrown something round his throat from behind him. Phineas understood well now that his friend was in the act of being garotted, and that his instant assistance was needed." One assailant ran away, but Phineas caught the other by the collar. "Didn't yer see as how I was a-hurrying up to help the gen'leman myself?" the villain said. But Phineas was not to be tricked, and hung on till in a couple of minutes a policeman took the ruffian into custody. "You've done it uncommon neat," said the policeman in congratulation. Phineas's career was helped by this intervention, though it happened that Kennedy, the man he saved, went on to be endlessly cruel to his wife.

Another Trollopean incident shows that the Victorians were realistic in their expectations of law and order in the nation's capital. In *The Prime Minister*, Ferdinand Lopez rescues Everett Wharton from three assailants in St James's Park at midnight. "As the night was fine, we, very foolishly, agreed to walk round St James's Park," Lopez explains in a letter to Everett's father. "It is a kind of thing that nobody does; – but we did it."

Lopez had separated from his companion (in fact they had quarrelled) and Everett "was attacked by three persons, a man and two women". Lopez says that he "was luckily in time to get up before he was seriously hurt. I think the man would otherwise have strangled him. I am sorry to say that he lost both his watch and purse." When Lopez meets Everett's father, the old man says: "It was very foolish going round the park at all at that time of night."

This time Trollope makes, not the victim, but the dashing saviour go to the bad. Lopez, in an atmospheric scene, ends up killing himself by jumping in front of a thundering steam locomotive.

INBRIEF

SEPTEMBER 14, 1855
In answer to the denunciations which have appeared in this and all the other morning papers against the road through St James's Park, an announcement has now been put out on authority that it was never intended to erect more than a footpath through the park, and a footbridge over the ornamental water. This is evidently an abandonment of the original design to popular remonstrances, for no one who has inspected the preparations may reasonably doubt that it was intended to cut a carriage-road through the prettiest of our London parks.

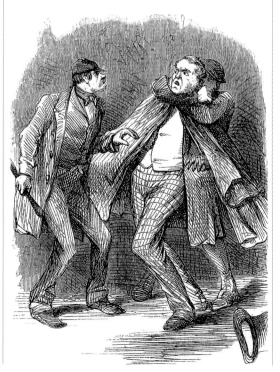

Garotting: 'Frequently, when the garotter had throttled his victim into unconsciousness,' said a contemporary report, 'the confederate struck the poor man crushing blows with a life-preserver.'

A NEW BREED OF CRIMINAL

The summer the Hooligan was invented

One hot August towards the end of the century gangs of young men threatened London with another 'reign of terror'

Hooligans were invented in the hot summer of 1898. No one quite knows where the word came from. It appeared in a music-hall song of the decade. Some said that a family by that name lived in Irish Court, Lambeth. Others said the word came from "Hooley's gang". By coincidence the big case of Ernest Terah Hooley in the Bankruptcy Court was headlined day after day in August 1898. In 1899, a book by Clarence Rook called *Hooligan Nights* became a bestseller, but by then Hooliganism was a household word.

Crime reporting was a large staple of all the newspapers, and on August 2, 1898 *The Daily Telegraph* detected a new trend. Two Southwark magistrates had announced their determination "to deal severely with the gangs of young roughs who infest the district, and who under the name of the 'Hooligans' have largely contributed to the existing 'reign of terror'."

The magistrates were, it said, sending them to jail at the rate of 10 or 12 a week. There was six weeks' hard labour for a 17-year-old who knocked down a workgirl in the Borough; a 20-year-old who assaulted and robbed a flower-girl was remanded for trial; a 15-year-old was remanded for trial for violent assault of an old woman who resisted him when he tried to "take liberties" with her.

This anti-social trend was characterised on the streets of south and central London by the gathering of small gangs of youths who went in for "larrikin" behaviour – annoying passers-by, forcing them off the pavement, knocking off their hats or jostling them. Sometimes it went further and people would lose their watches and money. Sometimes brutal violence was used. It could end in murder. The victims did not know how far things might go.

Just as "larrikins" were the roughs of Melbourne of the 1870s, so "Hooligans" were London's scourge at the end of the century. The press was soon alert to public concern – "terror" was a word often used – and magistrates' courts were monitored. The *Telegraph* ran regular reports throughout August, with a stream of letters from readers.

The archetypal Hooligan, with hair brushed forward over his sloping brow and a muffler round his neck, was portrayed in 1898 by William Nicholson in his frontispiece for the book 'Hooligan Nights'

It was no reflection of a dearth of news. The American-Spanish war was coming to an end, with the last shots being fired in Cuba and peace proclaimed in Manila. The British Army was engaging dervishes in Sudan. Bismarck died; the Pope was sick. Bicyclists were killed in accidents and a trombonist died when a bandstand collapsed at a Shrewsbury horticultural show. In parallel with the Hooligan coverage, a series of articles appeared about roughs on the racecourses, with Brighton a centre of violent lawlessness decades before Graham Greene's *Brighton Rock*.

The seaside was also the focus of daily reports headed BY THE SILVER SEA, as the nation paddled and ate ices. And the weather made news in itself, with the temperature well above 100F in the sun – a most unreliable measure. Eiffel Tower Lemonade

("Two gallons for fourpence halfpenny") took a full-page advertisement in the 12-page paper; it boasted an illustration – a rare thing – showing shirtsleeved men in boats rowing narrow-waisted, bonneted ladies, sheltering beneath parasols.

If there was a tendency to lump all street crimes together under the category of Hooliganism, the unsigned *Telegraph* commentator knew how to recognise the real thing. "The Hooligan savage may be known by the peculiar way in which he crops his cranium. How the operation is performed is a puzzle. The shears of the ordinary barber could not be made to bite so close to the scalp, but the whole of the head is not shorn. At the front, just above the forehead, a tuft of hair is left, three inches wide, maybe, and two long, and which brought forward, forms a hanging tassel between the Hooligan eyebrows. And when the eyes are close set, and the forehead is aslant, and the cheekbones prominent, the effect is something to remember."

Before the end of the month, the writer was an expert on Hooligan hairstyles. "What is known in street-ruffian circles as the 'crop-and-fly-flap' style is becoming quite the mode with the fraternity, and those barbers of the slums who are cultivating the tonsorial art from this aspect are said to be making a good thing of it, sixpence being the charge for a crop-and-fly-flap, whereas for a simple, plain hair-cutting in the same localities the fixed fee is but twopence. But the Hooligan worthy of the title is a thief as well as a rowdy, and has sixpence to spare."

On August 4 south London tradesman resolved at a meeting at Blackfriars "to form a league which would assist the police to put a stop to the reign of terror now existing in south London".

On August 5 two 18-year-olds were up at Worship Street magistrates' court, Clerkenwell, for assaulting and kicking a plumber and his foreman outside his shop. One of the accused, named Brummett, "scornfully cross-examined" the foreman.

—You was kicked about the head and face, was you?

—I was

—How many kicks, now, do you think you got?

—It is impossible for me to say.

—Anyways, according to you, your face was covered with blood?

—That was so.

—Well, what have you done with all the marks? Look at him! He looks like a man who has had his face kicked in, don't he?

Brummett was committed for trial and was removed from the court exclaiming: "And I s'pose, when I've done my bit for this, the police will be down on me again for something else I didn't do."

On August 8 the *Telegraph* reported on "a typical Bermondsey rough" up at Southwark police court. A constable gave evidence that the "prisoner and a number of other youths were 'larking' in Long-lane, pushing respectable people off the pavement and using obscene language". The policeman said he saw the youth assault several people but none would

INBRIEF

AUGUST 18, 1898

At Gainsborough, John Heinale, pork butcher of Gainsborough, was summoned for three offences against the general order of the Local Government Board prescribing regulations as to light locomotives. The allegations were that he drove a motor-car at a speed greater than was reasonable and proper; that he did not, at the request of a person having charge of a restive horse, cause the car to stop and remain stationary; that he did not by sounding a bell or other instrument, give audible and sufficient warning of the approach of the locomotive. A pony, driven by a coachman in the employ of a magistrate, shied onto the footpath, threw itself down, and the driver, named Hawkins, was pitched out of the trap.

Eventually the Bench decided to convict, but intimated that this being the first case under the Order the fine imposed would be small. For high driving the fine was 10s, and £1 17s 9d costs; and for not sounding the bell was also 10s, and the cost 12s 3d, the total penalty being £3 10s.

come to give evidence. The prisoner belonged "to a gang of young roughs calling themselves 'Hooligans'. They were a terror to the neighbourhood." The defendant was fined 40 shillings for disorderly conduct and using obscene language.

The next day the Home Secretary made a statement in Parliament. He acknowledged the importance of the matter, but did not think the police were unable to deal with it. The *Telegraph* began to publish readers' letters, almost all calling for harder sentences, often for the cat-of-nine-tails.

The paper pointed to a case in north London where a man was knocked down, tried to get away, was knocked down again so that his face hit the kerb; the defendant was heard to say, "I haven't killed the — yet," before throwing him on his head again. When sentenced to two months' hard labour, he left the dock laughing.

At Southwark, 20 cases on one day "arose out of the proceedings of the 'Hooligans' ". A witness to an assault on a flower seller heard the defendant say: "Here we are; we'll show them that we are the Hooligans." The flower seller said she went in fear of her life, and one of those threatening her since she brought the case was in court; the magistrate had him detained, to be charged.

As the days went on, the threat of Hooliganism was reported from all parts of London, and "nothing prompts him to commit his outrages so speedily as the unsteady gait of a pedestrian who is returning home in the small hours of the morning". On August 10, the magistrate at Newington sessions announced that he would do all he could to put down highway robbery. "A state of terror exists," he said, "which is appalling in a civilised country." In the first case, a Lambeth "larrikin" aged 18 pushed against a pedestrian and stole his watch worth £20. He was jailed for 12 months.

At Southwark the magistrate heard a case of a man of 74 being robbed in daylight, his arms pinioned and his watch taken. "It has made me very nervous," he said. "Can't you give him the cat?"

The prisoner (whining) said: "Oh do have mercy. You don't know what it is to be poor. I was in drink or I should not have done it."

The magistrate said he could send him for trial (before a jury), and there was a chance he'd be sentenced to the cat. But the man attacked would have to be able to give three or four days to attend the trial. "I wish I could," the old man replied. "It seems incredible that people can't walk the streets safely in broad daylight." So the larrikin got 12 months immediately instead.

That was not the end of the case, for the next week the *Telegraph* reported that the old man had received a threatening letter. "I am well acquainted with you, and also a gang who will, I swear, murder you! Murder! Yes, we will murder you as sure as I am an Anarchist. Prepare to meet your death, as I am about to take it, as you have not got a heart in you. Look upon this as you like, but you are a dead man before long." At the foot of the letter was a skull with cross-bones, two swords crossed and a heart with a dagger through it. But a letter-writing Anarchist hardly sounds the same as the typical unschooled Hooligan.

Was the whole thing being blown up out of proportion? A Criminal Investigation Department officer, Patrick McIntyre, for many years in Lambeth, told the *Telegraph* that it had always been the practice for juvenile roughs to "work" in such a fashion. He thought there was less rampant ruffianism in London than years before.

In Battersea in mid August, with the temperature in the upper 80s, a policeman gave evidence of the activities of the "Velvet Cap Gang" – Teddy Boys before the reign. On that Friday night a gang of 12 lads with sticks and belts all wearing velvet caps pushed pedestrians off the pavement, knocked on shop doors, and used obscene language.

Readers who wondered if they should fight back followed with interest events at Southwark police court, where George Clamp, 62, a Lambeth marble mason, surrendered to bail on August 8 to answer charges of stabbing a "Hooligan", Samuel Owen, on the evening of July 23, in Westminster Bridge Road. But the prosecutor (the Hooligan) did not appear; the police said he was "keeping out of the way".

A week later Clamp again appeared to answer the charge. The absent Owen had said that he accidentally jostled Clamp on the pavement, and was thereupon stabbed on the arm. Subsequent information showed that Owen had been following Clamp about for three hours, demanding money, and finally exasperating him beyond endurance. Clamp swore that Owen was one of three ruffians who molested and threatened him. The police gave Owen a very bad character. The lawyer for the prisoner asked the magistrate to discharge his client, and he was discharged.

The long-predicted fatality came towards the end of August. "A man named Thomas Collins," the *Telegraph* reported, "died in St Bartholomew's hospital late on Saturday night from the effects of brutal violence. On Friday night, three men dressed in fustians met the deceased in New North Road, Hoxton, near to East Road, and challenged him to fight. Eye-witnesses say the deceased tried to pass the men, but one of them at once tripped him, and he fell heavily to the ground. As he attempted to rise, he was kicked with great severity. When, at last, he got to his feet, two of the men pinioned him by the arms, while the other one pushed and kicked him until he was well-nigh insensible. He at last sank to the ground in a state of collapse, and was conveyed to the hospital, where he died from the effects of his injuries."

But a week later the spate of reports rapidly dwindled. Two big items dominated the news pages: the need for a retrial of Dreyfus, and the taking of Omdurman. Violent crime continued in Lambeth and Clerkenwell. The Hooligans did not disappear. A new word had entered the language and the debate on crime and punishment went on.

Readers' ideas for dealing with the Hooligans

The "cat" had solved problem of "the garotters in the early sixties", wrote T.R. Clapham from Lancaster, so bring it back to solve Hooliganism.

Many other correspondents agreed, and another advocated eight strokes of the birch in the presence of the boys' parents. "Ruffians are always cowards," wrote "A Lover of Justice" calling for "severe bodily pain" to be inflicted.

"H.W.G." from Wandsworth, rued the demise of corporal punishment: "We are now realising the result of the namby-pamby dealing with the young incorrigibles – they have now grown into lazy, drunken larrikins, hooligans etc, users of both knife and revolver."

One letter was even signed "The Cat", who wrote "I stamped out the garotter a few years ago. My son Jack, the birch-rod, would crush out these youthful pistol gangs." In reply the next day, H.O. Meyers of Hounslow wrote that he had seen the cat in use, and found any more than a dozen strokes a "barbarity". But Australian magistrates could order a dozen – "why not here?"

Above the signature "Cotswold Isys" another reader broke into verse on the subject:
Give them the cat,
And spare not the lash for their shrinking;
Five years of "hard"
They little regard,
And 10 they can bear without winking.

The classically angry response was encapsulated by someone called "A.J.P.": "Perhaps I should feel little more compunction in putting a bullet into a Hooligan 'bashing' a woman or child as I should in depositing it in the carcase of a mad dog."

A reader from Blackburn, Lancashire, signing himself "Medicus" was of a similar mind: "I can box a little myself, and could, perhaps, hold my own against eight out of 10 of the men one meets in the streets, but I confess that had I to walk the streets of Lambeth, or in similar places after dark, I should place more trust in a weighted stick and a loaded revolver than in my knowledge of fisticuffs... As far as I understand the law, a man is justified in protecting his own life at all costs. If that be so, am I not justified in shooting at a gang who are rushing towards me with clubs in their hands?" The enquiry was echoed by "Anxious" of London, who asked: "How can I, a small man of nine stones, 'keep my end up' without police protection in this manner. May I use a revolver?"

"An Ex-Champion Revolver Shot" thought such action eminently justified. "A little incident happened to me lately in Blackfriars, when my revolver saved me from being beaten and maybe

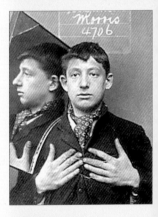

Young men in Wormwood Scrubs prisoner photographs show the haircuts and dress favoured by Hooligans

killed. I, in common with a lot of your correspondents, think that the time has come to go armed, since the law will not protect us, and the just complaints of long-suffering ratepayers are met with smiling scepticism and indifference by the authorities."

A different sort of letter came from the Dean of St Paul's, Dr Robert Gregory, which provoked a huge response from readers. "A quarter of a century since, I lived for 20 years in one of the poorest parishes in Lambeth," he wrote. "We had no disturbances of the kind." With the increase of education, the Dean wrote, we had a right to expect improvement in morals and behaviour of "the more dangerous classes". Yet it had become unsafe to walk in certain streets. "Under these circumstances, it is most desirous to do whatever can be done to trace the causes that lead to such crimes to their source. Where have these young villains been educated? What moral teaching have they received? Have they been compelled to attend school, what has been done by their teachers to implant in their minds the seeds of morality?" The Dean suggested that magistrates should be required to inquire, in cases of offenders under 21, as to the schools where they had been taught. His letter was taken by many as a criticism of "Board" schools set up under the Act of 1870 to supplement church-run schools.

In reply, readers said that children were not in fact being compelled to attend school. A correspondent signing himself "Old Fashioned" complained that children leaving a Board school bespattered his shop window with the filth of the street. A woman signing herself "La Douloureuse" wrote that she was one of 40 people living in a respectable row of houses who were "pestered by swarms of dirty little roughs", but if residents complained to parish officials or police they were met with "stolid indifference". A reader signing himself "Victim" wrote: "I am living in Hyde Park, not far from Gloucester Square, with a rental of £500 a year. For six years, these children have scratched and written on my street door and portals the filthiest words, and grossly immoral. I have applied to the police; but it is no use, as fast as I have the words removed, they appear again."

"I have two daughters, who have received all their education at Board schools,"countered R.M. Balmer Robson, from south-east London, "and I find that their education is sound and thorough. I prefer to send them there, because they are, by contact with other children, keen as razors; so sharpened and alert as to be better able to fight their own battle in after-life, instead of becoming the namby-pamby creatures one often finds turned out of the average middle class young ladies' seminary, half-educated and wholly conceited."

It wasn't just street violence, suggested J.A. Lawson of Edmonton, north London. "I have witnessed more brutality on the North London Railway during the last 12 months than in all my previous years. The officials make no attempt to stop it and seem to resent a report. I have seen respectable working men leave a compartment in a body to escape provocative aggression. Poor ladies sometimes hurry out of the carriage in dire confusion at the atrocious language and insinuations of some human wild beast."

The correspondence was in danger of moving away from the main question of Hooliganism. But the Revd Arthur Robins, Rector of Holy Trinity, Windsor, suggested a cause for the phenomenon. "There has been an obligation upon the Church for generations to call upon the State to get human habitations for the poor," he wrote. It was not schooling in decimals that was lacking; it was home life. "In London alone today there are some 50,000 families, each dwellers in one room apiece, in many instances within the limit of one bed. The life is made barbarous because the dwelling is but savage."

Though one correspondent wrote of the "baneful influence of the Society for the Prevention of Cruelty to Children", another thought that the society did not interfere enough.

A reader helpfully signing himself "Foreigner" looked on crime and punishment from another perspective: "With the greatest astonishment I have found it a widespread opinion among people in the most free and noble country in the world that flogging ought to be employed as punishment for street assaults. Do not these men see that every time the cat is used, society takes a step backward towards barbarism – towards torture and pillory? Society makes its own laws. The growing misery and crime in the big cities all over the world is a consequence of the likewise perpetually growing inequality in distribution of wealth."

On August 24 the Revd F.H. Reichardt, curate of St Peter's, Hoxton Square, a notoriously ragged area, put in a word for the virtues of rough youths. "For many years," he wrote, "I have been working as a clergyman among the roughest of them, and can testify to the splendid material of which some of them are built. In Kentish Town I had a brigade of 200 rough lads. I engaged an Army sergeant to drill them, but after one or two trials he decamped for his life. The lads, however, became attached to me, and I was able to present 125 of them to be confirmed by the Bishop.

"I have watched the lads carefully, and am still more or less in touch with them all, and I do not know of any case of a lad confirmed who has since gone to the bad. One of the wildest, a lad of 17, used to bring every penny of his hard earnings – only six shillings a week, for some 14 hours a day – to his sick mother during a trying winter.

"If you sow the wind you are bound sooner or later to reap the whirlwind, and if you neglect the street arab, don't be astonished when you find him developing and developed into the 'Hooligan'."

INBRIEF

SEPTEMBER 1, 1898

Mr E.N. Wood, Deputy Coroner, held an inquest last evening on Elizabeth Wellspring, aged 22 years, late cook at the Albion public house, Albion Street, Rotherhithe, who committed suicide on Monday by taking a quantity of rat poison.

Dr James Thomas McNamara, of Union Road, Rotherhithe, stated that deceased told him that she had taken two tablespoonfuls of rat poison. She added that she was very sorry, and did not know why she had done it. She swallowed enough poison to kill five persons. He wished to say that it ought not to be possible for a person to buy, unrestricted, a pot of rat poison containing sufficient phosphorus to kill half a dozen ordinary mortals. (Hear, hear.)

The coroner: I quite agree with you.

Witness: The stuff is called "Rough on Rats". On the box is given the antidote to be used for persons taking it, which is a little common salt in water. A person wishing to frighten somebody might take a dose of the poison, thinking that they could be cured by swallowing some salt and water. This, of course, is a fallacy. Such stuff is not only rough on rats but rough on human beings.

The jury returned a verdict of suicide whilst temporarily insane and added a rider as follows: "We desire the coroner to write to the Home Secretary, calling his attention to the unrestricted sale of poisons."

WANTED
Catching the Brighton railway murderer

The first newspaper artist's impression of a wanted criminal caused great national excitement and brought him to the gallows

The Telegraph's 'excellent likeness' of the 22-year-old murderer; 'sickly appearance, scratches on throat, teeth much discoloured'

In 1881, a murderer was arrested after *The Daily Telegraph* published an artist's impression of him. It was the first time a newspaper had published a sketch of a wanted man. He was caught after someone recognised him in the street. Indeed the keeper of his lodging-house, who sent for the police, had never seen the *Telegraph* sketch. But it had intensified the search for the murderer, and encouraged others seeking a reward to tell Scotland Yard of his whereabouts.

The crime became known as the Brighton Railway Murder and the suspect was Percy Lefroy Mapleton. In the first mention of him in the newspapers he was called "Lefroy", because he had given that name to police, and this version stuck.

"We give a sketch portrait by a gentleman who knew Lefroy and had frequent opportunities of noting his characteristics," the *Telegraph* announced on July 1. "It has been attested as an excellent likeness by several persons with whom Lefroy came into close contact."

The sketch certainly looked sinister. To help, a description from the police was appended: "Age 22, middle height, very thin, sickly appearance, scratches on throat, wounds on head, probably clean shaved, low felt hat, black coat, teeth much discoloured."

To this the paper added that: "He is very round shouldered, and his thin overcoat hangs in awkward folds about his spare figure. His forehead and chin are both receding. He has a slight moustache, and very small dark whiskers. His jawbones are prominent, his cheeks sunken and sallow, and his teeth fully exposed when laughing. His upper lip is thin and drawn inwards. His eyes are grey and large. His gait is singular; he is inclined to slouch, and when not carrying a bag, his left hand is usually in his pocket. He generally carries a crutch stick."

The help of "licensed victuallers, tobacconists, railway officials, stage carriage conductors, and cabmen" was particularly sought.

The crime was the murder of Frederick Isaac Gold, whose body was found near the mouth of the Balcombe tunnel in Sussex. A ticket collector had that afternoon found a man at Preston Park station wounded on his head and drenched with blood, complaining that he had been assaulted and robbed. The bloody man gave his name as Percy Mapleton Lefroy, and the ticket-collector, taking him for a victim, not an assailant, allowed him to go off and seek treatment for his wounds. By the time he was patched up, Gold's body had been found, yet Lefroy was not detained. Instead, a detective accompanied him back to London, but was persuaded to wait outside his lodgings at Wallington, Surrey. While the policeman waited, Lefroy disappeared.

After the *Telegraph* sketch was published an arrest was soon made on the mail train from Paddington – unfortunately the arrested man was a Mr Daw, found to be of unsound mind, as his brother, a draper in Tavistock, explained when he was summoned by telegram. Another man, in Sevenoaks, was actually charged with the murder, but was discharged after an acquaintance of the real Lefroy gave evidence that it was not he. Another man answering to the description was reported at the Cambridge Hotel at Shoeburyness, Essex.

The *Telegraph* soon reported that "innumerable wrong arrests" were being made. A man thought to resemble the sketch was picked up at Calais, the worse for drink. A Scotland Yard superintendent having received a telegram from the mayor of Calais, took the Channel ferry himself, only to find the suspect was known to Calais police as a local resident. He was charged with drunkenness. Another three or four people were arrested in London. By July 4 a rumour was circulating that Lefroy had assumed women's clothes.

On July 8 the real Lefroy was arrested in a house in a "shabby genteel" street in Stepney, east London. He had taken a room there after fleeing from Wallington eight days before, and had never stirred from the rented room in that time. He told his landlady that he was an engraver and was waiting for his luggage from Liverpool. He took all his meals in his room, which she did not like his doing. She suspected he was not going to pay his rent. She sent for the police after two things put her against him: he took another lodger's coat and sent a message to a City firm which, on her enquiring, denied any knowledge of him. She knew about the Brighton Railway Murder, but had not seen his likeness in *The Daily Telegraph*, otherwise, she said, she would have known him at once.

But a fellow lodger, who hoped for part of the £200 reward offered for Lefroy's arrest, thought that the police had hurried to the Stepney lodgings because he had spoken about their strange lodger to a friend in Brighton, who had got in touch with Scotland Yard. It was certainly the case that Scotland Yard had been given the Stepney address by an informant other than the landlady.

After his conviction, Lefroy confessed in Lewes jail to the murder of Lieutenant Roper of the Royal Engineers, who had been shot dead at Chatham in the February of 1881. Lefroy's sister had suspected him of that. He also confessed to crimes "which if his own condemnation can be believed, must rank him henceforward among the greatest malefactors of the age". But, the *Telegraph* warned, "much suspicion must, of course, attach to such of these statements as are unsupported by collateral facts".

Lefroy had given five contradictory versions of how he came to shoot Gold. From his statements as a convict awaiting execution, the *Telegraph* pieced together a version it judged to be true.

"He denies altogether that he entered the compartment in which he killed Mr Gold at the London Bridge Station, and positively declared that the evidence of the railway official, who swore he saw him take a seat in the carriage with the unfortunate gentleman, is false. According to Lefroy he took a seat in a carriage in which, curiously enough, there was another passenger sitting by himself, and that he was strongly tempted to murder him, but, owing to some strange fancy, he refrained from carrying out his intention.

"On the arrival of the train at Croydon he left this compartment and got into another – the one in which Mr Gold had taken a place. He had a short conversation with his victim, when Mr Gold put down the newspaper he had been reading and reposed himself in his seat as if to doze. While stretching himself out for this purpose he took a handkerchief from his pocket. In doing this Lefroy noticed that accidentally he pulled out his purse,

which fell on the floor of the carriage. Mr Gold did not hear the purse fall, and, placing the covering over his face, prepared for sleep.

"It occurred to Lefroy to take out his own pocket-handkerchief, throw it over the purse, and then, under pretence of picking up the handkerchief, to steal it. The noise, slight as it was, which he made in taking the purse, aroused Mr Gold.

"He instantly started up, and exclaiming: 'You scoundrel, do you want to rob me!' hit straight out at Lefroy, and struck such a severe blow that the thief was fairly hurled from one side of the carriage to the other. One effect of the blow was to open Lefroy's coat, and while he was getting up Mr Gold saw the butt end of the pistol projecting out of the inside breast coat pocket. "Directly he discovered that Lefroy was armed, Mr Gold shouted out: 'You villain, is it murder as well as robbery that you mean?' or words much to that effect. Jumping to his feet – or rather rushing at Lefroy – he snatched the pistol out of his coat pocket and fired at him twice. Neither shot struck Lefroy, who managed to close with his assailant and regain the weapon. He immediately fired two shots at Mr Gold.

"He believed the first of these struck the carriage near the bell pull, and the second inflicted the wound in Mr Gold's neck. At this point the convict's confession is rather confused, but as nearly as can be ascertained, they both fell to the bottom of the carriage, and then commenced the desperate struggle for life.

"It is declared by Lefroy – extraordinary as it must appear – that directly after he had shot Mr Gold, that gentleman did not fall to the ground insensible, on the contrary, he had strength enough to seize the pistol and deal his murderer a blow or two on the head, causing the wounds which were afterwards dressed by the Brighton surgeon.

"While the struggle was going on the two men had rolled up to the door of the carriage. With such vigour did the old man fight for his life that he pressed Lefroy against the door with one hand at his throat while he pulled out a pocket-knife with the other. He even opened the blade with his teeth. This effort, however, and the loss of blood from his wound, had exhausted him, and Lefroy succeeded in grabbing the knife, and hacking at his face.

"Lefroy tried to make out that he hardly knows who it was that opened the door – in fact, he thinks it was Mr Gold himself. He fancies, so he says, that his victim had a hope he would be able to push him out of the carriage. Lefroy, however, was now the stronger of the two, and pitched the unfortunate man onto the rails where his body was found."

To this account, the paper added that Lefroy said he had undergone a debate with the Devil from the time he took his pistol out of pawn to the time he entered Gold's compartment. The question he put to the Devil was "Poverty and honour – or wealth and dishonour". Perhaps Lefroy was mad, though the possibility was not pursued at the time; certainly he was very weird. At all events he ended up with poverty, and dishonour, and the hangman's noose.

INBRIEF

FEBRUARY 23, 1882

Directors of the Crystal Palace have started a course of lectures by Professor Silvanus P. Thompson of University College, Bristol, on electricity.

Professor Silvanus Thompson predicted that the present would be regarded as the age of electricity; that its application would soon enter every division of labour, and modify its condition; and that if the English nation is to hold its own in the commerce and industry of the world, the principals of this science must enter into the education of the workman. The electrical exhibition of the Palace, which will be far advanced towards completion when the Duke of Edinburgh visits it on Saturday, is an illustration of the truth of this remark.

From the **Telegraph**

The murderer hanged on the Sussex Downs

November 30, 1881

From our Special Correspondent

Just as the clock was striking half past eight this morning the little wicket gate of the lodge of Lewes jail was opened by a warder for the purpose of admitting some dozen and a half gentlemen who till then had lingered in the garden which belongs to the prison. A bright sunshine had succeeded a gusty night, and was rapidly driving away the mists that still hung over the South Down hills.

At last we came to the yard – the one for which we were particularly bound – a large irregular space, bounded on one side by the prison, and on three others by high walls, and containing at one end a row of celery trenches carefully banked up. At the end, however, facing that where the vegetables were grown, and closest to the corner of the prison, were two objects which forced themselves upon the view. In the right-hand corner as we looked upon them rose a couple of thick black posts, with a huge cross piece, from which dangled a staple and a long, thick rope; in the other, about 10 yards distance, an open grave.

As we filed into the yard, I noticed that we were being one by one saluted by a somewhat diminutive man clothed in brown cloth, and bearing in his arms a quantity of leather straps. There was nothing apparently in common between the grave and the gallows and the man, and for the moment I imagined that the individual who raised his hat and greeted each arrival with a "good morning, gentlemen," was a groom who had chanced to pass through the place, bearing a horse's bridle and headgear, and who was anxious to be civil. But to my horror, the man in the brown coat proved to be no stranger wandering about in the manner I had pictured, but the designer of the horrible structure on the right, and the official most closely connected with that and the open grave. William Marwood it was who thus bade us welcome, and the straps on his arms were nothing less than his "tackle".

I confess to a shudder as I looked upon the girdle and arm pieces that had done duty on so many a struggling wretch, and half expected that the man who carried them would have attempted to hide them. But no such thing! To him they were implements of high merit, and together with the gallows formed what he now confidentially informed his hearers was "an excellent arrangement". It was evident that in the gallows and the tackle too he had more than a little pride. He was even ready to explain with much volubility the awful instruments of his craft.

"That rope that you see there," quoth he, as he gazed admiringly at the crossbar of black wood, "is two and a half inches round. I've hung nine with it, and it's the same I used yesterday." Nor does he manifest the quaver of a muscle as he went on to point out certain peculiarities of design in his machinery of death. Had he been exhibiting a cooking apparatus, a patent incubator, or a corn mill, he could not have been more

complacent or more calm. "It's a running noose, you see," said he, "with a thimble that fits under the chin."

"The pit's all new," he went on to say; "new brickwork, you will see, and made on purpose." A glance revealed that it was new – as new as the grave. Formed after the ideas of Marwood himself, it certainly appeared to be complete as an engine of death. It consisted of two pits, connected with each other, one a broad and the other a narrow oblong, the broad one being immediately under the gallows, and covered by a black trapdoor that opened in the centre and was only supported by a long bolt; the other containing a brick staircase that led under the scaffold.

Above the trapdoor, or rather at the right-hand side of it, and close by the gallows tree, was a lever, something like the switch handle that one sees on railway lines, connected with the vault below the trapdoor. The rope that hung from the crossbar was coiled up; and although it had done duty so frequently, as Marwood said, seemed nearly new.

William Marwood, the hangman

To Marwood the whole thing evidently seemed a triumph of art; and as he moved hither and thither, explaining the superiorities of his design, he evidently expected that his handiwork would meet approval. All the while the bell dismally tolled. At length a warder came battling up, and with a bundle of keys in his hand beckoned to Marwood. It wanted about 10 minutes to 9 o'clock, and the doomed man was waiting.

"Ready for you," remarked the warder, and with an expectant look Marwood gathered up his "tackle" and followed. With an easy skip and a hop, as though he were answering an agreeable call, he left us, and disappeared towards the cell of the man about to die. I pictured him as he would move along the corridor, and present himself at the portal of the condemned cell, with that smile on his face and that ready step. I wondered mightily how he – the agent of death – could move so briskly, and after what fashion he would introduce himself to the human being he was going to strangle. Death is proverbially swift; in the guise of Marwood it moved with appalling celerity.

As it chanced, Lefroy knew nothing of this, and only saw his executioner as the latter with a bow entered the cell. Then it was probably too late for much thought. "I hope the rope will not break," was the only expression to which he gave utterance, possibly the result of some apprehension from what he had heard of the "Marwood long drop".

There was not time for more, the hangman was already busily at work, passing the leather belt round his body, fastening his elbows and wrists, and baring his neck. The bell was tolling, and nine o'clock had nearly come. It was time to be moving. The clergyman, in his white surplice, was ready; two warders had taken their places, one on either side of the condemned; Marwood, with one strap yet unused in his left hand, and his right hand firmly fixed on the leather belt that confined his victim, was prepared to move; the under sheriff, the governor of the jail, surgeon, and magistrate all were waiting; it was time for the burial service to begin. The corridor echoed forthwith to the sound of the death prayer. Slowly passing through the passage toward the door that led into the yard moved that awful

Hooded and pinioned, the condemned man stands on a trapdoor over the long drop in a pose arranged by Marwood's contemporary, James Berry

procession; and as the warder unlocked the door which opened close by the scaffold it emerged into the air.

I had chanced to see Lefroy on several previous occasions, and notably at the trial, and yet it was with a feeling bordering upon curiosity that I now looked upon him as he emerged into the open. There was much that operated against the producing of a favourable impression: he was attired, not, as had been stated, in a prison garb, but in a very old suit of greyish tweed; he was tightly pinioned, so tightly that, as I afterwards observed, his wrists were bruised; his hat was off, and his hair somewhat disarranged; he had not been shaved for some time; and he was being hurried along by his executioner at a disquieting rate.

But apart from all this, there was a pallor on his face so unearthly that he presented the appearance of one who was already dead, and I much doubt whether, but for the presence of the warders on either side of him, and the support which he gained from the hangman who pushed him forward, he would have been able to accomplish the distance from his cell to the grave. The words of the clergyman, rising and falling upon the ears of the spectators, were evidently lost upon him; he did not appear to hear the passing bell, but looked upwards as though in an agony of fear, and so stumbled helplessly along.

It was not far, only a few score yards in all, but the march to the grave, or rather to the scaffold, seemed terribly painful; all the bravado that was witnessed in the dock at Maidstone had gone; the terrors of death were in full force upon the hapless culprit. As he approached the scaffold this was particularly noticeable; he could scarcely take the step which was to place him where he had never stood before and from whence he would never step again, and Marwood, who at no instant left go of the belt, was fain once more to push him forward.

It was evidently not the moment for ceremony with the hangman, who was now once more very busy placing the tall young man, up to whose shoulders his own face scarcely reached, under the cross tree, stooping down to strap up his legs, and then fumbling about with a white glazed linen cap which he now assayed to put over the trembling youth's face.

I do not suppose for a moment that Marwood intended to be rough; he possibly was excited, and anxious to do everything as expeditiously as possible. But it certainly appeared to me that in attempting to fix the cap on Lefroy's head, and in pulling it down over his face, he hurt the prisoner somewhat unnecessarily. The worst of this was, however, yet to come. The long rope dangling about Lefroy had now to be adjusted, and the thimble through which the noose ran to be placed beneath his neck. I did not time it; it may have lasted only a few seconds; but to me it seemed appallingly long, while the swaying of Lefroy's body showed the agony he was enduring.

I cannot tell whether the sound of the clergyman's voice, which continued all the while the preparations went on, was of great consolation to him. His last look as the white cap was produced was lifted heavenward, his pallid face turned upwards, his lips moving as though in prayer; but so soon as the cap was over his face he began to sway, so much that I expected he would fall before the business was finished.

At last, however, all was ready, and Marwood, grasping the hand of his victim, stepped back; there was another awkward pause, apparently for the purpose of allowing the clergyman to finish the sacred invocation in which he was engaged; and then, the lever being pulled back, the trap doors opened, and Lefroy falls with a terrible thud into the cavern below. Down 10ft, as

was presently shown by the measurement of a tape line, he had dropped, the whole weight of his body falling upon the neck, which, receiving such a strain, was instantly broken so completely that the body never gave so much as one convulsive shudder, but, turning half round, hung swaying in the cold morning air, enveloped by a haze of steam rising from the corpse, and showing, by the visible disconnection of the vertebrae and by the open hands, how sudden death had been.

The preliminaries to the hideous spectacle had been painful in the extreme, to spectators and sufferer alike. But I think the actual death was as merciful as it could well be, if the agony of the two or three minutes from the leaving of the condemned cell to the fall of the scaffold be left out of consideration. Had there been an assistant to expedite the movement upon the scaffold, or had chloroform or another benignant anaesthetic been given to the condemned to lessen the pain of suspense, less fault might have been found with the miserable business.

As it was, without any feelings other than those of reprobation for the horrible crime for which Lefroy suffered, I felt that the agony of death had been unnecessarily prolonged, and that, compared even with the punishment of the guillotine in France, it was a tedious and horrible form of execution. It may, too, have been fancy; but it seemed that the actual falling of the trap doors and the long drop occupied a sensible period, though it is impossible to say how long the two seconds or so thus occupied may seem to one who is being thus awfully despatched.

But the whole of the spectacle connected with the Lefroy execution was not over. An inquest had yet to be held on the body of the dead man, and for this purpose a number of the inhabitants of Lewes had been summoned as jurymen. Thus, a little after 10 o'clock, we found ourselves – spectators of the execution, jail officials, coroner, and jury men – convened in the committee room of the prison once more, for the purpose of determining how Percy Mapleton Lefroy "now lying" to quote the words of the commission, "dead within the precincts of the jail," had come by his end.

The jury, sworn in, now proceeded to view the body, and were conducted to the infirmary of the jail, the same room in which, by the way, Lefroy was incarcerated prior to his trial – a large apartment, containing three or four beds and a bath. Here, on trestles, in a shell coffin, lay the dead body of the man, clad as we saw him when he emerged into the yard where he was executed, with his boots still on, and the same grey tweed suit. He had evidently been measured for his coffin while alive, and placed in it but a minute or two before we arrived.

A more horrible appearance than the remains presented is difficult to conceive. And, as though to add to the horrors of the scene, it appeared to be the duty of the jurymen to examine the body minutely, and by prods and pushes to satisfy their curiosity as to the physique of the dead man. In truth, his dead body did present the appearance of more strength than I had supposed, and there remained less cause for wonder in my mind as to how he contrived to kill a well built man such as Mr Gold.

The viewing over, the jury returned to the rooms, and there sat in solemn conclave, while the governor of the jail gave evidence of the identity of Lefroy, and the surgeon deposed to the effect that the deceased met his death by hanging; and then we filed out into the open air once more and the bright sunlight; the mists had gone from the Sussex hills, there was no cloud in the blue sky, and the day, so unusually ushered in to us, was as gladsome as though it had been the herald of spring.

From the Telegraph

The magistrate's warning to the child-beating stepfather

July 28, 1855

Guildhall. – Henry Wickstead, a cab driver, was brought up, charged with ill-using his stepson.

Henry Wickstead, a little boy, who appeared in a most weakly condition, said: The prisoner at the bar is my stepfather. Yesterday afternoon, he beat me with his strap; he is a cabman; he beats me because my brother told tales of me that were untrue; I was beaten on Saturday also with a broom handle; my brother is younger than I am; he told my father that I had taken money out of his pocket when I had not; he has beaten me before this; I have generally plenty to eat and to drink, but he put me into a room on Saturday, locked the door, and left me there three days without giving me anything to eat.

Defendant (in a most bullying tone): Now, sir, what have I beaten you for?

Boy (crying): Because my brother told stories of me.

Harriet Stallion was then called and said: I live on the second floor of the same house as the defendant. He lives on the first floor. I am a married woman, and my husband is a coppersmith. My attention was called by hearing the child screaming: "Don't, father." I entreated the prisoner not to beat the child. I told him that I had heard so much of it, I could stand it no longer. The boy came crying to me on Saturday and begged of me to give him something to eat. I have given him bread through the window. The boy's mother only comes home on Sunday.

Mr Phillips, the relieving officer of the West London Union (at whose instance the defendant was given into custody), said that when he saw the child yesterday, he was filthy.

William Smith, police constable 244, said: I am on this beat. I have known the prisoner for six or seven years. I never knew anything more against him than his being a violent man and addicted to drinking. There are complaints from nearly everyone in the square about his ill-using the child. I myself have witnessed him beating the boy with the strap of his badge.

Defendant: I cannot keep anything in the place. The boy goes about getting things of the different shops in my name. This is nothing more than conspiracy.

The mother, a respectable looking woman, came forward and said, it was true the boy had been punished but never more than was necessary. He was a very bad boy, much given to thieving.

Alderman Finnis (to defendant): I do not think this is a case that directly comes within the act; but I cannot help thinking that you do not give the boy the proper attention you ought to. You ought to send him to school. I regret that there is not corroborative proof that you shut this boy up for three days without food. Had there been, I should most certainly have sent you to prison for six months. I shall call upon you to find two sureties of £5 each to treat the child properly for six months. Mr Phillips, we are very much indebted to you, as the relieving officer, for bringing this case under our notice.

A burglar shoots a policeman on a London rooftop

July 15, 1885

Yet another outrage has been added to the list of murderous encounters between armed burglars and the Metropolitan Police. The present victim – Police-constable Owen Davis, 135x – is a man barely four and twenty years of age, and unmarried. He lived at Notting Hill police station. At 10 o'clock on Monday night, he went on duty, his beat taking in Kensington Park Gardens, a broad thoroughfare having terraces of tall houses on either side. At No. 37, a builder's ladder had been left standing, forming a means of access to the coping, behind which a wide gutter runs the entire length of the terrace.

It is the custom of policemen on night duty to give special attention to ladders, low walls, etc, and they have a secret system of placing a "mark" in a position likely to escape the notice of a burglar. It appears that shortly after 1am, Davis, who had been at the spot 20 minutes earlier, discovered that his "mark" had been tampered with. He attained the assistance of a fellow-constable, Prettyjohn, 320X, whom he stationed at the foot of the ladder, which he (Davis) himself commenced to ascend. He had to do this burglar-fashion i.e., from the back, the first 20 rungs being covered by a plank lashed in front in the usual insufficient manner for night protection.

According to the statement which Davis has been able to make to his superiors, when he stepped from the top of the ladder, he discovered, concealed in the spacious gutter, two men, one of whom wore a mask, which resembled a cap, in the peak of which two eye holes had been cut. His companion had

the appearance of a labourer, and it may here be mentioned that the marks of corduroy trousers were subsequently detected on the ladder.

The elder and more powerful of the two engaged in a fierce struggle with the policeman, which must have been prolonged for nearly 10 minutes. The constable drew his truncheon and struck his man a blow upon the shoulder, the force of which shivered the stout weapon.

With an imprecation and the threat, "I'll murder yer," the burglar, producing a revolver, fired four times. The reports were clearly heard by the alarmed inmates of No. 36, upon the roof of which house the exciting scene was being enacted, and the sound of the policeman's fall upon the slates was also distinguished amidst the din.

Meanwhile, the other constable, Prettyjohn, perceiving the danger in which his comrade stood, began to climb the ladder, which the younger burglar had been watching, having taken no part in the fight. As soon as this miscreant saw that help was at hand, he endeavoured to detach the ladder from its fastenings and throw it bodily into the street. Prettyjohn, half way up, felt the violent oscillation, and in self-defence, was compelled to slide down again to the pavement.

By this time, all the neighbourhood was astir. A messenger sent to the police station hard by brought back a posse of constables. Upon search being made, Davis was found on the roof alone, insensible and bleeding from the neck, his shattered truncheon lying beside him.

SHOCKING SCENES

Fenians blow up a street in Clerkenwell

In 1867 London was not accustomed to deliberate explosions that destroyed whole buildings. All at once that changed

In 1867, 12 people were killed when Fenians attempted to free two of their number imprisoned in the Clerkenwell House of Detention. The Fenian Brotherhood had been founded in 1859 a year after the Irish Republican Brotherhood was formed in Dublin. One of the Clerkenwell prisoners was Richard Burke, who in September had organised the successful escape of two Fenians from jail in Manchester, during which a policeman was killed. Burke was released during an amnesty in 1872.

"This latest Fenian exploit in Clerkenwell is a great folly," Karl Marx wrote to his friend Friedrich Engels the day after the explosion. "The London masses, who have shown much sympathy for Ireland, will be enraged by it and driven into the arms of the government party."

The Daily Telegraph was careful to advise its readers not to tar all Irish people, or Roman Catholics, with the Fenian brush.

In the following 130 years the *Telegraph* was to

Fearsome Fenians: the determined face of militant Irish nationalism was becoming familiar in the 1860s. James Donaghy, Henry Hughes and Hugh McGriskin of the Irish Republican Brotherhood were photographed in May 1866 in Northallerton jail, Yorkshire. In Manchester two Fenians escaped from jail, setting off a train of events that culminated in the outrage at Clerkenwell

spectacles. All the cells in the prison were lighted up; the wall in front was one great black mass, in the middle of which, low down, there was a huge cavity, through which you could descry the gas lamps in the prison yard.

"The debris of that yawning chasm in the wall had formed a high mound in Corporation Lane; and on the top of the hillock of broken bricks stood Captain Eyre Massey Shaw, directing, with his usual coolness and decision, the operations of the firemen.

"There was a strong detachment of the Scots Guards on the ground. The explosion was a madcap attempt on the part of the Fenians to liberate a member of their faction who was confined, on remand, in the House of Detention. The only eye-witness of the outrage was a boy, who was standing, about four o'clock in the afternoon, in front of No. 5, Corporation Lane, when he saw a large barrel close to the wall of the prison, and a man leave the barrel and cross the road.

"Shortly afterwards the man returned with a squib in his hand, which he thrust into the barrel. Some other boys had gathered round, and one was smoking; and he handed the man a light, which the recipient applied to the squib. When he saw that the squib was beginning to burn, he ran away. A police constable ran after him; and when he arrived opposite No. 5, "the thing went off".

"There were several people in the street at the time, and playing children. The explosion blew down several houses, and smashed most of the coarse glass panes in the windows of the prison; and the results of the outrage to the unoffending inhabitants of Corporation Lane were most shocking.

"I had passed through the cordon of police easily enough; but to get back to Fleet Street was a matter of considerable difficulty. The crowd was enormous; and the police, naturally, could not tell friends from foes, or Fenians from journalists; but cuffed and buffeted all the assemblage, impartially. I managed, however, to get close to the detachment of Guards, who were marching away from the scene of the explosion, and telling the officer in command who I was, he good-naturedly allowed me to "tail on", so to speak, to the detachment; and at the steady pace at which the soldiers were marching, we were soon clear of the crowds, and I was free to make my way to Fleet Street and write a description of what I had seen."

The Fenians suspected of having committed, or of being accomplices in, the Clerkenwell outrage were not tried until April, 1868, but all were acquitted; with the exception of one, Michael Barrett, who was hanged in front of the Debtors' Door, Newgate, on May 26.

This was the last public execution that took place in England. The year 1867 had come to an end with a very serious Fenian scare; other explosions had occurred, there was great public excitement, and nearly 30,000 special constables were sworn in.

report many more Irish Republican outrages, many of them worse than the bombing in 1996 at Marsh Wall near the *Telegraph* offices in Canary Wharf, which killed two men and injured 100. The blast from that explosion broke the clock in the editor's office.

The *Telegraph* journalist George Augustus Sala later recounted the experience of reporting the Clerkenwell outrage: "On the 13th December 1867, just as I was about to return to Putney, at the end of my day's work, I was intercepted at the Waterloo terminus by a nimble messenger from the *Daily Telegraph* office, who told me that an explosion had taken place at the Clerkenwell House of Detention, and that I was to repair thither at once. The swiftest of hansoms conveyed me to the prison. It was nightfall when I arrived at the House of Detention.

"There was a strong cordon of police round the scene of the explosion to keep off the mob; but the inspectors on duty knew who I was, and allowed me to pass. My eye lighted on the strangest of

INBRIEF

AUGUST 7, 1855
COLOURED CHILDREN IN UNITED STATES SCHOOLS
The legislature of Massachusetts has passed a law obliging the public schools to admit Negroes amongst their pupils.

From the **Telegraph**

'The doll and the baby's chair were in one broken heap'

December 14, 1867

The report and concussion of the air alarmed everyone within the radius of half a mile, and within a radius of half that distance the inhabitants appear as by one impulse to have rushed frantically into the streets. Over the scene of the catastrophe hung a funereal pall of smoke and dust, which almost suffocated those who had escaped more serious injury. For some few minutes the people in the neighbourhood were so terrified as to be unable to properly understand what had happened.

Women and children ran about screaming, making confusion worse confounded, and men with blank faces stared aghast at each other and asked, "What is it?" Some of these appear to have been little less terrified than the women and children, but others, and the great majority fortunately, were recalled to a sense of manhood by the cries of wounded men, the shrieks of women, and the pitiful wailings of tortured children.

Following the gallant example of a fine fellow named John Brasnen, a brick-layer's labourer – who, running to the spot from the place where he was at work, and seeing a human hand projecting from the ruins of the fallen house, mounted the debris between party walls tottering to their fall, and, at the eminent risk of his own life, extracted in succession an old woman and man and a young woman – they set to work to rescue those whose cries were filling the air with sounds of horror.

The two Fenians for whose rescue this bold outrage was committed were locked up in their cells at the time of its occurrence; had they been exercising in the yard, they would either have been killed by the falling wall of their prison, or, if they had survived they would in all probability have escaped.

In the lane immediately in front of the breach the explosion had torn up the roadway to a considerable depth; and the houses immediately opposite were in ruins. St James's-passage opening out of Corporation-lane, almost faced the breach in the prison walls. The corner house stands at present, but it is a mere shell; the side facing the passage has fallen down, the floors are gone, the windows are utterly destroyed and not an atom of furniture was discernible.

But, if the desolation of this house appeared complete, that of its neighbour, which had felt the full force of the explosion was still worse. This fine three-storeyed house gave a sudden shake, and then fell downwards in a horrible mass of ruins. All in the house fell with it; and to some death came instantaneously. So great was the force of the explosion, that the house appears as though it had been cut with one blow of some huge sword from between its neighbours.

A large number of firemen and police were clearing away these ruins at 6 o'clock in search of bodies. They worked by the light of gas jets, which flared from off the tops of broken gas pipes. All toiled with a hearty will, removing the bricks and raising the timbers. At the door of No 5 stood Thomas Young, who said he had a large workshop attached to his premises, in which he carried on the manufacture of cases for telegraphic instruments. The whole interior of his house was destroyed, and eleven persons who were in the different rooms, lodgers with their families, and others relatives of his, were so seriously injured that they had all of them to be taken to St Bartholomew's Hospital. Some small fragments of stone struck him on the forehead, slightly bruising him; he was stunned for a moment and when his senses returned he found that his left thumb was gone. A passing missile cut it off below the joint and it was dangling by a bit of skin. This was afterwards severed at the hospital and he returned to his wrecked home.

He stated that his wife and his sister, the first-floor lodger and four children, and the second-floor lodger and three children – all of whom were in the house at the time – were seriously injured. Every room in the house was a complete wreck and every atom of furniture was destroyed. The window frames were blown in, doors were broken, the partition walls were levelled, the stairs were ruined and great gaps ripped in the passage floors. A heap of finished telegraph boxes which were in the front room were blown about the place, the tables, chairs and sofas broken to pieces and the whole room covered with small fragments of glass. The little room at the back was so utterly destroyed that not more than head and shoulders could be introduced inside the door. A partition wall was blown across the bed, and the whole room completely wrecked.

Up stairs that were very rickety from the force of the explosion, rooms were entered which presented the saddest pictures in this house of desolation. On one floor were the rooms shortly before occupied by a mother and three children. All the little treasures of the household – the stuffed bird, the pictures of *Babes in the Wood*, the child's doll, and the baby's chair – were in one broken heap, bespattered with the blood of the poor children to whom they once belonged.

There was a young man acted as guide through this house, who could with difficulty restrain his tears, as he related how the little children clung about him when he carried them downstairs, and their blood flowed from them upon him, staining his clothes.

After the blast: 'The floors are gone and no atom of furniture remains'

Police stand outside the broken wall of the Clerkenwell House of Detention, with debris from the damaged houses of Corporation Lane all around

The Fenians are the enemy and not the people of Ireland

December 14, 1867

This latest act of the secret society will put to flight all that sentimental sympathy which has been lavished on them in some quarters. When they conspired in Ireland, when they made war in Canada, when they took the field in Kerry and Dublin, they were treated with a leniency that no other nation on earth would have shown. The lives of their leaders were spared, and the dupes who followed them were lightly punished. The clemency of the British people is first rewarded by the murder of a constable in the execution of his duty, and now by an unprovoked and savage outrage which scattered wounds and death among innocent and helpless households. Hitherto the Fenian conspiracy has not been regarded with any feeling much stronger than repugnance, but the Clerkenwell tragedy has revealed a depth of guilt that precludes all further mistake.

The detestable act of yesterday has a fearful value of its own, since it plainly discloses the true nature of the league, and the enormities which spring from it. British civilisation, fully warned, will now wake from its apathy, and take ample measure of its preservation.

December 16, 1867

We have to look at Ireland, not as the seat of the disease, but as the country to which the contagion has been brought. Were all Ireland Fenian at heart, we should have no alternative but to stamp down the sedition with the iron heel of military power or to give the country its independence. For with the Fenians there is no available middle course. But Ireland is not Fenian at heart. The whole Protestant Church, though inflamed by sectarian hatred, still closely clings to the English connection. The Roman Catholic middle classes are on the side of order and of law, as their verdicts against the Fenians abundantly proved. The Roman Catholics are, in their own interests, opposed to a Republican sedition that strikes at priests as much as at Kings.

When those allies are, naturally or accidentally, on our side, it will be a great blunder if, with the use of bad language in public places or in the press, we give them just offence by confusing together in one vulgar, silly popular anathema the whole Irish race and the whole Roman Catholic population. It would also be unworthy of the English nation if its anger against Fenianism should render it deaf to the just discontent of the Irish people against wrongs that English legislation still sustains – an alien Church, the creature of conquest, and the living memorial of the penal laws; and a land system that makes Irish agriculture miserably poor. We may hang convicted Fenians with good conscience but we should also thoroughly redress these evils.

A PRINCELY MEMORIAL

Sennacherib, Cheops and Prince Albert

The memorial to Victoria's consort was on the scale of a cathedral, but arguments had been fierce for a very different design

'A very few weeks had elapsed after the death of the Prince Consort," wrote the *Telegraph* looking back 10 years from 1872, "when that great meeting, which fully represented the voice of the whole country, was held at the Mansion House of the City of London."

The meeting was to decide upon a suitable memorial to Prince Albert "whose powerful and well regulated mind and great ability had for more than 20 years been unceasingly devoted to improving the condition of the humbler classes, to the development and extension of science and art, and to the judicious education and training of the Royal family."

The result was to be the Albert Memorial, but there was no reason at all why it should have ended up the Gothic extravanganza that has now regained some of its brilliance after years of restoration. Among the architects invited to submit a design, only George Gilbert Scott was wedded to the Gothic revival. Lord Palmerston had secured from Parliament a vote of £50,000 for the project (in addition to £47,000 subscribed in Britain and the colonies), and it was Palmerston who had forced Scott to build the new Foreign Office in Whitehall in the Italianate, not the Gothic style. The battle of the styles – between the Neo-Classical and the pointed-arched Gothic – was still raging fiercely.

One early idea for the memorial was for a 150ft monolithic obelisk – which would indeed have been impressive. But it proved hard to find a quarry to supply such a massive lump of stone. In 1863 Queen Victoria was shown the designs submitted by seven architects. "There were only two that would do at all," she said, "and only one that is really applicable" – and that wasn't Scott's but Philip Hardwick's. Scott's, she thought, was too like the Walter Scott memorial in Edinburgh "and too like a market cross".

Plans by other architects included a Greek temple with a stepped roof like the mausoleum at Halicarnassus and, as the architectural historian Gavin Stamp has pointed out, from Alexander Thomson an amazing unsolicited design – a soaring

Monumental scale: the brick undercroft beneath the steps (below, in a photograph from 1865) entailed the building of 868 arches – 'a curious, picturesque and intricate series of catcombs'. Here some of the workmen may be seen on the lofty wooden scaffolding. Masonry was transported about the site with the help of an overhead travelling crane (below, right). In the finished memorial, the Telegraph explained, 'the magnificence of the fleche and the vault of the canopy is due to the combination of Mr Skidmore's rich metalwork and the glass mosaics of Messrs Salviati and Co, of Murano, near Venice'

obelisk shape surmounted by an attenuated dome and flanked at the base by massive steps and guardian lions of more oriental appearance than those in Trafalgar Square. "For unspeakable, Semitic majesty," wrote one critic, "this design has no equal; in its ideal shadow, the executed design by Sir George Gilbert Scott appears as a cuckoo clock."

In 1863, though, Scott was not yet knighted, and the Queen yet to be convinced. His drawings for a Gothic memorial, taking as its starting point the "Eleanor Crosses" (marking the resting places of the bier of Queen Eleanor of Castile in 1290, as at Geddington, Northamptonshire), eventually won her over. This was despite Palmerston's renewed opposition and alternative suggestion of an "open Grecian temple".

"After Her Majesty had selected Mr Scott's design," the *Telegraph* recorded, "the Executive Committee, which was immediately formed, received a truly public spirited offer from Mr John Kelk, who expressed his willingness to undertake the construction of the Memorial entirely at cost price, his accounts being open to the supervision of the Executive Committee." Though Scott initially mistrusted Kelk, who some said was largely motivated by a desire for social advancement, his drive overcame the unforeseen difficulties of rapid construction. (The supplier of granite committed suicide when he found it impossible to ship supplies from his quarries; Francis Skidmore, responsible for the huge amount of metalwork, could not keep to the rates agreed beforehand.)

The memorial was more like a cathedral than a statue. "The central portion of the monument," the *Telegraph* explained, "is based upon a mass of concrete 60 feet square and 17 feet in thickness – indeed, in some parts it is of much greater thickness, owing to the inequalities of the ground. Upon this are laid two continuous courses of thick stone landings, bedded in Portland cement; and on this platform is erected the substructure of massive brickwork upon which the monument is based. The substructure supporting the steps and landings which surround the monument, though planned simply with a view to their practical uses, forms a curious, intricate and picturesque series of catacombs."

More visible was the "adornment of the Podium with emblematic or representative figures in alto rilievo". These showed heroes of painting, poetry and music, of sculpture and architecture. Included were Sennacherib, as the founder of the palace of Nimrod, King Cheops, and Hiram the builder of the Temple.

"It need hardly be said that the magnificence of the fleche and the vault of the canopy is due to the combination of Mr Skidmore's rich metalwork and the glass mosaics of Messrs Salviati and Co, of Murano, near Venice, with which revived form of skilful ornament the tympana, spandrels, and vaulting are adorned." Part of the inspiration for the rich craftsmanship came from the medieval metalwork reliquary in Cologne reputed to contain the relics of the Three Kings of Christ's nativity story.

The scale of the undertaking was indicated by "a few curious statistics" given by *The Daily Telegraph* when The Queen made a private visit to the completed structure on July 1, 1872. (She did not want to officiate at a public opening.) "The quantity of concrete used is 120,000 cubic feet, of which 61,200 cubic feet are a single block. Beneath the steps are 396 piers and 868 arches. The total length of granite steps is 11,879 feet, or two and a quarter miles, and the number of steps is 1,803. The sub-plinths of the bases of columns are two stones, each weighing 10 tons, and the bases themselves in single blocks weigh upwards of 15 tons each; the working of each of these stones occupied 12 men for 16 weeks, and cost £260. The length of polished granite columns is 791 feet in 56 stones; and the pavement of the platforms covers a surface of 23,803 square feet."

The *Telegraph* much admired the whole thing. "Now that the entire work is uncovered, and the lower portions, which for a long time have stood forth isolated and straggling, appear as one mass of masonry, the central monument, with its burnished gold pillars and its rich glow of Salviati mosaics, retires into a fitness of proportion scarcely imaginable by one who saw it merely surrounded by a number of white groups cropping up from a desert of timber planking."

During her visit the Queen was able to read the dedicatory inscription, "executed in mosaic, the letters being of blue glass with black edges, placed upon a ground of gold enamelled glass". It said:

QUEEN VICTORIA AND HER PEOPLE
TO THE MEMORY OF ALBERT, PRINCE CONSORT,
AS A TRIBUTE OF THEIR GRATITUDE
FOR A LIFE DEVOTED TO THE PUBLIC GOOD

To George Gilbert Scott the Memorial was "the result of my highest and most enthusiastic efforts". To Queen Victoria almost nothing could do justice to the memory of her husband, but among her words of praise for the Memorial was the undeniable judgment: "It can be seen from a great distance."

From the Telegraph

The Royal yacht collides, with the Queen aboard

August 20, 1875

From our own correspondent, Gosport, Thursday
The excitement occasioned by the unhappy event on Wednesday evening, when the *Alberta*, with the Queen on board, ran down the *Mistletoe*, has not abated. It now appears that Her Majesty was sitting on deck as the two vessels approached each other and therefore saw all that occurred.

It is understood that the engines of the *Alberta* slackened speed, and that her course was slightly altered with a view to run astern of the *Mistletoe*. The latter tacked when she should have kept a straight course, and the anxiety of the crew to dip the flag in honour of the Queen led to their neglecting the helm.

When the schooner was struck, Samuel Stokes, one of the seamen, caught hold of Miss A. Peel in order to save her; but the rigging carried her out of his arms. Stokes succeeded, not without difficulty, in climbing up the *Alberta*. When Commander Fullerton, of the Royal yacht, leaped overboard, he succeeded in finding Miss Peel but was obliged to abandon the hope of saving her.

The captain of the *Mistletoe*, Thomas Stokes, was at the helm. It was he who was carried in an unconscious state onboard the *Alberta* and the

Queen assisted personally in the endeavour to restore animation to the old man. He belonged to Poole, was about 75 years of age, and leaves a wife and five or six children. The man whose body has not yet been recovered, Nathaniel Turner, the mate, also came from Poole; he leaves a wife and two children.

It was well that the *Alberta* was built in water-tight compartments, or the event, melancholy as it is, might have acquired a national importance. As I telegraphed yesterday, her cutwater and bow sprits are gone. But, in addition to this, all her timbers are started.

The Royal steam yacht 'Alberta' (above), built in 1863, cut right into the schooner 'Mistletoe', in whose wreckage (below) Miss Peel's body was found. In 1901 the 'Alberta' was to carry Queen Victoria's coffin from Osborne

INBRIEF

APRIL 21, 1882

Charles Darwin is dead. Our great philosopher and naturalist departed this life on Wednesday at his residence in Kent. Thus passes away from the age which he has adorned and enlightened a man who, perhaps, more than any other among his contemporaries, stamped the sign of his genius upon current thought....

One great work must be dwelt upon, that entitled *The Origin of Species by Natural Selection*. The first edition of this remarkable production appeared in 1859, and no competent physicist now doubts that – whatever may hereafter modify, complete, enlarge, or even correct the main theories of the author – the book itself was "epoch making", and must ever form a landmark in the annals of human enquiry, not inferior in importance to the *Principia* of Newton in astronomy, or in metaphysics to the *Critique of Pure Reason* by Kant.

It had been universally accepted that the innumerable species of animals and vegetables, as geology reveals or as nature displays them, were separately created. Custom had stamped this view with a religious sanction, and it had become all the more unquestioned because it ministered to the pride of the race. Far more marvellous and more divinely subtle must it seem to bestow upon the material of life – physical and mental – gifts which will evolve from low and little beginnings the countless visible forms of beauty and youth and power, than merely to invent this or that shape and creature, fixed thenceforward for all time.

A BULLET FOR VICTORIA

Maclean shoots at the Queen, but is he mad?

He had been seen levelling his pistol at the Queen's carriage. The question remained whether he was sane when he did it

He must have been a madman to shoot at the Queen – or must he? Roderick Maclean shot at Queen Victoria as she was driven in her carriage from Windsor station on March 2, 1882. She accounted it the seventh serious attempt on her life. "There was a sound of what I thought was an explosion from the engine," she wrote in her journal that evening, "but in another moment I saw people rushing about and a man being violently hustled. I then realised that it was a shot, which must have been meant for me, though I was not sure."

Gladstone, the Prime Minister at the time, comforted her with the reflection that assassinations abroad were politically motivated, but in Britain such attempts were the work of madmen.

The idiosyncratic poet William McGonagall had his own view of the attempted assassination:

There's a divinity that hedges a king,
And so it does seem.
And my opinion is, it has hedged
Our most gracious Queen.

Maclean must be a madman,
Which is obvious to be seen,
Or else he wouldn't have tried to shoot
Our most beloved Queen.

Despite the force of McGonagall's argument, it was yet to be found that Maclean really was mad.

"A man who was standing in the crowd fired a shot from a revolver," the next day's Court Circular reported laconically in the *Telegraph*. The Queen was said to be "very well" and had not "suffered from the shock". Indeed Victoria, then 62, was well enough after a night's sleep to address the boys of Eton College, a pair of whom had helped to arrest Maclean, one having "beaten him with an umbrella" in the Queen's words. She drove out in her carriage that evening and "received everywhere a welcome of indescribable enthusiasm". The *Telegraph* reported outrage,

sympathy and loyal bunting in the streets of Marlow, Liverpool and Oldham.

The day after the shooting, Maclean was brought before the mayor of Windsor, as head of the magistracy, in Windsor Town Hall. The *Telegraph* went to town in its report, spending 200 words on the prisoner's clothes alone – a frayed, worn coat of "dirty brownish blue" closely buttoned, a dirty collar and a once-black scarf at his twitching throat. But his boots were good, and polished. His appearance "recalled in general the notorious Lefroy, with a shade of advantage in Maclean's favour".

From the first he said he had not meant to shoot the Queen. He asserted that he had aimed at the carriage wheel. When trying to explain the position of his arm when he had made to shoot, he asked the police superintendent in court if he would hand him the pistol so he could demonstrate. "No, thank you," the officer replied firmly.

Maclean offered to give all the help he could to "elucidate the mystery". He asked for legal counsel. "I haven't the technical knowledge to conduct my case," he declared, "although I may have the ingenuity." If Maclean was mad he was not raving.

Maclean was tried for high treason on April 19 at Reading Assizes. *The Daily Telegraph* reported the trial the next day in about 13,000 words.

The two judges sitting were Lord Chief Justice Coleridge (who in 1871 had appeared as a barrister in the extraordinary Tichborne claimant trial) and Mr Baron Huddleston. The Lord Chief Justice addressed the jury in high style. "State trials in this country," he said, "have become matters of singularly infrequent occurrence. The vast mass of the people of this island acquiesce contentedly in that form of Government established by law, and are very grateful for the virtue and character of the Sovereign who now fills the throne – illustrious in herself as well as in her great descent.

"Nevertheless, the possessor of the English throne, even when filled by a Sovereign of unsullied title and unstained character, is not exempt any more than the head of any other Government or State – a military monarch perhaps on the one hand, and a great republic on the other – from occasional assaults on the person; sometimes by madmen; sometimes by men whose object is to throw the whole state of affairs into confusion, utterly reckless of the cruelty of the crime, and the means they employ; sometimes by men who, either from real misery or fancied wrong, are dissatisfied, and who desire to force the world's attention upon themselves by an outrage upon the great person who represents the system they assail, and against which their energies are devoted. Such crimes by the law of England are high treason, and those who commit them are traitors."

After hearing a short history of the law on treason, the grand jury present in court retired, and found a true bill against the prisoner. Maclean was at once placed in the dock. He wore the same shabby clothes he had on "when he committed the crime" as the *Telegraph* put it, "but the treatment he had received in prison seemed to have done him a great deal of good. He had lost the wretched and ill-fed appearance his face had while he was before the magistrates in Windsor Town Hall, and looked altogether heartier and stronger".

He replied to the usual question with a stammering "Not guilty, my lord". A different, "petty" jury was then empanelled. The Attorney-General, Sir Henry James QC, MP, opened the case for the prosecution.

"It was on Thursday, March 2," he said "that the offence was committed. On the afternoon of that day the Queen, who had been absent a short time from Windsor, returned by train, and reached the railway station about 20 minutes past five o'clock. Shortly before five o'clock the prisoner was seen waiting at the station. He had given an incorrect account of the circumstances which caused him to be at the railway station, stating that he was there to meet a person who was to arrive by train.

"Nothing more appears to have been noticed in relation to his movements until after the arrival of the Queen. When the carriage left the door of the waiting-room it had to pass through a gateway and thence through a comparatively narrow passage, which leads to the high street of Windsor. The prisoner took up a position inside this gateway, mingling with the crowd which had assembled at the station.

"The Queen was accompanied in the carriage by Her Royal Highness, Princess Beatrice and by the Duchess of Roxburgh. The window on the side where the prisoner was standing was open, and Her Majesty's position must have been discernible by him. When the carriage was moving off, he seemed to have stepped forward slightly from the crowd amongst whom he had been, and then was seen to raise his arm, extend a pistol in the direction of Her Majesty's carriage, and fire a bullet.

"So far as we can judge, that bullet was aimed not only in the direction of, but directly to the very carriage in which the Queen was sitting. Next morning, March 3, the bullet was found in a direct line from the place where the carriage was at the time the shot was fired and the spot where the prisoner was standing. There cannot be any doubt that had the bullet not passed a little either above or beyond the carriage, most serious results would have taken place."

"The crime was apparently one of premeditation," the Attorney-General continued, but he soon demonstrated the prosecution's willingness to consider the possibility of Maclean's insanity. "The humanity of the law lays it down that if a prisoner is not accountable for his actions at the time of committing a crime he shall be acquitted on the ground of insanity. On this occasion the prisoner at the bar has the benefit of able counsel, and I will leave it to the counsel to trace the previous life of the prisoner up to the time of this deed.

"But I wish distinctly to say that there is no desire for one moment on the part of the prosecution to keep back one fact which has come into their possession with respect to the mental condition of the accused. I feel that this is the course which not only humanity suggests, but justice requires. And if it shall be found by you that at the time of the crime this unhappy man was not accountable for his act, I am sure there will be a satisfaction felt by every subject of the Queen that it was not within the ranks of those who are sane a person could be found to lift his hand towards her, except in the attitude of respect and veneration."

The question of Maclean's sanity depended in law on a ruling deriving from the famous case of The Queen vs McNaughten of 1843 (*see overleaf;* the spelling of McNaughten's name has never been satisfactorily resolved, and it still varies in official publications between anything from M'Naghten to Macnaughton.) Now, in his summing up in the case of Maclean, reported in the *Telegraph*, Lord Chief Justice Coleridge gave a plain summary of the McNaughten ruling, which asked whether a malefactor knew "that the act was a wrong act for him to do". But earlier in the hearing Coleridge enquired repeatedly about a different matter from his knowledge of right and wrong. He asked whether Maclean was "capable of moral restraint" – whether he "could control his impulses". This he asked of the defence witness Dr Hitchens, who had certified Maclean insane in 1880. In reply Hitchens said, "Not then, not two years before."

Montagu Williams, the defence counsel, next examined Mr T.S. Sheldon, a surgeon and assistant medical superintendent of the Bath and Wells Lunatic Asylum. A certificate was produced before the court that said: "R.S. Maclean, admitted January 2, 1880; discharged, recovered, on no probation." There was an accompanying note on the case: "Being convalescent some months; his habits being intemperate."

"As one of the medical officers," Sheldon told the court, "I saw the prisoner frequently during his confinement in the asylum. He was suffering from an indefinite state, partly mania and partly melancholia. When admitted he was excited, and the excitement continued some days. Reaction set in, and he became melancholy. During the last month I do not remember his delusions very accurately, but I have a strong impression they were the same as were recorded in the certificate, in which he was said to be suffering from homicidal mania – at all events, from a mania calculated to do injury to others."

In answer to a question from the Attorney-General, Sheldon said: "When he was discharged I was under the impression that he had recovered from the acute attack of mania."

Mr Williams: Would those delusions be likely to return? — Witness: Yes; I thought when I sent him out he would probably come back, or be taken to some other asylum.

The Lord Chief Justice: You say that, as far as you could ascertain, the prisoner was recovered. — Witness: That, as far as we can go. I thought

Maclean fires a shot as the Queen leaves Windsor station, an artist's reconstruction in an illustrated paper, based on a sketch by an eyewitness. 'When the carriage was moving off,' the court that tried him was told, 'he seemed to have stepped forward slightly from the crowd amongst whom he had been, and then was seen to raise his arm, and extend a pistol in the direction of Her Majesty's carriage'

THE PRISONER

THE PISTOL

CARTRIDGE

THE BULLET
ON LARGER SCALE

that any exciting cause, such as privation, would induce a return of insanity.

Did you think him safe to be at large? — Quite safe at the time.

At the time did you think his state of mind such that, from time to time he would be dangerous? — I thought it might be necessary to confine him again.

Does recurring insanity usually take the same form? — Not always; it is more likely than not.

Tell me this. You have "habits intemperate". How did you gather that? — I did not admit him. In all probability it was obtained from the relieving officer who brought him to the asylum.

He was not guilty of intemperance at Wells? — (laughter) — No, my Lord.

Then it was merely what you were told? — That is all. I have known symptoms of alcoholic mania.

In your judgment, as far as you can recollect, was he capable of moral control? — I think he was to a certain extent.

I mean, was he capable of resisting an impulse? — That is a difficult question to answer.

Of course it is. Supposing that he had an impulse to do some mischief to someone. Was he, in your view, in a state of mind to resist it? — I think his state of mind was weak; that his moral sense was weakened, and that he might not have the power.

Would he have had the power to do so? — I cannot say.

The Rev Archibald Campbell Maclachlan, of Newton Valance, Hampshire, told the court how, on February 23, a man had fallen down in a fit at his gate. That man was the prisoner.

"He was in a most exhausted condition when I came up. He was placed in a chair. He seemed half starved, and was in a cold perspiration. His eyes particularly struck me, as he turned them up and down again repeatedly. He could only speak in a low whisper." Maclachan's gardener's wife gave him some tea and the gardener gave him some bread and butter. Maclachlan was in Windsor on March 2, and was standing "halfway between Leighton's shop and the corner", and he saw the outrider coming. "I said: 'Here is her Majesty. It is a narrow street; we shall see her well.' Just then I heard a report and saw smoke. I then saw the man I had relieved carried up the street."

The medical superintendent of Laverstock Asylum, Salisbury, a Mr Manning, told the court he had had the management of the asylum for seven years, and had "large experience of lunatics". He had examined the prisoner in Reading Gaol on the 6th, and again on the 30th of March.

What conclusion did you come to? — That he was not of sound mind.

INBRIEF

JULY 10, 1885
PERAMBULATORS ON THE PAVEMENT
Esther Maydwell and Emma Hannaford, servants – the former in service in Ladbroke Grove Road, Notting Hill, and the latter at Shakespeare House, St Mark's Road – were summoned by the police for driving perambulators on the footway. – Replying to the magistrate, Maydwell said she did not know it was unlawful to drive perambulators side-by-side. – Mr Sheil, the Magistrate: How are the people to pass if you girls are gaping after soldiers and policemen? – The defendants were each fined 3s, with 2s costs, with an intimation that the next time the full penalty would be enforced.

From the Telegraph

The precedent that decided if the gunman was mad or sane

April 20, 1882
Lord Chief Justice Coleridge explains the legal grounds of insanity.

"In the celebrated case of The Queen v Macnaughten, Mr Macnaughten was a man who was under a delusion that Sir Robert Peel had done him a grievous bodily injury. He believed that his life was made miserable, that his whole existence was poisoned by Sir Robert. He bought a pistol and cartridges, and lay in wait day after day for the distinguished statesman. He came across his secretary, and mistaking Mr Drummond for Sir Robert Peel, he shot him when near to Charing Cross, in the back and killed him on the spot.

"Macnaughten was tried by three eminent judges. There was a great conflict of evidence, there was a great array of scientific gentlemen and the end was that Macnaughten was acquitted on the ground of insanity. The doctors who were called for Macnaughten said that he was unaware in fact of what he was about, and that he did not know the nature of the act which he was doing in consequence of the uncontrollable effect his delusions had upon him. Some of the most eminent men in the country were witnesses for the Crown on that occasion. They sat in court, they heard the evidence given by the medical men who were called for the prisoner, and they declined, as was to be expected from honourable and high-minded men, to give

evidence against their convictions, their convictions going with the medical men who had been called for the prisoner.

"Accordingly the Lord Chief Justice of the common pleas, on that occasion, stopped the case and Macnaughten was acquitted. Whether the Lord Chief Justice was right in stopping the case or not I will not presume to say, but it led to a great deal of discussion and disturbance of public opinion. The House of Lords did what they had a right to do – they called upon the whole of the judges of England to answer questions which they put to them in writing with respect to crimes committed by insane persons, and the questions which in such cases should be left to the jury.

"In answering these two questions, the judges laid it down clearly that in all cases the jury were to be told that every man is presumed to be sane, and to possess a sufficient degree of reason, to be responsible for his crimes until the contrary be proved to their satisfaction; that to establish a defence upon the ground of insanity, it must be clearly proved that at the time he committed the acts he was labouring under such a defect of reason from disease of mind as not to know the nature and quality of the act he was committing, that he did not know he was doing wrong.

"Now, what I ask you is this, has the prisoner made out to your satisfaction either that he did not know that the act which he was committing was wrong; did not know its nature and quality; or, if he did know – that is to say, if he knew he was shooting at the Queen, and that if he shot at her with a loaded revolver and hit her, he would kill her – did he know that the act was a wrong act for him to do? If he did know it he is liable to punishment; if he did not, he is entitled to be acquitted on the ground of insanity."

INBRIEF

NOVEMBER 1855

Sir – Perceiving that you have for your principle the administration of justice and redress of wrongs, I will expose a practice which is in daily use, and although opposed to the regulations of the railway companies, yet sanctioned (not without a consideration of some kind) by their servants, to the great annoyance of other passengers. I allude to persons smoking in first-class railway carriages, a habit not at all consistent with our present advanced state of civilisation.
I am, Sir, yours &c,
An Enemy of Tobacco,
Nov 12

Sir – Permit me also to declaim against the same nuisance in second-class carriages, of which my circumstances oblige me to travel in.
Another Enemy To Tobacco Smoking in Railway Carriages,
High Street, Notting Hill,
Nov 15

Sir – In the early part of the last summer, I was coming from Woolwich to Shoreditch second-class, there were four other passengers, men, two of whom, immediately on the train starting, commenced smoking short pipes. I remonstrated in vain, after complaining to the railway servants. It is of no use, for they either will not attend to what you say, or they slam the door in your face, and give the signal for the train to proceed.
A Third Enemy To Smoking In Railway Carriages,
Upper Ebury Street, Pimlico,
Nov 17

Sir – Having seen for some days past complaints of smoking in railway carriages, could you not use your influence, by representing the urgent want of one or two carriages with each train to be appropriated to smokers alone?
WM,
Surrey Place, Old Kent Road,
Nov 21

Did you make a report on him? — Yes.

Did you write a report? — Yes; I was instructed by the sister's family to do so.

The report stated that Maclean was rambling and disconnected, and did not realise the enormity of the crime he had committed. He was labouring under three delusions – first, that there was a determination on the part of the people of England to persecute him; that persons were in the habit of dressing in blue to annoy him; and that he was under the influence of a supernatural power, hearing from time to time voices mocking and debating with him. He could not tell whether it was a male or a female voice.

Referring to the crime, he said he had come to the conclusion that it would be better to put a bullet into the pistol to impress people with its gravity. From time to time he broke into loud laughter. He was "of very weak mind", and subject to delusions, especially that of being persecuted. Manning believed the delusions were in full force on March 2.

The Attorney-General: Of course there are different degrees of insanity. What do you say as to his knowledge of an act he is committing. Would he be aware of what he is doing? — I think he would.

What do you think as to his competency to know whether he is doing right or wrong? — Well, it is difficult to enter into the mind of another person.

But what is your own opinion? — My opinion is that he would be competent to distinguish between right and wrong. Decidedly he would know at the time he fired the pistol he was doing a wrong act.

Your opinion is that the prisoner is of unsound mind? — Yes.

And, impelled by particular delusions, would it be consistent with a person knowing that an act was either right or wrong? — I think it would.

Mr Williams, for the defence said: Supposing the prisoner to be suffering from homicidal mania impelled by delusion, would he have power to prevent it? — I think not. I may say that I have frequently asked persons who have suffered from homicidal mania as to the commission by them of certain acts, as to whether they were aware of what they had done, and the answer has been "Yes; I knew perfectly well what I was doing, and that I was doing wrong, but I had not the power to control it."

The Lord Chief Justice: Do you say that this man, at the time he presented the pistol to shoot the Queen, knew that he was doing wrong, but yet was unable, from mental or other causes to control his act, such as a strong man, not suffering from delusions, would have been? — Witness: I do.

Mr Williams: Then it is your opinion that people suffering from homicidal mania are constrained to act irresistibly? — It is.

Dr Edgar Shepherd, formerly superintendent of Colney Hatch Lunatic Asylum for 20 years, had examined Maclean in Reading Gaol on March 24 and April 10, for an hour each time. He told the court Maclean was "of unsound mind, unquestionably".

"First of all, I should say that the prisoner has very marked defects, which handicapped him very heavily. He has a very narrow head, with the high, arched skull so commonly associated with idiocy and insanity. He is not a man who could reach a fair standard of moral or physical health. He has a nervous hesitancy of speech amounting to a stutter – imperfect vocal articulation I should call it. He has a scar on the right side of his head, about two inches long, the result of an accident about 13 years ago. This scar is very tender on pressure. He complained to me of a shooting pain through the forehead.

"I found he had delusions of an unmistakable character. He said persons in blue were against him and always had been: that he had a mysterious connection with the number seven, and that blue and this combination of figures were always disastrous to him. He told me that a few weeks ago he went to Somerset House, in the Strand, to ascertain whether he was registered or baptised. Finding that he was neither the one nor the other, he thought himself more injured than ever, and he determined to bring his case under observation by taking the step he had done.

"I pointed out to him the inadequacy of his grievances to the measures adopted for redress, but he did not seem to see it at all. He said he had a perfect right to do what he had done, because it had been revealed to him in early life that he had a great and secret power over mankind. He also said he was related to the royal family as much as George IV, and that the crowd would have torn him to pieces the other day had it not been for Jesus Christ."

In a crucial reply to the Lord Chief Justice, Dr Shepherd said he did not think the prisoner had any power to distinguish between right or wrong.

When Montagu Williams addressed the jury with a summary of the case for the defence, he said: "The only thing you have to decide upon is – was the prisoner, at the time he committed the act, of sound or unsound mind? Was he a responsible person in the eye of the law? Was he capable of distinguishing what was the quality of his act, and did he know the difference between right and wrong?"

The Lord Chief Justice, in summing up the case, said: "The prisoner has been defended by a gentleman distinguished by experience and ability, and there remains for you practically but one question to determine. Because the learned counsel, in the exercise of his judgment – and in my opinion he has exercised the judgment most discreetly – has not contested any of the facts or circumstances of the case, not a single question has been addressed, by way of cross-examination, to any one of the witnesses of the Crown who came to prove the facts of the case. That means that in the mind of that distinguished gentleman he was unable to show that in any single particular the evidence had fallen short of what the law required.

"It is not because the facts have been made out that the prisoner is to be found guilty, because from the earliest times the law has always distinguished between persons capable of committing offences and persons incapable in law of committing them. Although the latter class of persons may do an act, the law, regarding their incapacity, does not inflict criminal consequences upon them as a punishment. The question you have to determine is whether the prisoner was legally answerable at the time he shot at the Queen.... The question here is whether you believe the prisoner was capable of deciding between right and wrong at the time he committed the deed."

After explaining the McNaughten ruling, and briefly reviewing the medical evidence for the defence, Coleridge concluded: "A verdict of insanity is a merciful verdict. It saves the man's life, as it ought to be saved, if he is not a moral agent, while on the other hand it protects society against a repetition of those outrages, because he will be placed under the control of the government, and will be kept in custody as long as it will be right for him to be kept....

"If you are convinced he did the act when he was responsible, no words could be too strong, no punishment too heavy for him. If he was not responsible for it, although the life which he put in danger was a life inestimably precious, he ought to be protected as much as if he had only committed the most trivial offence against the meanest subject of the realm. You must now consider your verdict, and say whether you find him guilty or not on the ground of insanity."

The jury retired at 23 minutes before five o'clock, and were absent five minutes. On their return, the Clerk of Arraigns said: Gentlemen of the jury, are you all agreed on your verdict?

The foreman: We are.

The clerk: Do you find the prisoner, Roderick Maclean, guilty or not guilty?

The foreman: Not guilty, on the ground of insanity.

The clerk: And that is the verdict of you all?

The foreman: It is.

The Attorney-General: I have to ask, my lords, that you make the usual order to detain the prisoner in strict custody during Her Majesty's pleasure.

The Lord Chief Justice: Let that be so.

The prisoner was then removed from the dock.

Maclean was sent to Broadmoor hospital.

From the Telegraph
An attempt by a mad cabinetmaker to upset the Royal train

July 12, 1855

William Groyne, the cabinetmaker charged with attempting to upset the train on the South Eastern line at Tonbridge when Prince Albert and the Duke of Cambridge were returning from accompanying the Emperor and the Empress of the French to Dover, was tried at the Quarter Sessions held at Maidstone on Monday. From the evidence it appeared that the train would not have been injured by the obstructions the prisoner had placed on the line, as the speed at the spot would have been very slow, and the prisoner was acquitted. He said he was unconscious of his actions at the time, but was now sane.

INBRIEF

JULY 15, 1855

The Temperance Societies of England held high festival at the Crystal Palace yesterday. It was their annual reunion – this year organised by the Good Templars – and if one were to judge from the number and bearing of the multitudes that filled the capacious building and covered its ample grounds, this country can boast of rapidly growing sobriety.

There were about 50,000 persons present yesterday. This particular Temperance order has over 80,000 adults and over 50,000 juveniles adherent in England alone; in Scotland 40,000 adults and 20,000 children and several thousand in Ireland and Wales. In round numbers there are over a million grown persons and about the same number of children, affiliated with the various Temperance societies.

A GIANT JUBILEE PICNIC
Meat pies and oranges for 30,000 children

Victoria's Golden Jubilee became, through a scheme of the Telegraph's, a chance to rejoice in a huge treat for children

Thirty thousand children enjoyed a picnic in Hyde Park to celebrate Queen Victoria's Golden Jubilee in 1887. "Were there any catastrophes, disasters, breakdowns, as some of the uncomfortable and envious amid us so eagerly predicted?" asked *The Daily Telegraph*, which organised the event. The uncomfortable might have had in mind the recent disaster at the Tsar's coronation in which 3,000 were trampled to death.

"None!" came the answer. "Nothing untoward happened, unless we except 15 cases of stomach-ache, which were tenderly dealt with, and successfully alleviated by the menial resources of science. To the 'lost children' tent came eight stray lads, but, their addresses being stamped on their sleeves, they were put into two cabs and safely taken home."

Naturally "faultless weather beamed upon the out-of-door festival" that June 22 – 50 years and two days after the 18-year-old Princess had pulled a cotton dressing-gown over her night-dress at six in the morning to find the Archbishop of Canterbury and the Lord Chamberlain falling on their knees in a sitting-room at Kensington Palace to tell her that her uncle was dead and she was Queen.

Now the 68-year-old Queen, perched in her carriage like an Easter egg wrapped in violet silk overlaid with lace, was driven through miles of cheering streets. The children in Hyde Park had been ready for hours. And, if addresses were stamped on their sleeves, "surprise, delight, and unmistakable happiness were stamped upon every young face from the hour when the children marched in long columns into the great green playground prepared for them, until the close of the day's pastimes and joys, when they filed forth again, chattering and laughing with each other, and each hugging a memorial cup tightly as a valued souvenir of the unexampled outing they had enjoyed".

Two teachers were detailed to look after every group of 10–20 children. "It was a pleasant feature of the great gathering," the paper noted "that the relations between pupils and instructors were manifestly and without exception of a cordial – we

Faultless June weather beamed on the Queen as she drove through miles of cheering streets

may safely say, of an affectionate – character. No rough words or over imperious commands were to be heard on the one hand; no insubordination on the other."

From Birdcage Walk, detachments were shepherded to marquees in Hyde Park, where "on tables were piled mountains of comestibles in snowy paper bags, each bag containing a meat pie of splendid dimensions and savoury contents, a square of cake, lavishly studded with plums, a bun, and an orange. Underneath the tables stacks of loaves were visible and behind them casks, ready spigoted and tapped, bearing the legends of 'lemonade', 'gingerade', and other attractive drinks."

"As soon as each group of boys and girls emerged from the red cloth covered tables, armed with the refreshing bag, down they settled in rings, with a teacher at their head, and investigated – tasted – approved – and consumed. The order of repast, was mainly pie first, next cake, thirdly bun, and the orange last; but here and there the plums in the cake betrayed the possessor into an injudicious reversal of the natural 'rotation of crops'."

The outing provided ample opportunity for *Telegraph* reporters to warm their readers' hearts. "There was a batch of blind children and a body of Jewish children among the 30,000. The little sightless boys and girls were led about by carefully appointed guides, and treated like gentle invalids, everything being explained to them, and every available pleasure imparted."

As for the Jewish boys and girls who "could not partake of food, especially meat, prepared without reference to the scruples of their religion", they found "bags of provision duly marked and certified, ready to their hand".

Interestingly, the East End children did not exhibit signs of coming from "slums and sickly homes" or of living "the miserable lives of Board School children". Instead, "lots of them were very pretty and graceful, with eyes as clear and bright as stars, rosy cheeks, and limbs robust and full of fresh strong life". Their schoolteachers declared: "We selected them, sir, by ballot. We could have turned out 10 times as many who would have pleased you quite as much."

After the children had cast aside their emptied paper bags, "they clustered like swarming bees round the Punch and Judy shows, which were in full force of that deathless and delightfully immoral tragical comedy on every side.

"There were the Aunt Sallys – which were not merely attacked but demolished, smashed, pulverised, massacred by the shower of sticks which the enchanted boys hurled at their devoted heads. There were races, leapfrogs, ball play, football, touch and cross, follow my leader, and all sorts of other improvised pastimes, with dances whenever the music struck up, and peep shows.

"'Oh dear, oh dear,' a small thing in white mob cap and yellow gloves from Archbishop Tenison School [in Kennington] was heard to sigh, 'I wish it would never be night. I shan't be able to play at half the things here.'"

There were a thousand skipping ropes served out of wagons, 42,000 prizes "to be scrambled for", and "beyond all, wonderfully exciting lucky-dip barrels of which here is an official list of the contents: Japanese balls, walking sticks, folding fans, pop guns, dressed dolls, china head dolls, Japanese figures, monkeys on sticks, fancy mounted money boxes, china-head walking sticks, Jubilee Queen's portraits, pan pipes, toy butterflies, cornets, large boxes of paints, scholars' companions with pens, paper, and blotter, etc, new drawing slates, boxes of coloured crayons, French kaleidoscopes, fancy wood money boxes, carved animals, coloured book cases, snakes, musical pears, whistle mallets, horse and carts, polished wood pencil cases, mechanical walking figures, bird statues, expanding figures, dolls in cradles, tin whistles, flageolets, tram-car whistles, puzzles, lotto games, Jubilee watches, pin cushions, assorted boxes of toys, skipping ropes and sailing boats."

The Queen at last arrived, her approach signalled by "the glitter of the escort, a rolling thunder of cheers from the people, and shriller cries of joy from the long lane of children". In response she "graciously bowed from time to time as her carriage passed on". Then followed a body of "swarthy representatives of the Indian Army and the final escort of Guards. The former were the objects of much admiration, wearing, as they did, their Oriental uniforms." The Queen was "looking well, and highly pleased with the scene around her".

She was presented with "a splendid bouquet of the loveliest orchids wrapped round with a silvered satin holder" It bore an inscription also written round the ornamental gateway through which her carriage passed: "Not Queen alone; but mother, Queen, and friend in one!"

IN OSCAR'S FASHION

Wildean advice on how men ought to dress

Oscar Wilde was almost at the peak of his fame when he chose the Telegraph in which to spread his ideas on men's clothes

Men were wasting their buttons, Oscar Wilde declared in a long letter to the *Telegraph* printed on February 3, 1891. "When a thing is useless it should be made beautiful, otherwise it has no reason for existing at all," he wrote. "Buttons should be either gilt, or of paste, or enamel, or inlaid metal, or any other material that is capable of being artistically treated. The handsome effect produced by servants' liveries is almost entirely due to the buttons they wear."

Indeed the whole lack of colour in men's dress was deplorable. "The uniform black that is worn now, though valuable at a dinner-party, where it serves to isolate and separate women's dresses, to frame them as it were, still is dull and tedious and depressing in itself," Wilde said.

"The little note of individualism that makes dress delightful can only be attained nowadays by the colour and treatment of the flower one wears. This is a great pity. The colour of the coat should be entirely for the good taste of the wearer to decide. This would give pleasure, and produce charming variety of colour effects in modern life."

Wilde was keen for his opinions to appear in the *Telegraph*. At 34 he was already famous, but neither *Lady Windermere's Fan* (1892) nor *The Importance of Being Earnest* (1895) had yet been produced. He sent a separate letter to Edward Lawson, the proprietor, stressing that "the subject of modern dress is worth discussing, and of course yours is the paper that is in quickest touch with the public". Wilde's brother Willie (1853–99) had not so long before been engaged as a leader writer and sub-editor. According to later memories in the office, he was known for working stripped to the waist – "a practice considered very much more peculiar then than it would be today", Lord Burnham remarked in 1955. By the end of the 20th century it had become unheard of, in the newsroom at least.

Wilde's letter was not signed, though "I am afraid everybody will know who the writer is," he wrote to Lawson, "one's style is one's signature always."

Wilde was responding to a long leading article of the day before pondering the changes in men's fashion, especially the advent of trousers in place of boots and breeches from about 1814. "It is notorious that when trousers first became popular they were vigorously resisted by Beau Brummell, who had a magnificent leg, upon which he prided himself not a little," the leader-writer observed.

Wilde noted that men's fashion had become static. "The dress of 1840 is really the same in design and form as ours. Of course, the sleeves are tighter and the cuffs turn each over them, as sleeves should be and as cuffs should do. The trousers, also, are tighter than the present fashion, but the general cut of the dress is the same. It consists, as ours does, of tail-coat, open waistcoat, and trousers."

Although during his tour of America 10 years earlier Wilde had sported silk stockings below knee breeches, as pictured here ("more comfortable and convenient"), he did not object to trouser-wearing in his letter to the *Telegraph*. Cloaks, however, were essential, as long as the style was correctly chosen. "We must wear cloaks with lovely linings, otherwise we shall be very incomplete."

As for coats, the *Telegraph* had wondered who it was that had decided the coming season's fashion should be "a frock coat with very long skirts and broad pointed lapels at the breast". Wilde remained more interested in the colour than the cut. "One will be able to discern a man's views of life by the colour he selects. The colour of the coat will be symbolic. It will be part of the wonderful symbolistic movement in modern art. The imagination will concentrate itself on the waistcoat. Waistcoats will show whether a man can admire poetry or not. That will be very valuable." For himself Wilde had sometimes often chosen waistcoats of velvet "as it catches the light and shade".

If the change that Wilde advocated, of doing away with black clothes for men in favour of colour, was to be brought about, he had an idea. "In Paris the Duc de Morny has altered the colour of coats. But the English dislike individualism. Nothing but a resolution on the subject passed solemnly by the House of Commons will do with us. Surely there are some amongst our legislators who are capable of taking a serious interest in serious things?"

The Daily Telegraph continued to be on easy terms with Wilde despite hints of the scandal to come. That May his volume of essays *Intentions* was reviewed cheerfully and from it "The Decay of Lying" was singled out as the piece in it which "for piquancy most people will agree with Mr Wilde in placing before all the others".

Wilde detected the hand of W.L. Courtney, and wrote asking if he might not review his novel *Dorian Gray*, which on its publication had been "very grossly and foolishly assailed as an immoral book". Courtney was able to oblige next month, calling *The Picture of Dorian Gray* "an extremely clever study, not always quite pleasant in tone, of a complex stage in modern culture".

Four years later Wilde was imprisoned, and he died while Victoria was still queen. He was 44.

INBRIEF

JUNE 23, 1891
LITERATURE OF THE DAY
The second volume of Mr Charles Booth's *Labour and Life of the People* has just been issued by Messrs. Williams & Norgate.

One or two of the results at which Mr Booth has arrived in his study of pauperism are very noticeable. Amongst them may be mentioned the fact that the deepest poverty is to be found, not in the East district, but in Central South London, among the riverside population between Blackfriars and London Bridge, where paupers form the enormous percentage of 68. In the East the percentage is only 58.

Mr Booth believes that in order to divorce industry from poverty we ought, in some fashion, to eliminate the very poor, casual class from the population of the metropolis. For it is always on the verge of crime and pauperism, and helps to swell the rates and keep down the scale of wages. A very interesting chapter deals with the immigration from the country into London, in which it is maintained that the instinctive desire to better themselves is the main cause which drives men from rural districts into the metropolis, and not, as has sometimes been maintained, want of work. We get the pick of the village in London, and it appears that they very rarely fall into the unemployed class.

'Waistcoats will show whether a man can admire poetry or not,' Wilde told the readers of the Telegraph. Dressed for his lecture tour of America, he was photographed in knee breeches ('more comfortable and convenient') and velvet coat ('It catches the light and shade')

EXCURSION TRAIN CRASHES

A day by the sea and a smash on the way back

Excursion trains were the making of the popular English seaside resort, but they proved an occasion of terrible accidents

Seaside holidays became a possibility for the masses thanks to railways, and particularly to excursion trains that moved large numbers at cut prices. As early as August 1840 an excursion train from Leeds had four engines pulling no fewer than 67 carriages; as it passed it seemed to an observer "like a moving street, the houses of which were filled with human beings".

The Great Exhibition of 1851 drew six million visitors in five months, with the help of hundreds of excursion trains. "Ramsgate, Margate and suchlike favourite Cockney resorts," the *Telegraph* noted in 1855, "have grown over-full, dusty and dear. Even remote little sea-side nooks, down away upon the western coasts, are becoming dotted with round hats and readers of new novels."

A decade later, apart from the regular summer traffic of holidaymakers flocking to seaside hotels and boarding houses, the annual total of excursion travellers reached perhaps three and a half million. Excursions caught on in Britain in a way not experienced on the Continent or in North America. In Britain the coast (or in the south, London as a destination) was near enough for huge numbers of urban workers to take a day's holiday by train.

There was a special danger in the business, because excursion trains disrupted the timetable, which, for a long time, alone protected trains from hurtling into one another. Although the Board of Trade was pressing the advantages of a block system of signalling, which allowed only one train on a stretch of line at any one time, in the early 1860s most lines relied on time-lapse. Yet to send off one train five minutes after another was risky. The Clayton Tunnel crash of 1861 showed how this system, even reinforced in stretches by the block system, could lead to frightful carnage.

"Terrible accident on the London and Brighton Railway" was the headline in *The Daily Telegraph* on Monday August 26 1861. Terrible indeed. It was at the time the worst crash that had ever happened. And the setting, inside a tunnel, made the event especially horrible. Two excursion trains and a

regular service that Sunday were travelling north from Brighton, bound for London. The Portsmouth excursion train (16 carriages) was due to leave the station at 8.05am, the Brighton excursion (17 carriages) at 8.15 and the regular train from Brighton (12 carriages) at 8.30. In fact they left at 8.28, 8.31 and 8.35. Clayton Tunnel lay four or five miles ahead, uphill.

Signalman Killick at the Brighton end of the tunnel was in contact with signalman Brown beyond it at the other end. Around the tunnel the block system was in operation, with automatic alarm bells alerting signalmen to any irregularity. The Portsmouth train went into the tunnel. The alarm rang at Killick's signal box to indicate a signal had failed to function. Killick then saw the Brighton excursion speeding closer. He waved a red flag as it passed, then telegraphed Brown: "Is tunnel clear?" Brown, seeing the Portsmouth train pass, telegraphed back: "Tunnel clear." The third train, the regular Brighton service, then passed Killick's box, to be waved through by him.

But the driver of the middle train, the Brighton

'Life at the Seaside (Ramsgate Sands)' showed the effects of cheap railway travel on English coastal resorts. The artist, William Powell Frith, later had great success with his big canvas 'The Railway Station'. After 'Ramsgate Sands' was feted at the Academy in 1854 it was bought by Queen Victoria. 'Ramsgate, Margate and suchlike favourite Cockney resorts,' said the Telegraph the next year; 'have grown over-full, dusty and drear.'

excursion, had seen Killick's red flag, and pulled on the brakes. The heavy train stopped half a mile inside the tunnel. The driver feared there was something wrong with the Portsmouth excursion train ahead, and began to ease his own train backwards down the slope in the tunnel, in order to discover from Killick what was wrong. Two or three hundred yards from the tunnel mouth, the reversing Brighton excursion was smashed into by the speeding Brighton regular service.

"There was not, the survivors say, enough light in the tunnel for a man to see his hand in front of his face," the *Telegraph*'s special reporter wrote for Monday's paper. "And the scalding steam and the dense smoke united with the painful darkness to endow the locality of the disaster with characteristics of the most terrifying description.

"Some persons, foreseeing the danger, had thrown themselves from the windows; others had got out of the carriages through the doors, which they had burst open [the carriage doors in those years being locked before departure with the guard's key]; and some came slowly to a consciousness of

the injuries they had received, and crept and crawled out into the darkness which was around them on every side."

The reporter drew attention to the times at which the trains had left the station. But whatever the cause of the disaster, he wrote, "in the reading room attached to the station, there lie dead 21 human beings". The final toll was 23. The next day the paper urged that "additional precautions for the safety of the living can be insisted on, and stringent regulations can be framed to mitigate the dangers of a so-called 'pleasure-traffic', which, as at present conducted, is too often a wild and reckless neck-or-nothing race after the half crowns of the poorer classes".

The Government inspectors pressed on, against commercial or ideological resistance to state interference. Jack Simmons, the great expert on railway history, analysed the proportion of accidents year by year that were attributable to the special dangers of excursion trains. In the decade 1855–64 the percentage averaged 8.6; in the decade 1865–74 it had been reduced to 2.9 per cent.

INBRIEF

JULY 16, 1855

On Friday morning, at about a quarter past five o'clock, as the night mail train from Edinburgh was proceeding to London at the rate of about 40mph, on the Great Northern Railway, about a mile north of Doncaster it came into collision with a coal train which was running in the same direction and a frightful concussion ensued, although, providentially, only two or three persons were hurt.

DICKENS IN A RAILWAY SMASH

Falling from the viaduct at Staplehurst

A typical railway timetable mix-up led to a crash that killed 10 and might well have done for Britain's foremost novelist

Perhaps the Staplehurst railway smash killed Charles Dickens. He was caught up in it on June 9, 1865 and was never the same again. "I am curiously weak, weak as if I were recovering from a long illness," he wrote afterwards. "I write half a dozen words and turn faint and sick." He feared railway travel for the remainder of his life. At anything like speed he would became convinced that the carriage was teetering, a delusion he found "inexpressibly distressing". He died on the fifth anniversary to the day of the crash.

Dickens had been on his way back with his mistress and her mother from France that day. The trouble was that the time of the train depended on the tides, since it had to meet the ferry – and there were engineering works at Staplehurst in Kent. But the foreman, used to getting the work done between regular services, misread the timetable for the anomalous "tidal" train. The only other man in the repair gang with a timetable had dropped it on the rails where an earlier train had run over it.

The gang was working on a viaduct over a muddy stream, replacing baulks of wood carrying the rails; of the 32 baulks only one more remained to to be replaced. A 21-foot section of line was missing. The accident was ready.

A crash had taken place at some track works at Rednal, Shropshire, killing 13, only two days earlier, and the talk in the papers was all of safety measures. In theory there were preventive measures at Staplehurst. As well as red flags, there were detonators to put on the track to warn any approaching train. But the man with the flag was only 500 yards from the bridge, and according to

The wooden carriages that fell from the viaduct (below) were embedded in the mud or splintered open. Dickens (right, in an engraving from the 'Penny Illustrated Paper'), using his travelling hat as a basin, brought water to the wounded

'No imagination can conceive the ruin of the carriages'

Tuesday, June 13, 1865
My Dear Mitton,
I should have written to you yesterday or the day before, if I had been quite up to writing. I am a little shaken, not by the beating and dragging of the carriage in which I was, but by the hard work afterwards in getting out the dying and dead, which was most horrible.

I was in the only carriage that did not go over into the stream. It was caught upon the turn by some of the ruin of the bridge, and hung suspended and balanced in an apparently impossible manner. Two ladies were my fellow passengers; an old one, and a young one. This is exactly what passed: – you may judge from it the precise length of the suspense. Suddenly we were off the rail and beating the ground as the car of a half emptied balloon might. The old lady cried out "My God!" and the young one screamed.

I caught hold of them both (the old lady sat opposite, and the young one on my left), and said: "We can't help ourselves, but we can be quiet and composed. Pray don't cry out." The old lady immediately answered, "Thank you. Rely upon me. Upon my soul, I will be quiet." The young lady said in a frantic way, "Let us join hands and die friends." We were then all tilted down together in a corner of the carriage, and stopped. I said to them thereupon: "You may be sure nothing worse can happen. Our danger must be over. Will you remain here without stirring, while I get out of the window?" They both answered quite collectedly, "Yes," and I got out without the least notion what had happened.

Fortunately I got out with

orders, the detonators were to be used only in fog. It was a sunny afternoon.

The 13-carriage train was going at 50mph when the driver saw the red flag. The guard applied the brake, but there was no time to stop. Amazingly the engine, tender and first van made it over the bare baulks without falling off. Five carriages fell from the gap, some embedded in the mud, some, being built of wood, splintered and opened with the force.

"The crash was terrific, and the destruction was complete," reported the *Telegraph* the next day. "Probably all the passengers were unconscious for several moments; but, from the accounts given by those who happily escaped uninjured it seems that the carriages were completely broken up and that such of the travellers as were not crushed by the fragments found themselves imbedded in the mud and slime of the river's bed."

"Let us join hands and die friends," cried Ellen Ternan, Dickens's companion, as their carriage hung by its coupling from the bridge. It didn't come to dying, for them, but 10 others were killed, and 49 injured. "There was no human being at the moment to give aid to the sufferers, many of whom were so hopelessly pressed into the yielding soil that on the arrival of assistance it was necessary to dig deep with spades in order to recover the bodies."

Dickens, after helping the dying and wounded, remembered he had the manuscript of the last part of *Our Mutual Friend* with him in the carriage, and climbed back to retrieve it. He added a joky postscript to the novel noting that "Mr and Mrs Boffin, in their manuscript dress" were "with me in a terribly destructive accident". They were extricated "much soiled, but otherwise unhurt".

great caution and stood upon the step. Looking down, I saw the bridge gone and nothing below me but the line of rail. Some people in the two other compartments were madly trying to plunge out at the window, and had no idea that there was an open swampy field 15 feet down below them and nothing else! The two guards (one with his face cut) were running up and down on the down side of the bridge (which was not torn up) quite wildly. I called out to them "Look at me. Do stop an instant and look at me, and tell me whether you don't know me." One of them answered, "We know you very well, Mr Dickens." "Then," I said, "my good fellow for God's sake give me your key, and send one of those labourers here, and I'll empty this carriage."

We did it quite safely, by means of a plank or two and when it was done I saw all the rest of the train except the two baggage cars down in the stream. I got into the carriage again for my brandy flask, took off my travelling hat for a basin, climbed down the brickwork, and filled my hat with water. Suddenly I came upon a staggering man covered with blood (I think he must have been flung clean out of his carriage) with such a frightful cut across the skull that I couldn't bear to look at him. I poured some water over his face, and gave him some to drink, and gave him some brandy, and laid him down on the grass, and he said, "I am gone", and died afterwards.

Then I stumbled over a lady lying on her back against a little pollard tree, with the blood streaming over her face (which was lead colour) in a number of distinct little streams from the head. I asked her if she could swallow a little brandy, and she just nodded, and I gave her some and left her for somebody else. The next time I passed her, she was dead.

Then a man examined at the Inquest yesterday (who evidently had not the least remembrance of what really passed) came running up to me and implored me to help him find his wife, who was afterwards found dead. No imagination can conceive the ruin of the carriages, or the extraordinary weights under which the people were lying, or the complications into which they were twisted up among iron and wood, and mud and water.

I don't want to be examined at the Inquests and I don't want to write about it. It could do no good either way, and I could only seem to speak about myself, which, of course, I would rather not do. I am keeping very quiet here. I have a – I don't know what to call it – constitutional (I suppose) presence of mind, and was not in the least fluttered at the time. I instantly remembered that I had the MS of a Novel with me, and clambered back into the carriage for it. But in writing these scanty words of recollection I feel the shake and am obliged to stop.

Ever faithfully,
Charles Dickens

FALL OF A CATHEDRAL SPIRE
Chichester's 270ft of stone fold into rubble

The third highest spire in England, after a desperate week's work to shore it up, came down straight as if through a trap door

"FALL OF CATHEDRAL SPIRE", read a headline in *The Daily Telegraph* for February 22, 1861. "Yesterday, at half-past one, the beautiful spire of Chichester Cathedral fell to the ground. The choir has been under repair and alteration for several months. The tower, surmounted by the spire, rested on four lofty piers, with four arches, some of the stone work being defaced. The broken stones were taken out; in doing this the south-west pier was found to be unsound, and a number of men were employed to strengthen it. The workmen were fortunately at dinner, and no one was injured."

That was that, as far as the news columns of the *Telegraph* were concerned. But in Sussex unanswered questions remained. Desperate work had been under way for more than a week before the collapse. Immense timbers were brought on creaking wagons, and 50 workmen laboured even on Sunday to strengthen the piers supporting the 270ft spire – the third highest in the country.

The day before the collapse the 13th-century spire was seen to oscillate and its Norman supports let out "doleful creaks". That Wednesday night the wind blew a gale. Next morning the Dean of the

The spire, instead of crashing lengthways into the nave, was swallowed up by the tower, leaving the transept (above) open to the sky. Five years later the rebuilt spire (below, left) was topped out with the weathercock made for it in 1678

cathedral wrote: "Our patient survived the fearful storm of last night. We had fifty men at work all night. There was some fearful oscillation of the tower, and the main pier sank. If we could only have a few days calm weather it would be a comfort. I walk about like a guilty man."

No calm weather arrived. At 1pm on the fateful Thursday a cry went up: "Escape for thy life!" (In the biblical language of the account by the sub-dean George Braithwaite.) The workmen were not just "at dinner" – they had cleared out because "the fall was the expectation of every minute".

Crowds had gathered in the street to watch. "At 1.30pm the tower opened its mouth – separating on both sides – and the spire gradually sank down within it, absorbed as though an earthquake had dug its grave." Just as, at the end of the century, the campanile of St Mark's in Venice collapsed politely across the square, leaving the neighbouring basilica unharmed, so the spire at Chichester providentially folded up like a telescope instead of smashing through the length of the nave. "The spire appears to have slipped through the transept, as if it had been let through a trap door," reported the *West Sussex Gazette*. "The organ, which is in the immediate locality, was not damaged at all."

A passenger in a passing train was supposed to have glanced up from his book to see the spire hurtling down. A sailor in the harbour, having taken bearings from the spire, looked up again and found

it gone. Or so the stories say; evidence was found to be lacking by the authors of the excellent *Chichester Cathedral Spire – The Collapse*, published by University College, Chichester, in 2002.

Next to the cathedral, the dean's wife saw the spire "reel and then go down". She went to tell her husband, who was in his study. "He was leaning over his table sobbing, his face buried in his hands."

A photograph of one of the four piers, taken when the initial clearing of debris had been done, shows an ashlar skin and a rubble core broken off like a stick of seaside-rock.

Chichester had undergone repairs throughout its history. Wren had installed an ingenious pendulum weight hanging from the inside of the spire, to provide resistance to prevailing south-west gales. The spire had been restored in 1813, and clamps inserted into defective piers. More thoroughgoing restorers in 1860 found that the clamps were doing no good, and the decay of the masonry was greater than thought. An iron rod could be poked five foot deep into the core of one cracked pier.

After the collapse people looked for someone to blame. Posters went up in Chichester reading: "THE SPIRE. Don't promise Subscriptions to build a Spire until a strict and searching inquiry has been instituted to discover WHY THE SPIRE FELL."

It was hardly the Dean's fault, for the restoration work had begun before he arrived at the cathedral. The architects overseeing the subsequent attempts to strengthen the piers also came in for undeserved blame. The cause of the fall seems to have been the insecure rubble infill of the Norman walls below the spire. Its Victorian inheritors were unlucky not to have made good the deficiencies before strong winds brought them down. George Gilbert Scott had intervened at more fortunate cathedrals – with iron bracing at Salisbury, and girders at Ripon.

Not everyone heeded the appeal to refrain from subscribing to a replacement. Prince Albert, who was to fall mortally sick later that year, climbed to the summit of the heap of debris to inspection the ruins. He and the Queen subscribed 350 guineas to the estimated £46,000 needed to rebuild the spire.

George Gilbert Scott got his son to spend six weeks marking rubble for re-use. "His task was, by the help of prints and photographs, to 'spot' and identify every moulded and carved stone found among the debris." So productive was his labour that "we were not left to conjecture for any detail of the tower, and much was refixed in the new work".

The first stone of the new spire was laid on May 2, 1865, and on June 28, 1866, framed in wooden scaffolding, it was topped out with the great gilded weathercock made for the cathedral in 1678.

The fall left two echoes in literature. One is Golding's *The Spire* (1964), in part a reflection of Salisbury's 404ft spire – the tallest left in England – with its extraordinary internal wooden structure. But the suspense in the gale at Chichester is paralleled in the novel, as it is in a work directly inspired by Chichester, John Meade Falkner's remarkable *The Nebuly Coat*, published in 1903.

INBRIEF

JULY 13, 1885

A considerable number of visitors assembled around Crystal Palace bicycle track on Saturday afternoon, when the Tricycle Championships were decided. The weather was all that could be desired and the cinder paths in excellent conditions for racing.

Under these circumstances, good performances were confidently looked forward to, and the record for both one mile and 25 miles were beaten. The struggle between Furnivall and Letchford in the final of the mile, and that between Gatehouse and English in the 25 miles, will not readily be forgotten.

THE CYCLING RAGE

From London to York, starting at midnight

A challenge of 200 miles in 21 hours 30 minutes was tougher than the Telegraph's renowned war correspondent bargained for

The challenge of the first York Run, in 1891, was to cycle the 200 miles from London to York in 21 hours and 30 minutes. The event caught bicycling fever at its zenith. Cycling was the rage as a spectator sport, with stadiums built for the purpose, and a fanatical pastime for millions of quietly prospering people of either sex.

The *Telegraph* sent its renowned war correspondent Bennet Burleigh to take part in the Great York Run. He had already distinguished himself in reporting the Sudan campaign, during which he was mentioned in despatches, and in future years reported from Ladysmith and from the Russo-Japanese war.

The ride began at midnight. "Exactly 25 gentlemen were at the 'meet'," wrote Burleigh. "They had foregathered an hour and a half previously at an hostelry of appropriate name – the

From the **Telegraph**

Is cycling dangerous? The evidence of the coroner's court

September 7, 1898

Last evening Mr John Troutbeck held an inquiry at Pimlico with reference to the death of Annie Marie Byles, aged 21 years, a domestic servant. On Monday afternoon the deceased and a fellow servant went out for a ride on their bicycles in Earls Court Road. The deceased fell off and both offside wheels of an omnibus passed over her body, killing her instantly. Verdict – "Accidental death".

Mr Troutbeck then inquired into the death of Henry James Harwood, aged 44 years, a butler, who was also killed whilst cycling. At midday on August 29 the deceased was riding a bicycle in Hamilton Place, Hyde Park, when a policeman stopped the traffic. Harwood was resting at a "refuge" when his hand slipped off the top of a post, and he fell under the wheel of a cart laden with bricks, which passed over him, inflicting terrible pelvic injuries, which caused his death in St George's Hospital. Verdict – "Accidental death".

From the **Telegraph**

Bennet Burleigh on his Rowe Paragon roadster safety with clincher tyres

June 22, 1891

By an Amateur Cyclist

Now, as the chief object of the North Road Cycling Club's ride to York was to show what can be done "on wheels", the experience of the writer, who is a novice, will serve to illustrate the contention that to cover 150 miles in a day is a comparatively easy task.

The members of the NRCC were chiefly mounted on pneumatic safeties but other types were also ridden. It was a piece of conceit, perhaps born of Fleet Street and Bohemia, that I – a stout, untrained, overworked man about town – should have attempted to have ridden for even the shortest distance with such champions. However, after a long and incessantly busy day and no supper, I found I had just time to catch the party of strapping athletes. My machine was a roadster safety, weighing 10lbs more than any of the racers and semi-racers ridden by the clubmen, being a Rowe Paragon, with clincher pneumatic tyres.

Spinning on, I was well among the front at Highgate. Climbing the hill a "follower" darted across my front, and, to avoid him and a tram-car, I turned, only to have my wheels skid from under me on the wet causeway. I came down without injuring myself, but the right crank was slightly twisted.

At Finchley I got once again within touch of the party. We were at least clear of the town and the crowds, and again the leaders quickened speed. Last Saturday there was a full moon, and such periods are always chosen for night journeys by the club. Clouds, however, obscured the sky, and once out upon the North road, beyond the gas lamps of London, the party took the highway on trust. A thick grey mist hung in the valleys, but the gentle north-east wind which blew in our faces cleared the uplands and kept everybody cool, I believe, but myself.

Whetstone was reached, and High Barnet, 11 miles out, at 1am sharp. There had been one or two mishaps to cranks and saddles that had caused the riders to dismount for a moment to put things right. W. Crosbie Wilson was sent back 200 yards to see who it was that lingered. He found me in the scene of the last battle in the Wars of the Roses. I was choking with dust and thirst, hot and uncomfortable. This good Samaritan, Crosbie, stuck by me, an utter stranger, showed me a fountain, waited whilst I snatched a drink, looked after the crank of my machine, oiled it, and then gave me an orange to suck as we together pursued the party.

Spurting on – for the North Road is less travelled upon than any other in England, I believe – we rapidly passed Hadley and thence through Hatfield, the clocks striking two…. The slow grey dawn was coming in soberly as we ran through Stanboro', where a few villagers had gathered. An enterprising "bobby" rushed out, staff in hand, and got Crosbie to relight his lamp.

At last, but just in time to miss the main body of the cyclists, who kept their time-schedule like a first-class railway company, we reached Hitchen, 34 miles out. I was thirsty and hungry beyond anything, and drank water and milk with equal pleasure, but the tea custards provided for the party could not stay my hunger, and in despair I fell upon the bread and cheese….

Buckden is a pretty sleepy hollow, and I wished much to relax after a 60-odd miles spin behind the crack men of the crack cycling club. I decided to have a good breakfast and follow on more slowly to Stamford, 29 miles north. Crosbie hastened on, leaving me to thoroughly enjoy my meal.

An hour later I resumed the trip, to learn there had been more breakdowns – Bateson, Waterhouse, and Child had burst their pneumatics. It took me a little over three hours to Stamford. The 21 and a half miles to Grantham took nearly two and a half hours. I had trundled 110 miles from London.

Champion, in Aldersgate-street – where they partook of a substantial cold English supper."

Burleigh wrote war reports in gripping prose, but here he falls back on the rather artificial style of light journalism in the 1890s – "foregathered", "an hostelry", "partook". It was partly the legacy of George Augustus Sala. But the readers must have been used to it, or even approved of it, for, in private letters of the time, such slightly contrived language is common. Although many must have known who wrote the report – a column and a bit – in the issue of June 23, it was only given the byline: By an Amateur Cyclist.

The ride was to be an annual event for the North Road Cycling Club, with 150 members, mostly renowned long-distance amateurs. "Amateur" was a badge of pride. Membership was limited to those who could ride 100 miles in 12 hours.

In the Champion public house, a Classics master called F.T. Bidlake was chosen as "captain" and leader for the journey. The start was from the General Post Office in St Martin's-le-Grand, in central London. When the cyclists got there "it seemed impossible to mount under the circumstances, for the people blocked footpath and roadway, and there was such an incessant din of horns and small bells that it was difficult to make oneself heard." But on the stroke of 12 the crowd made a narrow lane for them, and they were off.

"The party in single file shot rapidly up Aldersgate towards Goswell-road. English enthusiasm for sport showed itself then, for the crowd roared for 'a clear way', and the chaff and 'chi-hiking' were dropped for clapping of hands, cheers and shouts of encouragement."

The pace was 12 miles an hour. Burleigh's machine was heavy, he was not very fit and had evidently missed the late-night supper and "aerated water" toasts, for he was soon desperately thirsty and hungry. Though he was looked after by one of the club members, W. Crosbie Wilson, he had damaged a crank and he reached Grantham, 110 miles from London, at 2pm. There had been other casualties. Nine broke down through damage to pneumatic tyres; "Crosbie's seat-pillar got bent"; "A. Nixon, who rode a tricycle, had an axle give way".

Burleigh decided to take the train to York so as to be able to report the finish. "It was exactly 9.30pm when the ten leaders pulled up opposite the hotel at York, none the worse, apparently, for their long ride of 200 miles."

The Classics master, F.T. Bidlake, elected captain and leader for the York Run, putting his tricycle through its paces

From the Telegraph

Women driven astray on the Champs Elysées

October 30, 1897

By special wire from our own correspondent. Paris, Friday night.
The prevailing opinion among those whose avocations have led them to bestow some study on the question is that the cycling craze is very far from having attained its climax.

This being the case, matters of fashion in connection with the movement are pressing themselves more and more into the foreground. Now it is melancholy to have to repeat it, but the fact nevertheless remains, that the women in this acknowledged centre and fortress of feminine good taste have not as a class excelled in the production and in the wearing of cycling garments. In this respect, indeed, the great majority have, as a rule, gone terribly astray, as anyone who may have watched the samples of "the female form divine" which, perched on a bicycle, career in shoals through the Place de la Concorde and up the Champs Elysées on a fine Sunday afternoon, will have felt constrained to admit. There is no need to go into too cruel details, but the spectacle presented by these members of the fair sex, as, in tight blouses and knickerbockers, they bend over the wheel, is, to put it mildly, the reverse of edifying, so much so as often to evoke expressions of bewilderment, ridicule, and disgust from the beholders.

The knickerbocker costume is, we hear, to be gradually abandoned in favour of the skirt. Among those whom I have consulted on this subject is a high and recognised authority in things pertaining to the creation of ladies' costumes. "Certainly," he said, "we are making more and more of the new dresses. Now it is not the women of the higher classes alone who are patronising the skirt. There are symptoms that it is making its way into other social strata."

Bicycle thief chased through south-west London

August 15, 1898

Nelson Greenaway, 27, hawker, living at 11, Nelson's Row, High Street, Clapham, and William Donelly, 17, a seaman, giving an address at Deptford, were charged at the South-Western Police court with being concerned in stealing a bicycle, worth £10, belonging to James William Rose, saddler, of 29, High Road, Balham. Mr Nichols defended.

The prosecutor stated that on Friday afternoon he left his bicycle outside 165, High Road, Balham, and on coming out found it was gone. He saw a man riding away on it, being covered by a cart with a white pony. He ran after them as far as Balham Fire Station, and then hired a bicycle and rode in pursuit. He followed as far as Mitcham, where he saw Donelly dismount from the bicycle and jump into the cart in which Greenaway was sitting. The cart was then driven away at a furious rate.

Harry Clark, a bootmaker, of 49, Trinity Road, Tooting, stated that he was riding his bicycle in Balham High Road, and at the prosecutor's suggestion he followed the cart and the

bicycle. He swore that Greenaway and another man were in the cart, but he could not swear to the identity of Donelly as the rider of the stolen bicycle. At Tooting Broadway he observed Greenaway get out of the cart, and then both he and the rider of the machine tried to erase the name from the bicycle. Not succeeding, they proceeded on their way as far as Figg's Marsh. Witness passed them and rode on to see a policeman. He had not got far when the cart came up at a furious rate. They drove on in the direction of Mitcham Fair.

Police-constable Lewis, 402W, deposed to arresting the prisoners in the Windmill beerhouse, Mitcham. Donelly denied the charge, and Greenaway said, "This is hard on me. I have a wife dead at home."

Mr Francis ordered a remand, and refused to grant bail.

Pedalling outrage round the parish pumps

August 10, 1898

We are able to state, on high authority, says the *Bicycling News*, that a scheme for the registration of cyclists is now receiving the close consideration of the Home Secretary.

The information can scarcely come as a surprise. From north, south, east and west complaints have reached him of furious riding by cyclists; every little parish and district council has thought fit to pass resolutions and send them to the Home Office.

AN ACADEMY SENSATION

'Applicants for Admission to a Casual Ward'

Luke Fildes made his name overnight with what the Telegraph called 'a great picture', notable for its content as well as its style

Police had to hold back the crowds who on May 1, 1874 pressed forward in the Royal Academy to see *Applicants for Admission to a Casual Ward*, the painting that overnight made the name of Luke Fildes. A whole column of enthusiastic criticism in *The Daily Telegraph* contributed to the excitement.

The sudden celebrity of 30-year-old Fildes followed from the intense feelings that painting provoked in the later 19th century. "From today, painting is dead," the painter Paul Delaroche had exclaimed on seeing his first photograph in 1839. But controversy about painting grew hotter as Victoria's reign went on.

The Pre-Raphaelite Brotherhood had attracted the rage of *The Times* and the support of Ruskin in the years immediately before the appearance of *The*

'God help the man! – he looks cold to the very marrow of his bones,' wrote the Telegraph critic about the man in the tall hat speaking to the policeman in Luke Fildes's picture. Readers of art criticism cared as much about the condition of the poor as the latest techniques of painting

Daily Telegraph. Although the Pre-Raphaelites had some early influence on J.M. Whistler, the American's style had more in common with the French Impressionists whose first exhibition in 1874 attracted hostility. But the Impressionists' work was not widely familiar even in 1877 when Ruskin was to write violently against Whistler. "I have seen, and heard, much of cockney impudence before now," wrote Ruskin, "but never expected to hear a coxcomb ask two hundred guineas for flinging a pot of paint in the public's face." The ensuing libel case brought by Whistler entertained London vastly.

The painting that so annoyed Ruskin was shown in the new Grosvenor Gallery, soon identified with the aesthetic movement. In the Savoy opera *Patience* (1881) W.S. Gilbert mocked the aesthete as a "Greenery-yallery-Grosvenor-Gallery-foot-in-the-

INBRIEF

DECEMBER 11, 1867

Sir – Allow me briefly to call your attention to a very hard case, arising from the execution of the Metropolitan Streets Act, which shows the bad effect of placing uncontrolled power in the hands of the police with regard to the enforcement of that statute.

Mrs Davies, the keeper of the apple-stall in Westminster Hall, must be known by sight to many of your readers. She has occupied her present position for upwards of 30 years – inside the hall during the sessions of Parliament, and outside Palace-yard when the hall is closed. She has always borne a most excellent character and has become well known as almost one of the institutions of the place. It appears, from some cause or other, that one of the policemen has conceived a grudge against her (although she is highly respected by most of the officials), and has immediately used his newly-acquired power to forbid her from standing in her accustomed place outside Palace-yard, while the hall is closed.

The poor woman is thus deprived of her only means of gaining a living for half the year, and she is now too old to take up any other kind of work.

Surely, this is a case in which the Act should not be put in force. What makes this Act seem still more oppressive is that she is an Irishwoman and a Roman Catholic.

I am, sir, yours, etc

B.

grave young man". While these trends developed, the Royal Academy summer exhibitions remained the focus of English artistic debate.

Over a number of days, serious newspapers reviewed the pictures chosen. That summer of 1874 saw another reputation made there with the popular reception of the 28-year-old Elizabeth Thompson's *Roll Call* (see page 24), a scene from the Crimean war of two decades earlier. Strangely to us, Ruskin approvingly called the painting "Pre-Raphaelite", because it was painted from reality, in outdoor light. Queen Victoria made sure she got it.

The *Telegraph* launched into artistic controversy with the energy its readers expected. Printing technology did not allow it to reproduce paintings, so critics were in the same sort of position as radio broadcasters today. In a descriptive piece giving details that the readers could not see, the *Telegraph*'s critic came out in almost unreserved praise for Luke Fildes's big oil (eight feet by six). Once readers became aware of how well-received paintings were, they would subscribe to a large sale of black-and-white engravings, which both *The Roll Call* and *The Casuals*, as it became known, enjoyed.

The *Telegraph*'s ebullient bohemian, George Augustus Sala, in 1874 perhaps the best known journalist in Fleet Street, had already made friends with Fildes. ("I detest suppers," he responded to an invitation from Fildes to an evening party, "they interfere with steady drinking – thus your programme jumps with my humour entirely.") Now he hoped "to do justice to your good work" if his gout allowed him to get to the Academy opening.

The long review in the *Telegraph* is not signed, but reads like a piece by Sala. Other critics suggested the picture lacked finish; later generations detected sentimentality. Sala and the majority saw true sentiment, social realism and painterly skill.

Fildes had been thinking about this painting since he had published a wood-engraving *Houseless and Hungry* in the first issue of *The Graphic* at the end of 1869. Dickens was so struck by it that Fildes had been asked to illustrate the novel *Edwin Drood*, left unfinished at Dickens's death. The oil version of *The Casuals* required 21 life-studies of men and women, people that Fildes discovered during night-time wanderings in the London streets. Some, despite their misery, were suspicious of an invitation to sit at his studio. But the "big old Boozer", shown in the centre of the picture, proved only too happy to sit, a pint of porter regularly replenished at his feet.

The completed painting represented, "a simple and almost naked tragedy", to the mind of the *Telegraph* critic. "Of all the appalling sights in which this vast and luxurious metropolis abounds, there is not one more dreadful and more shameful than that of the beggars and tramps, the sickly and half-starved mechanics and labourers, with their wives and children, waiting at the gates of the police-stations for tickets which shall entitle them to a bed, a lump of bread, and a pannikin of gruel, in the vagrants' wards of the London workhouses."

Flourishing, in a gesture typical of Sala, a familiar

quotation from Dante, the critic exclaims: "*Lasciate ogni speranza* might be written over that station-house lamp, flaring feebly through the foggy sleet. It is true that these outcasts will be fed and housed, and that they will not die upon doorsteps, or under the lees of dead walls, for this night, at least; but afterwards, what is to become of them? What next!"

"A couple of policemen – bluff, hardy, but not hardened officials," he goes on, describing the canvas, "have marshalled this wretched troop into order, and are pointing out to them the way they should go. The contrast between the well-fed, warmly-clothed, cheerful-looking constables and the tattered, shivering crew around is very pitiable. Not one of these miserable men, women, and children is worth one single halfpenny in the world. Let the political economist lay the fact well to heart; let the ill-conditioned scoffer try to hammer the notion into his wooden head; they have Nothing, except their rags – no money, no food, no home, no friends, and no prospects. They are worse off than the wild beasts.

"But if these human wolves break the plate-glass window of a fashionable confectioner's shop and steal a Bath bun," the article continues, with moral indignation, "they must be locked up, and sent to the treadmill. Society cannot tolerate shop robberies; society cannot tolerate garotting. These are obvious truths, comprehensible to the meanest understanding; yet Society might have thought twice, perhaps, ere she set herself to the task of manufacturing criminals and paupers, of fabricating food for the gallows, the convict prison, and the warder's cat-o-nine-tails, by withholding education from the people – that education which is still withheld from them, all the School Boards in the country notwithstanding – by denying them decent homes in which to dwell, and by selling them as many penn'orths of gin as they can pawn their clothes and their tools, and ruin themselves or rob others to procure."

Garotting had been stamped out in 1862, and universal education imposed in 1870, but both phenomena would have been familiar as something modern to the paper's readers.

Fildes excelled, in the critic's judgment, both in what he showed and the way in which he painted it. "He has succeeded, in the most natural and unaffected manner, in bringing to the mind of the spectator the two physical and the two mental ideas governing the scheme of the work. First, actual and intense bodily cold and hunger; next, utter, abject pauperism and despair.

"There is a cadaverous boy here who might be carved in marble as a statue of Famine. There is a poor shivering devil of a foreigner, with a tall hat – such a hat! – with striped trousers – trousers that might have cost seven francs ten years ago in one of the second-hand shops of the Temple in Paris – an outcast too friendless and too poor to be sheltered even in the dog-hole garrets, or to be fed in the cat's-meat gargottes of Soho. He is a Communard, perhaps, a probable conspirator, a possible

incendiary; but – God help the man! – he looks cold to the very marrow of his bones. His nose is pinched, his lips are blue, the tips of his ears are nearly frost-bitten, his teeth chatter; you seem to divine even from the forward curve of his spine that his stomach is concave instead of convex, and that the cold has entered into his very vitals; and all this, be it observed, is done by the painter without the slightest affectation, exaggeration, or caricature.

"It is a very melancholy picture; but its ghastliness never approaches the grotesque. The technical merits of the work are very great; the ragged crew; the muddy slush of snow their poverty-hunted footsteps have trampled down; the fog, the sleet, are all skilfully but unobtrusively depicted. This is a great picture, and the modest young artist who has painted it must, if he works hard and studies intently, surely go very far indeed."

The success of *The Casuals* enabled Fildes to commission a remarkable house and studio in Kensington from Norman Shaw. But Sala warned: "Don't let your triumph in this picture lead you to cultivate exclusively this class of subjects." Fildes took the advice, or perhaps did not need it. He turned happily to sunny scenes from Venetian life, somewhat in the style of Alma-Tadema, and at last to state portraits of Edward VII and George V.

But two pictures remain that reinforce Fildes's reputation as an artist of Victorian social sensibility. One is a black-and-white double-page illustration for the 1878 Christmas Number of *The World*, run by the busy Edmund Yates. It is called *Found Dead on the Embankment*. The other is Fildes's best known picture, *The Doctor* – with a child lying sick at dawn in a dark cottage on a makeshift bed of two upright chairs. It was bought by Henry Tate for the national collection he was forming, and now hangs in the Tate Gallery. For a time, even before Fildes's death in 1927 it was hung in a basement. But the unfashionability of Victorian art receded and it can again, without shame, be appreciated in its own terms.

INBRIEF

JUNE 10, 1870

Charles Dickens is dead! Is there a breakfast table in the land around which the brief abrupt message – abrupt as the event it records was sudden – will not cast the shadow of a personal loss? Is there an English home – is there an American household – for which this day will not be a day of hushed and solemn stillness, as though a dear friend lay dead within the walls? Not merely had the fame and the genius of the departed won him love and honour among what we may term the reading classes of the nation; his rarely rivalled power to touch the deep springs of human feeling had made him a familiar friend in every English family. In the dwellings of the poor – the poor for whom his eloquent pen often pleaded, among whom he found some of his truest and most beautiful models – the works of Dickens moved simple hearts to ready laughter and to readier tears. And trace his hold on the minds – nay, more on the affections, the very daily life – of English men and English women up through all the graduations of our society – you will find the hold grow firmer, the affection and the familiarity more genuine, as the culture, refinement and sensibility become more marked.

From the Telegraph
Sir Arthur Sullivan at home

October 23, 1897

In the course of an interview with Sir A. Sullivan in the *Young Woman* for November, the writer remarks that it is difficult to believe that he was born 55 years ago, because of his extreme youthfulness, so far as the word indicates mental and physical alertness. "I found Sir Arthur at home," he continues, "on the occasion of which I am writing, at his town house in Victoria Street, and a veritable House Beautiful it is."

"As far as the greater public is concerned, I am not sure," continues the writer, "that it is not by such splendid pieces of melody as *The Lost Chord*, rather than by larger efforts, that the good work which Sir Arthur Sullivan has done will be best or more popularly remembered." *The Lost Chord* is, perhaps, the most successful song of modern times – at all events, it is one whose sale has, up to now, exceeded 250,000 copies.

A BOHEMIAN AGAINST IBSEN

London stages 'a dirty act done publicly'

Clement Scott, the leading drama critic of his day, opened fire with both barrels on the first night of 'Ghosts' in 1891

'An open drain; a loathsome sore unbandaged; a dirty act done publicly; a lazar-house with all its doors and windows open..." That was how *The Daily Telegraph's* critic, Clement Scott, characterised the first night of Ibsen's *Ghosts* on March 13, 1891. Scott was the most influential critical voice of his day. George Bernard Shaw, the complete Ibsenite and the most active champion in Britain of the Norwegian master, was delighted: the production would bathe in the controversy generated by the review. Indeed the *Telegraph* went at it with both barrels, carrying, opposite the first-night review, a leading article, which Shaw shrewdly suspected was the work of Scott with a hand from Edwin Arnold, the editor.

Ghosts was in truth strong meat even for the 1890s. A claustrophobic examination of sordid family secrets, inherited syphilis, adultery, incest, hypocrisy and religious repression, it was not performed on the licensed stage in Britain until 1911. The performances in 1891 were given at the Royalty Theatre by a group calling itself the "Independent

Henrik Ibsen (above), the author of 'Ghosts', was 'what Zola would have been without his invention' said the Telegraph in a leading article. As for the main characters (photographed in an early production, left), 'Who in their hearts cared for this "worm-eaten" prig of a boy, moaning and whining and blubbering about his fate, and talking heartlessly to his mother?'

Theatre", hoping as a club to evade the censorship of the Lord Chamberlain. It was a ruse that the *Telegraph*'s leader suggested was outside the law.

The paper's review, unsigned, but known by all as the work of Scott, was more restrained than its leading article. It made the point that the audience had come hoping to be shocked but had found their entertainment merely dull. It also made out the dramatic shortcomings of a play in which the characters "all preach and lecture and proclaim with wearisome iteration". The subject-matter even of *Ghosts* could be turned into tragedy by a great writer, Scott suggested, but Ibsen was not that man.

Clement Scott warned any budding dramatist against imitating Ibsen's preachy approach – a knock at Shaw, who was engaged in doing precisely that. In future years Shavian drama would become notorious for its lengthy set-piece speeches. Scott reserved his praise for the acting of Mrs Theodore Wright as the heroine of *Ghosts*, Mrs Alving, comparing hers favourably with good performances he had seen in productions of Ibsen's other plays, *A Doll's House*, *Pillars of Society* or *Rosmersholm*.

It was not as if Clement Scott were a narrow or philistine critic. Shaw called him a "sentimentalist", but that was merely a pejorative label plucked from his ideological store. Later writers on Ibsen tend to assume that Scott was "prejudiced and reactionary" (Miriam Franc, *Ibsen in England*, 1919) or was "what we think of as the typical late-Victorian of middle class" (Flora Elizabeth Emerson, *English Dramatic Critics of the Nineties*, 1953). But, like many of those associated with *The Daily Telegraph* in its first half century, such as its intrepid foreign correspondents George Augustus Sala and Bennet Burleigh, Scott was a self-confessed bohemian. Bohemia was still thriving four decades after the publication of Henri Murger's influential *Bohemians of the Latin Quarter*. For Scott and his friends it meant, if not quite starving in a garret, mixing easily with hard-drinking, raffish, matrimonially complicated actors, artists and writers.

Born in 1841, Scott had been a champion of the new naturalism of the dramatist Tom Robertson, who with plays such as *Caste* (1867) had brought a sharper realism to dialogue, plots, scenery and staging. Scott had left *The Sunday Times*, which found his criticism too outspoken, and joined the *Telegraph* in 1871. His early associates included Thomas Hood the younger, the editor of *Fun*, a rival to *Punch*; Frank Burnand, later editor of *Punch* itself; and W.S. Gilbert. He knew everyone in the theatre and was a successful playwright himself, writing for Squire Bancroft, the manager of the Prince of Wales theatre (which had staged Robertson's plays). To confirm his bohemian status he married in 1868 Isabel du Maurier, the sister of the artist who wrote *Trilby*, the tale of the mesmeric Svengali and his bare-footed singing protégée. Isabel and Clement Scott were married at the Brompton Oratory, for, like not a few journalists on the edges of society, Scott was a Roman Catholic.

Shaw made something of Clement Scott's religious outlook in his repeated journalistic attacks on him. In 1896, in a long piece in the *Saturday Review* (run by that Munchausen of sexual encounters Frank Harris), Shaw wrote that "Scott was the only critic whose attack on Ibsen was really memorable". Scott, he said, did not join with the complaints of the elderly, peevish and jealous, but "looking neither forward nor backward, gave utterance to his horror, like a man wounded to the quick of his religion, his affections, his enthusiasms – in the deepest part of him."

As Shaw put it on this occasion, the argument underlying *Ghosts* was one with which Scott might well have had some sympathy. If it had been presented as "a simple and direct plea for the right of a man of affectionate, easy, convivial temperament to live a congenial life, instead of skulking into the kitchen after the housemaid, and stealing a morsel of pleasure in the byways of drink and disease when his conscientiously conventional wife and her spiritual adviser were not looking, Mr Scott would be one of its most merciful critics".

At the same time Shaw declared that "Mr Scott is not a thinker", though by this he meant partly that Scott was not open to "ideas which were formerly only conceived by men of genius like Ibsen, or

'A vast body of readers conscious of his personality and anxious to hear his opinion' in the words of George Bernard Shaw, made Clement Scott (above) immensely influential as the Telegraph's theatre critic

intensely energetic spirits like Nietzsche". Scott's bent as a critic, he said, lay in feeling. "Whoever has been through the experience of discussing criticism with a thorough, perfect, and entire Ass, has been told that criticism should above all things be free from personal feeling. The excellence of Mr Scott's criticisms lies in their integrity as expressions of the warmest personal feeling."

It was to this that Bernard Shaw attributed Scott's pre-eminence. "Other men may have hurried from the theatre to the newspaper office to prepare, red hot, a notice of the night's performance for the morning paper; but nobody did it before him with the knowledge that the notice was awaited by a vast body of readers conscious of his personality and anxious to hear his opinion... His opportunity has of course been made by circumstances – by the growth of mammoth newspapers like *The Daily Telegraph*, the multiplication of theatres, and the spread of interest in them; but it has not been made for Mr Scott more than for his competitors; and the fact that he alone has seized it and made the most of it in a metropolis where every adult is eager to do his work for nothing but the honour and glory and the invitations to first nights, proves, you may depend on it, that his qualities for the work are altogether extraordinary."

Scott's practice in writing a review was to go from the theatre to the *Telegraph*, make for the room belonging to the proprietor, Edward Lawson, throw off his overcoat and coat, roll up his shirtsleeves, as if preparing for a fight, and set to work, fast. One day a messenger from the night editor came in and said: "Mr Le Sage's compliments, and will you please write as little as you can, sir, as he is so cramped for space tonight." Scott replied: "My compliments to Mr Le Sage, and tell him to go to hell; I shall write as much as I like."

The choicer abuse heaped on *Ghosts* by the press was gathered up by William Archer, the translator of Ibsen, and Shaw's ally for the time being. A selection was published in the *Pall Mall Gazette* on April 8. A third of the space went to extracts from the leader in *The Daily Telegraph*, but other opinions included: "Naked loathsomeness" – *Daily News*; "Revoltingly suggestive and blasphemous" – *Daily Chronicle*; "Morbid, unhealthy, unwholesome and disgusting" – *Lloyd's*; "Merely dull dirt long drawn out" – *Hawk*; "Maunderings of nookshotten Norwegians" – *Black and White*; "Garbage and offal" – *Truth*; "Nastiness and malodourousness laid on thickly as with a trowel" – *Era*; "Noisome corruption" – *The Stage*. It would have furnished a fine array of bills around the doors of any foyer.

Shaw gave a different version of the affair in his book *The Quintessence of Ibsenism* (revised 1913). He is more personally abusive than in his *Saturday Review* piece. He again makes the point that Scott was "an emotional, impressionable, zealous and sincere Roman Catholic" and then draws a picture of Scott having "in an almost hysterical condition, penned his share of this extraordinary protest. The literary workmanship bears marks of haste and

From the Telegraph

'It might be a noble theme; here it is nasty'

March 14, 1891

By Clement Scott

Women were present in goodly numbers; women of education, women of refinement, no doubt women of curiosity, who will take away to afternoon teas and social gatherings the news of the sensation play that deals with subjects that hitherto have been to most men horrible, and to all pure women loathsome. Possibly, nay probably, they were all disappointed. They expected to find something indescribably shocking, and only met with that which was deplorably dull. There was very little to offend the ear directly. On the Ibsen stage the nastiness is inferential, not actual....

Here we come to our great point, and it is this – that it is only the human scenes of Ibsen that are worth a brass button. There was scarcely a spark of interest in the play of *Ghosts* last night, except where Mrs Alving was on the scene. Why? Because Mrs Alving is a human creature, and because Mrs Theodore Wright touched everyone with her infinite womanliness. Who in their hearts cared for this "worm-eaten" prig of a boy, moaning and whining and blubbering about his fate, and heartlessly saying to his mother, "Of course I know how fond you are of me, and I can't but be grateful to you – and you can be so useful to me now that I am ill"? Oswald is a conceited, sensual and unnatural cub....

It is a wretched, deplorable, loathsome history, as all must admit. It might have been a tragedy had it been treated by a man of genius. Handled by an egotist and a bungler, it is only a deplorably dull play. There are ideas in *Ghosts* that would have inspired a tragic poet. They are vulgarised and debased by the suburban Ibsen. You want a Shakespeare, or a Byron, or a Browning to attack the subject-matter of *Ghosts* as it ought to be attacked. It might be a noble theme. Here it is nasty and vulgar....

Ibsen makes an attempt to convert Mrs Alving to Ibsenism, but he soon gives it up. There is a wild idea of making her a mouthpiece of freethinking, but the master thinks better of it. The others preach; Mrs Alving acts. ... She is rewarded for her unselfishness and self-sacrifice by being told by her cub of a son, whom she adores, that he would sooner be nursed by his sister, whom he incestuously adores, than by her mother, because she will have to die and leave the unnatural little monster.

INBRIEF

SEPTEMBER 1, 1897

Ellen Sinclair, 24, a stylishly dressed and good looking young woman, described as having no fixed address, was charged, at Marlborough Street, with stealing from George Warschauer, a merchant, living in Randolph Crescent, Maida Vale, the sum of £7. Mr A. Leslie, solicitor, defended.

The prosecutor stated that three months ago he was walking along Piccadilly with his cousin, when the prisoner accosted them and he again accidentally met her about 11 o'clock on the night of Saturday, July 31, when she came up to him and said: "I think I have seen you before, and have taken a great fancy to you. Will you see me as far as Oxford Street?"

He engaged a four-wheel cab and drove with her towards Oxford Circus. At the Circus she said: "Let us go round the corner," and the cab man was ordered to drive in a different direction. They soon arrived at Shaftesbury Avenue where the prisoner said she must get out, adding: "Don't come out of the cab or my mother will see you." (Laughter.)

She got out of the vehicle and went away and he shortly afterwards discovered that £7 in loose gold had been abstracted from his pocket. He had seen the money safe at the Empire a few minutes previously. Last night he saw the girl again in Regent Street, and gave her in charge.

Mr Hannay, the Magistrate: Is there any corroboration to the evidence of the prosecutor?

Detective Sergeant Gregory: No, Sir.

Mr Hannay: In these cases there must be some corroboration. The prisoner is discharged.

which, however, only heighten the expression of the passionate horror produced in the writer by seeing *Ghosts* on the stage."

Yet as Shaw's argument develops he concludes that Scott's objections to Ibsen's play are actually based on intellectual differences of principle. "A clergyman and and a married woman fall in love with one another. The woman proposes to abandon her husband and live with the clergyman. He recalls her to her duty, and makes her behave as a virtuous woman. She afterwards tells him that this was a crime on her part. Ibsen agrees with her, and has written the play to bring you round to her opinion. Clement Scott did not agree with her, and believed that when you are brought round to her opinion you have been morally corrupted."

Shaw did not reveal in his published journalism that, even before the production of *Ghosts*, he had been gunning for Scott, as shown by a letter to the actor Charles Charrington on March 30, 1891. In February he had taken part in a discussion of Ibsen at the Playgoers' Club, and an American actress called Elizabeth Robins had retailed the proceedings to Scott: "Bernard Shaw had got up in the Playgoers' Club and thanked his almighty God that Ibsen would be the end of Scott and all his works." Shaw commented that this, "except for my Almighty God, was very much what I actually had said". His account of the evening in his diary for February 17 was laconic: "I spoke, attacking Clement Scott, the dramatic critic of *The Daily Telegraph*, violently for his hostility to Ibsen. Dinner (at Orange Grove) 10d. Cocoa &c (same place) 7d."

So the row between Shaw and Scott was partly a matter of principle, but partly a clash of styles. Shaw might be challenging "middle-class morality" but his own life was the antithesis of bohemia, for he neither ate meat nor drank strong drink, he dressed in healthy, breathing Jaeger cloth and his sex life was expressed almost entirely by epistolary means.

Scott was a hard-living daily journalist, full of camaraderie, accustomed to late suppers and late mornings, and fully identified with the theatrical life, not just with plays on a page as a vehicle for ideas. Something of his character can be gathered from an incident one day when, as Scott was going to bed, a man arrived in a cab with a message from the night editor Le Sage, asking him to dictate on the spot an obituary for his friend the actor Walter Lacy. Scott's wife heard his response. "My friend – my friend – dead – Walter Lacy – my friend – to die at this hour. Why the hell couldn't he choose a reasonable time? Le Sage knows damned well that I can't dictate articles – that I never could dictate – blast Walter Lacy, dear old fellow. I'm not going to write a single line. I don't intend to write at all – of course I'll do it – who else can write about him as I can? Damn him – confounded, cursed nuisance to go dying like this, one of my best pals."

Another row that Scott was drawn into came when the dramatist Arthur Wing Pinero demanded, through a lawyer, an apology from him for a piece he had written in the *Illustrated London News* about

The Second Mrs Tanqueray. (It was not published in the *Telegraph*, because Scott had been away in America on the first night.) *"That interesting play/ The Second Mrs Tanqueray"* was the one that Matilda's parents had gone to see when she was burnt to death in Hilaire Belloc's Cautionary Tale; it was the smash of 1893. It embodied for Scott the wrong kind of realism, a pessimism that he loathed.

What annoyed Pinero, though, was Scott's drawing attention to the similarities between his play and one in German by Paul Lindau. By chance Pinero and Scott had the same lawyer, a eirenic man who wrote to each of the warring writers: "Come along and have a chat with me at twelve o'clock on Wednesday morning." Once he had got them together in his office, he made them shake hands and "promise to be better boys in the future".

Scott also had a brave falling out with the actor-manager Beerbohm Tree. He had praised Tree's performances, but then Tree hit a series of plays in which Scott pointed out his shortcomings. Tree complained to Edward Lawson, the paper's owner. Worse, Tree sent no review tickets for his next production, *Trilby* at the Haymarket, in October 1895. The implicit contract between producer and critic had been breached; it was an insult. Scott's interest in the play would have been all the greater because it was adapted from the runaway bestseller by George du Maurier, the brother of his first wife.

INBRIEF

OCTOBER 23, 1897
Benjamin Hitchen, one of the oldest and most trusted engine drivers in the employ of the London and North Western Railway Company, has died at Crewe. When the accident occurred he was driving the Scotch Express between Crewe and Carlisle and when Winsford, in Cheshire, was reached, a stone, thrown from a bridge under which the train passed struck him on the forehead.

She had died in 1890, and Scott had a new wife. They bought tickets themselves, for the second night. When the house manager came over and offered them a box, mumbling an apology for the review tickets having gone astray, Scott told him to go away in robust terms. But the next day Scott's review was as generous to Tree as any actor could have hoped for: his keen, incisive and effective study of Svengali made the play an emphatic success.

As for Shaw, he remained on surprisingly good terms with Scott, apologising freely after mistakenly attacking him over an article about stage censorship that had in fact been written by someone else. But Shaw had a sort of revenge for the *Ghosts* incident by turning Scott into the character Joseph Cuthbertson in *The Philanderer*, one of the "Plays Unpleasant". The stage direction that introduces Cuthbertson calls him "a man of fevered idealistic sentiment, so frequently outraged by the facts of life that he has acquired an habitually indignant manner". *The Philanderer* was Shaw's second play, written in 1893 when he was fully under Ibsen's influence, but it was not produced until 1905.

By then Scott was dead. In 1898 he had left the paper in a huff and started a weekly called the *Free Lance*. It failed. After a long illness he died in 1904. His widow Margaret published a feeble memoir in 1919. It was called *Old Days in Bohemian London*.

From the Telegraph

Ghosts: 'a lazar-house with all its doors and windows open'

March 14, 1891

From the leading article after the first night

Dramatic art never had enemies more deadly than those who have clubbed together to bolster up the reputation of the Norwegian writer Henrik Ibsen. Mr Grein, manager of the Independent Theatre, poses as a friend of high dramatic art. "*Ghosts*," he says, "is not beautiful – in the ordinary sense – but it is artistic, because it is a powerful play, written in human language, because it is as simple as a tragedy of the Greeks."

Ay! The play performed last night is "simple" enough in plan and purpose, but simple only in the sense of an open drain; of a loathsome sore unbandaged; of a dirty act done publicly; or of a lazar-house with all its doors and windows open. It is no more "Greek" and can no more be called "Greek" for its plainness of speech and candid foulness, than could a dunghill at Delphi.

The framework theory of this Norwegian's "inspiration", is said, by his own panegyrists, to be expressed in his play *An Enemy of the People* where the hero, Dr Stockmann – declared to be the portrait of Dr Ibsen himself – observes, "The great discovery I have made within the last few years is the discovery that all our sources of spiritual life are poisoned, and that our whole society rests upon a pestilential basis of falsehood."

The passage which gives its title to the piece of offensive pessimism performed last night is couched thus: Mrs Alving, the heroine, says, "Ghosts! When I heard Regina and Oswald in there I seemed to see ghosts before me. I almost think we're all of us ghosts, Pastor Manders, it's only what we have inherited from our fathers and mothers that 'walk' in us. It's all sorts of dead ideas and lifeless old beliefs, and so forth."

Human society itself is for Ibsen but a vile crowd of actors and actresses walking shamefully on the thin crust of a quagmire called "Law and Order." There is nothing new, and nothing true, and it does not signify. Henrik Ibsen of Skien is what Zola would have been without his invention and analysis, Carlyle without his genius and piety, or the "melancholy Jacques" without his culture and wit, if they had been born of a seafaring family in a poor fishing village upon the Western Fiords.

It is difficult to expose in decorous words – the gross, and almost putrid, indecorum of this play of *Ghosts*. Suffice it to indicate that the general situation is that of a son exposing to a mother – herself, in past days, a would-be adulteress – his inheritance of a loathsome malady from a father whose memory the widow secretly execrates while she publicly honours and consecrates it. Even the Lady of the Camellias – that hectic harlot – coughed her frail soul away with some external propriety; but Ibsen's patients expectorate, if we may venture to say so, in public, and air on the stage matters that a blind beggar would hide under his patches.

In the name of outraged Art let these people – author, actors, and admirers – keep to themselves their clinical confessions and scenes which appertain to Mercury rather than the Muse. If their food be such carrion, let them devour it apart; but, in whatever measure they bring their crapulous stuff into the light of day, we trust that public opinion, backed, if necessary, by the law, will rebuke and restrain the novel and perilous nuisance.

THE WESTMINSTER AQUARIUM
The Indiarubber Legmaniac and Frederick's Cats

Opposite Parliament stood a huge building that staged increasingly outlandish music-hall acts as its fortunes dwindled

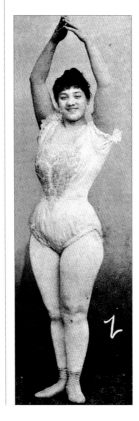

The vast Aquarium, viewed from the door of Westminster Abbey, boasted Madamoiselle Zaeo's trapeze skills

F or such a big building where such strange things happened, it left surprisingly little memory behind. The Royal Westminster Aquarium was 600ft long and 160 broad, opposite Parliament and the Abbey, stretching down Tothill Street. It was built purely as a commercial venture.

Part of its site is now taken up by the bulk of Methodist Central Hall, which hardly evokes the weird sights once seen there – Farini's Earthmen, the Polar Walrus, the Missing Link, Mademoiselle Paula performing in the Tank with huge Alligators and Snakes, the Russian Giantess, the Wonderful One-Legged Acrobat, Captain Constentenus

(Tattooed from Head to Foot in Chinese Tartary), Frederick's Cats, the Intelligent Seals, Neet the Indiarubber Legmaniac, and the Cannibals of Tierra del Fuego ("fed at 2.30, 6.00 and 10.00"), all brilliantly lighted by Electricity and the Pompeian Albo-Carbon Light.

Royal it was, because it was opened by the Duke of Edinburgh – Queen Victoria's second son, Prince Alfred, "poor Affie" who she thought had been "ruined by Society". He had just married the Tsar's daughter, no Russian Giantess. The Aquarium opening was in January 1876 and "a brilliant gathering, as the term is commonly employed, could hardly have been expected", the *Telegraph* commented, because "Society", ruinous or not, was still absent from town.

It was an inauspicious start. Bands played "God Save the Tsar" and "not a cheer was raised by a crowd who, then and afterwards, exhibited the extreme of coolness and apathy". No one could hear the Prince's speech. "I need hardly remind you," the printed text said, "that the earnest desire of the Prince Consort was ever to encourage any enterprise which could conduce to the moral and intellectual progress as well to the material welfare of the people."

"The extensive aquarium," the Duke of Edinburgh thought, "cannot fail, if properly directed, to stimulate the love of natural history and the acquirement of scientific knowledge." But it did fail. In any case, from the first there were no fish.

"Fishes are cold-blooded animals," said *The Daily Telegraph*, "but they must have felt a thrill of pride when news was flashed through the ocean depths last Saturday that a Royal Prince and some thousands of people had, with form and ceremony, opened an aquarium in the heart of London. Whether the fishes would have been flattered had they known that not one representative of their class was present at the opening ceremony is doubtful.

"There was music to hear; there were pictures to look at; plants and flowers to delight the eyes; and even sundry counterfeit presentment – some of them in a strangely dilapidated condition – of land animals; but no fish, only rows of empty tanks, of which, by and by, fish are to take possession."

Still, the fishless surroundings were striking. More than 25,000 plants adorned the building, in beds along each side of the nave, and in baskets hanging from that great span of glass and iron. Alfred Bedborough, its architect, "must also be credited with an effective use of colour upon the interior. Everywhere a chocolate brown prevailed, relieved by lines of blue picked out with gold, the result of this combination being that the superabundance of light from the enormous roof of glass is so toned down as to avoid the fatigue of the eye".

Even without marine life, the Duke of Edinburgh declared inaudibly, there remained "access to a

Captain Constentenus is described on the poster below as a 'Greek Albanian tattooed from head to foot in Chinese Tartary as punishment for engaging in rebellion against the King'. The reasons given for his striking appearance varied from season to season

useful reading room, the daily performance of good music by a well-chosen orchestra, the periodical exhibition of such a collection of paintings as we see around us – agencies which cannot but exercise a most beneficial influence in refining public taste."

That was not how everyone saw it. Even the arrival of assorted fish for the 30 tanks, including "the largest salt-water tank in the world" did not bring in paying customers. The royal links were maintained when in 1882 there was an informal "christening" by the Prince and Princess of Wales of the baby alligator "Jack". But the place got a reputation for shadiness, despite the brilliant illumination. Westminster was then a haunt of prostitutes, and Society stayed away from the arcades of potted plants. Arthur Sullivan had been appointed musical director but no lady would be seen promenading within earshot of the orchestra.

A sign of slipping standards was a Japanese marionette show against which a manufacturer of gas-meters felt obliged to bring a prosecution for indecent gestures that "could not be witnessed by wives and children". Lively entertainments introduced to tempt wider audiences seemed to some a scandal under the nose of Parliament.

"The importation of a lady who obligingly allowed herself to be fired out of a cannon twice a day proved greatly to the taste of a jaded public appetite," the *Telegraph* remarked in later years, when the place had fallen on harder times. "With this novel 'sensation' the Aquarium management secured an invaluable free advertisement from the Home Secretary, who wrote that he would hold them personally responsible for any mishaps that might befall the intrepid lady.

"To a clever showman like Mr Wybrow Robertson, the opportunity was far too good to be lost. Thus, within 24 hours, the London hoardings provided the population with food for much innocent merriment in the placarded copies of the astute manager's reply to the Home Secretary, in which he united his assurances that the performance was destitute of danger with a kindly offer to fire the Right Hon Gentleman out of the gun at any time he might find it convenient to submit himself to that ordeal, so as to satisfy himself personally of the safety of the feat."

On New Year's Day 1883 an eye-catching single-column advertisement in the *Telegraph* proclaimed:
ROYAL AQUARIUM – Krao, The Missing Link.
ROYAL AQUARIUM – Krao. What is it?
ROYAL AQUARIUM – Krao. Twice daily, 2–6 and 7–9, commencing Jan 1 – admission: afternoon 2s; evening, 1s.

In its editorial columns the paper thought Krao "undoubtedly worthy of public attention and careful scientific examination" as the proposed "missing link between man and the monkey" that Darwinism lacked. Krao was "apparently not more than nine years old, of feminine sex, and has nothing repulsive in her appearance, while the disposition of this so-called 'human monkey' seems gentle and affectionate, though it is said that when anything

FARINIS LATEST NOVELTY

ROYAL

AQUARIUM

CAPTAIN COSTENTENUS,

THE GREEK ALBANIAN!

TATTOOED FROM HEAD TO FOOT

IN CHINESE TARTARY, AS PUNISHMENT FOR ENGAGING IN REBELLION AGAINST THE KING.

offends her she shoots her lips out like a chimpanzee, and darts angry looks around. Her head is adorned with thick, jet-black hair of a rather coarse texture, and her limbs and body are enveloped in a natural soft fur of a dark colour."

The poor thing had apparently been "discovered by the well-known traveller Carl Bock in Laos and brought with some difficulty, but with due authority, through Siamese territory for exhibition in England, as a proof of the existence of a hairy race long asserted to exist in remote parts of the country". She had already picked up "a few words of English".

Even when the arrival of the Polar Walrus was announced in the autumn of 1883, its attractions had to be eked out by Ethardo and Son (acrobats), Professor Grant (ventriloquist), the Onzelins (horizontal bars) and Captain Ureck, the Hungarian Giant (base vocalist). At its fishiest the Aquarium spent £100 a week on feeding aquatic creatures; better value proved to be *not* feeding Jacques "The Fasting Man". In 1891 he held out for 50 days (six more than David Blaine in his glass box further down river in 2003).

On March 21, 1893, the *Telegraph* carried at the top of its front page, where advertisements for the Aquarium always appeared, this "Important Notice – Professor THOMAS BURNS (the World Champion High Diver, Ornamental and Long Distance Swimmer) has undertaken to, THIS DAY, dive from beneath the Aquarium Dome into a tank of water below the ground level. The time appointed for the dive is 4.45. The management expects the feat will be accomplished, but will not guarantee its taking place." But he did it, falling flat on his back 83 feet below in the great tank. Those tanks also came in handy for the act of "Professor Beckwith's lady swimmers – as graceful and pretty as it is free from the least indelicacy or grossness".

A little too free in displaying her pale but muscular legs for the taste of the Central Vigilance Society for the Repression of Immorality had been the dextrous Mademoiselle Zaeo the trapeze artist – British by birth, but the toast of the Trieste sawdust ring – dressed only in a damasked corset. In 1890 a correspondent in the *Telegraph* described her image in costume on a thousand public posters as a "harmless picture of a beautiful acrobat". Emboldened, Captain Molesworth, the manager of the Aquarium, had a mind to defend Mlle Zaeo from prosecution under the Indecent Advertisements Act, passed the previous year. Finding the London County Council against him, and the Aquarium filled thanks to the publicity, he decided instead to take the posters quietly down.

The Easter attractions of 1898, all for a shilling, made the Aquarium practically delirious in an announcement printed in tiny type: "Thought Reading Dogs, Educated and Talking Donkeys and

The poster for the Grand Opening Ceremony of the theatre at the Aquarium promised a farce, an Original Address written expressly by Clement Scott, the drama critic of The Daily Telegraph, and a stage adaptation of Dickens's 'Bleak House'. It wasn't enough to keep the seats full

Dogs, doing all sorts of marvellous things blindfolded, and without their trainers being present. A Minstrel Dog Orchestra, dogs playing drums, cymbals and various instruments. A very special illusion, that has taken Professor Valadon many years to perfect: human living beings will be precipitated through space, and how done it will be impossible to tell. The Champion Lady Jumper of the World (Miss Parker) has undertaken to jump off an ordinary brick 'placed end-up' over a horse 15 hands high without upsetting the brick, and Professor Parker will perform other remarkable feats in jumping. The Marvellous Flying Sisters Ongar reappear in a series of sensational feats of almost miraculous achievement. The renowned Arthur Lloyd and Sketch Company, Jewel's Clever Royal Marionettes, Jolly John Nash is retained to sing his old and most successful song and Tootle-Tootle Cornet Solo. Amongst Animals' Performances are three Troupes of Performing Dogs – Buer's, Victor's, and Kriesel's. The comic business is strengthened by the Jones-Amonda Troupe of Pantomimists; Joe Colverd, Jolly John Bull; Osmond and Kloof, Clown Instrumentalists; Baby Loftus, Serio-comic; Neet, the Indiarubber Legmaniac; Fred LeNore, Elliott and Warne, the Otto Troupe of Knockabout. The lady Serio-comics are May Wentworth, Reany Wilson, Lily Lilias, Laurie Wallis, Elsie Trevor, etc. There will be Military Drill. Fun in a Gymnasium by Ros and Ros, Shadowgraphy and Juggling by Tregetour, Hectors on the Tightrope, the Cardownie Troupe of National Dancers, Prof. North and Life-Sized Ventriloquial Figures; Willis, Comical Conjurer etc. There will be Living Freaks and all sorts of Side Shows, Klondike Experiences, a Boy with Three Legs, etc. For sensation nothing in London will compare with the Jackley wonders, the marvellous Flying Vol Becques, the Three Charms and the Sisters Ongar, the Great Dive by Annie Luker, headfirst from the Dome, and Finney, who dives headfirst tied up in a sack with the sack set fire to."

But it was no good, even with the sack set fire to. The Aquarium managed to last just 27 years, outliving the Duke of Edinburgh, who died as Duke of Coburg before his mother Victoria in 1900. It closed its doors on January 10, 1903, when "one of the biggest crowds ever gathered within the Aquarium walls discreetly refrained from any departure from good manners such as might have called into action the extra police specially drafted in". That night an early moving film, referred to as the bioscope, "unfolded the glories of the Coronation Procession" of Edward VII, the godfather 21 years earlier of the alligator Jack. In 1908 the auditorium was reassembled in Canning Town, as the Royal Albert Music Hall, and when that fell through became a cinema.

TWO EMINENT VICTORIANS

Finding a bone to pick with The People's William

Gladstone was a hero with whom the Telegraph fell out. For W.G. Grace it expressed its admiration in shillings

W hen the *Telegraph* was founded it was far more radical than William Gladstone. In its first five years, he was wondering which Cabinet to join – the Conservatives' or the Liberals'. He didn't get on with Palmerston and still rather leant to his old party, the Conservatives.

In 1858 and 1859 he was sent by Lord Derby's Conservative Government as a commissioner of the Ionian Islands, giving everyone a breathing space. When he came back, Disraeli was dug in as the leading Conservative in the Commons. In any case

the Conservatives were out of power. So Gladstone accepted a post in Palmerston's Government.

Soon Gladstone, as he always did, threatened to resign, but first he must get through a Bill to remove tax on paper – newsprint for the *Telegraph*. He corresponded with Thornton Leigh Hunt, the editor, whom he had met in 1860, and the Paper Bill hugely benefited the *Telegraph*, selling at 1d.

The *Telegraph* supported Gladstone throughout the 1860s, and Edward Levy was credited with coining the nickname "The People's William". Gladstone was, the *Telegraph* suggested in 1862, the next leader of the nation: "The failing hand of the Premier [Palmerston] will relinquish the helm of state. It would be ill for England, in prospect of such a day, if she had not one pilot at least to whom she could look with happy confidence. She can, she does, so look to GLADSTONE, because in all a long career of public life he has never swerved from the path of manly and straightforward policy."

"Straightforward" was an odd word for William Gladstone, who, even when honest, puzzled his best friends by his motives. He swerved enough in the 1870s. Thornton Hunt, whom he met almost daily during the Reform Bill debates of 1867, died in 1873. Edward Levy still saw Gladstone sometimes, and the *Telegraph* backed him in the 1874 election, which the Liberals lost. In 1877 came the rift.

The grounds were not "straightforward". Turks had massacred Bulgars, who sought independence. In his pamphlet *Bulgarian Horrors*, of 1876,

Alfred Morgan entitled his painting 'An omnibus ride to Piccadilly Circus – Mr Gladstone travelling with ordinary passengers'. By 1885, when the picture was finished, the Telegraph had parted company with The People's William

Gladstone caught popular support by demanding the Turks leave Bulgaria "bag and baggage", but for him there was a subtler question. Were the Bulgarians, encouraged by Russia, justified in throwing off the rule of the Greek church and establishing an independent exarchate (which they had tried at first to do with the aid of the secular power Turkey)?

With this in mind, Gladstone had in 1877 written twice to a Greek merchant in Constantinople called Negropontis (referred to in Parliament as "Negroponte"), who had asked him for comments. They were cautious: "It was and is far from my intention to pronounce between Greek and Slav."

Gladstone wanted the Bulgarians freed. "Let the daily power of the Turk in Bulgaria be destroyed," he said in 1878. But his letter to Negropontis of July 1877 was described by the *Telegraph* as "inciting the Greeks to rise against the Turks". The letter had been shown to the British ambassador in Constantinople, A.H. Layard, who had passed on its contents orally to the *Telegraph* correspondent. The paper's consequent reports caused uproar in Britain. Gladstone had, the *Telegraph* said, urged the Greeks to "unite with the Slavs in an attack on the Turks".

Then Negropontis denied that Gladstone's letters had said any such thing. Gladstone complained. The *Telegraph* was at a loss, since it had no copies of the letters; but the damage was done. In March 1878 the Commons debated a motion viewing "with regret" the action of the ambassador. It was defeated by 206 to 132, but it marked a parting of the ways for W.E. Gladstone and Edward Levy-Lawson's *Daily Telegraph*.

Giving Grace 100,000 shillings

In 1895 W.G. Grace returned to the form that 30 years before had made him the pre-eminent cricketer of his time. He changed the very standard of batsmanship. Before his time it was unusual to score 50 on the rough wickets of the day and most rare to gain a century. Grace made centuries and double centuries. In 1876 he made 400 not out in a match against Grimsby.

At the beginning of the 1895 season Grace was 46, and made his 100th century in first-class cricket, batting for Gloucestershire against Somerset. He reached his 1,000th run of the season by May 30, and was greeted enthusiastically in the field and in the press. The Prince of Wales wrote to congratulate him.

It was then that the *Telegraph* came up with the idea of opening a "shilling fund" for his benefit. The paper had long organised charitable collections for good causes. In 1862 the distressed Lancashire cotton workers, hit hard by the American Civil War, received more

In 1895 W.G. Grace, at the age of 46, scored his 100th century in first-class cricket. The public, the Prince of Wales and the Telegraph wanted to show their appreciation

than £6,000 raised by *Telegraph* readers. In later years a bigger readership raised enormous sums: £255,275 for widows and orphans of the South African War; £231,209 during the First World War for King George's Fund for Sailors.

The shilling fund for Grace was devised to allow people who could not afford a large donation to become part of the wave of gratitude to Grace for his achievement and for the glory that he had shed on the game of cricket. Everyone joined in, from the Prime Minister down. Lord Salisbury sent £5 accompanied by a letter saying: "I beg to enclose a centenary of shillings to use the current phrase. I have not touched a cricket ball for more than 50 years – so I am afraid that I can only claim a *locus standi* as owner of a village cricket ground."

Grace was by profession a doctor, a fact which the satirical magazine *Moonshine* (a kind of *Punch*) played on in publishing a cartoon of Sir Edward Lawson, the *Telegraph*'s proprietor, presenting Grace with a cheque for £5,000. "Don't mention it, doctor," it has the newspaperman saying, "and thank you for what you have done for my circulation."

It was a marketing stunt, but Lawson was no doubt sincere in the words he wrote to Grace with the cheque representing 100,000 shillings. It was, he said, "a very notable and emphatic expression of the general love for those out-of-door sports and pursuits, which – free from any element of cruelty, greed, or coarseness – serve so admirably to develop our British traits of manliness, good-temper, fair play, and the healthy training of mind and body; at the same time giving pleasure and amusement to the greatest possible number".

Grace as a "Gentleman", not a "Player", was obliged to uphold the standards of amateurism, eschewing the financial benefits that flood in for modern-day sportsmen. The £5,000 would be a welcome gift. "I permit myself to regard the progress and result of the 'National Shilling Testimonial'," Lawson wrote, "as a manifestation, by classes and masses alike, of their abiding preference for wholesome and honest amusements in contradistinction to sickly pleasures and puritanical gloom, thus conferring upon you the happy distinction of a substantial personal tribute, which is at the same time a public approval of your example to the youth and manhood of your time."

"I can only marvel at the prodigious number and generosity of my friends," Grace wrote back in a letter reproduced prominently in the *Telegraph*. "I think and believe, with gratitude and pride, that I must have more than any other man ever possessed."

Four years later Grace played for England for the last time. He severed his long connection with Gloucestershire and took up a position as manager of cricket at the Crystal Palace. His appearance at the Oval in 1908 brought to a close his first-class career of 43 years, with a score of 54,896 runs. He was to die in 1915.

EXTREMES OF WEATHER

A snowbound train dug out by 300 navvies

Thousands enjoyed winter skating on London's frozen lakes in the 1890s, when summers made pith helmets desirable

The 1890s saw some extremes of climate in Britain. Surprising weather had always been a staple of the *Telegraph*'s news columns, and the paper regularly carried little charts of variation in pressure for readers to compare with the barometer in the hall. The frost at the beginning of 1891 was sharp, and by January 6 the ice on the Serpentine in Hyde Park was reported to be between six and seven inches thick. People flocked to the frozen lake and on that day 30,000 skaters and sliders made use

Boys clamber over the Thames at Deptford, frozen into fantastic shapes in the hard frosts of 1895, during a decade of extreme heat and cold

From the Telegraph

Deaths from exposure and skating by lantern light

February 13, 1895

In London yesterday the lowest temperature was 14 degrees. On the Thames the suspension of traffic continued. The quantity of ice in the stream goes on increasing, especially below London Bridge, thus greatly augmenting the risk to which all light craft are exposed. Yesterday, a barge containing 90 tons of sugar foundered near the Tower Bridge.

The ice in the West-End parks continues to increase, and yesterday, it was deemed safe to throw open to skaters the whole of the 40 acres of the Serpentine. Skating by torchlight on the Serpentine, which has been

indulged in since Sunday last, was rendered additionally picturesque last night by the large number of Chinese and other coloured lanterns which were carried suspended from the ends of sticks by the skaters.

Deaths from want and exposure continue to be reported.

of the ice there, including 5,000 who came after dark. Another 15,000 took to the Round Pond in Kensington Gardens, and no accidents were reported. The Thames was thick with ice floes and barge traffic came to a standstill.

In March cold weather returned suddenly, with a great blizzard. "Never since railways were constructed have trains been snowed up in the southern counties in the month of March," the paper remarked on the 11th. "The Zulu Express," it reported two days later, "which left Paddington Station on Monday afternoon at 3 o'clock for Plymouth, is still snowed up near the little station at Brent, Devonshire. Three hundred navvies are now doing their best to clear a way."

Another train was trapped in the middle of Dartmoor. "The train left Princetown at 5.35pm on Monday with four men and two women passengers. It was missed on Tuesday morning, but owing to the fearful weather no one could venture out in search of it.

"The second night was passed by the passengers in the utmost wretchedness. The windows were tightly closed, the ventilators fastened, and the curtains drawn, but the snow beat in all directions. All the compartments of the carriages, although the doors and windows were closed, were filled with snow up to the hat-racks.

"At daylight on Wednesday the weather cleared, and they were espied by a farmer who was rescuing his sheep from the snow, and who gave friendly assistance. His house was only 200 yards off, but the snow had been falling so thickly that he had not noticed the train."

In 1895 the Thames froze. As far down as Gravesend, the *Telegraph* reported in February, "drift ice extends from shore to shore. The steam launches belonging to Her Majesty's Customs, Board of Trade, and River and Sea Pilots have been laid up. There is no communication with Tilbury except occasionally by a screw-tug. All the

watermen's boats have been placed in the Ordnance Yard for safety."

In 1898 the summer heat was unbearable. On August 7 it was only 52F in London and by August 14 it was 85F. In the sun, a rather unscientific measure, it reached 127F, and the people felt it. "Miss Amelia Evans, residing at Brixton, was suddenly overpowered while cycling in Battersea Park, and falling from her machine, sustained a nasty scalp wound."

The hospitals saw cases of heat-stroke and apoplexy. "Men employed on outdoor work found the heat so great as to make it imperative to discontinue, while several policemen on duty became incapacitated. Some of the horses attached to the buses and heavily-laden wagons suffered terribly from the excessive heat."

The heatwave went on for days. "Some shops are offering pith helmets and Indian fabrics to broiling Londoners, but the demand for these articles has not been large." Readers had their own remedies. "Once again we are reminded by correspondents that orange colour is the best tint for resisting the sun's rays, and that the straw hats, regarded as a protector for the head during the weather recently experienced is a snare and delusion."

An anonymous *Telegraph* journalist, who had weathered summers of 103F during war in Bulgaria, proposed a more rational dress in place of the black frock coats and woollen trousers of City men: "A light pith bowler, tolerably high in the crown and triply lined with green gauze; a thin silken shirt and drawers, the former loose at the throat and the latter securely buckled around the waist; no waistcoat or cummerbund, for both are heating; a linen, jean, or nankeen jacket and trousers; closely-fitting socks of spun-thread or gossamer silk; and low-quartered shoes of canvas.

"Thus attired, a healthy man, whose 'pulse beats temperately' has nothing to fear from the utmost extravagances of an English summer."

From the Telegraph

The London Particular: fog plus the products of combustion

October 29, 1897

By an investigator

The scientific description of the "London Particular" would probably be: fog plus certain products of combustion, and injurious for two reasons. First, on account of the tarry products present, which envelope the drop of moisture and thus obstruct evaporation, hence the dryness of a London fog. Second, because the amount of carbonic acid in the air is largely increased during its prevalence, owing to the smoky vapour preventing its diffusion.

It was the "London Particular" which over-hung the metropolis during the greater part of yesterday. No difference of opinion could exist on that point, for the "products of combustion" settled in the corners of one's eyes in a way which would be impossible with the more respectable class of fog.

Don't labour any longer under the delusion that November is the favourite month of fogs. Mr Robert H. Scott, MA, FRS, whose zeal in the cause of weather statistics is well known to learned men, has compiled some elaborate tables dealing with fogs in London from 1876 to 1890. From these we learn that during the 15 years in question 834 fogs were recorded. The greatest number took place in December, which boasted 143; January 131; whereas the much abused November stands third on the list with only 117.

"It seems to be generally assumed", I said to Mr Scott, "that fogs in London have been increasing in frequency and severity."

"Some people say so," replied Mr Scott. "But I assume nothing of the kind. As a matter of fact, I believe there has been actually less of fog since 1890 than in the years immediately preceding."

In his opinion, the alleged increase of fog, especially in the South Western district of London, is attributable to the extension of building during the last quarter of a century. [Fog on the Embankment is pictured below in 1896.] This has increased the number of chimneys and whereas 20 years ago the fogs which reached the Chelsea Nursery Gardens were apparently innocent country fogs, they have of late years assumed the urban character, with all its deleterious attributes.

Finally, I directed my steps to the headquarters of the South Eastern Railway. Here I obtained information which had the advantage of corroborating the statements already made to me at several of the Great London termini. Namely, that the "block system" of signalling during a heavy fog works admirably. It is true that train services must be revised and some "fixtures" must be removed, but the idea of danger to passengers was everywhere scouted.

Victorians abroad

The Telegraph matched the enterprise of the explorers of its day, sending Stanley to
Its correspondents stood beside Burnaby cut down in battle and rowed along beside

THE BABYLONIAN NOAH

The deluge story discovered in Mesopotamia

George Smith astonished Gladstone with
new texts of biblical history. Could he find
a missing tablet to complete the account?

*The fashionably bearded
George Smith was 32
when his lecture spurred
the Telegraph to send him
to make new excavations
in search of cuneiform
tablets among the carved
remains of Babylonian
kings at Nineveh (top)*

The Prime Minister was excited by the
time the lecture came to an end. He felt
moved to make a speech, though he had
not intended to do so. Since the Prime
Minister was William Gladstone,
excitement came easily and the speech was greeted
by cheers. But he had reason to be moved, for he
had just heard read to him passages from ancient
Babylonian cuneiform inscriptions that gave an
independent account of the deluge that drowned
the world, as the book of Genesis told in the Bible.

Part of the tale of this Babylonian Noah went
thus: "I sent forth a dove, and it left. The dove went
and searched and a resting place it did not find, and
it returned. I sent forth a swallow, and it left. The
swallow went and searched, and a resting place it
did not find, and it returned. I sent forth a raven,
and it left. The raven went, and the corpses on the
water it saw, and it did eat, it swam, and wandered
away, and did not return."

To any half-educated Victorian this rang a
thrilling bell. Genesis said: "And it came to pass at
the end of forty days, that Noah opened the window
of the ark which he had made: And he sent forth a
raven, which went forth to and fro, until the waters
were dried up from off the earth. Also he sent forth
a dove from him, to see if the waters were abated
from off the face of the ground. But the dove found
no rest for the sole of her foot, and she returned

unto him into the ark, for the waters were on the
face of the whole earth: then he put forth his hand,
and took her, and pulled her in unto him into the
ark. And he stayed yet other seven days; and again
he sent forth the dove out of the ark; And the dove
came in to him in the evening; and, lo, in her
mouth was an olive leaf pluckt off: so Noah knew
that the waters were abated from off the earth. And
he stayed another seven days; and sent forth the
dove; which returned not again unto him."

There were differences, but the similarities were
amazing. On December 4, 1872 the *Telegraph* gave
big coverage to the events of the night before at the
Biblical Archaeological Society. The lecturer was
George Smith, of the British Museum. He was a
remarkable man. From a poor family he had been
apprenticed as an engraver of banknotes, but
developed a fascination for the oriental archaeology
carried out by Austen Henry Layard and Henry
Rawlinson. He began to spend his dinner hours at
the British Museum, and Rawlinson's faith in him
was rewarded when he discovered, among the
fragments brought back by the archaeologists, texts
that shed new light on Babylonian history.

By 1872, when he was 32, Smith, now on the staff
of the museum, had been turning his attention to
"Assyrian" clay tablets containing mythological
material. The *Telegraph* had been keeping an eye on
him, aware that news was in the offing, and on that
night it was revealed to an eager public.

"He had obtained a number of tablets," the paper
reported, "giving a curious series of legends and
including a copy of the story of the Flood. On
discovering these documents, which were much
mutilated, he searched over all the collections of
fragments of inscriptions, consisting of several
thousands of smaller pieces, and ultimately
recovered 80 fragments of these legends, by the aid
of which he was enabled to restore nearly all the
text of the description of the Flood, and
considerable portions of the other legends. These
tablets were originally at least 12 in number,
forming one story or set of legends, the account of
the Flood being on the 11th tablet."

According to Smith, "The Biblical account is the
version of an inland people, the name of the Ark in
Genesis means a chest or box, and not a ship; there
is no notice of the sea, or of launching, no pilots are

Africa and publishing the young Churchill's despatches from the North-West Frontier. Captain Webb as he swam the Channel

spoken of, no navigation is mentioned. The inscription belongs to a maritime people. The Ark is called a ship, the ship is launched into the sea, and it is given in charge of a pilot."

"In conclusion," reported the *Telegraph*, "he remarked that this account of the Deluge opened a new field of inquiry in the early parts of the Bible history. The question has often been asked, 'What is the origin of the account of the antediluvians, with their long lives so many times greater than the longest span of human life? Where was Paradise, the abode of the first parents of mankind? Whence comes the story of the Flood, of the Ark, of the birds?' The Cuneiform inscriptions are shedding new light on these questions, and supplying material which future scholars will have to work out."

"It would be a mistake," it suggested, "to suppose that, with the translation and commentary on an inscription like this, the matter is ended. Beneath the mounds and ruined cities of Chaldea, now awaiting exploration, lie, together with older copies of this Deluge text, other legends and histories of the earliest civilisation in the world."

As it happened, Gladstone had mythological theories of his own. Homer, he thought, had been given a kind of classicist's revelation from God, parallel to that of the Bible. So another pagan version of the biblical events sent his heart racing. "Every day must begin for me with my old friend Homer," he told the meeting, "from whom I hope never to be parted as long as I have any faculties or any breath in my body. The course of recent discoveries, both in Assyria and in Egypt, has tended to give a solidity to much of the old Greek traditions which they never before possessed. I don't know whether it is supposed that the enquiries of archaeological or other sciences are to have the effect of unsettling many minds in this our generation; but I must say, for myself, that on every point at which I am enabled to examine them, they have a totally different effect (Cheers)."

The effect did not make Gladstone lose his head. Whoever was going to pay for the excavation of the cities of Chaldea, it was not going to be the Liberal Government. "It has been the distinguishing prize of this country," Gladstone told the crowded meeting, "to do many things by individual effort that in other countries can only be effected by what

INBRIEF

JULY 22, 1885
Our Portsmouth correspondent writes.
The village of Emsworth has been visited by a remarkable plague of flies, which simultaneously covered an area of one mile. At some places it was impossible to move without closing the eyes and mouth. Around every lamp in the town the spectacle was most curious. Attracted by the light, thick swarms abounded, and their buzz resembled that of a hive of bees. At the post office, where the upper portion of the door is open for ventilation, and where necessarily the light is kept burning till the early morning, the insects covered the sorting boards, letters, and bags, and had to be continually swept off with brushes. At one lamp they simply hung down in clusters. In the window of the office they are now to be seen in thick bunches. Bicyclists coming from Havant were in several instances compelled to alight, so thick was the swarm; and at the auction mart at the bottom of the town, the tray in which the money was taken was covered an inch thick.

Sir Robert Peel used to call the vulgar expedient of applying to the Consolidated Fund – (a laugh) – or to whatever in those other countries correspond with that well known institution of our country.

"If you," he continued, turning to Sir Henry Rawlinson, who was chairing the meeting, "are disposed to elect me individually as a member of this society, I shall be extremely happy to take my place in its ranks (Cheers)."

For a task from which the Treasury shrank, *The Daily Telegraph* happily stumped up, especially when it meant securing a story that was as mesmerising to the Victorian mind as the theories or Darwin or the fossil discoveries of Charles Lyell. Smith's lecture spoke of a missing part of the "Deluge Tablet". What if the *Telegraph* could send him off to Nineveh, in ancient Babylonia, modern Iraq, to find it?

"The newspaper came forward," Smith recalled in his book *Assyrian Discoveries*, "and offered to advance a sum of a thousand guineas for fresh researches at Nineveh, in order to recover more of these interesting inscriptions." The trustees of the British Museum gave Smith six months' leave. "It would have been better to wait until the autumn before starting," Smith wrote, "but I desired there should be no disappointment to the proprietors of *The Daily Telegraph*" – who sought results while the subject was fresh in the public mind.

Smith got useful advice for travelling in what was still the Ottoman Empire from an old Eastern hand and friend Edwin Arnold, already on the staff of the *Telegraph* and in the coming year to become its editor. On January 20, 1873 Smith set off. After the usual difficulties (donkeys, rivers, natives, officials), at nine in the morning on March 2 he reached the ruins of Nineveh.

On May 14 he had time to examine the cuneiform inscriptions gathered from a trench he had dug. "On cleaning one of them I found to my surprise and gratification that it contained the greater portion of 17 lines of inscription belonging to the first column of the Chaldean account of the Deluge, and fitting into the only place where there was a serious blank in the story."

He hurried off to seek a telegraph, and on May 19 at 6pm despatched a telegram which *The Daily Telegraph* printed in its issue of May 21. "I am excavating the site of the King's Library at Nineveh;

which I found without much difficulty. Many fresh objects of high importance have rewarded my search. Since my last message I have come upon numerous valuable inscriptions and fragments of all classes, including very curious syllabaries and bilingual records. Among them is a remarkable table of the penalties for neglect or infraction of the laws. But my most fortunate discovery is that of a broken tablet containing the very portion of the text which was missing from the Deluge Tablet."

The paper was elated: "It will be gathered from the supremely interesting telegram which we have received from the scene of Mr George Smith's labours at Nineveh that a success, eclipsing all his other good fortune, has crowned the energy and ability of our indefatigable Commissioner. He has discovered the missing portions of the famous 'Eleventh Tablet', and this primeval legend of the Deluge will now be completed."

It was "as though certain duodecimo volumes were lying *perdu* under the South Downs, and a few months had been allowed to a party of excavators for the purpose of hitting upon them."

"Mr Smith's errand is thus obviously and successfully fulfilled, so far as regards the Deluge Tablets," the paper judged. In fact, the extra parts of the tablet were to prove less arresting and less like Genesis than those already in the Museum.

The *Telegraph* made a curious statement with which Smith was to take issue: "In reply to his request for instructions, we have desired him to close his labours and to return home. The hot season is now impending, when even at Kouyunjuk and Nimroud work becomes impossible."

This judgment rested on the latter part of Smith's telegram as published: "Immense masses of earth and debris overlie whatever remains to be brought to light in this part of the great Mound. Much time and large sums of money would be required to lay it open. I therefore await instructions from you and the Museum, as the season is closing."

But according to Smith's later account, "from some error unknown to me, the telegram as published differs materially from the one I sent. In particular, in the published copy occur the words 'as the season is closing', which led to the inference that I considered that the proper season for excavating was coming to an end. My own feeling was the contrary of this, and I did not send this." Poor Smith had no choice but to come home.

The British Museum was to pay for his return to Mesopotamia in 1874, and again towards the end of 1875, to excavate the remainder of Assurbanipal's library. But on reaching Baghdad he found to his great disappointment that the disturbed state of the country would allow no excavation. He was worn out by anxiety and fatigue, and his health broke down. He was brought as far as Aleppo, where he died at the British consulate on August 19, 1876.

He left a wife and family, and in October 1876 the public purse was at last opened, to give them a civil list pension of £150 a year, in gratitude for George Smith's "eminent services to biblical research".

INBRIEF

OCTOBER 8, 1897

One million and a half subscribed from private sources to the relief of the Indian famine, and the total expenditure incurred in combating that terrible calamity the vast sum of £10 millions sterling! Such were the splendidly impressive figures submitted yesterday afternoon, at the Mansion House, to the committee presided over by the Lord Mayor. It was the most pleasant of all the meetings which that body have held, for it was the last: their work of mercy is done. The gaunt enemy with whom the Indian Government, nobly seconded by private benevolence at home, has struggled so long and with such magnificent success is at last beaten from the field. Lord George Hamilton was able some time ago to inform Sir George Faudel-Phillips that the fund might now be closed. The rainfall has been propitious, the autumn crop is secure, the prospects of the winter crop are good. It is true that there are still some million and a half of persons in receipt of relief; but these are decreasing week by week by leaps and bounds, and in a few more weeks the relief works in most of the provinces will be discontinued. It has been a long fight this battle of England for the lives of her Indian subjects, which has been thus crowned with such complete victory.

H.M. Stanley (right) in the photographer's studio, dressed as he was the day he found Dr Livingstone. Now, three years later, he was to walk across Africa for The Daily Telegraph

STANLEY IN AFRICA

Uganda – a field for mission and enormous profit

A bloodstained bundle of despatches brought an appeal from an African king that stirred the British imagination

The man renowned for finding Livingstone in the middle of Africa, Henry Morton Stanley, set off on a further journey of exploration "through the Dark Continent" as a result of "strolling over one day to the office of *The Daily Telegraph*".

By Stanley's account it happened like this: "While I was discussing journalistic enterprise in general with one of the staff, the Editor entered. We spoke of Livingstone and the unfinished task remaining behind him. In reply to an eager remark which I made, he asked: 'Could you, and would you, complete the work? And what is there to do?'

"I answered: 'The outlet of Lake Tanganyika is undiscovered. We know nothing scarcely – except what Speke has sketched out – of Lake Victoria; we do not even know whether it consists of one or many lakes, and therefore the sources of the Nile are still unknown. Moreover, the western half of the African continent is still a white blank.'

"'Do you think you can settle all this, if we commission you?'

" 'While I live, there will be something done. If I survive the time required to perform all the work, all shall be done.' "

It was April 1874, not three years since Stanley had spoken the words "Dr Livingstone, I presume" at Ujiji, a week's march from Lake Tanganyika. The discovery had brought him fame, but also jealousy and criticism. Some accused him of stealing Livingstone's papers; some refused to believe he had met Livingstone at all; others said someone else, called Rowlands, had made the discovery. Poor Stanley was cut to the quick, for his birth in Wales had been registered as that of "John Rowlands, Bastard"; it was surname he had forsaken as an adult when the took that of a benefactor, Henry Hope Stanley, whom he met as a young man in America.

Now, when H.M. Stanley visited England he was frozen out by the Royal Geographical Society. But one man who did not shun him was Edwin Arnold. Arnold, who had joined *The Daily Telegraph* in 1861, was a poet and student of oriental religion, but he was also an adventurous traveller who had braved

the terrors of the Indian Mutiny. He struck up a friendship with Stanley, whom he hoped to recruit as a foreign correspondent or "commissioner". This Arnold was able to do when he became a chief editor of the *Telegraph* after the death of Thornton Hunt in 1873. The ground had been prepared by John Le Sage, the reliable engine of the paper's news coverage. He had gone to Marseilles to intercept Stanley on his return from Africa.

In 1874 Livingstone died and his sun-dried body was brought back for an English funeral. Stanley was one of the pall bearers. And Arnold was at the funeral. Arnold shared Stanley's enthusiasm for a new exploration of the African interior, but there was a question of money.

Edward Levy, as he was still called, the future Lord Burnham, not only held the purse-strings of the *Telegraph* but also acted in effect as its editor. Levy realised that he could get Stanley for half price if he shared expenses with the *New York Herald* – with which in any case Stanley had in theory a contract. So Levy sent off a telegram to James Gordon Bennett of the *Herald* – "Would he join *The Daily Telegraph* in sending Stanley out to Africa, to complete the discoveries of Speke, Burton, and Livingstone?" Back came the reply: "Yes. Bennett."

"Two weeks were allowed me for purchasing boats," Stanley wrote, "a yawl, a gig, and a barge – for purchasing equipment, guns, ammunition, rope, saddles, medical stores, and provisions; for making investments in gifts for native chiefs; for obtaining scientific instruments, stationery."

Before setting sail, Stanley was given a farewell dinner by the *Telegraph*, and there he met Captain Fred Burnaby (see page 120), who half promised to meet him at the sources of the Nile. Stanley also acquired, at Arnold's suggestion, the services of two English boatmen, Ted and Frank Pocock, the sons of a Kent fisherman. "Both Mr Arnold and myself warned the Pocock family repeatedly that Africa had a cruel character," Stanley was to recall. Ted died in Africa the next year, and Frank in 1877.

Once Stanley was back in Africa he sent regular despatches to the *Telegraph*, which it honourably shared with the *Herald* week by week. The one that made the biggest impact was Stanley's appeal for a mission to Uganda, where the king had apparently embraced the Ten Commandments. "Where is there in all the Pagan world a more promising field for a mission than Uganda?" asked Stanley.

This despatch, sent in April, was not published till November 1875, and it was exceedingly lucky that it was ever received. Stanley had entrusted his manuscript to Colonel Ernest Linant de Bellefonds, a French explorer travelling with a party of 40 men, who undertook to send it on via British forces on the Nile. "I hope I may see Stanley again, and have the happiness of spending several days with him," Bellefonds wrote in his journal. But his party was set upon by Bari tribesmen and only four lived to reach a British Army station; he was not among them.

Even by November, the *Telegraph* was uncertain how the despatches had got through despite the

INBRIEF

AUGUST 19, 1898
ADVANCE ON KHARTOUM
A new sunbonnet, a sort of poke headgear, has been designed and tried on a thousand camels. Out of these animals, which have marched all the way from Assiout, only one died from the effects of the sun, and that was a camel which had lost its hat.

massacre. "Whether one of the survivors kept possession of the papers, or whether they were flung aside in the forest by the robbers and afterwards found by the detachment sent out by Colonel Gordon, is not even now certain; but the tattered condition of the covers – upon one of which the Italian postmaster, astonished at the blood-stained envelope, has inscribed a memorandum to the effect that it came to hand in that state – leads to the belief that these letters actually lay for days in the African jungle, where they had been thrown away by the ignorant and superstitious savages."

From Stanley's manuscript, the *Telegraph* concluded that he "enjoys at the present hour, we venture to assert, the extraordinary distinction of having revealed to geographers the actual and ultimate fountain of the Nile in the same water-worn Uplands of Central Urimi which he has depicted so well, and from which he tracked the winding Leewumbu – unnamed and unknown before – the stream he afterwards found flowing as the wide Shimeeyu into the Victorian Lakes, the mother source of the Nile."

But it was Stanley's appeal for a Christian missionary initiative that stirred the imagination of the British people. The King of Uganda was ripe for conversion, Stanley averred. "Until I arrived at Mtesa's Court, the King delighted in the idea that he was a follower of Islam; but by one conversation I flatter myself that I have tumbled the newly raised religious fabric to the ground, and, if it were only followed by the arrival of a Christian mission here, the conversion of Mtesa and his Court to Christianity would, I think, be complete."

"Mtesa has determined henceforth," Stanley wrote, "until he is better informed, to observe the Christian Sabbath as well as the Muslim Sabbath, and the great captains have unanimously consented to this. He has further caused the Ten Commandments of Moses to be written on a board for his daily perusal – for Mtesa can read Arabic – as well as the Lord's Prayer and the golden commandment of our Saviour, 'Thou shalt love thy neighbour as thy self'. This is great progress for the few days that I remained with him, and, though I am no missionary, I shall begin to think that I might become one if such success is feasible."

"Here, gentlemen," he urged his readers, "is your opportunity – embrace it! The people on the shore of the Niyansa call upon you. Obey your own generous instincts, and listen to them; and I assure you that in one year you will have more converts to Christianity than all other missionaries united can number. The population of Mtesa's kingdom is very dense; I estimate the number of his subjects as two million. You need not fear to spend money upon such a mission, as Mtesa is sole ruler, and will repay its cost ten fold with ivory, coffee, otter skins of a very fine quality, or even in cattle, for the wealth of this country in all these products is immense. The road here is by the Nile, or via Zanzibar, Ugogo, and Unyanyambe. The former route, so long as Colonel Gordon governs the countries of the

Upper Nile, seems the most feasible." The Nile route did not remain free from dangers; Stanley was not to know that 10 years later Gordon would die at the hands of fanatical followers of the Mahdi.

In the meantime Stanley got down to practical details, the profits to be made and the supplies needed: "I would suggest that the mission should bring to Mtesa as present three or four suits of military clothes, decorated freely with gold embroidery; together with half-a-dozen kepis, a sabre, a brace of pistols, and suitable ammunition; a good fowling piece and rifle of good quality, for the King is not a barbarian; a cheap dinner-service of Britanniaware, an iron bedstead and counterpanes, a few pieces of cotton print, boots, etc. For trade it should also bring fine blue, black and grey woollen clothes, a quantity of military buttons, gold braid and cord, silk cord of different colours, as well as binding; linen and sheeting for shirts, fine red blanket and a quantity of red cloth, with a few chairs and tables. The profit arising from the sale of these things would be enormous.

"For the mission's use it should bring with it a supply of hammers, saws, chisels, axes, hatches, adzes, carpenter's and blacksmith's tools, since the Waganda are apt pupils; iron drills and powder for blasting purposes, trowels, a couple of good sized anvils, a forge and bellows, an assortments of nails and tacks, a plough, spades, shovels, pickaxes, and a couple of light buggies as specimens, with such other small things as their own common sense would suggest to the men whom I invite. Most desirable would be an assortment of garden seed and grain; also white lead, linseed oil, brushes, a few volumes of illustrated journals, gaudy prints, a magic lantern, rockets, and a photographic apparatus. The total cost of the whole equipment need not exceed £5,000 sterling."

The details read like something out of Robinson Crusoe's account of his salvage from the shipwreck. The prospects attracted both those who hoped to save the souls of the "savages" and those who sought "enormous" profits. Perhaps only the fate of the courier of the despatches and his companions cast a shadow on the enterprise.

Certainly the *Telegraph* despatches gave a new brilliancy to the renown of Stanley the explorer, who had another 14 years of African travel in him, concluding with the farcical rescue of the German explorer known as Emin Pasha, who did not in the end want to be rescued. The people of equatorial Africa were indeed brought some missionaries, but the Congo basin fell under the control of Belgium, whose appalling misdeeds were to give Stanley much pain in his old age.

"*The Daily Telegraph* gave Stanley the largest newspaper circulation of the time in this or any other country," Lord Burnham, Edward Levy's grandson, was to write half a century after Stanley's death. "Stanley's articles did more than give Victorian readers thrilling stories of adventure; they had a considerable part in the inspiration of the 19th and early 20th-century development of Africa."

INBRIEF

OCTOBER 18, 1897

NOTES FROM THE SHIRES

Daily experience reveals the unwisdom of paying any great amount of heed to popular belief or current gossip. A few years ago we were assured that fox-hunting, as a sport, was on its last legs. Its final doom was sealed – so, at least, croakers and pessimists persisted in asserting – when wire-fencing came to the front as an effective and cheap and, therefore, generally popular form of protection from the reckless invasion of stock, during the sultry days of springtime and summer. In the Autumn it is customary to send fat stock to market; the great need, then, for the continued erection of what is such a blemish to the landscape in mid-Winter being done away with, what more simple remedy than its temporary removal – such removal being carried out under the superintendents of hunt committees, with, of course, the sanction of farmers themselves? Moreover, the expense involved in taking the wire down and putting it up again at the close of the season is equally, of course, defrayed by subscriptions from those directly benefited. This course has been adopted of late years in the Shires, and has been found to work excellently.

A MONSTER CORRESPONDENT

George Augustus Sala: bombast round the world

Loud and ugly, his nose broken in a fight about champagne, this friend of Dickens knew everything and went everywhere

George Augustus Sala was a monster. A loud, hard-drinking special foreign correspondent, he was proud always to wear a clean white waistcoat each morning, to write two long articles every day and devote much of the night to champagne and the ladies.

He was 28 when he joined the *Telegraph*, two years after its foundation, and like many early *Telegraph* writers he had theatrical connections, his mother being a singer at the Opera House. But Sala was proud of his intellectual strength as well as his bohemian energies, picking up languages easily and never fearing to quote from Shakespeare and the ancient classics.

There was a gentler side to his tastes, for his early career was spent in drawing, he was an extravagant collector of old china and, in a typically over-compensatory way, he made a hobby of detailed engraving although he had the sight of only one eye.

He was an ugly, heavy man with a bulbous nose made less shapely in a famous late-night fight near Leicester Square, after an argument with a brothel-keeper about the price of champagne. At the height of his reputation he was remembered for bursting into the room of the editor-proprietor Edward Lawson late one night, pretty well oiled, and shouting "You bladdy Jew, give me some money!" Indeed the only surviving *Telegraph* archive records of Sala's career are a file of letters requesting advances on salary.

His outlandish behaviour was put up with because of his tremendous energy at home and success in despatching news from foreign assignments; and in any case bohemian journalists were not expected to behave otherwise.

Sala knew the popular market. He had at the age of 20 become the editor of *Chat* – "Facts, Fun, Fiction, and On-Dit, for Rail, Boat, Bus and Cab. Full of Original and Surpassing Wit. Price, One Halfpenny – worth One Shilling".

Later he had worked on Dickens's *Household Words*, and for the *Telegraph* kept off politics, preferring "human and descriptive social essays". He fancied that he knew about everything, and some of his long leading articles read like it. He represented an aspect of the "New Journalism" that antagonised Matthew Arnold: shallow Philistinism behind a facade of learning. In *Friendship's Garland*, Arnold parodies Sala while describing him: "He blends the airy epicureanism of the salons of Augustus with the full-bloodied gaiety of our English cider-cellar."

Sala wrote vividly but his prose is usually fatally full of purple touches and "bombastic circumlocutions" (in the phrase of the biographer Sidney Lee). Among the frequent foreign phrases, not always correctly spelled, elegant variations ("succulent bivalve", "crimson stream of life") alternate with misty archaisms ("withal", "morn", "verily"). Sala must have had some idea of the effect, for *Punch* allowed him to write parodies for them of his own prose. It is also fair to remember that Sala was read with great pleasure by many thousands, and that many younger writers imitated his style.

During his early days with the *Telegraph*, Sala had found time to start the magazine *Temple Bar* in rivalry to the successful *Cornhill*. There was some irony in its name, for one of the achievements of which he was most proud was the later demolition of Temple Bar itself after a campaign of leading articles in the *Telegraph* over several years. Beyond the obstacle that it presented to traffic, Sala's objection to this baroque monument marking the City boundary in Fleet Street was chiefly that Sir Christopher Wren had not known his business in designing it in the first place.

Sala encapsulated his wandering life in a telegram of instruction from the office that he received in Warsaw in 1876: Go Odessa see mob go Constantinople. (In this celebrated telegram, it should be noted that "mob" was short for "mobilisation".) He sent lengthy reports from the American Civil War, from chaotic Spain, from Garibaldi's camp, from the Franco-Prussian War, from St Petersburg and Constantinople, from the United States and Australia. He was well paid – two thousand a year – and thought he earned it.

He spent more than he earned. In the 1890s there was a deterioration of his career with the *Telegraph*, for which he had always contributed as a freelance, never joining the staff, and in 1892 he set up his own paper, *Sala's Journal*. This failed financially. His 15,000 books and his china collection had to be sold; he died at the end of 1895, after being received into the Catholic Church.

Sala togged out in fur coat and boots, with essentials strapped to him in a small bag, ready to 'Go Odessa. See mob.'

From the **Telegraph**
The essential Paris à la mode

April 9, 1899

By a Parisian

Never before, perhaps, has dress been kinder to those who have taste and judgement than at present; never before has it been fuller of pitfalls for the unwary, who, seeking to obey the most stringent dictates of La Mode, have only succeeded in making themselves ridiculous.

Such a pitfall is the up-to-date skirt. Fashion chroniclers urge that it be tighter and tighter, more wispy and raggy each week. Take no heed, for in the multitude of counsellors there is no trust. The well-cut Paris skirt is neither skimpy nor raggy; it is accurately shaped to the hip, but so cut on the bias that it looks neither tight nor strained. This same bias causes it to fall in graceful flutes from the knees, resting well on the ground, and measuring about four yards round at the hem.

Needless to say, this length of skirt necessitates care in one's movements, and craves wary walking, otherwise the result is much tripping and stumbling, neither dignified nor elegant.

Flounces and furbelows are obsolete in the gay capital; plain skirts are the rule, though the tunique is very well worn, and will be even more so, as soft materials such as foulards and voiles come more to the fore.

The illustration (far right) is a gown in the Princesse shape, which will be the leading style throughout the summer. It is in heliotrope pastelle cloth, with yoke and revers of white satin, embroidered in pale blue silk and silver braid; the embroidery is carried down the skirt.

The Princesse style is one to be adopted with

GE FOR WOMEN

discretion, and when well made, and on a good figure, it is the most graceful of modes; but this, again, is another example of the fact that whatever Worth may do for the man, dress does not always make the woman, but the woman does sometimes make the dress, by her personality and her manner of wearing it, converting the most simple garb into an elegant toilette.

Stitching is the ornamentation of the moment in self colours as well as in contrasting, and as it necessitates much time and labour on the part of the workwoman it is not likely that its adoption by the belles of the East End will incur the frowns of West End dames just yet.

Elegant costume, and one which fashion smiles upon just now, is a fine black-faced cloth, the skirt plain trimmed round the hem with several rows of cream silk stitching, fastening on the left side with small silver buttons. The coat is worn open, but caught together at the waist with silver chains and buttons, very short in the basque, with revers of white satin, lightly powdered with embroidered violets, and opening over a blouse of cream satin, with old lace cravat and paste buckle.

It must be remembered that a smart black dress is an essential in a wardrobe of even the most moderate pretensions. It is never out of season, never old-fashioned and always *comme il faut*.

'The well-cut Paris skirt (left), cut on the bias, falls in graceful flutes from the knees.' This fashion piece appeared in the short-lived Sunday Daily Telegraph

THE CHANNEL AND NIAGARA

With Captain Webb, out of sight of land

Matthew Webb swam from Dover to Calais, but then he accepted the challenge of the whirlpool rapids at Niagara Falls

Matthew Webb, the first man to swim the English Channel, was a doctor's son who had learnt to swim in the River Severn. The year before the Channel swim he had accepted a wager to stay in the sea longer than a Newfoundland dog. The creature was pulled from the water "nearly drowned" after an hour and a half, with Webb still going strong.

In 1874 he was awarded a Royal Humane Society medal for jumping from a steamer to try to save a seaman who had fallen from the rigging. In 1875 he was appointed to captain the *Emerald*, of Liverpool. For the rest of his life he was referred to as Captain Webb.

Great public interest was aroused by Webb's announcement of his intention to swim the Channel. An attempt had been made in 1872, and a successful Channel crossing made by Captain Paul Boynton, an American, in May 1875 – but he had been wearing his "patent dress", a sort of lifejacket.

Webb himself failed on August 12, 1875, but tried again on August 24. By the rules, he was not allowed to touch either the sailing boat or two rowing boats that accompanied him, one of which carried the *Telegraph* correspondent.

Webb was 27, 5ft 8in and weighed 14 stone 8lb. He rubbed porpoise grease on his body. He ate nothing during the 21-hour 45-minute swim, but drank ale, beef tea, brandy and hot coffee.

Captain Webb dived off the Admiralty Pier, Dover, at four minutes to one o'clock on that Tuesday afternoon. According to the correspondent, "His pace averaged 26 strokes to the minute" in the ebb tide. "At 1.45 slack water commenced, and Webb being still fresh, he was able with this advantage to increase the direct distance between himself and the shore rapidly. His strokes now averaged 22 per minute, and that speed he continued regularly for several hours. At 2.30 a little rain fell, but it speedily passed off, and a quarter of an hour later the swimmer took his first refreshment, consisting of a small cup of ale.

"At 4 o'clock the floodtide had brought the captain back again abreast the point at which he started, and in the three hours it was reckoned that he had made a direct advance towards the opposite shore of four-and-a-half miles. A thick haze at this time almost hid the heights of Dover, but the weather was warm and calm, and the sea perfectly smooth.

"When Webb had been at his task three-and-a-half hours one of the referees inquired how he felt, and he replied: 'All right,' whereupon the party in the lugger gave a ringing hurrah.

"At 6 o'clock we were a mile outside the South Sands Head light ship, and at that point a large screw steamship, the *Ville de Malacca*, passed uncomfortably close. The swimmer was watched from the poop with astonishment, but our hail was not answered.

"Things went on well until 9.30 when Webb called out that he had been stung on the shoulder by a jellyfish, and he asked for some brandy. At that time there was a perceptible weakening of his strokes, and it was feared that eight-and-a-half hours in the water and the chilly air of the evening were beginning to tell on him." Webb was then about half way.

"At 11.50 the Calais mail steamer *Maid of Kent* came out of her course to pass within hail. The people on board cheered heartily, and the captain reckoned that Webb was then 13-and-a-half miles from the nearest English land."

At two in the morning the referee reported that Webb was growing weaker. "The diver prepared himself and took his seat in the row boat ready for any emergency. Meanwhile a good dose of old brandy was administered, Webb called out: 'All right,' and the diver dressed again.

"Dawn appeared at 4 o'clock, when we lost the Cape Grisnez light altogether. We had indulged the hope that daylight would show Webb some land to cheer him; but for the next hour there was no more sign of land than if we had been in mid ocean. A voice from the row boat requested the skipper to get some hot bricks ready, which seemed ominous of failure.

"At half-past-five, high land loomed through the mist. This land proved to be a bold point to the west of the seaside village of Sangatte. Webb was much gladdened on seeing it, and struck out bravely in that direction. The tide, however, was carrying us to the north east, and land seemed to get no nearer.

"A waste of sand stretching right up to Calais then became the land ahead. It was now 7.30 and Webb had been in the water 18 hours. He was evidently thoroughly fagged, and much distressed by the waves beating in his face.

"The breeze increased, and the lugger had to tack to avoid running away from the swimmer. In passing him at 8 o'clock, he seemed dreadfully distressed, and a contrary wind and tide were buffeting him sorely. The point at which he was aiming seemed to drop away to the south, while the tides driving him towards Calais Sands left him apparently as far from shore as he was an hour

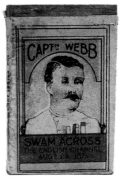

Captain Webb matches bore a more or less accurate image of the hero, with the date of his conquest of the English Channel

In his official photograph, one of the medals pinned to Webb's costume was from the Royal Humane Society, for trying to save a man overboard

earlier. At 9.30 a large row boat with eight persons on board came out and heartily applauded Webb, and, what was more valuable, they rode on the weather side and saved the seas from breaking over him. Up to the last the excitement was most painful; for even when Webb was within 200 yards of the shore it was feared his strength would not hold out to reach it. In strict accordance with the arrangements, no one assisted him in the least.

"As a last encouragement, the rowers pushed down their long oars to show that they could touch the bottom. The excitement increased to the close and when at last Webb did touch ground, the men in the boats around him jumped into the water and fairly hugged him with delight. The news of his approach had spread in town, and a crowd ran down to shore to welcome him, while a carriage stood on the margin of the water ready to drive him to his hotel.

"On landing he was very weak, but, as the boatmen expressed it, 'jolly in his talk' up to the end. He was enveloped in wraps, and driven to the Hotel de Paris, where after being well rubbed down, he drank three or four glasses of old port wine. He went to bed immediately and slept soundly.

On July 24, 1883 Captain Webb set out to swim the rapids and whirlpool at the foot of Niagara Falls. He was then 35 years old. The whirlpool was about a mile below the Old Suspension Bridge, beneath the Grand Falls. "The river narrows considerably here," the *Telegraph* reported, "and the huge volume of water rushes through the rocky gorge with tremendous force and velocity."

"I am going to swim the whirlpool rapids," he told an American reporter who called upon him before the date fixed for the venture, "and I will say it is about the angriest bit of water in the world. They are rough, I tell you, and the whirlpool is a grand one, but I think I am strong enough and skilled enough to get through alive."

Webb's motive was to win the $10,000 prize put up by the railway companies whose lines converged at the Falls. "The people at the Niagara Falls," the *Telegraph* reported, "told him he would be simply committing suicide."

"It was thought, when he saw the terrible torrent of the rapids, with jagged rocks jutting threateningly from each side, and the rush of water so constrained that the middle of the current bulges to a height of 30ft above the sides, with the gruesome whirlpool just beyond, that even he would quail." But he did not.

"When I strike the whirlpool," he said, "I will strike out with all my strength and try to keep away from the suck-hole in the centre. I will begin with the breast stroke and then use overhand strokes. My life will then depend upon my muscles and my breath with a little touch of science behind them."

He was rowed in a small boat to about 300 yards above the Old Suspension Bridge. "He dived into the river at 4 o'clock in the afternoon, and on entering the rapids was almost turned over by the force of the water. He swam the rapids, however, with great determination, being now and again caught sight of by a few of the spectators. When last seen he was entering the whirlpool, and at first appeared to be doing well, but very shortly afterwards threw up his arms and disappeared. He was not seen again."

Captain Webb left a widow and two children.

AMONG THE DERVISHES

The remarkable Fred Burnaby's last adventure

In 1885 an outstanding war correspondent found himself in the thick of a desperate battle next to a very unconventional soldier

I t falls to few war correspondents to report the death of a famous officer stabbed by a Sudanese spearman a few yards away while fighting for his own life with a revolver in a close-run stand against a swarming foe. But in 1885 Bennet Burleigh succeeded in sending some of "the most brilliant war telegrams to be found in the records of journalism" as the *Telegraph* itself claimed at the time. In days when correspondents' names were rarely mentioned, Burleigh's star billing was remarkable. He was to report on 24 wars for the *Telegraph*, but Sudan was very nearly his last.

On January 17, 1885 he was with a force near the Nile in Sudan under Major-General Sir Herbert Stewart on its way to relieve, if there was still time, General Gordon at Khartoum. The evening before, he had talked into the night with another man who was glad to be taking part in the dangerous venture – Colonel Fred Burnaby. Burnaby and Burleigh had chatted at a party a year earlier at the opening of the *Telegraph*'s grand new offices in Fleet Street with their opulent "Pillar Hall". Now one of these two men was to die before another day passed.

Six foot four inches with a 46-inch chest, Burnaby was said to be one of the strongest men in Europe, in his youth once carrying a pony under his arm, and regularly using a dumbell of 1·5 hundredweight.

Burnaby was no conventional soldier. "His voice was thin and piercing," wrote his biographer, "his features Jewish and Italian, and his unEnglish appearance led him to resist attempts to procure portraits of him." Yet in 1870 the fashionable painter James Jacques Tissot caught something of his languorous bravura, as he lounges in the uniform of a captain of the Household Cavalry. It now hangs in the National Portrait Gallery.

Burnaby punctuated his Army career with feats of travel, once setting off for Russian-controlled central Asia immediately he heard the Tsar's government had forbidden Europeans to enter the region. He related his journey in the bestselling *Ride to Khiva* (1876), and another Russian-teasing venture in *On Horseback through Asia Minor* (1877).

In 1885 he was 42, and determined to make one

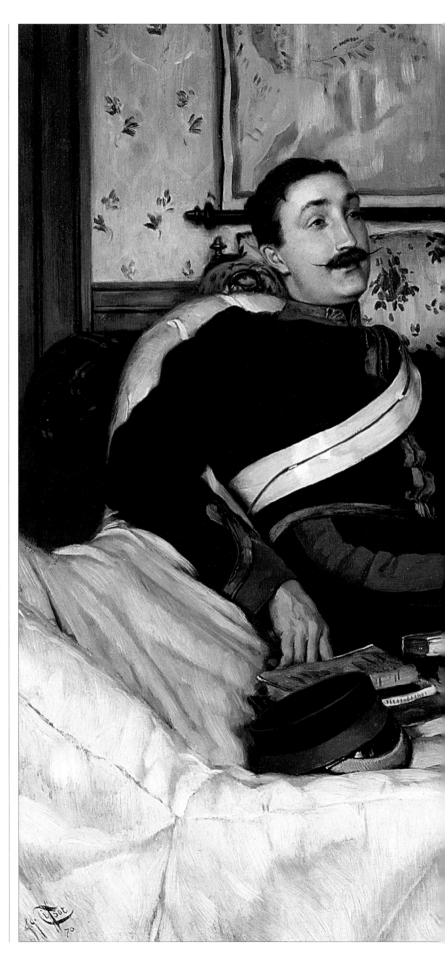

more daring venture – to come to Gordon's rescue. Knowing he would be forbidden the enterprise by headquarters, he put it out that he was on his way to Bechuanaland, and popped up at Abu Klea in Sudan in mid January, expressing his delight to Burleigh that he had arrived in time for the battle against the Mahdi's men.

All Britain, from the Queen down, was in extremities of suspense at the fate of the national hero General Gordon. "Gordon to be saved at any cost", ran one *Telegraph* headline on a Cabinet decision. On January 24, as the relieving force drew nearer Khartoum, the country was jolted by a terrible shock – two dynamitings, one in the House of Commons and one in the Tower of London. No one died; much damage was done, at the heart of Empire, and the Fenians were to blame. Three years earlier, Lord Frederick Cavendish had been knifed down in Phoenix Park, Dublin. The Clerkenwell outrage of 1867 had shown what Fenian dynamite could do. In 1885 Westminster Abbey and the Queen were said to be targets.

The nature of foreign reporting at the time added to the air of suspense. Newspapers carried short telegrams from Sudan a couple of days after the event, but while the outcome of battles or the death of officers were known soon, it took weeks for full details to reach London in despatches sent by post. The news of the British victory at Abu Klea, 80 miles from Khartoum, was known on January 21, and with it the death of Colonel Burnaby. But Bennet Burleigh's full report was strangely delayed. Khartoum had fallen, Gordon was confirmed dead, and the death from wounds of Sir Herbert Stewart himself was known in London before at last on March 4 the *Telegraph* was able to publish Burleigh's account of that desperate day at Abu Klea.

The British force under Stewart there numbered 1,800, including 135 cavalry. There were 2,888 camels and three big guns. They spent the night drawn up in a square with their camels in the centre, in sight of the enemy, who were beating their tom-toms, "beyond all discordant noises successful in irritating a sensitive ear", as Burleigh noted. The men, resting with bayonets fixed, were disturbed by three false alarms of attack during the night. But not all the whizz of bullets above their heads could keep them from an exhausted sleep.

Next morning at 9.30, as the British advanced in a strict square formation over undulating ground, 4,000 or 5,000 of the trained troops of the Mahdi, urged on by Dervishes on horseback, advanced on them "like a vast wave of black surf", their white teeth shining and their arms flashing like thousands of mirrors. Burleigh takes up the story (right).

Previous page: James Jacques Tissot played up Frederick Burnaby's careless languor in his portrait of 1870, with the young captain's plumed cavalry helmet standing beneath a map of the East, and books jumbled beside him on the sofa. Fifteen years later, his opponents were to be the sword-wielding tribesmen of the Sudan (below)

From the Telegraph
The wild strokes of a brave man dying hard

March 4, 1885
From Bennet Burleigh's despatch
Colonel Burnaby himself, whose every action at the time I saw from a distance of about 30 yards, rode out in front of the rear of the left face, apparently to assist two or three of our skirmishers, who were running in hard pressed. I think all but one man of them succeeded in reaching our lines. Burnaby went forward to the men's assistance sword in hand. He told me he had given to his servant to carry that double-barrelled shotgun, which he had used so well against the Hadendowas at El Teb, in deference to the noise made in England by so-called humanitarians against its use. Had it been in his hands Burnaby would easily have saved other lives as well as his own, but they would have been English lives at the expense of Arabs'.

As the dauntless colonel rode forward on a borrowed nag – for his own had been shot that morning – he put himself in the way of a sheikh charging down on horseback. Ere the Arab closed with him a bullet from someone in our own ranks, and not Burnaby's sword thrust, brought the sheikh headlong to the ground. The enemy's spearmen were close behind and one of them suddenly dashed at Colonel Burnaby, pointing the long blade of his spear at his throat. Checking his horse and slowly pulling it backward, Burnaby leant forward in his saddle and parried the Muslim's rapid and ferocious thrusts; but the length of the man's weapon, eight feet, put it out of his power to return with interest the Arab's murderous intent. Once or twice I think the Colonel just touched his man, only to make him more wary and eager.

The affray was the work of three or four seconds only, for the savage horde of swarthy negroes from Kordofan, and the straight-haired tawny-complexioned Arabs of the Bayuda steppe, were fast closing in upon our square. Burnaby fenced smartly, just as if he were playing in an assault at arms and there was a smile on his features as he drove off the man's awkward points. The scene was taken in at a glance – with that lightning instinct which I have seen the desert warriors before now display in battle while coming to one another's aid – by an Arab who, pursuing a soldier, had passed five paces to Burnaby's right and rear. Turning with a sudden spring, this second Arab ran his spear into the Colonel's right shoulder.

It was a slight wound – enough, though, to cause Burnaby to twist around in his saddle to

defend himself from this unexpected attack. Before the savage could repeat his unlooked-for blow – so near the ranks of the square was the scene now being enacted – a soldier ran out and drove his sword-bayonet through the second assailant. As the Englishman withdrew the steel, the Arab wriggled round and sought to reach him. The effort was too much, however, even for his delirium of hatred against the Christian, and the rebel reeled and fell.

Brief as was Burnaby's glance backward at this fatal episode, it was long enough to enable the first Arab to deliver his spear-point full in the brave officer's throat. The blow drove Burnaby out of the saddle, but it required a second one before he let go his grip of the reins and tumbled upon the ground. Half a dozen Arabs were now about him. With the blood gushing in streams from his gashed throat, the dauntless Guardsman leapt to his feet, sword in hand, and slashed at the ferocious group. They were the wild strokes of a proud, brave man dying hard, and he was quickly overborne and left helpless and dying. The heroic soldier who sprang to his rescue was, I fear, also slain in the mêlée, for – though I watched for him – I never saw him get back to his place in the ranks.

The charge of the Arabs carried many of them into the centre of our square and among the camels. There death and havoc rioted for two or three minutes, whilst our men moved off from the inextricable mass of wounded, dying, and dead camels. It was an awful scene, for many alas! of the

In the fierce mêlée at the battle of Abu Klea, Burnaby was unhorsed by an Arab spear, and with blood pouring from his throat slashed with his sword at the ferocious group assailing him. Fred Burnaby was 42 and looking for one more adventure to add to his extraordinary career

wounded left behind on the cacolets and litters perished by the hands of the merciless Arabs, infuriated by their sheikhs, whose wild hoarse cries rent the air, whilst the black spearmen, entangled among the animals, ran hither and thither thirsting for blood.

Amid the general calamity there were many providential escapes. Lord St Vincent, who, with another wounded man, was being borne upon a pair of camel-litters, was overturned with his camel, and fell underneath; the wounded man, who was on the opposite side, was killed, and Airlie owed his life to the accident. Trifling as was the obstacle offered by the heap of helpless animals, it was enough to break the rush of Arabs. So great at this moment was the peril of the situation that officers in the Guards and Mounted Infantry placed their men back to back to make a desperate battle for life. The Martini-Henrys never ceased, for hundreds of men kept firing with good aim at the enemy. There were others, I regret, who were neither discreet nor careful as to the direction of their fire.

At this stage, seeing the Arabs were no respecters of person, I myself took up a Martini-Henry, but the third cartridge stuck, and I had to resort to my revolver. Our men were now nearly all clustered around the circular mound, with a swarm of Arabs fighting upon what was originally the left and rear faces of the square; the others were still hanging back undecided among the wreck of camels. The column kept backing with their faces outward towards the top of the low mound, until they were wedged in a compact mass. To me, who was outside on the right face, they appeared to spin and turn slowly around the mound, a whirlpool of human beings.

The position luckily enabled them to deliver a heavy and withering fire into the dense mass of Arabs. Soon the enemy showed signs of wavering, and with cheers and shouts our men redoubled their fire. A young officer, whose name I did not learn, rallied a number of men on the right rear and these being soon joined by others were able to deliver an excellent and most telling transverse fire into the enemy's ranks. The strained tension of the situation had lasted nearly 10 minutes, when at last the Arabs, two or three at first, then in twenties and fifties, began to trot off the field. In five minutes more there was not an enemy to be seen standing within 300 yards of us. With cheer upon cheer, shouting ourselves hoarse we hailed our victory, dearly won as all knew it to be.

We found our losses during the day were, roughly, including native camel drivers, over 100 killed and about 200 wounded. Of the enemy, five or six hundred lay heaped in front of and around our dead camels, and I think nearly as many more fell on the hillside and in the wady.

YOUNG CHURCHILL

Forceful letters from the North-West Frontier

Winston Churchill in his early twenties wanted fame in battle, a start in politics and an income. He turned to the Telegraph

That Winston Churchill should at the age of 22 be writing war reports for *The Daily Telegraph* from the North-West Frontier of India at £5 a column came about by a coincidence of chances. Churchill was seeking fame and fortune in some war; he had already taken a look at the war in Cuba. Then, as an officer of the Fourth Hussars, he went out to India.

In the summer of 1897 the tribesmen of Swat and neighbouring valleys north of Peshawar, stirred up by the Mad Mullah, had rebelled, and it was the task of General Sir Bindon Blood to put them down. Churchill had made friends with Sir Bindon a year before and got him to promise that if he led another expedition he would allow him to join it.

Now he read in the papers of the general's new task, which became known as the Malakand campaign, from a settlement on a tributary to the river Swat. Churchill immediately set off from leave in England for India, wiring the general as he went. Within three weeks Sir Bindon was good enough to write from his camp in Upper Swat, unable to offer a staff post, but advising Churchill to come as a press correspondent.

But for which paper? Churchill got his mother to act as his agent. *The Times* had already asked Lord Fincastle, but she had better luck with Edward Lawson, the *Telegraph*'s proprietor, who replied to her letter by telegram: "Tell him to post picturesque forcible letters." The pay was £5 a column, half what Churchill had hoped.

He was to have 15 letters published, from the first week in October, under the name "A Young Officer". Letters they were, being a month old by the time they were printed. The headline news from the campaign was published within a day or two via telegraph. Churchill was not happy. "I will not conceal my disappointment at their not being signed," he wrote to his mother. He had aimed at "bringing my personality before the electorate." Hardly anything in the *Telegraph* at that time was signed; only some of the poetry of Sir Edwin Arnold, or a survey of drama by Clement Scott.

And £5 was not enough: "I will not accept less

Churchill in the uniform of the Fourth Hussars. His posting to India promised a chance to earn money from journalism. His mother wrote to the Telegraph's proprietor, who replied: 'Tell him to post picturesque, forceful letters.'

than £10 a letter and I shall return any cheque for a less sum." It is not known that he did. "I do not think that I have written anything better." It was all so frustrating: "When I think of the circumstances under which those letters were written, on the ground in a tent temperature of 115 degrees or after a long day's action." Then what should he find but that in one letter the paper had printed "the word 'frequent' where I wrote 'pregnant'. This of course makes rubbish."

The letters are indeed pretty good writing. Since Churchill was seconded to a punitive expedition, in the Mamund valley 50 miles west of Malakand, the account of burning villages reads rather uncomfortably to a modern eye. But the hard details are there – the smoke from the thatch "blue against the mountains, brown against the sky". And there is none of the bombast that mars the writing of Sala and his school.

Sir Bindon made good use of Churchill, whom he mentioned in despatches, though he did not win the VC that Sir Bindon hoped. Lord Fincastle did, and wrote a book on the campaign. Churchill survived, and the despatches he wrote for the *Telegraph* helped him put together his own book, *The History of the Malakand Field Force*, which sold 8,500 copies in the succeeding year.

From the **Telegraph**

Churchill reports on a strange war on the edge of India

October 14, 1897

By a Young Officer, Camp Inayat Kila, September 17
We were breakfasting at Nawagai when everyone was surprised by the arrival of a native officer with an escort of 11th Bengal Lancers who had ridden "trot and gallop" with the news of the night's fighting. "Three British officers and 12 native soldiers killed and wounded – six hours' action – and a cavalry pursuit," such were the outlines of the message.

Permission having been granted me to accompany the returning escort and join the second Brigade for the impending engagement, I selected a scanty but judicious outfit – of which the most important items were chocolate, a waterproof, and a toothbrush – and started. Presently we emerged into the broad plains of Nawagai, and looked around for signs of the camp.

Right across the spacious plateau lay a long brown string of marching men and mules. The Brigade was moving into the Watelai Valley to a convenient camping ground from which to direct the punitive operations against their assailants of the night before. The blazing thatch of three or four fortified villages sent a high column of smoke into the air – blue against the mountains, brown against the sky. The troops were halted on the site of their resting place for the night, and as the small party with which I was riding arrived, the cavalry came back from the pursuit and began to look to their horses. The bright steel of the lance points was here and there dulled by red streaks and blotches. A sowar displayed his with pride. "How many altogether?" was the question asked on all sides. "Twenty-one, but they are still game; there will be another attack tonight," answered an officer.

Everyone was eager to talk of the events of the night before. How they had had no sleep. How they had lain prone while the bullets whistled in from all quarters. Of the daring of the enemy. Of the composure of the troops. Of the general discomfort and danger. The doolies of the field hospital passed, each with its pale, stricken occupant. One contained poor Harrington, so dangerously wounded that while I write his life is despaired of. The tents showed many bullet-holes, and everyone looked tired and drawn.

"You were lucky to be out of it last night," they said; "but there's plenty more coming." The camp showed that this belief was general. Everyone was digging a hole – a kind of soup-plate – in the earth in which to sleep. The shelter trench thrown up all round the sides was higher than usual. The hospital was protected by flour bags and boxes. It was not difficult to realise what all this meant.

But the expected attack did not come off.... Desultory firing continued at intervals throughout the night – some 200 or 300 shots were fired – without injuring anyone, and without awakening those who had been up the previous night. The

North-West Frontier: setting up a Maxim gun

camp was full of noise. The challenges of the sentries, the squeaking of the mules, the firing of the picquets, divested the night of all solemnity.

Here was no place for reflection. It displayed a life lived only in the present. There might be fighting tomorrow. Some people might be killed or wounded. It was sufficient to be alive for the moment; and the camp shrugged its shoulders, and, regarding the past without regret, contemplated the future without alarm.

October 26, 1897

By a Young Officer, Inayat Kila, October 2
It was evident, as the Guides cavalry approached the hills, that resistance was contemplated. Several red standards were visible to the naked eye, and the field glass disclosed numerous figures lining the various ridges and spurs. The squadrons, advancing as far as the scrub would allow them, soon drew the fire of isolated skirmishes. Several troops dismounted and returned the salute with their carbines, and at 8.45 a dropping musketry fire began.

The action was begun by the Guides Infantry storming the ridges to the left of the enemy's position. These were strongly held and fortified by stone walls – called sangars – behind which the defenders were sheltered. The Guides advanced briskly, and without much firing, across the open ground to the foot of the hills. The tribesmen, shooting from excellent cover, maintained a hot fire. The bullets kicked up the dust, or whistled viciously through the air; but the distance was short, and it was soon apparent that the enemy did not mean to abide the assault.

When the troops got within a hundred yards and fixed bayonets a dozen determined men were still firing from the sangars. The Afridi and Pathan companies of the Guides – uttering shrill cries of exultation, culminating in an extraordinary yell – dashed forward, climbed the hill as only hillmen can climb, and cleared the crest. On the side of the next hill the figures of the retreating tribesmen were visible. A good many fell, subsiding peacefully, and lying quite still, and their fall was greeted by strange little yelps of pleasure from the native soldiers. These Afridi and Pathan companies suggest nothing so much as a well-trained pack of hounds, for their cries, their movements, their natures are similar.

The village was carried with the bayonet and partially destroyed. But the pressure of the enemy now became so strong that the brigadier ordered the retirement to commence. As usual the enemy pressed the withdrawal, but with less vigour than on former occasions. This close fighting leads to heavy loss, but it tells equally on both sides.

The loss in killed and wounded was four officers and 56 men. It may be thought that this list of casualties does not justify the employment of such expressions as "severe fighting", "heavy loss", etc. But the severity of an action should be judged by the proportion the casualties bear to the number engaged.

This is a strange war and the more I see the more do I realise the difficulty of conveying a true picture to the Englishman at home.

BUDDHA ON THE DISTRICT LINE

The orientalist who wanted to be Poet Laureate

Edwin Arnold seemed an unlikely editor, carrying a bag of jewels and writing his books of verse on the Underground

To be an expert in oriental languages and the author of a biography of Buddha in verse were unusual accomplishments for the editor of a popular London newspaper even in the 19th century. Edwin Arnold (1832–1904) was to give the *Telegraph* much of its flavour in Victoria's last four decades.

He fell into journalism even more carelessly than most. In 1860, aged 28, he and his wife returned from India, where he had been principal of the Deccan College in Poona during the days of the Indian Mutiny, uncertain times even if the uprising did not engulf the city. While boating in Falmouth harbour Arnold picked up a copy of the *Athenaeum* magazine and saw an advertisement for a leader-writer on *The Daily Telegraph*. "Shall I apply?" he asked his wife. "If I do it will probably be given to me."

Arnold's confidence might have seemed ill-founded when he was interviewed by Edward Levy, acting as editor and proprietor.

"Have you ever been inside a newspaper office?" asked Levy.

"No."

"Have you ever written a leading article?"

"No, but I've written some poetry."

"Do you think you could do a leading article?"

"I think so. But at any rate, if you like, I'll try."

"Very well. Go into the next room and write me something about the threatened war between Denmark and Prussia."

What Arnold produced must have pleased Levy, for he found himself immediately on the staff of the paper. According to a variant tale by his son Julian, Arnold's task had been writing two articles, one on "blush roses", the other on "steel filing". The subjects were no less likely than the Prusso-Danish war, given the vast range that Arnold tackled over the following 40 years. In his first week he wrote six leaders, each a rambling affair of 1,200 or 1,500 words.

The blustering foreign correspondent George Augustus Sala says in his memoirs that Arnold's prose displayed "an Oriental exuberance of epithets". It was a little unfair, commented Levy's grandson, Lord Burnham, to be accused by Sala of all men of such a trait. Arnold was undoubtedly an energetic writer, who displayed great concentration as he sat at a small table in the centre of the room in the old *Telegraph* offices, beneath "a single window, seldom washed save by London's sooty rain", scratching away with pen and ink. He'd as happily use the kitchen poker, so long as he could get his thoughts down. Printers had to be cryptographers in those days of scrawled longhand. All Arnold asked was not to be spoken to while he wrote. "If the string of thought be suddenly broken," he said, "the pearls that were strung thereon are scattered, and none may find them again."

That sentence illustrates something of his weakness. His prose is clichéd, artificial and nebulous. It was no worse, though, than many contemporary journalists', and he had some things to say. Tastes have changed, and Arnold's literary reputation was already established. As an Oxford undergraduate he had won the University's Newdigate prize with a poem on Belshazar's Feast, which he declaimed in the baroque splendour of Wren's Sheldonian Theatre. It formed the centrepiece of a volume of poetry published in 1853, when he was still only 21. "In America, many years later," wrote a contemporary, "Matthew Arnold found himself credited to an embarrassing extent with the poetical baggage of his namesake."

Edwin Arnold was quietly convinced of his own poetic skills. When Tennyson died, in 1892, he was one of three informal claimants to succeed him as poet laureate whose names were put to the Prime Minister, W.E. Gladstone, who had just formed his last administration. The other two were Lewis Morris and Alfred Austin. George Augustus Sala, opined that Arnold's poetic star shone only less brightly than Algernon Charles Swinburne's, and that next in order came Alfred Austin, Lewis Morris and William Morris.

Gladstone was not so sure. At first he wanted John Ruskin, even though Ruskin had denounced him in print. But Ruskin, he learned, had lost the use of his reason. He then favoured William Morris or Swinburne. But it would have been impossible to propose their names to the Queen, for William Morris was technically a Communist and Swinburne contained elements of "licentiousness". Lewis Morris's poetry was found wanting, as indeed it might.

The post was left unfilled for nearly four years, and the next Prime Minister but one, Lord Salisbury, after Kipling had declined the offer, plumped for Austin. At least Austin was better than is suggested by his present reputation among people who have not read him. Arnold sent him the remarkable telegram: "Accept my heartiest congratulations with which no grudge mingles, although I myself expected the appointment."

Arnold had a practical side, as a carpenter, a traveller and yachtsman. Into old age he liked to dress in a loose dark-blue yachting suit, his pockets

INBRIEF

JULY 25, 1885

If the Mahdi be really dead, he has done civilisation a good service. What a weird majesty there was about this man, who controlled, as if with Solomon's signet ring, the evil genii of ruin, carnage, and fierce fanaticism! How spectral was his appearance upon the scene, far away in the Southern Sudan! He stepped out from his cell on the riverbank and, facing the Mollahs and the dervishes, said: "I am He." They scoffed at him; but he went forth into the Desert and told the dwellers in tents, that he was the Mahdi, the herald of the Millennium – that first "blast of consternation" which the Muslims say precedes the Resurrection, levelling the infidel people as a hurricane lays the corn, and thrilling the faithful as with the sound of an archangel's trumpet. And they presently believed him; put on his uniform, braided with those texts from the Koran which promise everlasting Paradise to such as die for the Faith in fight against the unbeliever. Tribes rallied to him for his name alone. All Islam was up at the sound of it. The Mollahs and the dervishes vainly said: "This is not He," and set to work with computations of time and commentaries on prophecy to prove that they were right. Victory in battle was Mahomed Achmet's answer. Was not all the Sudan in his hand? Lower Egypt itself was threatened; Arabia became ripe for outbreak; the Turks grew troubled. Alone, this one man, a penniless dervish, had let loose the torrent which more than once in history has been the terror of the human race. Everything appeared to lie within his grasp. The hour of triumph was already striking – had, indeed, struck – when, on a sudden – Azrael whispered in his ear, and Mahomed Achmet "the Mahdi" the "Guided one," and Guider, laid down dominion and power, and turned and went forth with the Angel of Death.

Edwin Arnold liked to relax with a pipe and text in Persian, which he had mastered, along with Hindi, Urdu, Sanskrit and Turkish, as well as the usual European languages, living and dead

behind Stanley's being sent back to walk across Africa; he arranged for George Smith to go to Mesopotamia and dig for cuneiform tablets recounting the story of the Deluge; he sent H.H. Johnston to climb Kilima-Njaro (as the *Telegraph* spelled it) in 1884. Whatever his own writing style, he was valued as a re-write man *avant le mot*, and it was said that Bennet Burleigh's standing owed a good deal to Arnold's presentation of his despatches.

But Arnold's enduring reputation rests on *The Light of Asia* (1879), his book-length verse interpretation of the life and teaching of the Buddha. T.S. Eliot read it as a child, and it suggested to him a future passage in *The Wasteland*. It sold a million in the United States, from which Arnold profited not a penny, the copyright laws being then unsettled.

Arnold composed some of the poem in his bungalow at Southend and some on the District Line of the Underground as he travelled to and fro, between his house in South Kensington and Fleet Street. He would write fragments not only on the margin of the newspaper he carried or on the insides of envelopes torn open, but even on his shirt cuffs, so that many of those pearls were lost in the wash. He then assembled the surviving scraps of paper into codices or bundles which he called "brick piles". From these he copied the final work into a blank book.

The Light of Asia received some denunciations from the pulpit and one full-length book in rejoinder, not so much because it explicated Buddhism as because it implied a less than universal claim for Christianity.

In 1891 Arnold published *The Light of the World*, on Jesus. The subject was thought to be familiar, the poetry was less exotic and the sales were a disaster.

"I remember him as a rugged, rather ugly old man in a black velvet skull-cap," wrote Lord Burnham 50 years after his death. "This was not a habit of old age, as he had worn it for many years."

"It seems strange to say," remembered Margaret Scott, the wife of the paper's renowned drama critic, "but when speaking to me of death, as he did on many occasions, Edwin Arnold appeared to await it with almost eager curiosity." He outlived two wives, and after his second bereavement in 1889 left the office where he had been "a chief editor" for 16 years and set off as a travelling "commissioner" or correspondent.

With his daughter he roamed the Pacific coast and his beloved Japan. There he found a third wife, Tama Kurokawa from Sendai, aged 20, and they returned to England. Even a decade after the Japanese Exhibition in London, knowledge of Japan among the English had generally not gone much beyond *The Mikado*. Tama Arnold appeared pretty but isolated to visitors to her new home in Bolton Gardens. There she remained amid the cherry blossom of South Kensington when in 1904 Arnold breathed his last.

bulging with carpenter's tools. Above a grizzled beard his face was tanned from the sun and wind. He had an ungrasping attitude, sometimes giving away the libraries of books he had collected; he liked to relax after a hard day's writing with a pipe of tobacco and Persian text.

A truly unusual habit of Arnold's was to carry jewels, cut and uncut, about with him – not for the sake of their value, but for their colour. In the bazaars of Ceylon he had bought a bagful of sapphires, garnets, rubies, emeralds and other gemstones.

With his carpenter's tools he would bore a small hole in the edge of a sideboard, the back of a chair, the newel-post of the stairs, and there set a jewel. Members of the family would find a topaz in the handle of a hairbrush or a piece of purple spar in an umbrella handle.

Arnold mastered Hindi, Urdu, Sanskrit, Persian and Turkish, apart from the usual European languages, living and dead. (As a little boy he had hidden a Greek New Testament inside his prayer book to beguile the hour of Sunday service.) He put his interests in exotic lands to good use. He was

PART 2
Edwardians and Georgians 1901-1952

News for the million

Welfare and warfare

*Soldiers of the British
Expeditionary Force at
Southampton station on
their way for embarkation
at the beginning of the
Second World War,
under a sign promising
'News as it is'*

News for the million

The first half of the 20th century was peculiarly shaped by the press, which worked a growing audience. From a newspaper for a solid middle-class core, the Telegraph

OUT OF THE DOLDRUMS

From 100,000 to a million circulation

Less stuffy than The Times, less vulgar than the Mail, the Telegraph recruited a new kind of reader – and crossword solver

The *Telegraph* ran into the doldrums before its revival in 1928 under the ownership of the Berry family. It was caught between the populism of the halfpenny *Daily Mail* (founded 1896) and the establishment claims of *The Times*, revived by the *Mail*'s owner, Lord Northcliffe.

"I read *The Times*, but I suppose that is because I was brought up on it," said the future King George V when he visited the *Telegraph* offices as Prince of Wales. "The Princess reads the *Telegraph* and tells me what is in it."

The First World War pushed the *Telegraph*'s price up to 2d. Ten years after the Armistice its circulation had fallen to 84,000. The front page, as with *The Times*, was all small advertisements. There was no regular use of photographs, even in the Twenties, except for events such as the sinking of the *Titanic* in 1912 or for the death of kings.

In 1901 the editor was John Le Sage, if anyone. He was vague about the matter, noting in *Who's Who* only that he had been "managing editor for many years". While Edward, now Sir Edward, Lawson was still around, he called the shots. But in 1903 he accepted a peerage, and as Lord Burnham kept his shots for the pheasants, of which 3,937, with the help of George V, died one day to mark his 80th birthday. Hundreds were presented to members of staff.

By then, editing under Burnham's son Harry Lawson, Le Sage was in his seventies. "His appearance was that of a rather dull and stupid man," remarked the Fourth Lord Burnham later, "but he was far from being either." The trouble was, he wouldn't go, but stayed on till 1923 to complete his 60 years in Fleet Street. He died in 1926, aged 88.

The paper wasn't entirely moribund, and an enduring selling-point, the crossword, was introduced on July 30, 1925 – well before *The Times* first published one on February 1, 1930. The *Telegraph* announced its entrance only by the heading TO-DAY'S CROSSWORD PUZZLE. There were no instructions as to what to do with it. Readers would have seen examples in magazines, since crosswords first appeared in America at the end of 1913. They had become something of a craze.

The early crosswords were practically quiz-words. A typical clue was: "Wrote *The Rape of the Lock*" (answer: Pope). The solution appeared next day, as now, written into a reduced grid. Later, for some years, answers were merely listed, to save space.

No one thought of giving a number to each day's crossword until a couple of years later – on June 6, 1927. That was No 530. I hope someone had worked out the number carefully.

The weirdest passage in the *Telegraph* crossword's history came in 1944, when answers to clues gave code-names connected with the D-Day landings on June 6. On May 3, 1944 the answer to 17 across ("One of the US") was Utah. This was the code-name of a landing beach. On May 22, the answer sought was Omaha, another beach. On May 27 the solution to a clue was Overlord, the name for the whole D-Day operation. On May 30, it was Mulberry (a type of floating harbour to be used). Lastly, on June 1, the answer to a clue was Neptune, the code-name for the naval assault phase.

It was too much to be coincidence, although it is hard to see how it could have helped the enemy, who did not know where the invading force would strike. MI5 sent two men to call on Leonard Dawe, the compiler of the crosswords. Poor Dawe felt grateful not to be shot, but could provide no explanation.

In 1984 Ronald French came forward with the information that he had been a schoolboy at the

New owners built monumental offices in 1930 (top), on the fifth floor of which the proprietor's lawn was tended. In 1925 came the first crossword (right, solution on page 256)

in partnership with the cinema and radio to create celebrities and package news for transformed itself into a daily that was read by millions

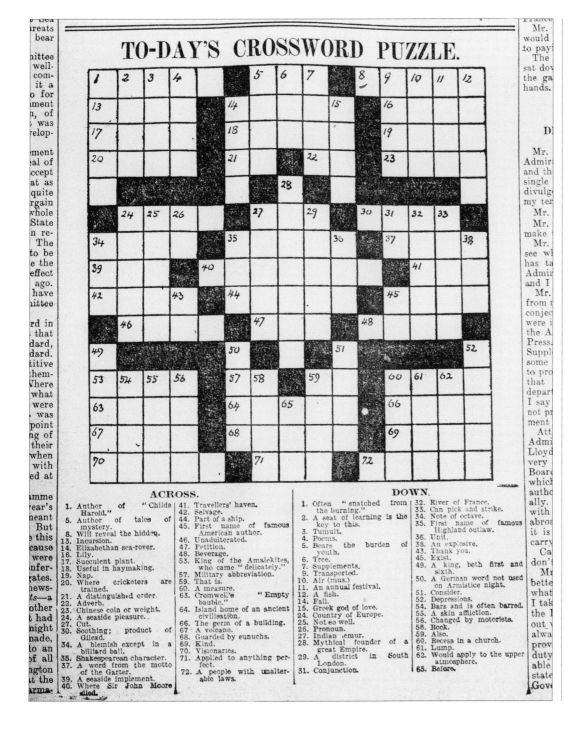

TO-DAY'S CROSSWORD PUZZLE.

ACROSS.

1. Author of "Childe Harold."
5. Author of tales of mystery.
8. Will reveal the hidden.
13. Incursion.
14. Elizabethan sea-rover.
16. Lily.
17. Succulent plant.
18. Useful in haymaking.
19. Nap.
20. Where cricketers are trained.
21. A distinguished order.
22. Adverb.
23. Chinese coin or weight.
24. A seaside pleasure.
27. Cut.
30. Soothing; product of Gilead.
34. A blemish except in a billiard ball.
35. Shakespearean character.
37. A word from the motto of the Garter.
39. A seaside implement.
40. Where Sir John Moore died.
41. Travellers' haven.
42. Selvage.
44. Part of a ship.
45. First name of famous American author.
46. Unadulterated.
47. Petition.
48. Beverage.
53. King of the Amalekites, who came "delicately."
57. Military abbreviation.
59. That is.
60. A measure.
63. Cromwell's "Empty bauble."
64. Island home of an ancient civilisation.
66. The germ of a building.
67. A volcano.
68. Guarded by eunuchs.
69. Kind.
70. Visionaries.
71. Applied to anything perfect.
72. A people with unalterable laws.

DOWN.

1. Often "snatched from the burning."
2. A seat of learning is the key to this.
3. Tumult.
4. Poems.
5. Bears the burden of youth.
6. Tree.
7. Supplements.
9. Transported.
10. Air (mus.)
11. An annual festival.
12. A fish.
14. Fall.
15. Greek god of love.
24. Country of Europe.
25. Not so well.
26. Pronoun.
27. Indian lemur.
28. Mythical founder of a great Empire.
29. A district in South London.
31. Conjunction.
32. River of France.
33. Can pick and strike.
34. Note of octave.
35. First name of famous Highland outlaw.
36. Unit.
38. An explosive.
43. Thank you.
45. Exist.
49. A king, both first and sixth.
50. A German word not used on Armistice night.
51. Consider.
52. Depressions.
54. Bars and is often barred.
55. A skin affliction.
56. Changed by motorists.
58. Rock.
59. Also.
60. Recess in a church.
61. Lump.
62. Would apply to the upper atmosphere.
65. Before.

INBRIEF

APRIL 2, 1910

By Mrs Eric Pritchard

It is the fashion today to look young. A century ago women were content to give up their youth (as far as appearances were concerned) at 40; today we practically have no old ladies, and to be old just when we have learnt the secret of youth and the art of dressing would be an insult no less to modern intelligence than to dressmakers and beauty specialists.

With what a short reign those charming ladies of Early Victorian era were content – they wore bonnets and caps at 40. What would they think of the motor bonnet and the lace bedroom cap worn by the women of the same age today?

What would perhaps astonish them most would be the fact of married women dancing in short frocks. As a matter of fact, this is not a suitable or dignified style of dressing for the older woman. For the debutante who has no experience of managing a train it is an admirable fashion, and especially designed to meet her needs; in fact, for evening wear till this season the dress of the girl and the matron were too similar to point to the necessary contrasts.

For no matter how young women are, and how young they look today, they do not want to pose as debutantes unless they happen to be so. Therefore, it is as well to consign the short dancing frock to youth.

school where Dawe was headmaster, which had been evacuated to Effingham, Surrey. French said that Dawe would sometimes ask boys to help fill in blank grids for crosswords, for which he would then devise clues. The young French had, by his account, learnt some D-Day code-words from Canadian and US servicemen camped near the school; he remembers the words being fairly common knowledge there. "Hundreds of kids must have known what I knew," he said.

But newspapers don't live by crosswords alone, and again, as in 1855, a price cut came to the aid of the circulation. It was the brave action of Sir William Berry (who had just taken control of the paper from the Lawsons) to reduce the price to 1d at the end of 1929. From 100,000 in November 1929 circulation leapt to 200,000 in January 1930, and rose by 50,000 a year or more from then on. Circulation in wartime was limited by paper shortages, so the magic number of a million was delayed until April 1947. "This is the first time in the newspaper history of the world that any quality newspaper has achieved a million sale," the front page proclaimed.

It was a job to print so many each night. The Berry family had installed new presses when they bought the paper two decades before, and a more visible change was the demolition of the high-Victorian office building in Fleet Street and its replacement in 1930 with a splendid and gigantic Art Deco pile. A small lawn was tended for the proprietor outside his fifth-floor office.

When the Berry family bought the paper, they retained Arthur Watson, who had been editor since 1924, and on the staff since 1902. He was to remain editor until 1950, under William Berry, later Viscount Camrose, as editor-in-chief. The history of the paper under its new owners has been well sketched by Duff Hart-Davis in his book *The House the Berrys Built* (1990).

Camrose wielded his power responsibly, opposing the appeasement of Hitler at a period when *The Times* gained some popularity by pursuing the contrary policy. The *Telegraph* showed sympathy for the unemployed during the depression and kicked against the post-war government's interference in personal liberties.

The readers didn't care who the editor was, and probably did not notice when Colin Coote took over in 1950. Not all the staff cared for his Olympian manner. "Oh, if only I shared the editor's utter indifference about what appears in this newspaper," remarked the satiric Malcolm Muggeridge, in his short-lived post as deputy editor.

Still, the Tories won the election the next year. Lord Camrose was, in his early seventies, still active. Circulation and advertising were booming. Then, on February 7, 1952 the *Telegraph*, with a special eight-page supplement tucked inside, carried the biggest headline it had ever run, over all eight columns. DEATH OF KING GEORGE VI. It was unexpected. His daughter, now the Queen, was in a Kenya game reserve 5,000 miles away. With her long reign a new age had begun.

THE MUST-HAVE CORSET
Perfection with the kindness of the New Curve

Wasp-waisted corsets had exerted a cruel tyranny in Edward's reign. With the new king a softer outline was more desirable

The female figure was required to grow narrower and narrower in the waist as the reign of Edward VII progressed. By 1908 a fashion writer exclaimed, "The present figure aimed at is calculated to drive despair to the heart of the irretrievably buxom." The corset became obligatory, even under bathing costumes. "The corsets are now cut so deep," one sufferer complained, "that to sit down appears an impossible feat."

There was money in corsets. In 1912, with George V on the throne, the Royal Worcester corset company was taking full-page illustrated advertisements in *The Daily Telegraph* to announce, after 50 years' development, "the undeniably perfect corset". Prices ranged from 10s 11d to 42 shillings – the weekly wage for a labourer.

Corsets gave quite a pictorial lift to the pages of type in 1912 when the *Telegraph* carried no pictures at all in most issues. With their elaborate structure, corsets were deemed permissible in a family newspaper; a coupon with the advertisement offered a "Souvenir Booklet" for the more curious.

Women feared they had done permanent damage with the wasp-waisted corsets of the day,

The American advertisers of the 'Royal Worcester' corset regarded the good conditions in their factories – 'where every stitch is guided by conscience' – as almost as much of a selling-point as the endlessly adaptable virtues of the corsets themselves

THE UNDENIABLY PERFECT CORSET—THE ROYAL WORCESTER
Which has exerted so Vast an Influence on Corsage and Dress during the past Half-Century

ROME WAS NOT BUILT IN A DAY. NEITHER IS A GOOD REPUTATION. EVERY ROYAL WORCESTER CORSET IS BACKED BY FIFTY YEARS' SUSTAINED REPUTATION. PROVED MERIT OUTLIVES MERE CLAIMS.

Model 961. Price 42/- FOR FULL FIGURES   *Model 951. Price 49/6 FOR AVERAGE FIGURES*   *Model 962. Price 21/9 FOR FULL FIGURES*   *Model 928. Price 27/6 FOR AVERAGE FIGURES*

Carelessly-developed Figures

WORK IS BEAUTIFUL

THE HOUR, THE MAN, AND THE CORSET

THE HOUR

THE MAN U.S.A.

DAVID H. FANNING, the Founder and

COMPARATIVELY FEW ARTICLES OF ANY NATURE HAVE ATTAINED THE INTERNATIONAL REPUTATION AND PRESTIGE ENJOYED BY ROYAL WORCESTER, BON TON, AND ADJUSTO CORSETS

Model 568. Price 10/11 FOR SLENDER FIGURES   *Model 581. Price 10/11 FOR AVERAGE FIGURES*   *Model 639. Price 12/11 FOR AVERAGE FIGURES*   *Model 919. Price 21/9 FOR AVERAGE FIGURES*

What is "The New Curve"?

THE NEW CURVE follows the lines of the naturally perfect figure—

THE NEW CURVE aims to idealise nature.

THE NEW CURVE produces the graceful straight-hipped silhouette.

THE NEW CURVE, by a masterly stroke of design which is the secret of Royal Worcester Corsets, attains the perfect interpretation of the exquisite mode of 1912 without restriction of any kind—it therefore overcomes absolutely the well-based objections which have so long pre-

THE NEW CURVE is the doom of:—

The made-to-measure corset—

The freak corset embodying the ideas of self-styled professors—

The pernicious system of buying corsets from registered numbers.

To get the new fashion you must get Royal Worcester Kidfitting Corsets with THE NEW CURVE. They have faithfully caught the spirit of the new mode, and have thrown open the Gate of Fashion to EVERY lady, no matter of what

---

and a selling point of the Royal Worcester was the supposedly kinder "New Curve". In any case, "the corset that may have served very well for a season or two back is no use whatever for the 1912 mode, with the New Curve".

"What is The New Curve?" the advertisements asked on the readers' behalf. "The New Curve follows the lines of the naturally perfect figure. The New Curve aims to idealise nature. The New Curve produces the graceful straight-hipped silhouette. The New Curve, by a masterly stroke of design which is the secret of Royal Worcester corsets, attains the perfect interpretation of the exquisite mode of 1912 without restriction of any kind. It therefore overcomes absolutely the well-based objections which have so long prevailed against the long corset." Such as not being able to sit down.

The copywriters brought in an up-to-date analogy. "What beautiful pictures lie hidden in the undeveloped photographic negative," it declared, "only too often to be ruined by careless developing. What possibilities of figure-beauty are similarly lost by

INBRIEF

APRIL 1, 1903

KLEPTOMANIA:
THE FATAL ATTRACTION OF DEPARTMENT STORES

One of the most mysterious of feminine shortcomings hitherto known to medicine and law has just been cleared up.

It was heretofore known as kleptomania – an irrational impulse in ladies out shopping to extract things which they seldom needed, never used, and could almost always afford to buy. A specialist for mental disorders, Dubuisson, tells us the scene of these petty thefts is invariably an enormous store. A curious point is that so-called kleptomania is almost exclusively a woman's failing. Out of 120 cases which Dubuisson inquired into, there were but nine men implicated.

Another peculiarity is that the moment they were caught in the act they not only admitted their guilt, but usually confessed to other similar misdeeds. The purloined articles were found, not in use, but hidden away wholly untouched, with price tickets still attached.

careless development – careless corseting!"

The "Worcester" in the Royal Worcester was a town in Massachusetts where one David H. Fanning had set up his one-room corset factory half a century before. A greybearded, bespectacled man of 81 but described as "in his prime", Mr Fanning stared out from his engraved portrait in the middle of the page upon Model 568 ("for slender figures") and Model 962 ("for full figures") and the figures in between.

The American origins of the Royal Worcester phenomenon might perhaps be detected in the concern to portray the 2,000 happy, egalitarian and industrious workers busy in producing "the wonderful perfection of the Royal Worcester Kidfitting Corset". One illustration showed happy bloused and skirted workers in the "white-tiled dining hall", another represented a vast but orderly stitching room, "light as the lightest day" with "marvellous machinery which is kept up to date year by year at immense cost".

"Contrast the conditions at Worcester, where every stitch is guided by conscience, with the ordinary factories where amid squalor, polluted air and crowding, the work is scamped through at so much a dozen pairs!

"Thus it comes that there exists between employers and employed a spirit of cordiality and co-operation, the ideal of which is to uphold the supremacy of Royal Worcester corsets against the world.

"There is no lady in the kingdom whose figure cannot be improved by wearing a Royal Worcester Kidfitting Corset." It almost sounded a comfort and a work of philanthropy at the same time.

From the Telegraph

The girl who became the Speaking Clock

June 22, 1935

The voice came through, cool, clear, delicately inflected, giving to Milton's lines their full rhythmic beauty. The judges listened and deliberated: and, a short time after, Miss Ethel Cain, aged 26, of Croydon, a telephone operator at Victoria Exchange, was acclaimed the Girl With the Golden Voice for whom the General Post Office had been searching for many weeks.

She will not – alas! – recite *L'Allegro* to subscribers. But one day in the not too far distant future if you are on a go-ahead exchange you will be able to dial T-I-M and listen while a sound film of her voice tells you the time. And I, who have heard her speak, can recommend you do so, as an aesthetic experience.

The finals of the Post Office competition were held at St Martin's-le-Grand yesterday morning. The judges were Mr John Masefield, the Poet Laureate, Dame Sybil Thorndyke, Lord Iliffe, Mr S. Hibberd (the chief announcer of the BBC), and Mrs E.D. Atkinson, recently chosen as the perfect telephone subscriber.

The finalists spoke a passage from Milton, another from Stevenson's *Treasure Island*, and a third test, giving nine different times. She will soon begin recording the 132 separate hours, minutes, and seconds which are required.

She told me yesterday that she had studied elocution for some years and was an enthusiastic amateur actress.

Miss Ethel Cain, The Girl With the Golden Voice

INBRIEF

DECEMBER 28, 1910

From our own correspondent, New York, Tuesday

American optimism was strangely exemplified yesterday, when 20 members of the Alimony Club now in seclusion in New York's Gaol because of default in the payment of allowances to their wives, from whom they have separated, participated in the Christmas festivities. These alimonists are not treated like ordinary prisoners and the warden of the gaol allowed them to carry out the annual custom of dining together upon turkey and plum-pudding, with plenty of beer and cigars to round off the feast. The warden himself presided, bidding the refractory husbands eat, drink and be merry, and with the assistance of a harmonica they joyfully obeyed.

It was apparently the most convivial affair in the club's history. Only one or two discordant notes were struck. One member possessing a vestige of sentiment, requested permission to sing *Home, Sweet Home* but the motion was lost by a vote of 9–1, and an amendment in favour of *We're Here Because We're Here, and We're Glad Because We're Here* was substituted unanimously. Addresses delivered by many of those present were all to this effect, that if they had known how pleasant it was in gaol they would have got locked up long ago.

Then they sang the club anthem, written by a veteran member and jealously preserved in the archives, entitled *We'd Rather be in Gaol than Married.* This anthem was encored, and was sung with greater fervour each succeeding time.

OVERTAKING CRIPPEN

Daily bulletins on the fate of a fleeing murderer

Wireless telegraphy led to the arrest of a poisoner and secured exclusive despatches from the ship where he was trapped

When Dr Crippen was caught, fleeing to Canada aboard the liner *Montrose*, *The Daily Telegraph* boasted: "Our Special Correspondent supplied the details of one of the most dramatic arrests that has ever been effected."

Crippen won a place in Madame Tussaud's and the nation's chamber of horrors that has outlived widespread exact knowledge of his crime. In February 1910 he had killed his wife with poison, cut up her body and buried it in the cellar of 39 Hilldrop Crescent at Holloway, the respectable London suburb of clerks such as the fictional Mr Pooter and of professional men such as the homoeopathic physician Hawley Harvey Crippen. It was the separation of his wife's bones and flesh that had gripped the imagination of the public.

After murdering his wife, Belle, an annoyingly stagey and unsuccessful singer, Crippen invited his secretary, Ethel Le Neve, with whom he had been having an affair, to live in his house. People saw her wearing Mrs Crippen's jewellery.

When the police investigated, Crippen – an American by origin – said, first that his wife had gone to America and died, and, later, that she had left him for another man. He admitted his affair with Ethel.

Crippen's nemesis was Chief Inspector Walter Dew of Scotland Yard, a figure whom the newspapers could invest with all the qualities of the dogged sleuth. In early July, Dew questioned Crippen at Hilldrop Crescent, and before he could return for another interview, the couple had fled. The police dug up the dismembered Mrs Crippen from the cellar, wrapped in her husband's pyjamas.

Henry Kendall, the captain of the *Montrose*, was also a natural for a crime story: "Captain Kendall as Sherlock Holmes", read a headline in the *Telegraph*. The paper declared a scoop in printing an account by the captain of the moves leading up to the arrest. "This is the only message I have sent today to the Press," he telegraphed to the paper.

Crippen and Ethel Le Neve had embarked under

the name of Robinson, she disguised as his son. The captain saw through them and telegraphed Scotland Yard. If an historic dimension to the events was sought (to justify curiosity in this tale of romance and murder), it was to be the first arrest made thanks to wireless telegraphy. Marconi was pleased as punch with the publicity, and so was Canadian Pacific, who owned the *Montrose*.

Captain Kendall's wireless messages to Scotland Yard enabled Dew to pursue the liner in a faster steam ship. While the *Montrose* was still in the open sea, Captain Kendall sent an account to the *Telegraph* of the trap to be sprung. "I believe we have located Crippen," he said in a "Marconigram" as he willingly called it. "The man seems hopeful enough so far, but at times he glances landwards with a look painful enough to suggest that the very roots of his hair are being pulled up.

"He slept very little last night, and was on deck at 5am this morning, under close observation, as usual. He has a haggard appearance and is full of nerves. He walks the deck alone, and often pauses to listen to the snapping of our Marconi wireless apparatus, exchanging messages between ship and shore."

Miss Le Neve never made a convincing boy. This "queer-looking, girlish companion was the topic of frivolous speculation from the first".

"I chatted with the suspects yesterday," Kendall told the readers of *The Daily Telegraph*. "He asked if the water used aboard ship was distilled, and I told him no. He replied: 'I thought all the ship's water was distilled,' and added that he had used a lot of it for mixing medicine.

"Yesterday he and I came up the staircase together, just after lunch. We stood for a moment.

Crippen, muffled in hat and collar, is led down the gangplank after his arrest on the 'Montrose'

Here I saw a French woman sitting on the cushions reading a French newspaper. I noticed that she was busy with an account of 'Le Crime De Londres. Curieuses suppositions de la police anglaise'. I noticed my companion's face began to twitch. Later I secured the paper, and hid it."

Kendall obtained a description of Crippen from Scotland Yard that included the information that the wanted man had false teeth. The captain came up with a plan. He invited him into his cabin and told him funny stories. When Crippen laughed aloud, Kendall could see his teeth were false.

On July 31, 1910, off the Canadian coast at Father Point, at 9am local time, Inspector Dew approached in a rowing boat dressed as a pilot to allay Crippen's suspicion, and accompanied by Canadian lawmen.

The telegraphic account sent to *The Daily Telegraph*, said: "Crippen was walking on deck. Inspector Dew approached him from behind, and touched him on the shoulder.

"Crippen turned round sharply, and there was a mutual recognition between him and the inspector. 'There's your man!' said Inspector Dew to one of the Canadian officers, and Crippen accompanied his captors to a cabin, where he was formally arrested. 'I am rather glad the anxiety is over,' appears to have been the only remark he made.

"The inspector then went to Miss Le Neve's cabin. She was reading a book, and on looking up at her visitors immediately guessed what their purpose was. She is said to have uttered a piercing scream, then grew suddenly calm, and submitted to arrest."

Crippen was tried at the Old Bailey and hanged on November 23. Ethel Le Neve was acquitted and lived until 1967.

THE SIEGE OF SIDNEY STREET

Armed battle with anarchists in the East End

At the time, the use of troops and a Maxim gun in London were seen as 'unparalleled in the history of English civilisation'

O n the night of Friday December 15, 1910 three policemen were shot dead when they tried to arrest burglars in the act of tunnelling into a jeweller's shop in Houndsditch, on the edge of the City of London. England was not used to policemen being shot, and it soon emerged that these were no ordinary burglars, but "Russian Anarchists". Within a month the incident had led to the Siege of Sidney Street, which saw Winston Churchill dodging into doorways to avoid the bullets.

In the meantime there was an excited debate about whether the police should be armed and what controls should be put on aliens.

As the *Telegraph*'s issue dated Saturday December 17 was being put to bed at 2am it was known that a police sergeant had been shot dead and four men wounded, but no arrest had yet been made.

The house where the burglars had been surprised backed on to the jeweller's shop. "Some two or three weeks ago this particular house in Exchange Buildings was rented," the paper reported that morning, "and there went to live there two men and a woman. They were little known by neighbours, and kept very quiet, as if, indeed, to escape observation. They are said to have been foreigners in appearance, and the whole neighbourhood of Houndsditch containing a great number of aliens, and removal being not infrequent, the arrival of this new household created no comment.

"The police, however, evidently had some cause to suspect their intentions. The neighbourhood is always well patrolled. Shortly before 11.30 last night there were sounds either at the back of these newcomers' premises or at Mr Harris's shop that attracted the attention of the police." The burglars were surrounded but "rushed out, and as they ran up the narrow cul-de-sac fired right and left. Both of the men are said to have had revolvers, which they used with deadly effect. What became of the woman no-one seems to have noticed."

Monday morning's paper reported that the two other policemen shot had died in hospital, bringing the police losses to three. But after a tip-off a man

Armed police – two of the thousand called out – stand ready as Winston Churchill, the new

Home Secretary, confers with a police inspector (in bowler, carrying an umbrella) outside the house where the anarchists were trapped

had also been found dead in a house nearby where his fellow escaping burglars had left him.

Nine days later the affair was given a deeper political dimension by the discovery of an "Anarchist arsenal in the East End" by police seeking the two men and the woman wanted over the Houndsditch murder. In a house formerly occupied by the dead burglar, known as Gardstein, police found "a complete arsenal for the manufacture of explosives. Amongst the materials – most of them contained in glass bottles to preserve their effective strength – were quantities of nitric acid, sulphuric acid, nitro-glycerine, liquid mercury, potash, and phosphates."

But that was not all, the *Telegraph* revealed. "Anarchist literature, in sufficient quantities to corroborate the suspicion of the police that they are face to face with a far-reaching conspiracy, rather than an isolated and unpremeditated attack on civil authority, is stated to have been recovered.

"It is reported, in addition, that a dagger was found and a belt, which is understood to have had placed within it 150 Mauser dumdum bullets – bullets, that is, with soft heads, which, upon striking a human body, would spread and inflict a wound of a grievous, if not fatal character."

Before the week was out, the affair was to reach its dramatic climax. There was just time for an *entr'acte* that kept on the boil discussion of armed criminals and the role of Churchill as Home Secretary. "A labourer, named Charles Arthur," the paper reported, "was charged at the Tower Bridge police court with attempting to break into a public house in the Borough in the early hours of the morning, and afterwards with attempting to murder Constable Haytread by shooting at him with a revolver. This is not the case of a foreign Anarchist, but of an English hooligan, who to escape arrest whipped out a revolver and fired shot after shot."

The arrest of Arthur found its own heroine, Mrs Frances Wright, aged 36, who told her story to the *Telegraph*. "I had left my house and was crossing the road to a neighbour's when I saw a man double round the corner and run towards me. The constable was close behind him. The man turned around and fired. The policeman did not stop and the man fired again.

"The policeman called out, 'Help me, missus.' I

said, 'How?' and he said, 'Get the whistle'. I tried to catch hold of the whistle but in the struggle I could not get it. Then the man got his hand free and put his revolver to the policeman's forehead. I struck his face – I can't remember how often – and with the other hand I pulled at his collar from behind. The revolver clicked but did not go off.

"Then I managed to break the last two links of the chain and get the whistle. I blew it for all I was worth. When I could blow no more I ran to the door of a house, where some people were standing looking on, and asked them to blow it, but this they would not do. Then a man I knew came running up, and I gave the whistle to him, and he ran into Dover Street and blew it until help came."

Asked whether she was not frightened when she intervened, Mrs Wright said: "I thought of those poor fellows shot in Houndsditch. I wanted to save this one if I could. When I was struggling and the man was trying to use his revolver, I prayed God He would spare me for the sake of my children, and He did."

Her struggle, the *Telegraph* said, "has naturally given a shock to her nerves, from which she was suffering considerably yesterday. She is also unable

Churchill, as Home Secretary (leading, in tall hat), takes cover in a gateway as the siege progresses. 'He and a photographer were both risking valuable lives,' said Balfour in the House of Commons. 'I understand what the photographer was doing. But what was the right honourable gentleman doing?'

From the **Telegraph**

London has a narrow escape as the police strike is settled

September 2, 1918

The police strike is over and done with. It has been settled with a promptitude and a decision which are in the sharpest contrast with the dilatoriness and procrastination out of which it directly

arose. For that, London has to thank the Prime Minister [David Lloyd George], and its congratulation will be sincere as the prospect of the capital being denuded for any length of time of its guardians – or, rather we should say, of its regular guardians, for a large majority of the Specials nobly stuck to their posts – was sufficiently disquieting.

The whole situation arose so suddenly that everyone was taken by surprise, including, perhaps, the disorderly elements in the population, who, if they had had greater warning, might have turned to their profit such abnormal conditions and gathered in a rich harvest of plunder. All Friday night London lay at the mercy

The crowds watching the siege 'warmly cheered every detachment of soldiery as it appeared'. Here, with every balcony filled with spectators, the police hold back people in the street as Scots Guards marksmen take up position. Three spectators were hit by stray shots

to make free use of her hands owing to the fact that the fingers of her left hand were badly torn in wrenching away police-constable Haytread's whistle, the chain of which she was forced to break before she could put the whistle to her lips."

But what struck the paper in its editorial comment columns was the statement of the man arrested to the police. "Mr Churchill is going to alter things," he had said, "and we shall have a better chance, instead of being worried by you people."

"Such expressions," the *Telegraph* commented, "can bear but one interpretation. They mean, if this man be a fair example of his kind, that the Home Secretary, and no doubt, his friend the Chancellor of the Exchequer [Lloyd George], are 'the favourite statesmen' of the criminal classes."

Churchill the Liberal had a reputation as a reformer of the criminal justice system, and the *Telegraph* made the most of the trigger-happy Arthur's remarks. "What does the ignorant man naturally think when he hears that the Home Secretary is arranging for lectures and concerts to be given in the convict prisons, and for the drastic reduction of those periods of solitary confinement which prisoners most cordially detest?

"If they misunderstand him, and look towards him with hope and admiration as a sort of revolutionary leader, who will lead them to the plunder of the rich, and to the righting of those who are unfortunate enough to have 'done time', the mistake is not altogether one which we can wonder at."

Churchill was to lose some of that image as "a sort of revolutionary leader" during the events of January 3, 1911. BATTLE WITH ANARCHISTS IN THE EAST END OF LONDON, ran the top headline in the *Telegraph* on January 4. And beneath that, the headlines, diminishing in size in the style of the day, read:

DESPERATE MURDERERS AT BAY

SEVERAL HOURS FIGHTING WITH THE SCOTS GUARDS AND POLICE

MAXIM AND FIELD GUNS READY FOR ACTION

HOUSE SET ON FIRE

ASSASSINS RESIST TO THE DEATH

KILLED IN THE BLAZING RUINS

The newspaper had no doubt of the importance of the day's events. "Yesterday a scene unparalleled in the history of English civilisation was witnessed in the very heart of one of the most congested parts of the East End of London," the report began. "For about four hours what amounted to a pitched battle was waged between about 1,000 armed police and military and two or three Anarchists who are believed to have been connected with the Houndsditch outrage of three weeks ago."

The story was told in outline and there followed column after column of vivid detail, accompanied by large photographs, which were not usually carried at all in the paper at that time. These showed the troops, and the artillery, and Winston Churchill taking cover from the anarchists' fire.

That day was incidentally a triumph for the journalist Ellis Ashmead-Bartlett. He had been a successful war correspondent, at the age of 18 accompanying the Turks in the Graeco-Turkish war, and six years later acting as a correspondent from Japanese positions in the Russo-Japanese war. As the bullets flew at Sidney Street, he succeeded in getting the stories of more than one eyewitness – and keeping them away from other reporters and, indeed, the police, until he had sold the story to the *Telegraph*. At the same time he sold his own services

of its so-called "criminal classes", but the number of burglaries committed was very small, and there seems to have been no increase at all in the graver crimes. For this chivalrous forbearance we are duly grateful, and there is room also for legitimate satisfaction at the way in which London "carried on" during the daylight hours. The self-control of the traffic was almost as perfect as the ordinary police regulation – so ingrained is the habit of obedience and so strong is the force of custom.

But we trust that no false inferences will be drawn therefrom. Nothing could be more mischievous and dangerous than the idea that a strike of the Metropolitan and the City Police is a light

matter. A much truer view to take of this deplorable incident is that the capital has had an exceedingly narrow escape.

This strike is an unhappy and an evil precedent. It ought never to have taken place, because the men's demands should have been properly met long since. Their claims for increased pay and allowances had only to be stated publicly to ensure them the sympathy of the public, for, compared with the general rates of wages now ruling, the police rates were scandalously low and even as they will be under the Prime Minister's award, they are still quite moderate considering the responsibility and the exacting nature of the men's duties.

to the paper, going on to be a renowned foreign and war correspondent until his early death in 1931.

The siege began after the police had been given a tip that men wanted for the Houndsditch murders were living at 100 Sidney Street, Stepney. "The miscreants were apparently sleeping, with revolvers handy. They awoke just after the police officers had cleared the premises, and poured on them a heavy fire.

"Later in the morning a cordon, four or five men deep, was drawn at some distance round the building so as completely to isolate it, and the battle began. The besieged men fired persistently at the police, who were fortunately able to reply.

"As the morning advanced, additional police were drafted on to the scene and, at length, when the utter desperation of the Anarchists was realised – a detective-sergeant having been seriously wounded, and constables injured – word was sent to the Tower of London for troops. Some picked shots of the Scots Guards, with a Maxim gun, soon arrived.

"Thus, soon after London had settled down to the day's work, in this narrow street off the Mile End Road, the spectacle was presented of a party of Guardsmen mounting a Maxim gun on its tripod and gravely filling the ammunition belts, just as they might have been called upon to do in active service; and a little later a contingent of Royal Horse Artillery from St John's Wood Barracks, cheered as they came by thousands of spectators, appeared upon the spot, with a couple of quick-firing guns.

"These guns were not as a matter of fact used, but from the road and from adjacent buildings police and soldiers maintained a continual fire on the desperados, who replied briskly, unfortunately with some lamentable casualties.

"Soon smoke was seen to be issuing from the house. The premises were rapidly involved, and firemen and engines were promptly on the spot ready for action. Mr Churchill, who had been watching the proceedings, issued instructions that the fire brigade was only to 'stand by' to prevent the fire from spreading to adjoining premises.

"Even when faced with certain destruction by burning, the miscreants refused to surrender. The

flames soon enveloped the house, then the roof fell in, and the rooms from top to bottom were soon gutted. Two charred bodies were discovered. One of these is believed to be that of 'Fritz', one of the men 'wanted' for the Houndsditch murders."

As a footnote to its main report, the paper told the story of how the two men came to be trapped in the building. "Some time ago an English girl living in the East End was lured into a house by a couple of foreigners and ill-treated. The girl knew quite well who her assailants were, and they had known her for some time previously, but for a variety of reasons no complaint was made to the police. Quite recently, however, the girl again met her persecutors, and as a result of that meeting a male relative gave information to the police. This was to the effect that the aliens in question were none other than the man 'Fritz' with his companion 'Peter the Painter', together with a third man called 'Rozen'. All three were members of an Anarchist club in the East End, and at that moment they were in hiding in a house in Sidney Street."

In a separate short report the *Telegraph* noted that "the police have reason to believe that the man known as 'Peter the Painter' is not one of the two Anarchists killed yesterday in Sidney Street and that he is still at large." He never was caught, and his identity remains a mystery to this day.

The police almost had another fatality on their hands. Leeson, the detective-sergeant who had been following up the clues in the case, was shot in the chest after what seems to have been an unwise stirring-up of the anarchist hornet's nest. Just after daybreak one of the policemen outside 100 Sidney Street threw a handful of small stones at the top-floor window.

There was no response. Leeson picked up a bigger stone and hurled it through the window of the room occupied by the wanted men.

"Instantly a couple of revolver shots rang out," the *Telegraph* reported. "Then in rapid succession came four others, the sounds indicating the muffled discharge of the automatic pistol. The hands which fired them were not seen, but that the aim was deadly was soon demonstrated when Sgt Leeson

From the Telegraph

Gunman barricaded in burning building dies after 15-day siege

Ninety-two years after Sidney Street another East End siege ended as fire engulfed a house where a gunman had defied police
January 10, 2003

Eli Hall, 32, who was wanted in connection with two shootings, died after firing at officers and setting fire to the building in Hackney, east London. It is thought he may have died because he was unable to escape the blaze after barricading

himself inside following the escape of his hostage on the 11th day of the stand-off.

Scotland Yard sources said Hall, who was armed with two guns, a bag of ammunition and at least one petrol bomb, was not believed to have been shot.

The final 24 hours of the siege, which is estimated to have cost more than £500,000, began with Hall opening fire at officers manning a roadblock and then setting the building – a shop with bedsits above – ablaze. The fire burned for much of the day, and after it started attempts to establish contact with Hall – described by police as "a hostage negotiator's nightmare" – produced no response.

Police fired baton rounds to break windows and enable firemen to tackle the blaze and at 5pm fired CS gas into the building.

INBRIEF

APRIL 17, 1912

MR W. T. STEAD

By T.P. O'Connor

[The journalist W.T. Stead, see page 38, was among those who had drowned in the *Titanic*.]

In some of the characteristics of a journalist Stead was equal, if not superior, to any journalist of his time. He could paint a picture with extraordinary vividness; he could pile up a case with a wealth at once of detail and of imagery in a very brief space of time; never could he be dull, even in a line; and his point of view, though often wrong-headed, was always striking and original. Without any self-questioning, always inspired by some strong purpose, he could make his way to the presence of anybody. He could interview a Tsar or an Emperor. He was so strong a personality that people never thought of him as a man of this class or that, of his profession.

He was drawn to the German Emperor by certain common qualities of restlessness and dreams, and... took an active part in promoting the exchange of visits between the journalists of England and Germany. Stead would be in his element in such gatherings. Getting up without hesitation and without a trace of embarrassment, he would deliver with extraordinary fluency a speech half English, half ungrammatical but intelligible German, amid laughter and applause.

fell, pierced with a ball through the chest. He was borne through the stable yard, and assisted up a ladder on to the roof of outbuildings to the wall overlooking the large open yard at the back of Messrs. Mann & Crossman's bottling stores.

"When this wall was reached, the ruffians had the officers again under fire. There was a tremendous fusillade for a moment or two while the brewery workmen were bringing steps for the party to descend, but none of the bullets did more serious damage than to cut off the rim of Sgt Hallam's hat, and the wounded man was carried to the London Hospital on the brewery company's ambulance."

Under the headline DOCTOR'S THRILLING STORY, the paper, probably thanks to Ashmead-Bartlett, told the exciting tale of Leeson's rescue through the eyes of Dr M. Nathaniel Johnstone. "I was called about half-past seven o'clock by a man who said a policeman had been shot in Sidney Street. When I got there I was taken into the brewery yard, and had to climb over a gateway, up ladders, and scramble over the roof of outbuildings, to get to the place.

"Firing was going on the whole of the time. I found poor Leeson lying on a couch in a room. His shirt was open and I saw a wound in the left breast. I found that the bullet had made its exit from the right breast, having gone across the body, with a slight downward movement.

"I attended to him, and he spoke about his wife and children, and asked me if it was 'All up with him'. I said, 'No, you will be all right.' We gave him some brandy, and he revived. He put his hand into his pocket and produced his revolver, saying, 'Here is my revolver; it is no more use to me.' I put it in my hip pocket. The question then arose, how we were to get him to the hospital, for all the time the firing was going on. Someone suggested that we should get him over the wall.

"We put him on a stretcher and were sliding him gently along the coping when we heard bullets whizzing past. Just before we got to the edge of the coping the patient turned round on the edge of the stretcher and slid down the wall onto the ladder, out of the line of fire.

"It was extraordinary. A bullet hit the wall very near my face. I got down under cover, and we were able to get him to the hospital without anybody else being hit."

Three people from the crowd that gathered to watch the show were hit by stray bullets. "By every species of public conveyance – train, tram and bus – spectators journeyed to the scene. And what a scene it was! What man present had ever witnessed soldiers firing ball cartridge in the streets of London?

"Profoundly engrossed as it was, it was unmistakably a good-natured crowd. It was, indeed, a multitude, surprised into silence as one might say, by the wholly unusual character of the day's events. Yet not always silent. Impelled by instincts that were manifestly on the side of order, it warmly cheered every detachment of soldiery as it appeared and greeted with unstinted acclaim the alacrity and dash with which the firemen got to work."

Churchill was, fortunately, not hit, but his exposure led to widespread criticism of his behaviour, not least by the Conservative Opposition. Everyone had seen photographs of the Home Secretary in Sidney Street. "He was, I understand, in a military phrase, in what is known as the zone of fire," said A.J. Balfour in Parliament. "He and a photographer were both risking valuable lives. I understand what the photographer was doing. But what was the right honourable gentleman doing?"

If Churchill was carried away by the excitement of the day, it did not panic him into instant action against aliens. He heard from Buckingham Palace that George V hoped that "these outrages by foreigners will lead you to consider whether the Aliens Act could not be amended so as to prevent London from being infested with men and women whose presence would not be tolerated in any other country".

Churchill went as far as circulating a draft Bill to the Cabinet, though he admitted in an accompanying memorandum that it included a "naughty" principle of making "a deliberate differentiation between the alien, and especially the unassimilated alien, and a British subject". In any case, no time was allocated to the Bill in the Commons, and it fell by the wayside.

At 9.25pm firearms officers launched 12 "distraction grenades" into the upper floors to create a diversion and provide an opportunity to examine the interior.

Two officers with torches climbed ladders to look inside but teams could not enter the building, fearing it might be structurally unsafe following the extensive blaze. A structural surveyor was examining the building last night.

There had been no contact with Hall, who told police repeatedly that he was determined not to go to prison where he had previously been held for what is believed to be a sex offence, since Wednesday night.

"He was of resolute mind then that he was not coming out," said Cdr Bob Quick, the officer leading the police operation. "If he did, he would seek recourse to firearms." Hall had told police earlier in the siege, which began on Boxing Day, that he was on a "mission from God" to kill as many policemen as possible.

Police tactics had been to wear down Hall's resistance in the hope that he would give himself up. The electricity and water supply to the flat were switched off and Hall responded by burning furniture to keep warm.

The stand-off started a debate in the Metropolitan Police, with some officers believing that it should have been ended when the hostage came out on day 11. It is expected to lead to a major review of hostage operations in the force. A source said last night: "This man was obviously a danger to police if we went in but the firearms specialists believed it could be handled. No one wanted to make the decision to end it."

THE WAR IN THE AIR

Zeppelins bring the conflict to the home front

In 1915 a 23-year-old airman won the VC for shooting down a German airship. Ten days later he was dead

On June 8, 1915 King George V sent a message to a British airman on active service: "I most heartily congratulate you upon your splendid achievement, in which you single handed destroyed an enemy Zeppelin."

It was indeed an amazing feat. In his Morane monoplane, Sub-Lieutenant Reginald Warneford of the Naval Air Service braved fire from German positions on the ground as he pursued a Zeppelin flying past Ghent on its way back to base at dawn.

Warneford swooped down on the airship and dropped six 20lb bombs as he did so. "He was more successful than he believed possible," the *Telegraph* reported.

"Before he had time to do more than begin his upward curve, the explosion of the gas envelope took place, and the assailant was swept from his airway by the sudden up-blast. The swift and unexpected tornadoes of his own creation swept his machine upwards and over as if it had been a feather. It was a moment when only the utmost coolness and skill could save him."

The pilot managed to perform a complete loop, and returned his aircraft to a level trajectory. But the aerobatics had drained the petrol supply for the engine, which cut out. Warneford made a landing in a field in occupied territory and refilled the forward tank from a fuel reserve at the rear of the aircraft. He then succeeded in taking off again from the field. He was just in time to evade German pursuit and made it safely back to the British lines.

The burning wreckage of the Zeppelin fell on to the convent school of Amandsberg. The nuns tried to get the children to a place of safety. Two sisters who had run outside with children in their arms were badly hurt, and one nun was killed.

Ten days later came the news of Warneford's death. He had taken up an American magazine writer from the Buc aerodrome, near Versailles, and at 600ft the biplane was seen to rock; its wings met, and it plummeted down. At 250ft, both men appeared to jump, according to witnesses. Warneford was still alive when they reached him,

but "nearly every bone in his body was broken" and he died on the way to hospital. He was 23.

But his achievement remained. "Never, probably, was heroic deed in time of war surrounded by more of sheer glamour than was the feat of Lt Warneford," the *Telegraph* commented. Warneford had been working for the P&O shipping line when war broke out; he obtained a commission in the Navy and by February 25, 1915 had won his pilot's certificate after only four flying lessons.

It was less than six years since Bleriot had become the first man to fly the Channel, but aviators had come into their own. Victory against a Zeppelin had a symbolic significance, for the monstrous airships were bringing death and destruction from the air for the people back home in England. The first raid was on the stretch of East Anglian coast from Yarmouth to King's Lynn on January 19, 1915. The airships could fly at 10,000 feet at 50mph and carry two tons of bombs; their weakness was the inflammable hydrogen that kept them airborne.

"Hostile aircraft visited the Eastern Counties and the London district last night, and dropped incendiary and explosive bombs," reported a Press Association despatch published by the *Telegraph* on September 10, 1915. "At midnight a few casualties had been reported and some fires, which were then well under control." That night 20 were reported killed and 86 injured; the raid accounted for almost two thirds of the damage inflicted by the Zeppelin campaign, which in all amounted to 159 raids, dropping 270 tons of bombs and killing 557 people. But that September night there was no telling how much more was to come.

The next day insurance offices were busy. "Owners of properties stood two and three ranks deep at insurance counters," the *Telegraph* reported. "Under the Government scheme for aircraft and bombardment insurance, in which the insurance companies are co-operating, the rate for owners and occupiers of residential property has remained fixed at 2 per cent, against aircraft risks. For an extra 1 per cent, insurance can be obtained against bombardment by hostile guns not landed on British territory."

A fortnight later came news of the downing of a Zeppelin "in Essex" as the paper had to say vaguely for reasons of war. About half an hour after midnight a raiding Zeppelin was spotted and the guns began to fire.

"Shells could be seen bursting above and below it in a most tantalising way, and it was obvious that the raider was making for home again with all possible speed. Then a red spot – it appeared to be no more – appeared in the dark heavens. That red spot just as suddenly developed into a ball of fire, and the Zeppelin commenced to burn. The people cheered, sirens started screeching, factory whistles commenced to blow, and in a moment all was pandemonium.

"The flames crept along the back of the Zeppelin, which appeared to light up in sections, until in about a couple of minutes it was burning

Sub-Lieutenant Reginald Warneford, of the Naval Air Service, was 23 when he won the Victoria Cross for single-handedly destroying an enemy Zeppelin. A monoplane was dwarfed by the bulk of the airship (as shown in the image below of a later atttack in 1917), but had the advantage of manoeuvrability

from end to end. Then it appeared that the cars beneath had broken its back by their weight, and it seemed to the observers to buckle up. It wavered for a few moments, and then pointed nose downwards to earth.

"In a perfectly perpendicular position the Zeppelin, which was then one red mass of flames, dived slowly to earth. Those few moments afforded a wonderful spectacle. Flames were bursting out from under the sides and behind, and, as the gas bag continued to fall, there trailed away long tongues of flames, which became more and more fantastic as the falling monster gained impetus."

For those living nearby it was a terrible moment. "Where would it fall?" was the obvious question. "We hurriedly got our children downstairs," one eye-witness told *The Daily Telegraph*, "and then watched in suspense, until the flaming torch had passed out of the danger zone, as far as we were concerned.

"Very soon after the airship fell, the fire brigade arrived on the scene. The vessel had smashed a tree in its descent, and was partially hung up, which gave the flames a better chance. It burnt furiously, but fortunately there was a plentiful supply of water from a pond close by and the brigade got the fire under control very quickly."

"Special constables found numerous dead bodies in different parts of the field," the *Telegraph* reporter wrote. "Some were scorched and charred beyond recognition, but others were scarcely burnt at all, and had apparently been killed from shock. The commander, who was wearing the Iron Cross, was identified by the superior texture of his uniform."

A farm labourer had been woken by the drone of the Zeppelin's engine. ("A noise to which residents of this part of the East Coast have now become accustomed," the *Telegraph* noted.) The man said that as the vessel descended there was an explosion. "It didn't hurt any of us, but it smashed the front windows of my house and those of my neighbours. I found afterwards that all the hair was singed off the back of my dog, which was in a kennel outside."

In another incident in Essex, a country policeman, alone and unaided, arrested the entire crew, commander and all, of a German airship. When he saw it coming down, "he went at once to a telephone office in a certain village and ordered the people in charge to telephone for troops to be sent to the spot. While he was in the office a German officer came in and said: 'May I send a telephone message?'

" 'Excuse me,' said the police constable, 'but aren't you a German?'

" 'Yes,' replied the German officer, 'I am the commander of an airship which has just made a forced descent, and I wish to telephone to give myself up.'

"Said the constable, 'No, you come along with me. How many of you are there?'

"The German commander told him, 21. Thereupon the constable of the Essex Police collected the 21 and marched them away."

From the Telegraph

Rudyard Kipling reports from the mountain trenches of Alsace

Wednesday September 15, 1915

Very early in the morning I met "Alan Breck" with a half-healed bullet-scrape across the bridge of his nose, and an Alpine cap over one ear. His people a few hundred years ago had been Scotch. He bore a Scotch name, and still recognised the head of his clan, but his French occasionally ran into German words, for he was an Alsatian on one side.

"This," he explained, "is the very best country in the world to fight in. It's picturesque and full of cover. I'm a gunner. I've been here for months. It's lovely."

It might have been the hills under Mussoorie and what our cars expected to do in it I could not understand. But the demon-driver, who had been a road racer, took the 70hp Mercedes and threaded the narrow valleys, as well as occasional half-Swiss villages full of Alpine troops, at a restrained 30mph. He shot up a new-made road, more like Mussoorie than ever, and did not fall down the hillside even once. An ammunition-mule of a mountain-battery met him at a tight corner, and began to climb a tree.

"See! There isn't another place in France where that could happen," said Alan. "I tell you, this is a magnificent country."

The mule was hauled down by his tail before he had reached the lower branches, and went on through the woods, his ammunition boxes jinking on his back for all the world as though he were rejoining his battery at Jutough. One expected to meet the little Hill people bent under their loads under the forest gloom. The light, the colour, the smell of woodsmoke, pine needles, wet earth, and warm mule were all Himalayan. Only the Mercedes was violently and loudly a stranger.

"Halt!" said Alan at last, when she had done everything except imitate the mule.

"The road continues," said the demon-driver seductively.

"Yes, but they will hear you if you go on. Stop and wait. We've a mountain-battery to look at."

They were not at work for the moment, and the Commandant, a grim and forceful man, showed me some details of their construction. When we left them in their bower – it looked like a Hill priest's wayside shrine – we heard them singing through the steep, descending pines. They, too, like the 75s [the French field gun], seemed to have no pet name in the service.

It was a poisonously blind country. The woods blocked all sense of direction above and around. The ground was at any angle you pleased, and all sounds were split up and muddled by the tree trunks, which acted as silencers. High above us, the respectable, all-concealing forest had turned into sparse, ghastly blue sticks of timber – an assembly of leper-trees round a bald mountain top. "That's where we're going," said Alan. "Isn't it an adorable country?"

Blind mazes

A machine-gun loosed a few shots in the fumbling style of her kind when they feel for an opening. A couple of rifle shots answered. They might have been half a mile away or a hundred yards below. An adorable country! We climbed up till we found, once again, a complete tea garden of little sunk houses, almost invisible in the brown-pink recesses of the thick forest. Here the trenches began, and with them for the next few hours life in two dimensions – length and breadth.

You could have eaten your dinner almost anywhere off the swept dry ground, for the steep slopes favoured draining, there was no lack of timber and there was unlimited labour. It had made neat double-length dug-outs where the wounded could be laid in during their passage down the mountainside; well tended occasional latrines properly limed; dug-outs for sleeping and eating; overhead projections and tool sheds where needed and, as one came nearer the working face, very clever cellars against trench-sweepers.

Men passed on their business; a squad with a captured machine-gun which they tested in a sheltered dip; armourers at their benches, busy with sick rifles, fatigue-parties for straw, rations and ammunition. Long processions of single blue figures turned sideways between the brown, sunless walls. One understood after a while the nightmare that lays hold of trench-stale men, when the dreamer wanders forever in those blind mazes till, after centuries of agonising flight, he finds himself stumbling out again into the white blaze and horror of the mined front – he who thought he had almost reached home!

In the front line

There were no trees above us now. Their trunks lay along the edge of the trench, built in with stones, where necessary, or sometimes overhanging it in rugged splinters or bushy tops. Bits of cloth, not French, showed, too, in the uneven lines of debris at the trench lip, and some thoughtful soul had marked an unexploded Boche trench-sweeper as "Not to be touched". It was a young lawyer from Paris who pointed that out to me.

We met the Colonel at the head of an indescribable pit of ruin, full of sunshine, whose steps ran down a very steep hillside under the lee of an almost vertically plunging parapet. To the left of that parapet, the whole hillside was one gruel of smashed trees, split stones and powdered soil. It might have been a rag-picker's dump heap on a colossal scale.

Alan looked at it critically. I think he had helped to make it not long before.

"We're on the top of the hill now, and the Boches are below us," said he. "We gave them a very fair sickener lately."

"This," said the Colonel, "is the front line."

There were overhead guards against hand bombs which disposed me to believe him, but what convinced me most was a corporal urging us in whispers not to talk so loud. The men were at dinner, and a good smell of food filled the trench. This was the first smell I had encountered in my long travels uphill – a mixed, entirely wholesome flavour of stew, leather, earth and rifle oil.

Frontline originals

A proportion of men were standing to arms while others ate; but dinner time is slack time, even among animals, and it was close on noon.

"The Boches got their soup a few days ago," someone whispered. I thought of the pulverised hillside and hoped it had been hot enough.

We edged along the still trench, where the soldiers stared, with justified contempt, I thought, upon the civilian who scuttled through their life for a few emotional minutes in order to make words out of their blood. Somehow, it reminded me of coming in late to a play and incommoding a long line of packed stalls. The whispered dialogue was much the same: "Pardon?" "I beg your pardon, monsieur." "To the right, monsieur." "If monsieur will lower his head." "One sees best from here, monsieur," and so on.

It was their day and night-long business, carried through without display or heat, or doubt, or indecision. Those who worked, worked; those off duty, not five feet behind them in the dug-outs, were deep in their papers, or their meals, or their letters; while death stood ready at every minute to drop down into the narrow cut from out of the narrow strip of unconcerned sky. And for the better part of a week one had skirted hundreds of miles of such a frieze!

The loopholes not in use were plugged rather like old-fashioned hives. Said the Colonel, removing a plug: "Here are the Boches, look and you'll see their sandbags." Through the jumble of riven trees and stones one saw what might have been a bit of green sacking. "They're about seven metres distant just here," the Colonel went on. That was true, too. We entered a little *fortalice* with a cannon in it, in an embrasure which, at that moment, struck me as unnecessarily vast, even though it was partly closed by a frail packing case lid. The Colonel sat him down in front of it, and explained the theory of this sort of redoubt. "By the way," he said to the gunner at last, "can't you find something better than that?" He twitched the lid aside. "I think it's too light. Get a log of wood or something."

Handy trench-sweepers

I loved that Colonel! He knew his men and he knew the Boche – had them marked down like birds. When he said they were beside dead trees or behind boulders, sure enough there they were! But, as I have said, the dinner hour is always slack, and even when we came to a place where a section of trench had been bashed open by trench-sweepers, and it was recommended to duck and hurry, nothing much happened. The uncanny thing was the absence of movement in the Boche trenches. Sometimes one imagined that one smelt strange tobacco, or heard a rifle bolt working after a shot. Otherwise they were as still as pigs at noonday.

We held on through the maze, past trench-sweepers of a handy light pattern, with their screw-tailed charge all ready; and a grave or so; and when I came on men who merely stood within easy reach of their rifles, I knew I was in the second line. When they lay frankly at ease in their dugouts, I knew it was the third. A shotgun would have sprinkled all three.

"No flat plains," said Alan. "No hunting for gun positions – the hills are full of them – and the trenches close together and commanding each other. You see what a beautiful country it is!"

Kipling wore these civilian clothes for his reporting tour; a month later his son was killed in action

And there came a priest, who was a sub-lieutenant, out of a wood of snuff-brown shadows and half-veiled trunks. Would it please me to look at a chapel? It was all open to the hillside, most tenderly and devoutly done in rustic work with reedings of peeled branches and panels of moss and thatch – St Hubert's own shrine. I saw the hunters who passed before it going to the chase on the far side of the mountain where their game lay.

A bombarded town

Alan carried me off to tea the same evening in a town where he seemed to know everybody. He had spent the afternoon on another mountain top, inspecting gun positions; whereby he had been shelled a little – marmité is the slang for it. There had been no serious marmitage and he had spotted a Boche position which was marmitable.

"And we may get shelled now," he added, hopefully. "They shell this town whenever they think of it. Perhaps they'll shell us at tea."

It was a quaintly beautiful little place, with its mixture of French and German ideas: its old bridge and gentle-minded river, between the cultivated hills. The sand-bagged cellar door; the ruined houses; and the holes in the pavement looked as unreal as the violences of a cinema against that soft and simple setting. The people were abroad in the streets, and the little children were playing. A big shell gives notice enough for one to get to shelter, if the shelter is near enough. That appears to be as much as anyone expects in the world where one is shelled, and that world has settled down to it. People's lips are a little firmer, the modelling of the brows is a little more pronounced and, maybe, there is a change in the expression of the eyes; but nothing that a casual afternoon caller need particularly notice.

Cases for hospitals

The house where we took tea was the "big house" of the place, old and massive, a treasure house of ancient furniture. It had everything that the moderate heart of man could desire – gardens, garages, outbuildings, and the air of peace that goes with beauty in age. It stood over a high cellarage, and opposite the cellar door was a brand new blindage of earth packed between timbers. The cellar was a hospital, with its beds and stores, and under the electric light the orderly waited ready for the cases to be carried down out of the street.

"Yes, they are all civil cases," said he.

They come without much warning – a woman gashed by falling timber; a child with its temple crushed by a flying stone; an urgent amputation case, and so on. One never knows. Bombardment, the Boche textbooks say, "is designed to terrify the civil population so that they may put pressure on their politicians to conclude peace".

In real life, men are very rarely soothed by the sight of their women being tortured.

A WOMAN'S VIEW OF WAR
A capacity for doing more than knitting socks

Mary Billington was a veteran reporter. With the outbreak of war she immediately investigated the changing role of women

Six-foot tall and keen on horses, Mary Billington (pictured above in the frontispiece to her book, 'Woman in India') saw a portent of war in 'the attendance of women at boxing matches'. The New Yorker Gertude Ederle (right), on the brink of her record swim, felt 'like a prize-fighter before he gets into the ring'

Mary Frances Billington was a forceful woman. The daughter of a Dorset rector, she was six foot tall and accustomed to travelling alone to the outposts of Empire. In the *Telegraph* office she liked to be called "Billington". She gave her recreation briefly as "horses".

Journalism was the coming thing for women. *The Daily Mirror* was founded in 1903 as a paper for women written by women. It was not a success, but perhaps its owner Alfred Harmsworth had not given it a chance. "Women can't write and don't want to read," he declared, as he counted his losses and sacked the female staff.

Mary Billington had a different notion. She had joined the *Telegraph* from the illustrated paper *The Daily Graphic* in 1897. The *Telegraph* provided a forum for "advanced" views, opening its columns in 1898 to an interminable debate about the role for women. "Wife or lover?" asked the headlines. For Mary Billington the answer was neither.

For her the First World War was not merely a clash between states. She had seen its portents in "the strange waves of restlessness, demands for excitement, the rage for garish colourings, the amazing eccentricities of fashion, the extravagances in all forms of luxury, and the aberrations of futurists." Even fancy-dress balls gave her cause for uneasiness. "Not less significant was the attendance of women at boxing matches."

The war, she thought, gave women a chance to show their true qualities of self-sacrifice. In 1915 she described what women were doing at the front or at home in a book, *The Roll-Call of Serving Women*, incorporating her first-hand reporting for the paper. In those first months of war, the sufferings of Belgium still figured prominently in readers' minds. *The Daily Telegraph* started a "Shilling Fund", of the kind organised for W.G. Grace (see page 107), to help the many Belgian refugees. Grace had received £5,000; readers gave more than £200,000 for the Belgians.

Among women's voluntary efforts, Queen Mary's Needlework Guild could appear slightly ridiculous in turning out 970,000 pairs of socks. But in a war where thousands of men were disabled by trench foot – the destruction of blood vessels and flesh through prolonged cold and wetness – a pair of dry socks was more than a comfort.

Mary Billington had no illusions about the demands of nursing men with hideous wounds. "Talk about the 'glories' of war," said a Quaker nurse she interviewed, "one felt only the terror and ghastliness of it." But she also reported the initiative of Dr Louisa Garrett Anderson and Dr Flora Murray in running a hospital in France. "If you make a success of the work you are going to do," said Dr Garrett Anderson's mother, a pioneer among women doctors, "you will advance the position of medical women by a hundred years." Succeed they did.

At home, women were recruited for armament manufacture. "A most interesting aspect of the women's work is shaping and sewing the covering and 'wing' – to employ a non-technical word – of aircraft." But in other trades there was opposition from male employees, as when women were engaged as bus conductors. As more and more men joined up, these attitudes were to change.

SHE SWAM THE CHANNEL
Smeared in sheep fat and swollen-tongued

Gertrude Ederle was the sixth person to conquer the Channel. All the others were men, and she swam faster than any of them

The first woman to swim the Channel also broke the men's records. Gertrude Ederle was only 18 when she made the crossing in 14 hours 30 minutes, on August 6, 1926. Five people had swum the Channel before, including Captain Webb in 1875 (see page 118), and Gertrude Ederle made it faster than any, beating by an hour and 57 minutes the record set by the Italian Enrico Tiraboschi in 1923.

Her father had taught her to swim after she had almost drowned at the age of seven. She tried the Channel in August 1925, giving up in white-capped seas about seven miles from her goal on the English coast, despite, or perhaps because of, a jazz band that played to her at intervals from an accompanying tug. For her renewed attempt the plucky young New Yorker set off from France, at

Cape Gris Nez, just after seven in the morning. "I'm ready, let's go; don't see how I can wait much longer to flirt with old Mister Channel," the *Telegraph* next day reported her saying. "I just feel like a prize-fighter before he gets into the ring."

"After six hours' swimming," the paper said, "she was about 10 miles off the French coast, but well to the eastward. The sea at that time was rough, the wind breaking up the seas into little white-capped waves.

"At a quarter-to-five she had progressed so well that her position was about seven miles south-east of Dover, with the Goodwin Lightship bearing two miles north-west. The wind was moderating and sea conditions slightly better than throughout the day. Then a stiff breeze knocked up and rain fell. But the girl swam on…

"Even when nearing the coast, the completion of the task seemed impossible," the *Telegraph* commented, "but by a superhuman effort she cleared the tide and gained the beach, breasting the waves with vigorous strokes.

"Miss Ederle landed about 50 yards to the north of the Lifeboat Station at Kingsdown, near Deal. It was dark, but there was a small crowd to welcome her, including Mr Sutton, coxswain of the lifeboat, and his wife. Miss Ederle, says Mrs Sutton, was in 'absolutely perfect condition'."

It might not have seemed so to Gertrude Ederle, smeared in sheep fat, her tongue swollen through the effects of the salt water. She had sucked a block of sugar every hour or two to soothe the soreness, and also managed some chicken broth and two slices of pineapple as she swam.

On her return to New York hundreds of thousands welcomed her in a wild ticker-tape parade down Broadway. But her fame brought little fortune. She made a film, *Swim, Swim, Swim*, but suffered isolation from increasing deafness caused by childhood measles. She fell down some steps in 1933, injuring her spine, which doctors immobilised in a cast for two years. Although she was told she'd never swim again, she made a public return to the water at the New York World Fair in 1939, but gave up competitions.

She devoted herself to teaching deaf children to swim. "Since I can't hear either," she said, "they feel I'm one of them."

She died unmarried in 2003.

D.H. LAWRENCE'S PAINTINGS

'A man with one hand always in the slime'

The novelist's latest book had been confiscated as obscene. The Telegraph's diarist sent his canvases the same way

An exhibition of paintings by D.H. Lawrence attracted the ire of *The Daily Telegraph*'s column "London Day by Day" in June 1929. "Probably no greater insult has ever been offered to the London public than the exhibition at the Warren Galleries," the column hazarded. "To encounter a friend, particularly a friend of the opposite sex, in the Warren Galleries is, to say the least of it, highly embarrassing. It must be a standing source of amazement that the authorities permit the public display of paintings of so gross and obscene a character."

The amazement did not continue for long, as the police, having read *The Daily Telegraph*, removed 13 of the pictures. Lawrence, sick and living abroad, went through weeks of trouble to persuade a magistrate to return them to him.

The exhibition had been nearly a year in the planning, because, to Lawrence's annoyance, Dorothy Warren, the gallery owner, dithered with arrangements. In the meantime, *Lady Chatterley's Lover* was published, and confiscated as obscene. Lawrence reflected in a letter to Dorothy Warren that since so many people had been "mortally offended" by the novel, an exhibition might make things worse, although to his way of thinking "such skunks should be offended to the last inch".

After the police raid, Lawrence, sick in Florence, found himself "depressed and nauseated" about the whole episode. To make matters worse, no one wanted to buy the pictures at the prices he thought right. He feared they would be burnt and wanted them shipped abroad. Eventually he settled for having them sent to his sister's house in Ripley, Derbyshire, where they could be stored in the attic.

"London Day by Day", signed "Peterborough", a name taken from the alley running beside the *Telegraph* offices, took an interest in obscenity. Earlier in the year, it had applauded the Home Secretary for banning Radclyffe Hall's lesbian novel *The Well of Loneliness*.

The next year Lawrence died, and Peterborough took another bite at the cherry. "The kink in the brain developed early," the column judged, "and he came to write with one hand always in the slime.

"His later books and poems were rightly banned by the Censor, like the unspeakable pictures which were brazenly exhibited in London last summer... The man was ill, the mind diseased, and the two maladies slowly gathered strength together."

'Boccaccio Story' was one of the 13 pictures taken away by the police after the 'Peterborough' column called them 'gross and obscene'

A WORK OF ART DESTROYED

Chiselling off the mosaics at Westminster

Images on the apse above the high altar of Westminster Cathedral were smashed after a campaign in The Daily Telegraph

In 1935 *The Daily Telegraph* helped to destroy a huge work of art – the mosaics covering the High Altar apse at the east end of Westminster Cathedral. Or, viewing it from a different perspective, the paper was responsible for saving the cathedral from an entirely unsuitable blemish.

Westminster Cathedral was substantially complete when its architect John Francis Bentley died in 1902, but the internal decoration was entirely lacking, the great arches and domes remaining in grey brick and dark cement. The intention was to finish the work on the interior as money became available. Some of the architect's ideas were dumped never to be revived, such as the wonderful scheme for a marble floor inlaid with the outline of fishes. Bentley's plan was to have the whole interior surface of the roofs and apses covered with golden mosaics in the Byzantine style.

Under Cardinal Bourne, who became Archbishop of Westminster in 1903, some mosaics were designed by a Royal Academician, Gilbert Pownall, and were installed in the Lady chapel in 1930. More than three million Venetian glass tesserae were pressed into the mastic cement on the walls of the chapel before its mosaics were complete.

By 1934 a model of the next task, Pownall's design for the great apse behind the High Altar, was put on public display. Above the arched windows were to be large figures of the Apostles, and between the windows scenes from the life of Christ, with at each side Old Testament scenes such as Moses and the Burning Bush, and Pharaoh's army foundering in the Red Sea.

Work began in the autumn of that year, but by then the first broadside had been fired in the pages of the *Telegraph* by the art critic Edward Hutton. As an historian of Italian and Byzantine art, Hutton knew what he was talking about. As a convert to Catholicism five years earlier, with enough money to endow new churches, his voice was not to be ignored.

In 1923 Hutton had built the Arts and Crafts church of Our Lady and St Peter at Leatherhead, with its carved stone Stations of the Cross by Eric Gill and its fine stained-glass windows by Paul Woodroffe (including a nativity scene featured in 1992 on the annual British set of postage stamps for Christmas).

In a letter to the paper, published prominently in its news columns next to a large piece about Prohibition in America, on December 7, 1933 Hutton drew attention to developments at the cathedral, "a building which especially interests us all as one of the finest of our time, and as a monument of our world city, used on many national, imperial and international occasions".

After noting the cathedral's "beautiful and moving Stations of the Cross, now famous all over the world" by Eric Gill, Hutton went on to say that "there are other things which have recently appeared in Westminster Cathedral which can, I feel, be regarded only with anxiety, and now with dismay". He meant the apse mosaics.

Hutton did not pull his punches. "In the large mosaic which fills the semi-dome," he wrote, "the design as a whole is meaningless, weak and incoherent; the figures are mean and very poorly and clumsily drawn; the drapery ugly; the colour inharmonious and crude."

He then showed off some of his academic knowledge of the matter. "We are told the style of these mosaics has been suggested by, or based upon, the work of the Second Golden Age of Byzantine art as we see it at Palermo, for instance, 'with an undertone' of today. It does not need more than a single glance at the work at Cefalu, or in the Martorana, in the Cappella Palatina, or even at Monreale or at Venice, to discover the poverty, feebleness and vulgarity of this work at Westminster."

Under the cross-heading "Ruining a great building", Hutton then came

A model of Gilbert Pownall's designs for the mosaics in the great apse at the east end of Westminster Cathedral. Work on them was stopped in 1936 and the work that was completed hacked off again

to his unequivocal climax. "Dismay and grief will not allow me to remain silent in view of the vast mosaic which is now uncovered upon the arch of the great sanctuary of the church. In the empty puerility of its design, the weakness and clumsiness of its drawing, and not least the ugliness and crudity of its colour, it would seem to involve the whole great church in little less than ruin."

According to Patrick Rogers, the present-day historian of the cathedral, Cardinal Bourne was irritated. He himself had been to see the mosaics at Monreale, one of the sites mentioned in Hutton's letter.

In an issue of the cathedral magazine, the Cardinal said he expected "a golden mean between the sixth-century mosaics of Ravenna and those installed a thousand years later at St Peter's, Rome". In any case, he wanted his cathedral to be not a museum of art, but a house of prayer, so that "everything should assist the piety of the ordinary faithful Catholic".

But within a year Cardinal Bourne was dead. Edward Hutton soon pressed his case with his successor, Archbishop Arthur Hinsley (who was made a cardinal in 1937). In December 1935, the *Telegraph* reported that Hutton had gathered a posse of big names in the art establishment to send a stern memorandum to the Archbishop of Westminster. The signatories asserted that the new mosaics were "lacking in the finer qualities of art", and the finished work they could "only consider with dismay", which was a favourite word of Hutton's.

The memorandum was signed by the presidents of the Royal Academy and the Royal Institute of British Architects, the director of the National Gallery (Kenneth Clark) and other well known names such as Sir William Rothenstein and Charles Holden. Even Eric Gill signed.

According to the *Telegraph*, "the Archbishop had replied in extremely cordial terms". Hinsley was willing to let himself be persuaded. His other concern was that money was being spent on decoration that could have been spent on schools for the poor. He cautiously announced the establishment of a "small advisory committee of art experts to consider all questions relating to the interior decoration of the building".

Work on the mosaics was stopped and the aggrieved Pownall was paid £2,000 in compensation. As the boys of the cathedral choir sang in their stalls in the great apse, little tesserae of mosaic would occasionally fall onto their music sheets.

In 1936 the completed mosaics were hacked off by workmen. At one moment it seemed that Eric Gill might design mosaics to replace them. He wanted to keep the design simple and geometrical. He also mused: "How beautiful the Cathedral would look whitewashed." But Gill died in 1940. Seventy years on, the smooth surface of the apse half-dome remains bare still.

INBRIEF

MARCH 15, 1949

Dr Fisher, Archbishop of Canterbury, for the second time in 15 months, publicly dissociated himself last night from actions and political utterances of Dr Hewlett Johnson, Dean of Canterbury. The Dean is a member of the editorial board of the Communist *Daily Worker*.

In a statement issued from Lambeth Palace Dr Fisher said: "In December, 1947 I found it necessary to issue a statement dissociating myself from the political opinions and activities of the Dean of Canterbury.

"Nonetheless it has recently been supposed by many people in Canada and the United States during the Dean's visit to those countries that he speaks for the Archbishop of Canterbury or with my approval. I therefore repeat that the supposition is entirely incorrect. It is a matter of great regret that the Dean should advocate views which are so insensitive to the true facts of the situation.

"Since it is frequently asked why the Dean is not removed from his office because of his opinions, I must say first that for removal from office the law requires a trial and conviction in some civil or ecclesiastical court and that the Dean has not rendered himself liable to a charge in either court.

"Secondly, in this country we greatly value the right to freedom of speech and the law is slow to curtail it, even when it proves inconvenient, irksome or hurtful. Its suppression is one of the grave charges against those totalitarian and police states which enjoy the Dean's confidence."

THE STONE OF SCONE STOLEN

Westminster Abbey burgled by nationalists

It had been in England since 1296 but in 1950 four young Scottish nationalists smuggled it away in the boot of a car

'The Coronation Stone was stolen early on Christmas morning from under the Coronation Chair in Westminster Abbey, where it had rested for 650 years," the *Telegraph* reported on December 27, 1950. "Scottish nationalists are suspected."

The paper's chosen name for the stone remained "the Coronation Stone". Others called it the Stone of Scone or the Stone of Destiny. "It is of sandstone," the *Telegraph* explained, "26½in by 16¾in by 10¾in and weighs 468lb (over 4cwt)." In fact it weighs 336lb. Baselessly reputed to be the stone that Jacob used as a pillow, it had been stolen from Scotland by King Edward I of England in 1296.

In 1950 the thieves had apparently hidden in the Abbey overnight, removed the Stone and forced their way out with a crowbar through the door at Poets' Corner. Scotland Yard warned police to watch for the Stone and for a Ford Anglia car driven by a woman, aged about 25. With her was a man of about 29. Both the man and the woman spoke with Scottish accents. Airfields and seaports were told to keep watch for any heavy packages, particularly those labelled "geological specimens".

On December 28, Holy Innocents Day, the paper reported a radio appeal by the Dean of Westminster for help in the Stone's recovery. "You may imagine my feelings," said Dr Alan Don, "when early on Christmas morning, of all days, the Clerk of the Works rushed into my bedroom and told me that the Coronation Stone had gone." It was an "act of sacrilege" and "senseless crime", carried out with "great cunning". The King was "greatly distressed".

On December 30, the Serpentine having been uselessly dragged, the paper reported a "petition to the King, whose authors claim to be the persons who removed the Coronation Stone".

"As proof of their *bona fides*, the petitioners said the mainspring of the wristlet watch found in the Abbey when the Stone was missed on Christmas morning was recently repaired."

Then the trail went cold until April, 107 days after the theft, when the Stone was suddenly delivered to

the ruined Abbey of Arbroath by three unknown men who drove up to the gates in a black saloon car at 12.20 pm.

"The three men took out the Stone," wrote the *Telegraph*'s reporter, "resting on a four-handled wooden litter. They deposited it in the presence of the custodian at the base of the high altar where King William the Lion of Scotland lies buried. Here Robert the Bruce signed the Scottish Declaration of Independence in 1320.

"It was draped with the blue St Andrew's flag. Bareheaded, the men carried their 4cwt burden 100 yards across the lawn. After calling the attention of the custodian to two letters lying on the flag they left. Less than three hours later Angus county police took the stone in a van to Forfar.

"Mr James Wishart, the Abbey custodian, said: 'The three men asked if I would take delivery of the Stone and I agreed at least until the police came. In the excitement, I forgot to ask them their names.' "

Among many Scots there was no appetite to apprehend the thieves. The King, at a lunch in Preston, was handed a note giving him the news of the Stone's return. "He smiled broadly and passed the note round." The clerk of works of Westminster Abbey hurried to Scotland, bringing, to check the match, a small piece chipped off the Stone when it was stolen.

A letter that was left with the Stone read: "Unto his Majesty King George VI, the Address of his Majesty's Scottish subjects who removed the Stone of Destiny from Westminster Abbey and have since retained it in Scotland

The Stone in place in the Coronation Chair during the crowning of King George VI in Westminster Abbey in 1937. At each end of the buff-coloured lump of coarse sandstone (below) ancient iron rings are set, attached by staples secured by lead run into the fixing holes

humbly showeth: That in their actions they as loyal subjects have intended no indignity or injury to his Majesty.

"That they have been inspired in all they have done by their deep love of his Majesty's realm of Scotland and by their desire to compel the attention of his Majesty's Minister to the widely expressed demand of Scottish people for a measure of self-government.

"That in removing the Stone of Destiny, they were restoring to the people of Scotland the most ancient and most honourable part of the Scottish regalia which for many centuries was venerated as the palladium of their liberty and which in 1296 was pillaged from Scotland in the false hope it would be the symbol of their humiliation and conquest.

"That the Stone was kept in Westminster Abbey in defiance of a Royal command and despite the promise of its return to Scotland.

"That by no other means than the forceful removal of the Stone from Westminster Abbey was it possible even to secure discussion as to its rightful resting place.

"That it is the earnest hope of his Majesty's Scottish people that arrangements for the proper disposition of the Stone may now be made after consultation with the General Assembly of the Church of Scotland, who as successors of the Abbot of Scone are its natural guardians.

"That it is the earnest prayer of his Majesty's loyal subjects who have served his Majesty both in peace and war, that the blessing of Almighty God be with the King and all his peoples, so that in peace they may enjoy the freedom which sustains the loyalty of affection rather than the obedience of servility.

"GOD SAVE THE KING."

On St Andrew's Day 1996 the Stone was returned to Scotland by the British Government. It looked "surprisingly small and fragile" wrote Andrew Gilligan in *The Sunday Telegraph*.

By then the theft of the stone from Westminster Abbey seemed more a source of pride than a "senseless crime". Kay Matheson, 22 when she took part in the theft, told *The Daily Telegraph* in 1996 how she had dodged the police in 1950 with the Stone in the boot of her car. "I had to lie low in Scarborough for a while," she remembered. "There were police roadblocks on all the roads over the border. I drove it back to Scotland once the initial storm had died down a bit."

She was pleased by its return to Scotland, but suspected that John Major, Prime Minister at the time, was trying to win votes. Ian Hamilton QC, the best known of the stonenappers, called its return to Scotland a "circus" for clownish politicians. The two other Glasgow University students in on the theft were Alan Stuart and Gavin Vernon.

The Stone stayed on show at Edinburgh Castle, despite a petition to house it at Moot Hill in the grounds of Scone Palace. The understanding was for it to be lent to Westminster Abbey for the next coronation.

THE HOTTEST DAY

So hot that MPs sat in their shirtsleeves

In 1911 the thermometer hit a hundred degrees – but not officially. It was never to rise higher in the 20th century

'All previous official readings of maximum temperatures were exceeded, and August 9, 1911 was officially and unofficially declared to be the hottest day experienced in the metropolis in the past 70 years," reported *The Daily Telegraph* the next day.

There was a reading at Greenwich of 100F, and it was officially 97F in the shade at South Kensington, Camden Square, and Hillington, Norfolk. "The sun blazed out from an almost cloudless sky. Scarcely a breath of wind was blowing and that which was experienced came from the sunny South."

"I have kept a record for some years, and have a Kew-certified instrument in a screen in my garden," wrote Mr G.T. Phillips of Wokingham to the paper on August 10. "The soil is gravel, and I am 225 feet above sea level. On Wednesday, at 12.45pm, it stood at exactly 100 degrees, and remained so until 2.30pm."

These extremes invited extreme responses even among the elected representatives of the people. "At a meeting of the Grand Committee of the House of Commons which is considering the Coal Mines Bill," the *Telegraph* reported on August 11, "one member, in rather a hesitating manner, removed his coat. The example was no sooner set than other members did likewise, and the discussion was carried on with half the members of the committee, about a score, in their shirtsleeves."

Some weren't so lucky. "Whilst working on a barge off Battersea during the tropical heat on Wednesday, Henry Alfred Petch, 49, of Britannia Place, Battersea, suddenly became ill and ran into a house, where he collapsed," the paper reported. "At the inquest yesterday, Dr Prior said it was due to heart failure following apoplexy, caused by the sun's rays."

"Everyone is asking," the *Telegraph* commented on August 12, "when the present heat and drought are coming to an end. Sensational statements have been made regarding both. A rigid scrutiny reveals the fact that, after a fairly normal but somewhat cool June, we have now had during the last 40 days a distinct general drought over the middle and south

The seaside comes to town for these young women cooling off in the Serpentine, Hyde Park, in the record-breaking August heat of 1911. On an August day, 92 years later, the temperature rose to an even higher record, with 100.6F (38.1C), at Gravesend, Kent

of England. This has been accompanied by temperatures which in July gave us no fewer than 17 days with over 80 degrees, and four days with over 90 degrees in the shade at Greenwich."

As for drought, it pointed out unconsolingly, worse had frequently been known. "Between 1815 and last year 10 great droughts have been recorded at Greenwich in the spring and summer, each averaging 83 days in duration, with 13 rain days, and a total average rainfall during each period of only 1.07 inches. The longest of these droughts was 120 days in 1893; the shortest was 62 days, in 1834; and the one which combined the greatest number of days

SPANISH INFLUENZA

The epidemic that killed more than the war

As the Great War came to an end a deadly outbreak of flu swept Britain. There were plenty of ideas for remedies. None worked

In the spring and summer of 1918 virulent influenza had swept the Western Front. It gained the name Spanish Flu, although Spain was not its origin. By the autumn the new form of virus began to hit towns and cities at home. The outbreak was to kill some 228,000 in Britain, more than any epidemic since the cholera of 1849. In foreign countries millions died, many more than all those killed in the First World War.

The coming of the influenza to London was reported with a mixture of stoicism and frustration. "Influenza continues to spread in London," reported the *Telegraph* on October 23, "but it is stated that the majority of cases are of a somewhat milder type than those of a week or two ago."

"A strong protest against the inaction of the Government in reference to the shortage of medical men was made by Dr Armstrong at a Hackney inquest yesterday," the paper reported next day. The father of a sick 12-year-old boy went to fetch a doctor, but found "a long queue of patients outside the surgery". The doctor promised to call after surgery hours, but before his arrival the child died.

The coroner said he "wished publicly to declare that the present shortage of medical men was scandalous and disgraceful. He protested against the part of the Government in the matter and said it was time the latter sent the medical men home from the front."

It probably wouldn't have helped, yet there was a feeling that surely something could be done. But what? On October 25 "at some schools it had been necessary to close several departments owing to shortage of staff. The schools were not being closed generally, because it was considered that the children were no more likely to fall victims in well ventilated buildings than they were running about the streets or packed together in picture theatres."

On October 26 the paper wrote: "Although at the moment the indications are that in London the high watermark has been reached, influenza continues to claim fresh victims daily. In the 24 hours ending at 7 o'clock yesterday morning the County Council

with the smallest total rainfall (only 0.53 inch) lasted for 101 days, from March 15 to June 23, in 1844."

Still, things were bad enough. "In parts of East Kent pasturage is practically burnt up. The root crops, especially turnips, are becoming mildewed. At a stock sale, held at Newingreen, near Hythe, lambs were sold at as low a price as one shilling each, the owners having no feed for them."

The next year, August harvests were destroyed in many parts by floods.

In 2003 the highest temperature ever recorded in Britain rose to 100.6F (38.1C), at Gravesend, Kent, on August 10.

INBRIEF

FEBRUARY 11, 1903

"Aldwych" and "Kingsway" were approved by the London County Council as names for the new streets which will result from the Strand and Holborn improvements.

ambulances conveyed to hospital 25 persons stricken with sudden illness in the streets."

Twenty-five policemen had died in London, and "Dr Thresh, medical officer of health for Essex, reported that influenza is spreading along the lines of railway from London to Southend, Epping, Waltham, Colchester, and Cambridge. This he attributes to overcrowding in railway carriages."

"There is no abatement of the influenza epidemic in London," was the news on October 28, "and the local authorities are becoming perturbed."

Still the epidemic grew. On October 29 it was reported that "all the members of the Wimbledon Fire Brigade, numbering about 20, are incapacitated." On October 30 that there were "thousands of patients in the Government departments alone, and the work is being carried on under great difficulties by the staff who remain. Most doctors are working night and day in the endeavour to attend to their patients."

Theories of disease-avoidance abounded. But "according to an authority, the idea that a smoker is more immune from the epidemic than the non-smoker is a fallacy," the *Telegraph* said. "The view he expressed was that a smoker's throat was always more or less relaxed and unhealthy, and consequently more ready to absorb disease germs."

"The Borough of St Pancras has been placarded with posters, advising the public to keep warm and rest in bed on the first appearance of symptoms," it was reported. "A gargle is recommended, consisting of a teaspoonful of salt in half a glass of water, coloured purple with a weak solution of permanganate of potash." Some people queued at chemists for quinine.

Under the headline EAT FAT BACON, the *Telegraph* reported the views of Dr Howarth, a medical officer of health for the City of London. "For the last three years," he said "the proportion of fatty substances consumed by the public has decreased – the meat supply has not been so generous; butter, margarine, and lard have been scarcer; milk is not easy to obtain; cream is prohibited. People have lost weight due entirely to the lack of fatty substances. Although not suffering from the effects of malnutrition, the public are in such a physical condition that they are more prone to the effects of chills. I would therefore suggest that the public should avail itself of the present abundant supply of bacon, particularly fat bacon."

There was advice too from Mr E.W. Morris, house governor of London Hospital. "Do not be frightened," he said. "There is nothing to be frightened about if you take the following precautions. If you get a cold or bad throat or feel feverish, go to bed and stay there four or five days. Influenza only becomes dangerous when you do not go to bed.

"Don't try and fight it and keep about – just go to bed. Send for a doctor if you do not feel better.

"Dissolve a teaspoonful of common salt in a tumbler of warm water, and gargle your throat and mouth with this two or three times a day. Do not go into crowds more than you can help. Wear warm clothes. Eat well, but do not drink spirits. Go to bed early and have as long nights in bed as you can. Remember that you catch disease most easily when you are cold, wet, hungry, and tired.

"Don't talk about influenza. It is already wearing itself out, and will go all the sooner if you don't talk about it. Influenza is a disease that likes to be noticed." That autumn it had certainly succeeded.

INBRIEF

SEPTEMBER 2, 1918
LENIN'S FATE – REPORTED DEATH
On Saturday afternoon the Admiralty issued, via Wireless Press, the following Russian official wireless message, sent at 10.16pm on Friday: "To all. A few hours ago a criminal attempt was made on the life of Mr Lenin at Moscow. Lenin has been wounded."

LENIN REPORTED DEAD
Copenhagen, Sunday.
A telegram which has reached here direct from Petrograd announces that Lenin has succumbed to his wounds.
– Exchange Telegraph Company.
A memoir of Mr Lenin, with other Russian news, appears on page nine.

[But he wasn't dead. Lenin died in January 1924.]

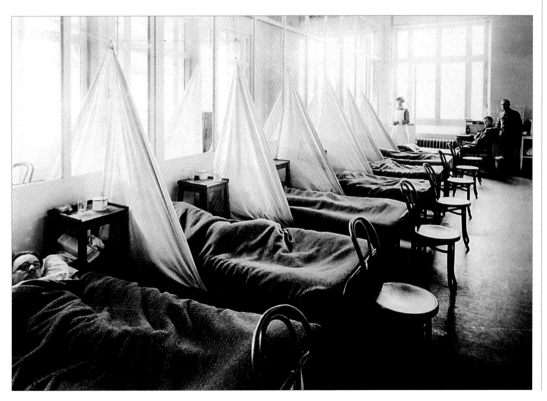

The influenza epidemic first made itself felt on the Western Front. Here servicemen lie in Hospital No 45 in Aix-les-Bains, their beds separated by curtaining

THE DAY LONDON FLOODED

Thousands are made homeless by rush of water

Some drowned in their beds, others fled a surge of water down the streets as the Thames overtopped its embankments

Using a makeshift raft the day after the Thames flooded streets on both the north and south banks in January 1928

T he flood that hit London in the early hours of January 7, 1928 made 4,000 families homeless. The Houses of Parliament became an island. Several people were drowned, some when the basements where they lived filled with water as they slept. The crisis came suddenly for those living

near the Thames. "The flood pursued and overtook them as they ran, and at times it was only with a struggle that they kept their feet. Alarmed householders looked out of windows and saw a raging torrent at their doors. Some took refuge in upper rooms. Others grabbed their children, and, scantily clad, ran for the safety of streets away from the river. Others, less fortunate, were caught like rats in a trap in basement rooms and were drowned."

The trouble, according to that day's *Telegraph*, was an unusually high tide meeting an "immense volume of flood water" coming down from the upper reaches of the Thames after snow thaw. Both sides of the river were inundated, at Westminster and Poplar, Battersea and Greenwich.

"Shortly after 12.30am water was seen to be coming on to the roads near the Temple Station of the District Railway, which is one of the most low-lying parts of the Embankment," it reported. "Little waves were washing against the wall of Temple Gardens and in at the gate." At the Houses of Parliament "water came in great volumes on to the Terrace, then down into the open space at the foot of Big Ben, and over the whole of Old Palace Yard, which was over a foot underwater at 1am."

As the water swept halfway down Vauxhall Bridge

Road, flooding scores of basements, "disconsolate tenants of the houses, aroused by the noise of rushing water, could be seen standing outside their premises watching the firemen at work – work which was mostly in vain".

When day came, 14 people were found to have been killed. Basement dwellers "were either trapped in their sleep and drowned or had just time to make a hasty flight to the upper floors bereaved of all their belongings".

In the basement of the Tate Gallery many Turners were damaged, while the vaults of the Houses of Parliament flooded and the moat of the Tower of London filled. Water poured into the Blackwall Tunnel, and put out of action Lots Road power station, which produced the electricity for the Underground.

The disaster had begun ominously at midnight with the training ship *President* floating menacingly at the level of the parapet of the Embankment. Once that was overtopped, water rushed in with great speed. Outside the Tate Gallery "great blocks of stones were hurled many yards away and the roadway torn up. As the flood surged on, the flight of panic-stricken men, women, and children continued, and when at last the onward rush of water ceased there was five feet of water in Horseferry Road."

Next day from her hospital bed Miss Marjorie Frankeisse told an heroic tale from an incident at Putney in which two girls, Irene and Dorothy Watson, lost their lives. "I heard a sound as if water was being let out of a bath," she said. "When I got out of bed I found that it was swirling round my feet and furniture was floating about in it. I knew that I could not get out into the passage, and I had a brainwave and thought of the window.

"Before I got out I heard Irene Watson go to the telephone in the passage and shout something, and then rush back to her bedroom. Dorothy, who was sleeping in the same room, and was a strong swimmer, got out into the passage, and that was the last I saw of her. As I left the place I shouted, 'Get through the windows.' I saw Irene standing on her bed, which was floating in the water. I got outside, and as I passed the window of Irene's bedroom I heard the smashing of glass as if someone were trying to get out.

"Billy Watson and Peter, my brother, had already got out into the basement area, and Billy was in a bad way. Three times he went under, and I had to grab him to keep him afloat. Two men and three women from the flat above had tied three sheets together and lowered the end into the water. I managed to get Billy to the sheet, and he was hauled up. I knew that Mrs Watson, who is a big woman, was in her room, so I grabbed the sheets and swung myself into her window. At that time there was only about a foot of space between the top of the water and the ceiling. I could see Mrs Watson scrambling towards me, and as she did so her dog Tony, evidently anxious to get to his mistress, pushed her back into the water. This happened several times.

"Still clinging to the sheets held by the five people upstairs, I swung backwards and forwards, holding Mrs Watson until she could grasp the sheet sufficiently to be hauled up to the flat above. Everything happened in a few minutes. I was half-dazed, and in the darkness it was difficult to see what was happening. How we managed to get out I do not know."

The Daily Telegraph's conclusion after the event was that the disaster could hardly have been foreseen. The chairman of the Thames Conservancy Board commented that "to guard against a tidal disaster the only solution he could see was the construction of a barrage across the river – at Tilbury, for example". It was not until 1982 that the Thames Barrier at Silvertown was completed. It was perhaps the greatest achievement of the Greater London Council (1965–86).

THE LOCH NESS MONSTER

The head of a seal and the body of an eel

In the year Hitler became Chancellor of Germany, the people of Britain showed a desire to believe in a monster of their own

As science progressed – towards a foreseeable war – the 1930s developed an alternative interest in phenomena "unknown to science". In 1933 it was the turn of the Loch Ness Monster. The first sighting was made in April by Mrs Aldie Mackay, who managed the Drumnadrochit Hotel. She was being driven by her husband along the new motor-road on the north side of the loch when she saw a whale-like hump in the water. By the time the car stopped it had gone.

"The story of the Loch Ness Monster progresses," reported *The Daily Telegraph* on December 6. "Many people allege that they have seen it. Mr Hugh Gray, a fitter at the aluminium works at Foyers, claims to have photographed it five times – with one success out of the five negatives.

"The negative was described as revealing a creature about 30ft long. It has a head like a seal, and an elongated body like an eel, with two lateral fins. Mr Gray was out walking on the afternoon of Sunday, November 26, when he saw the monster in the loch about 100 yards away. Fortunately he had his camera with him.

"He states that the object was two or three feet

INBRIEF

MARCH 7 1931

From The Children's Telegraph page:

How many leaves do you think a tree has? If there's a wood or park near you go and look at some of the trees and make a guess. The number varies enormously.

A beech tree of average size has 119,000 leaves, but a fir tree has nearly 40,000,000 leaves. An elm tree may have 7,000,000 leaves, and a pine tree from 20,000,000 to 40,000,000 leaves. Of course, in the pine the needles are the leaves.

A birch tree has only some 200,000 leaves. The 7,000,000 leaves of an elm tree, if all put together, would make a surface of about five acres.

We have had a good deal of snow this week, and many of us have been playing at snowballs and making snowmen. The snow seems very light when we pick it up, but when there is a heavy fall hundreds of tons descend on quite a small area.

An inch of rain falling on an acre means 100 tons of water, or 64,000 tons to the square mile. Now a foot of snow is equal to about an inch of rain.

During the last weekend something like a couple of inches of snow fell on an average over perhaps a quarter of the area of Great Britain. That area is 56,214,327 acres, and a quarter of it is 14,053,582 acres. If two inches of snow fell on those acres then about 234,000,000 tons of snow fell on Great Britain in a few hours. What a good thing it is that this does not fall all at one time, and on one place!

The monster made a splash internationally. 'Prehistoric monster or mass hallucination?' asked the French magazine 'Je Sais Tout...' in February 1934

above the surface of the water. 'I did not see any head, but there was considerable motion from what I thought was the tail. The object only appeared for a few minutes. It was of great size.'"

Although the photograph had been snapped up by the Glasgow *Daily Record*, the *Telegraph* explained that a print had been shown to Professor Graham Kerr, a biologist at Glasgow University. "I see nothing in the photograph with a head like a seal," he said, "nor do I see a body like an eel, nor do I see two lateral fins such as have been described by the photographer. What I do see is a curved shape in the water, with the appearance of vertical splashes rising up from it. I find this picture which you have shown to me utterly unconvincing as a photograph of any living creature."

People were not to be dissuaded. The Secretary of State for Scotland was urged to take steps to protect the monster in Loch Ness from the irresponsibly curious. "The Chief Constable of Inverness-shire, has offered to cause warning to be given to as many of the residents and visitors as possible for the purpose of preventing any attack on the animal if sighted," he told the local MP obligingly.

On December 21 the *Telegraph* carried a classified advertisement. "Monster of Loch Ness," it ran. "Two ex-officers, Intelligence (Naval and RE), have devised practicable scheme for securing this creature alive. Monster will be the sole property of sportsman, scientist or syndicate providing necessary expenses with suitable honorarium if successful. Perfectly good references."

"Are there two monsters in Loch Ness?" the paper asked on December 29 after two sightings the day before on opposite sides of the Loch, 15 miles apart. Two women driving along said they had seen it "cleaving through the water" a little north of Foyers. Two men in a lorry said they had had a clear view of the "creature" near Fort Augustus.

The next day 12 Boy Scouts arrived at Foyers to keep a lookout for the monster. They were put up in the local church hall. Even on the train bringing them from Glasgow they were told by a woman from Foyers that 35 years earlier her father had seen the monster floating about the loch.

"The number of visitors here is growing," reported the *Telegraph*. A French journalist telephoned daily reports to his newspaper; there were dozens of cameramen and some film companies.

"A number of bones which were found on the shores of Loch Ness near to the ancient castle of Urquhart have now been identified," the *Telegraph* mentioned. "They were sent to the Royal Scottish Museum, Edinburgh, and have been identified as (1) recent ox – or cow – teeth and the jaw of a pig; and (2) probably a piece of bone of a large bird, broken and weatherworn, but probably of no great age."

At 11.30pm on December 31, 1933 the Boy Scouts left the church hall and launched their outboard motorboat into the Loch. "As the local church bells chimed 12, the boys dipped their mugs into the loch and drank," the *Telegraph* reporter wrote. "They

then fired dummy revolvers. That is how they brought in the New Year. Earlier they had made their first voyage up the loch in the hope of catching a glimpse of the monster." The scouts' leader Captain Wright, though, formed the conviction that ripples, "with their humps", caused by wind on the water, had been mistaken for a strange creature.

A startling development hit the news pages on January 6. An Edinburgh veterinary surgeon, Mr Arthur Grant, said that while motorcycling along the north side of the loch by moonlight early that morning he had almost run into a strange great beast on the road at Abriachan. This was opposite the place on the south side of the loch where Mr Spicer, of London, and Mrs Reid, the wife of the postmaster at Inversarigaig, had previously seen a monster on land.

"The animal took fright, went down the bank in two great leaps, plunged into the loch, and disappeared," the paper reported. "This is his description of the creature he saw: length 15 to 20ft; large body; long neck with small, eel-like head; large oval shaped eyes just on top of head; flippers, two sets, apparently webbed; tail probably five to six feet, rounded at end."

"It was a bright moonlight morning," Mr Grant said. "Some 40 yards away, under the shadow of the hills near Abriachan, I saw what appeared to be a large black object on the opposite side of the road. I was almost on it when it turned what I thought was a small head on a long neck. The creature, apparently taking fright, made two great bounds across the road and plunged into the loch.

"I had a splendid view of the object. In fact, I almost struck it with my motorcycle. The body was very hefty. I distinctly saw two front flippers. There were two other flippers, which seemed to be webbed, behind. Knowing something about natural history, I can say that I have never seen anything in my life like the animal I saw."

On January 11 the monster was seen between Drumnadrochit Bay and Urquhart castle by two Inverness women motoring on the Dores-Inverness road. The women were Mrs Margaret Cameron, of Porterfield Bank, and Miss Ila Tinnock, daughter of a warder at Inverness prison. They described the creature as having a big grey back standing 2ft out of the water and setting up a great wash. It brought to 15 the number of people who had reported sightings that week.

On April 2 it was the turn of members of the East of England women's hockey team. Miss Warwick Peterborough told a *Telegraph* reporter: "When we were about three miles from Invermoriston, returning to Inverness, I distinctly saw the head and tail of some creature about 200 yards out in the loch. I called to my companions, but the object disappeared quickly, and all they saw was a great movement of the water."

But no one caught the beast, nor were there indubitable photographs of it. A sonar scan of the loch in 1987 proved inconclusive.

CRYSTAL PALACE BURNS

Molten glass pours down as flames leap up

One night the 25-acre wonder of Victorian engineering crashed into incandescent ruins as crowds risked their lives to watch

The Crystal Palace was destroyed by a spectacular fire on the night of November 30, 1936. The great glass building, 1,850ft long, and covering 25 acres, was ablaze from end to end within half an hour of the alarm being raised.

The Crystal Palace, in which the Great Exhibition had been held in 1851, had been moved with its 293,655 panes of glass from Hyde Park to Sydenham Hill in the following year. Now flames rose 300ft

into the air, and the fire was seen from the Devil's Dyke, near Brighton, and from an aeroplane over the English Channel.

The fire broke out at about 8pm, and although the structure was of glass and iron, flames spread with astonishing speed through the huge transepts and galleries divided by wooden partitions and filled with furniture. A waxworks exhibition in one hall melted and fed the flames. Within half an hour, the north transept, 175ft high, had fallen in with a roar audible for miles. At 8.55 the end wall of the south transept fell. "A spiral staircase inside made an incandescent pillar," wrote the *Telegraph* reporter.

"Hundreds of thousands of people flocked to the scene," *The Daily Telegraph* reported, "and fire engines had great difficulty in getting through the congested streets. More than 90 fire appliances, with 500 fireman, were engaged – a record for any London fire." Streams of molten glass poured down outside the building, forcing the firemen back.

Owing to the height of the Palace there was great difficulty in obtaining adequate water pressure. Domestic supplies were cut down over a wide area, but the loss of water pressure meant that the firemen had to leave the central parts of the building to burn themselves out.

The heat was so great that the firemen sprayed water on each other to prevent their tunics from scorching. "Their efforts were greatly handicapped

Palm trees and gigantic statues adorn the Egyptian Court at the Crystal Palace after its move to Sydenham, as pictured in 1854 in one of a series of photographs by Philip Delamotte. In the fire of 1936, statues 'crashed one by one with tremendous thuds into the furnace below'

Such was the heat that firemen had to play their hoses on one another to stop their tunics scorching. The next morning, beneath a surviving tower, all that could be seen was a smoking tangle of iron and molten glass

by the large number of buses and private cars on the Palace Parade. The buses were pushed by the firemen on to pavements and cars were even run into front gardens.

"Hundreds of spectators were imperilled when the south tower, 282ft high, threatened to collapse into the streets from which they were watching. With difficulty mounted police forced them back. The crowd, not realising the danger and thrilled by the spectacle, refused to be pushed back and the efforts of the police were greeted with catcalls. Finally, 3,000 police threw a cordon round the whole area."

Houses near the tall tower were evacuated, and to save it from the flames buildings at the foot of the tower were blown up with dynamite. "An orchestra practising in the palace had a narrow escape," the *Telegraph* reported, "leaving the building just before the great Centre Transept crashed with a roar that was heard for miles, burying the cars of several members."

After one explosion within the blaze, broken glass showered on Penge West railway station, half a mile away. "Bicycles, on which thousands had ridden to the scene of the fire, were forced out of their owners' hands and many were trampled on when the crowd surged backwards."

Thousands of birds in an aviary in the palace were released. They rose in a flock through the lurid smoke and circled around in an attempt to get clear

of the blaze. Many could be seen fighting their way upwards, only to be overcome by the smoke and come fluttering down into the flames. Hundreds of fish in the aquarium were boiled.

Almost from the start of the blaze aeroplanes were circling round the palace and over the fire. Some had been chartered from Croydon by parties wishing to obtain an aerial view of the spectacle, and others carried photographers. Several narrowly escaped, caught in the columns of heated air.

At 2am a rising wind, blowing from the south, swept the flames with new vigour into the north transept. Huge yellow and red tongues turned the transept into a raging inferno. In the red glow, huge stone statues, lining the walls, stood out blackly and, as their supports collapsed, crashed one by one with tremendous thuds into the furnace below.

"By three o'clock this morning," the paper reported on December 1 in a late edition, "the towers were all that was left of London's amusement palace. The rest of the great building was a mass of twisted red hot metal, from parts of which flames were still leaping. Molten glass dropped from the great girders into the ruined halls beneath." Apparatus in the research laboratories of the Baird Television Company was also destroyed.

The surviving towers were demolished during the Second World War lest they guide enemy aircraft to their bombing targets.

INDIAN MUTINY DINNER

Veterans eat plum pudding in the Albert Hall

Fifty years on, six hundred old soldiers commemorate 1857 with a grand Christmas dinner. But dozens live in the workhouse

Commemorating the Mutiny, an angel representing peace, by Carlo Marochetti, surrounded by a Gothic screen by Henry Yule, now stands at All Souls church, Cawnpore, having been moved there from the site of a well in which massacred women and children were thrown in 1857

The Albert Hall was filled with tables for a grand Christmas dinner for 600 old soldiers 50 years on from the Indian Mutiny of 1857. Piper Angus Gibson of the Black Watch, the last survivor of those who played in the relieving forces to Lucknow after a 90-day siege, led a contingent of pipers in *The Campbells are Coming*, the very tune that half a century before had told the besieged that Sir Colin Campbell and his men were coming to their aid.

Then came a dinner of Victorian heartiness. Everyone ate mock turtle soup, roast turkey, ham, tongue, roast beef, salad, plum pudding and mince pies. The officers drank hock, claret, whisky, brandy and punch, with cigars; the men drank ale, stout and punch and had the advantage of being issued with a souvenir pipe to smoke their tobacco. "They fell to in as brisk a fencing bout with victuals as ever clattered on plates like blade on buckler."

Next day, December 24, a complete page was devoted to the names of officers who had accepted invitations. The whole thing was reported in column after column of the cheerfully elevated prose thought proper to the occasion. "The band played. Waiters skipped up and down the gangways with flagons of ale and stout, and I beheld one veteran take up his flagon mightily with both hands, and not lower it again until he had dealt with its contents in such fashion as might instruct the men of these degenerate days.

"They had *Rule Britannia!* to dessert. And the band went on playing. They had *Pomp and Circumstance*; and pipes and snuff and punch, which they considered a symphony worthy of Elgar."

It was all *The Daily Telegraph*'s doing, and they had recruited Field Marshal Lord Roberts, veteran of the Mutiny itself, of Kabul in later years, and then of Pretoria, to chair the crowd of ancients. Lord Curzon, the Viceroy from 1899 to 1905, made a stirring speech, telling a well-worn anecdote of Sir Colin Campbell during the Mutiny asking who the young Lieutenant Roberts was; he soon found out when Roberts recaptured the colours in battle, winning a Victoria Cross. Rudyard Kipling was

there, his black coat standing out among the bright uniforms, and he had written a poem for the day.

Today, across our fathers' graves
The astonished years reveal
The remnant of that desperate host,
Which cleansed our East with steel.

Forty years after the dinner, India was to gain its independence. The Mutiny itself is now called the First War of Independence by some.

In 1907 imperial perspectives were different. The commemorative dinner took some arranging, because there was no central record of where the survivors of the Mutiny were. Most were dead. "The scene had been conjured up out of an apparent oblivion, from which it seemed only a few months ago no commemoration could ever be rescued," the *Telegraph* said. "It has been brought together when the dispersal of the veterans who composed it had seemed beyond gathering."

The reporter sent to cover the arrival of the veterans at King's Cross station adopted an uncertain Trollopean line in dialogue. "The first two stepped out of the train at 10 minutes past 3am," he wrote, "when King's Cross was a compound of ghostliness and gloom, the latter perhaps predominating. 'Eh, it's a big place London,' said one as they walked towards the courtyard. 'You could put Middlesbrough in here an' it would never be missed.' ''deed you could,' rejoined the other, 'an' 20 Middlesbroughs.'

"Installed in the station hotel, they drank hot coffee gratefully, for the journey had been long – 12 hours for one from start to finish. But the rain poured dismally on the pavement outside, and the sight dispirited them. Like children, they grew suddenly tired, and presently went off to bed."

But the next contingent displayed more stamina. "We're just fine here," they protested, "if ye'll alloo us to crack by this fire we'll be muckle obleeged till yee."

The old soldiers were transported en masse from the railway terminus in buses across town to the Albert Hall. "The minds of the old fellows wandered as happily and gaily as ever through the almost illimitable field of their recollection, and not the suddenest sway or most violent bump daunted or even interrupted them."

" 'Have you both got tickets?' asked one of the stewards of a couple of seasoned warriors as they presented themselves at the entrance to the Albert Hall. The elder of the twain displayed on his breast the blue rosette which singled out the invited veteran from the rest of the world; the other, and the younger, had modestly concealed under his overcoat the medals which were the reward of military service in Afghanistan and in Egypt. 'I unfortunately have no ticket,' said the latter, uncovering his decorations at the steward's request. 'But wouldn't you like to be inside?' asked the steward, who was evidently a man of sympathy who grasped the pathos of the incident. 'I should give anything to be inside,' said he; 'this is my father.' And forthwith a seat was found for the younger man, to the evident delight of both. The crowded hour that ushered in yesterday's celebration fairly teemed with incidents such as these."

In his speech Lord Curzon "called for honour to the women who faced the perils of 1857 with fortitude and heroism equal to that of the men, and no sentence was greeted with more sincere enthusiasm. By the little band of ladies who were present it was heard with gently bowed heads in a sense of womanly pride."

But in the reports next day the paper pointed out that "in many ways the most pathetic feature" of the event was that more than 100 of those eligible to attend were living in workhouses. Friends helped to buy clothes for them to wear to the Albert Hall, lest they be shamed. The *Telegraph* paid fares for those with no friends with any money. Those too infirm to travel were sent hampers. "It cannot be right," the *Telegraph* declared, "that any of the heroes of 1857 should be left to die in a workhouse."

GANDHI ARRESTED
The Mahatma taken from the Bombay train

The Telegraph man alone witnessed the arrest. After the scoop a policeman called at Fleet Street to demand the source's name

The arrest of Gandhi (above), who had instigated a campaign of civil disobedience, led to mass protests, like this one (top), which stretched for two miles down Sandhurst Road, Bombay

'**S**hould the Government of India resolve to arrest Gandhi," wrote the *Telegraph*'s political correspondent on May 1, 1930, "that step would be endorsed in London. In some quarters it is thought that a decision may not be long delayed."

Those two sentences sent the British Government into a panic. On the same day, the *Telegraph* had alarming news to report from India, thanks to its resourceful special correspondent Ellis Ashmead-Bartlett, the man who had joined the paper's staff during the siege of Sidney Street.

"I learn," Ashmead-Bartlett said in a telegram from Bombay, "that all European women and children in the north-west Province, the Punjab, and the United Provinces, where there is general unrest, have received instructions to be ready to evacuate their homes." Two platoons of Royal Garhwal Rifles had refused to fire on a riot at Peshawar. It was something like mutiny.

India had been brought to a high pitch of excitement by the campaign of civil disobedience instigated by Gandhi. A general uprising against British rule was feared. At last on May 5 Gandhi was arrested. Ashmead-Bartlett was "the only representative of a British newspaper present at the deserted spot when the Mahatma was taken from the Ahmedabad-Bombay train", the *Telegraph* noted. "The affair was conducted on both sides with complete equanimity and courtesy."

There was far less equanimity at home within the administration of Ramsay MacDonald. It was bad enough the *Telegraph*'s exposing the Government's uncertain grip in India, but for it to know in advance the decisions of the Cabinet was alarming. A policeman was sent to Fleet Street to demand from the editor, Arthur Watson, the name of the source for what was alleged to be a State secret.

Not until a week later did the readers come to know of the Government pressure. "The police were acting on Government instructions under the provision of the Official Secrets Acts," the paper explained in a news column. "The reason given for taking action in this case was that the premature announcement of Gandhi's arrest might result in organised resistance and bloodshed." But Gandhi, immediately after his arrest, had actually been put on a public train, the *Telegraph* pointed out, and no disturbance of any kind occurred.

The intervention raised the question: "whether only such political information is to be allowed to be published as members of the Government may themselves think fit".

What the public did not know then, or for many years, was that the source of the story, written by W.J. Foss, was none other than the Home Secretary, J.R. Clynes. Quiet negotiation between *The Daily Telegraph* and the Home Office secured an undertaking that no such action under the Official Secrets Act should be taken in future without the agreement of the Attorney General.

SUFFRAGETTE ARSON

Yarmouth pier burnt down in votes campaign

In one night Suffragette firebombs were set off in a theatre, a factory, a stately home – and a pier. Only war halted the epidemic

O n the eve of the First World War, British Suffragettes engaged in a campaign of arson. Perhaps the best remembered Suffragette image today remains one of which film footage survives – Emily Davison throwing herself to her death beneath the hoofs of the King's horse Anmer at the Derby in 1913. But in 1911 Emily Davison had set fire to pillar boxes, and this tactic was continued in 1913 and 1914.

On April 17 there was an "epidemic" of firebombs, one of which completely destroyed "the handsome pavilion on the Britannia Pier in Yarmouth", as *The Daily Telegraph* reported next day.

In the early hours of the morning a fire was also discovered at the Empire Theatre, Kingston upon Thames, with thousands of pounds of damage caused to the stage and furnishings. There were fires on the same day at Columbia Market, Shoreditch; at Kempton Park race course; at Staines Linoleum Works, with £15,000 of damage; at Nidd Hall, Ripley, Yorkshire, the house of Lord Furness; at a Bolton cotton-waste warehouse; and at Penzance, where a cinema or "picture palace" was destroyed.

Yarmouth for reasons known only to the Suffragettes had been a frequent target in those months, with attempted damage to the golf links, a fire at the scenic railway, an attempt to set ablaze Wellington Pier, and then the destruction of Brown's Timber Yard on the same day as the Britannia Pier pavilion.

"Nothing now remains of the structure that was at once a pleasant attraction to townsfolk and visitors, and a brilliant landmark by night to sailors at sea, except a grotesque framework of steel girders, so twisted as to give an absurd appearance of fragility," the *Telegraph* commented. "It is a grim relic of a campaign which Yarmouth is never likely to forget."

After the fire, Suffragette literature was found scattered about. "Among it was a postcard, bearing the printed words, 'McKenna has nearly killed Mrs Pankhurst. We can show no mercy until women are enfranchised.' On the reverse side was the battle

The 'pleasant attraction' of the pavilion on the Britannia Pier, Yarmouth (above), and (top), after the arson attack, the 'grotesque framework of steel girders, so twisted as to give an absurd appearance of fragility'

cry, 'Votes for Women'. Later today Mr Harry Tunbridge, the manager of the Britannia Pier, received a letter, bearing the Great Yarmouth postal mark, timed 1.15pm, with a single word, written inside in a woman's handwriting, 'Retribution'."

The reference to McKenna was to the Home Secretary who in 1913 had introduced brutal forcible feeding for Suffragettes in jail on hunger strike, and these included Emmeline Pankhurst, the founder of the Women's Social and Political Union. The first number of the *New Statesman* in April 1913 expressed the outrage her treatment caused: "The fact that Mrs Pankhurst can make him unpopular by dying on Mr McKenna's hands does not give him a right to add one ounce to the weight of her sentence. If she will not eat, he can charge her with an attempt at suicide by starvation. If she is sentenced to an additional month for that, and she repeats the attempt, he can get her certified as insane if he can induce any doctor to make an obviously false declaration, in which case Mrs Pankhurst would, we presume, be fed in an asylum by properly qualified persons without deliberate attempts to 'break down her resistance' by hurting her as much as possible."

But with the outbreak of war, Mrs Pankhurst turned her energies to recruiting soldiers. In 1915 *The Suffragette* paper changed its name to *Britannia* – not after the burnt pier. In 1918 a limited franchise was granted to women, and the pillar boxes of Britain were left uncharred until the IRA campaign on the eve of the Second World War.

IRA KILL FIELD-MARSHAL

Shot dead in London outside his front door

In 1922 a First World War commmander was murdered in daylight by two gunmen who opened fire as they were pursued

'Vengeance for loyal devotion to the cause of Ulster' was in the Telegraph's view the motive for the murder of Field-Marshal Sir Henry Wilson

Two IRA men shot dead Field-Marshal Sir Henry Wilson, who had been Chief of the Imperial General Staff in the last year of the First World War, outside his house in Eaton Square, London, on June 22, 1922. He had left the Army and was at the time MP for North Down, a staunch Unionist.

"This infamous crime," the *Telegraph* said, "was, beyond doubt, a political murder, committed as an act of vengeance upon Sir Henry Wilson for his loyal devotion to the cause of Ulster."

Wilson had just returned by taxi after unveiling a war memorial at Liverpool Street Station. The *Telegraph* ran an eyewitness account of his murder from a workman repairing the road outside the corner house. "The Field-Marshal got out of a taxi at the kerb, and, looking up, I saw one man standing on the corner of the road, close to the house, and just near the door was another man. As the Field-Marshal turned from the taxi they both let fly with revolvers. The Field-Marshal quickly stooped as if to dodge the shots, and hurried across the pavement as though about to insert his latchkey in the door. One of the two men then fired a second shot, and the Field-Marshal again ducked. This time the shot appeared to take effect, for he staggered across the pavement away from his door, and fell into the gutter. I think the bullet went into his head."

That might have been the appearance, but a report by the celebrated pathologist Bernard Spilsbury showed later that Wilson had been shot nine times: in the left forearm, twice in the right arm, twice in the left shoulder, in both armpits, twice in the right leg. Both shots to the armpits caused fatal wounds to the lungs.

The murderers shot two others, one a policeman, as they fled. "The fall of Constable March and a civilian who had been shot in the leg naturally made the pursuers keep a respectful distance. The two men, with the revolvers in their hands, continued their way down the terrace, crossing over Eaton Gate Road. They passed some painters at work on a house, who thought there had been a fight. The workmen noted that the smaller man was loading a revolver as he was passing.

"The two men turned into Chester Place, and were accosted by a man standing in the doorway of a public house, who asked, 'What is the matter?' One of them replied: 'They are after us.' They passed into Ebury Street, and had gone about 50 yards when a young constable threw his truncheon at the smaller man, causing him to fall to the ground. 'Kill him! Kill him!' shouted the infuriated crowd, who rushed forward to get hold of him.

"There were, however, a large number of constables up from Gerald Road police station, and many of these gathered round the fallen man and secured him. The bigger man was brought down by a constable who, without coat and waistcoat, had joined in the pursuit from Gerald Road police station. Dashing out of a side street, he struck the man a violent blow with his truncheon, and crumpled him up.

"The crowd instantly bore down both on the constable and the man, and it would have gone hard with the latter if other constables had not been at hand. A spectator says the capture of one of the men was expedited by a bottle accurately flung by a milkman striking him on the head."

The two men were Reginald Dunne (also known as John O'Brien) and Joseph O'Sullivan (also known as James Connelly), both 24. O'Sullivan had lost a leg at Ypres. They were tried in July and hanged on August 10, 1922. In 1976 their remains were sent to Ireland for reburial. Sir Henry Wilson is buried in the crypt of St Paul's Cathedral.

THE WORLD'S LARGEST LINER

The strange history of the Queen Elizabeth

Doubtfully christened, the ship carried 750,000 troops across the wartime Atlantic before her stylish decade of glory

T here was a suspicion at the time that the world's largest liner, the *Queen Elizabeth*, had been launched without being named as planned by the Queen. By September 27, 1938 Elizabeth, the consort of George VI, had been

queen for less than two years, after the abdication of her brother-in-law, Edward VIII. King George had to cancel his engagement to witness the launch because of the crisis of Germany occupying territory in Czechoslovakia; war was feared daily.

The Queen travelled alone to Clydebank to name the 40,000-ton ship, but the ceremony had to wait until the tide was at its height. "Suddenly there came the thunderous crunch of breaking timbers," the *Telegraph* reported, "and the ship began to move. There was a great shout of 'She's going'. Swiftly the vast hull slid away.

"The Queen, apparently taken by surprise, glanced upwards to where the bottle of Empire wine, bedecked in red, white and blue ribbon, still hung from its mast. In another moment it would have been too late. With quick presence of mind, the Queen turned to where a cord was stretched before her and cut it.

"The bottle swung down just in time to catch the last extremity of the bows, and a tremendous cheer greeted its breaking." The Queen was supposed to have said: "I hope that good fortune may ever attend this great ship and all who sail in her. I am very happy to launch her and to name her Queen

The 'Queen Elizabeth' being towed down the Clyde after her naming by Queen Elizabeth, the consort of George VI. As the vast hull slid away, the Queen managed to send a bottle of Empire wine smashing on to the last extremity of her bows

Elizabeth." But none of the 30,000 in the yard had heard her voice naming the ship. Lord Aberconway, chairman of the shipbuilders John Brown, told the *Telegraph* reporter: "As the ship went down the ways, I said to the Queen, 'Quick, Your Majesty, please name her before she reaches the water.' The Queen replied, 'It is all right, I have done so already.' Apparently, by some mischance, the microphone went out of action at that moment, and so the Queen's voice naming the ship remained inaudible even to those near her."

The liner had her good fortune tested when she made a secret maiden voyage across the Atlantic in wartime. On March 7, 1940 British readers learned that the ship had made a safe passage and was to dock at New York.

"The secret of her extraordinary maiden voyage had been well guarded," the *Telegraph* reported. The *Queen Elizabeth* had left her fitting-out basin on Clydebank on February 26. A high enough tide to negotiate the river was expected only twice a year.

Despite the dangers of enemy attack, no attempt at an unusually high speed was made for the Atlantic crossing, but the ship carried no passengers or cargo. On March 9 a report circulated in New York saying that 30 seamen had left the ship at Greenock because they feared the dangers of the Atlantic crossing. Cunard responded with a statement that when it was made known that New York was the destination, "some of the crew, chiefly for domestic reasons, were unable to make the longer trip and asked to be allowed to return to their homes".

"Could not such a fast ship be employed as an auxiliary cruiser in wartime?" the *Telegraph* asked in a question-and-answer article that day. "Speed alone is no qualification for such duty," came the answer. "Not only would the ship present a tremendous target, but there are few berths which could accommodate her when not at sea. She would be neither handy nor economical in any service but that for which she was designed."

But in November 1940 the liner sailed for Singapore where she was fitted out as a troop-transport, able to carry 15,000 men at a time. She shuttled across the Atlantic, carrying more than 750,000 troops before being refitted for her proper purpose in 1946.

The *Queen Elizabeth*, unlike her sister-ship the *Queen Mary*, never captured the Blue Riband for the fastest Atlantic crossing. But the 1950s were her glory days, with 800 passengers sitting down for dinner in her 110ft-square dining-room at 7.30 each night.

"The first hint of trouble to come was late in 1959," the *Telegraph* noted in 1972 in a piece looking back on her career. "A news item indicated that for the first time the number of seats on transatlantic jets exceeded space in ocean-going liners."

In 1968 the ship retired from the Atlantic route and was sold for £3,585,000 to a company that showed her off to more than a million tourists at a berth at Port Everglades, Florida. Then in 1969

came a report in the *Telegraph* that she had been "closed to trippers because the local fire chief, Mr John Gerkin, considers her a fire hazard".

In 1970 the businessman C.Y. Tung bought her for £1,333,000 to become his Seawise University in Hong Kong. But two years later the *Telegraph* reported her destruction by fire. "The liner *Queen Elizabeth*, once the symbol of Britain's maritime glory, was a listing hulk in Hong Kong's harbour early today, with her decks caved in and masts fallen as flames consumed her from stem to stern.

"The 82,998-ton former Cunarder had been burning for almost 24 hours after a fire which began inexplicably near the stern swept through her with staggering speed. But 300 people on board escaped without loss of life.

"In the darkness the stricken liner had glowed like a huge lantern. As dawn broke the flames were less intense, but she had a list of 20 degrees and appeared to be falling apart internally. Explosions aboard are thought to have been caused by fuel from her oil tanks. They had been 'pretty well filled', ready for a short sea trial in five days time to test her boilers before she began a new career as a floating university." Firemen stopped hosing her for nearly two hours for fear of increasing the risk of capsize.

"The disaster is likely to become the worst fire in maritime history – bigger even than the sinking of the liner *Normandie* in New York Harbour in 1942. Insurance claims will probably exceed £3 million – most of it placed on the London market."

By then the 963ft *Queen Elizabeth II* had been in service for three years. In January 2004 the *Queen Mary 2* entered service. With a gross tonnage of 150,000 tons she easily outdid all preceding liners, and her length of 1,032 feet beat the *Queen Elizabeth* by one foot.

INBRIEF
JULY 5 1951

THE LAST TRAM
Tonight the last tram of all, a No. 40 leaves Woolwich at 11.57pm, arriving at New Cross via Charlton and Greenwich, at 12.29 am.

Business was brisk and a good time was being had by all except the conductors as hundreds of people took their last-day-but-one opportunity to travel in London's trams yesterday (*below*). A favourite trip was a spin along the Embankment between Blackfriars and Westminster. There were long queues at the main stopping places.

Lord Latham, chairman of London Transport, had stated in a personal letter to every member of the staff yesterday that not only did the organisation again not pay its way in 1951, but that it was in the red for the year by a much larger amount than in the previous year.

Road services were in deficit by more than £2 million, of which more than half was accounted for by losses on trams.

IMPOSING THE DRIVING TEST

A 30mph limit to counter huge toll of road deaths

With more than 7,000 a year dying on the roads, restrictions were put on motorists. The Telegraph was not at all convinced

In 1933, 7,202 people were killed on the road in Britain. This was twice as many as were to die each year by the end of the century, and considering that there were only a million and a half registered vehicles, moving much less quickly, the mortality was alarming.

In 1934 the Government decided to introduce measures intended to reduce the toll. A speed limit of 30mph would apply in towns, and new drivers would have to take a test. In London, crossing places for pedestrians would be provided at junctions.

"At first it is not intended to make the use of the crossing places compulsory," reported *The Daily*

Telegraph. "But if the London pedestrian walks dangerously compulsion may be applied and penalties imposed for neglect."

The speed limit was the great surprise of the Road Traffic Bill. The trial of a 30mph limit in Oxford was indicated as a successful precedent. But it was apparent "that the proposal will arouse the opposition of motorists, and will give rise to acute controversy in Parliament".

Sir Stenson Cooke, secretary of the Automobile Association, put up a robust resistance to the Bill. "Speed limits," he told the *Telegraph*, "have been proved over a period of nearly 30 years to make not the slightest contribution to road safety. Their enforcement is a matter of great difficulty. The proposals to introduce driving tests will presumably require a large and expensive administrative organisation. It has yet to be proved that tests of this sort serve any useful purpose."

Under the driving test provisions, the paper reported, "a new driver shall not only have some acquaintance with the mechanical part of driving, but shall know something of road matters and the Highway Code".

In an editorial, the *Telegraph* expressed reservations about the speed limit. "The true protection lies in more prosecutions for grossly careless driving," it opined, "and more severe sentences on conviction. If the Ministry, however, has made up its mind that a speed limit is necessary in areas where, *ex hypothesi*, accidents are likely to happen, 30 miles is too high. The careless motorist will at once plead that he was not travelling at that speed."

The driving test meant driving lessons. 'It has yet to be proved that tests of this sort serve any useful purpose,' the Telegraph declared

TELEVISION'S DANCING IMAGES

On a little frosted screen, shadows of things to come

The world's first television columnist foresaw in 1935 that every happening on the Earth's surface would one day be screened

John Logie Baird, whose early television apparatus was described by the Telegraph's correspondent. 'The machine was made of a circle of cardboard cut from a hat-box, 16 bull's-eye lenses from bicycle lamps and a selenium cell,' he reported. 'Old bicycle parts, pins and needles, and even bits of driftwood were utilised.'

In 1935 the *Telegraph* became the first newspaper in the world to run a regular television column. "These images dancing and gesticulating on a frosted screen in the darkened room were only the shadows of what is to come," wrote the newly appointed critic L. Marsland Gander on February 7. "As the set was tuned, strips of light raced across the screen. Slowly a jumble of spots and bars resolved into the caption 'BBC'. Then Leonie Zifado in a black crinoline, with white flounces, which televised well, slowly advanced to a close-up and sang soprano solos."

Leonard Marsland Gander, despite his quaint name, was a forward-looking journalist. He was to be a courageous war correspondent, travelling 50,000 miles between 1941 and 1943. In February 1935 he had just celebrated his 33rd birthday and landed the job of television correspondent, adding it to his post as radio correspondent. (He insisted on that title instead of the "wireless correspondent" proposed.) That first day in his new job he was summoned by the go-getting assistant editor Oscar Pulvermacher, who said: "We want a television set in the office tomorrow. Not next day or the day after. Tomorrow."

"But there aren't any," Gander stammered, adding what he took for a clinching afterthought: "And if there were, there's no transmission."

Gander knew that his reply was not entirely true, for the BBC was already transmitting on the low-definition 30-line system. It was the high-definition 240-line transmission that was not yet on the public air, though it was planned for later in the year. "The system may be likened to reproduction of photographs in newspapers," he explained to *Telegraph* readers. "Reproduction in a newspaper is effected by a series of dots forming the images, and the greater the number of dots in a picture the better and clearer it becomes. So with the number of 'lines' in a television image."

So Gander had to settle for the Baird mirror-drum type of receiver. He had known the brilliant inventor of television John Logie Baird since the days of his experiments in an attic in Frith Street,

Soho. "The machine was made of a circle of cardboard cut from a hat-box, 16 bull's-eye lenses from bicycle lamps and a selenium cell," Gander recalled. "Old bicycle parts, pins and needles, and even bits of driftwood were also utilised."

At that stage Gander was far from convinced that there was a future for the dancing shadows he saw. By February 1935 he was converted. The BBC had undertaken to give "a fair and equal opportunity" to the competing technical models for television tansmission. Half of the development was to be paid for out of the annual 10 shilling licence fee and half by the Treasury.

In a leading article the *Telegraph* foresaw the synchronisation of radio and television transmissions until "the two things are harmonised as they are on the cinema screen". This was indeed possible eventually, with simultaneous transmissions on BBC radio and BBC television, such as the *Last Night of the Proms*. But with the introduction of digital broadcasting such synchronisation again became in effect impossible.

"It is questionable whether for long the 'inlookers' [as viewers were known] will be content with the short programme to be offered to them," the *Telegraph* thought in 1935. Gander pointed out that in the first broadcast he reviewed "the best full-length pictures were those of Tatiana Semenova's toe dancing; and the best close-up was that of Gerald Kassen, the bass-baritone, in Russian dress". Even for audiences used to Reithian rigour, an hour or two of this would hardly satisfy expectations.

In a piece that he wrote for the paper that month, John Logie Baird predicted that every wireless would in future have its own television screen. He was right about the universal appeal of television, but wrong in not foreseeing that radio would continue to have a future even without pictures.

The developing Baird system would allow outside transmissions – horse-racing perhaps, if the BBC would allow it in those days when off-course betting was still illegal. The technology also permitted the transmission of ordinary feature films. The problem was to overcome copyright difficulties and a corporate resistance to the commercially attractive.

In any case, the *Telegraph* took an optimistic view: "The technical difficulties that limit the range of transmission will be overcome, and the cost of apparatus will be reduced as the demand for television sets increases." And so it turned out, but not immediately. With the coming of war in 1939 transmission was suspended. Even the remaining tower at Crystal Palace, at 700ft above sea level an invaluable transmitting station, was demolished lest it prove a beacon for enemy bombers.

Only with the televising of the Coronation in 1953 was the public once again able to take advantage of the new device. Soon afterwards, those with a long memory could test the prophecy of *The Daily Telegraph* in 1935. "The day may come," it predicted, "when all important happenings on the Earth's surface will be within sound and sight of the whole world."

GREYHOUNDS AND RAMBLERS

The people's pastimes in town and country

Mancunians flocked to a new track for greyhound racing in 1926. More active types took to the mass-trespass movement

A new leisure pursuit for the urban proletariat got off in style with the opening of a greyhound stadium at Wembley in 1927. More than 50,000 crowded to the first night on December 11. "Many well known people were at the reception," reported *The Daily Telegraph* vaguely.

"Ten weeks ago the property now owned by the Wembley Stadium and Greyhound Racecourse Company was a waste of broken masonry and partly demolished buildings. From those ruins, under the supervision of Sir Owen Williams, who was principal engineer to the British Empire Exhibition [of 1924], has arisen kennels having accommodation for 136 dogs, a 20-acre car park, a new main road, and three new roads for pedestrians. Inside the Stadium, the old running track has been remodelled for greyhound racing."

Greyhound racing had attracted a new audience after the development of an oval track at Belle Vue in Manchester in 1926. The following year, White City stadium in west London, built to seat 68,000 for the 1908 Olympics, began to stage greyhound races too.

At Wembley it was not just a lot of men in hats and coats standing around a cinder track. Eight bars licensed for the sale of alcohol had been installed behind the banked seating. "To many present, the interest in the dogs was second to their interest in the palatial club, which occupies the whole of the main terrace front, and the gathering was in the nature of a social event."

The floodlighting that made evening meetings possible worked well. There was one hitch: "One occasion – in the Bermuda Hurdle Race – the leading dog overtook the 'hare', and, to the surprise of those watching, actually passed it without attempting a 'kill'. The dog then stopped suddenly."

Railway companies (not nationalised until 1948) which had stations nearby offered cheap fares for those going to the dogs.

In Manchester, which was only a bus-ride away from open country, rambling became a mass pastime provoking warm feelings. It acquired a

Left-leaning image, reinforced by campaigns to gain access to private land. The political aspect of rambling appealed to folk singers such as Ewan MacColl, who celebrated it in his song *The Manchester Rambler*.

On April 24, 1932 "an army of 400 ramblers, men and girls, bent on gaining access to privately owned moorland by 'mass trespass' stormed the slope of Kinder Scout, the Peakland mountain, and fought their way through a cordon of gamekeepers and moor wardens".

Fur-coated Tallulah Bankhead being presented with a greyhound called Moor Court. The hare awaits. Meanwhile, armies of ramblers, 'men and girls', like the contingent below, took to the hills, even when they were on private property

INBRIEF

FEBRUARY 2, 1932

Those privileged to be present at 10 Downing Street yesterday morning when the Prime Minister inaugurated the South African telephone service carried away a pleasing impression of Mr MacDonald's gift for friendship.

"Is that you, Hertzog?" was his cheery opening. With much feeling, he continued: "My dear Hertzog, I can imagine I am again visiting you as I did over a quarter of a century ago in that beautiful old farmhouse at the back of Table Mountain, where we met first of all."

There was a touch of anxiety in Mr MacDonald's voice as he referred to the Disarmament Conference. "The times are not exactly what we should call auspicious, Hertzog," he remarked.

General Hertzog expressed his happiness at hearing Mr MacDonald's voice. While he had to express the fear that Mr MacDonald's patience would be sorely tried at Geneva, he hopes the Disarmament Conference would succeed in what the world was expecting.

"There is nothing sadder," he continued, "than the reluctance with which the nations of Europe seem to concentrate even the mere discussion of the reduction of armament. If this atmosphere of suspicion of one another and lack of confidence in the League and the peace of the world is continued much longer, I fear it can only have one result – the non-European nations will be driven to look somewhere else than to Europe and the League for a world of peace."

A substitute for the more orthodox tea gown

From the Telegraph

Pyjama vogue

April 2, 1928

By the Hon Mrs C.W. Forester

For the real traveller there is much to be said in favour of the elegant sleeping suit. At their best, such things are very decorative and fairly inexpensive.

The length of jacket should be determined by the figure of the wearer. Slim women may choose the more shaped trousers and short coat, but those of stouter build should select the satin three-piece, with the top and wide trousers of soit washing satin in pink (or purple for travelling), and wear a long coat of printed gaily-coloured crepe de Chine with a border of the satin, so that to all appearances it is a slim coat-like dressing gown.

For more dressy occasions and boudoir wear thin fabrics and glorious colourings transform the pyjama suit into a substitute for the more orthodox boudoir wrap or tea gown.

Trespassers from the Lancashire branches of the British Workers Sports Federation marched from Hayfield to the bottom of William Clough, where the 20 or 30 leaders "with shouts of enthusiasm began scrambling up the boggy heather-clad slopes of Kinder Scout". Eight or 10 keepers armed with sticks met them, and "trouble followed immediately". By the time the main body of ramblers caught up, a free fight was in progress.

One keeper "rolled some distance down the slope, twisted his ankle, and was badly shaken. One rambler fetched water for him, and after a few minutes he was able to limp away."

Near the top of Ashop Head a detachment of 30 ramblers from Sheffield joined the main body, reporting a trouble-free trespass over the moors via Edale. After holding a "victory" gathering undisturbed the party returned to Hayfield. But there they were halted by a cordon of police across the road. Gamekeepers who had taken part in the struggle on the mountain inspected the ramblers and picked out five. These were arrested by the police and taken to Hayfield police station.

The leading spirit of the trespass, Benny Rothman, a communist, was sentenced to four months' imprisonment. He remained a keen walker into his eighties and died in 2002, aged 90.

Welfare and warfare

After little more than a decade of peace the shadow of war returned with the Nazi Second World War transformed Britain, and even before it was won, plans were

SOMETHING MUST BE DONE

Christmas presents for poor children

If poverty could not be abolished at a stroke, at least toys could be sent to those who had none. Readers bought 214,000

'Something must be done," the new king, Edward VIII, was reported to have said on November 18, 1936 when he toured the unemployed areas of South Wales. Some things were done, but the depression continued and families remained short of clothes and food and cheer as Christmas approached a year later. By then the King had abdicated.

In December 1937 *The Daily Telegraph* started a fund to buy Christmas presents for 150,000 children of poor families in the depressed industrial and mining regions of Durham, Tyneside, West Cumberland and South Wales. The scheme had been tried with great success the year before by the *Morning Post*. That newspaper had been swallowed up by the *Telegraph* in November 1937, and with it came W.F. Deedes, a 24-year-old reporter. He had masterminded the Christmas-present appeal on the *Morning Post* and was charged with doing it again on a bigger scale.

William Deedes wrote to all the head-teachers in the depressed areas asking for their help in compiling names and addresses of children between the ages of three and 13 with unemployed fathers.

Within five days of the *Telegraph* publishing its appeal enough had been raised to buy toys for 50,000. "Each toy," the paper promised, "will be addressed personally to the boy or girl and will be delivered by post as nearly as possible on Christmas morning."

The new king, George VI, and Queen Elizabeth were among the donors, and on December 10 the King's mother, Queen Mary, visited the newspaper's offices in Fleet Street.

The Queen was shown "dolls and picture-books, puzzles of all kinds, toy soldiers, model aeroplanes, cowboy outfits, boxes of conjuring tricks, table tennis sets, electric torches, and dozens of games", divided into six categories for different ages. One present that caught her attention was a "Princess Elizabeth" doll, with which came a number of dresses to be cut out and fitted to it, including a copy of Princess Elizabeth's Coronation robe.

Among the thousands of letters from people who had sent money was one from an anonymous donor, who might have found a job in advertisement copy-writing to judge by the little rhyme wrapped round his half-crown:

A drop less beer,
A bit less baccie,
A half-a-crown,
And a youngster happy.

Busy typists were at work addressing labels, each accompanied by the words, "Do not open until December 25."

In the same issue as the news of the Queen's kind interest came a heart-rending report "From a special correspondent, in a Depressed Area". "The children in this scarred, wind-bitten district play any game that costs nothing, look at anything that costs nothing to look at, and do not realise that Christmas – which brings so much happiness to other children – is approaching.

"The arrival in the depressing streets of a postman with a Christmas gift would be a stupendous and unbelievable event! No one could possibly say, for instance, what such a completely unexpected happening would mean to a child I saw hopping on one thin leg in the mysteries of some chalk game on the greasy pavement.

"This mite of seven, shrunken to the size of a much younger child, had a wizened, almost adult

Bread and tea on a Wigan table,

threat. The Telegraph refused to endorse the popular policy of appeasing Hitler. The
being made for a new society embodying the Welfare State

in a photograph by Kurt Hutton

sense of humour. Rose – incongruous name in such a district of desolation – looked at me and drawing her patched and too-large man's jersey round her, said: 'Can't hang up my stocking, mister. Ain't got one!' "

William Deedes had managed to persuade several department stores to provide toys at reduced prices. Marshall & Snelgrove, Gorringe's, the Civil Service Supply Association and Peter Robinson all joined in, giving hours of their staffs' time in sending and packaging toys.

By December 15, £11,000 had been raised, enough for 100,000 presents. The tireless special correspondent had found in Sunderland the tragic case of Robert. "He has been in hospital and had three operations for a tumour on the brain. His mother died while he was away. Twice a week his father has cycled the 12 miles to Newcastle to see him.

"Robert has come home for Christmas. But his father is worried because he knows that Christmas in hospital meant festivities and presents which will not be forthcoming in an unemployed home."

By Christmas Eve "the most exciting day of the year for all children who believe in Santa Claus", the *Telegraph* had found more addresses for children who needed cheering up, and a total of 214,000 packets were going out, even to Liverpool, Blackburn, Barnsley, Wigan and Redruth.

"Unless there are unforeseen delays the toys will reach their destination tomorrow morning," it promised in those days of reliable deliveries even on Christmas Day.

A postmaster at Whitehaven, Cumberland, told the *Telegraph* reporter about the 1,000 parcels that had arrived at his office. "It took us all Tuesday to sort them out. We cursed and blessed you all with alternate breaths, but the children were full of glee and that's a fact."

It was the same story in the Welsh Valleys. "In a little town in the Western Valley," a correspondent wrote, "I walked up to cottages with postmen late at night and heard the glad cries of children as we knocked on the doors.

"'Mother, go quickly, it's Santa Claus,' came the shrill treble of a little boy at one cottage. Then, as we stood talking to his mother, we heard: 'Is it Christmas yet? May I open it?'

"Some moments later I peeped into his room and saw the little boy sleeping with a teddy bear, almost as big as himself, clutched tightly in his arms. On his face was a smile of absolute content.
It was, his mother said, 'Tommy's first real toy.'"

The special correspondent was going great guns, with despatches that could surely leave no eye tearless. He found himself in Haltwhistle, Cumberland, on Christmas morning. "So neatly dressed in her thin blue Sunday coat and hat," he wrote, "Doris, aged 10, stood on a patch of broken ground at the top of the main street overlooking the valley and the pit, which has been silent for six years.

"A great portrait painter might have captured the

picture she made – her new handbag clasped tightly in one hand, her shining eyes lighting an otherwise expressionless little face, behind her the sweeping hills of the valley through which the River Tyne begins its course.

"Doris, whose right leg will never get well, spoke shyly about the other children and their pleasure; how the parcels had come – 'We didn't know, you see' – how the news had eventually leaked out, and how they agreed, she and her friends, to keep their parcels closed until Christmas morning.

"It was only half past nine, with the sun hardly up, but everyone seemed to know what everyone else had got."

If the campaign had been good for sales, it was not without a genuine effort on the part of the *Telegraph* staff, not to mention the postmen. It was four years before *How Green Was My Valley*, and 10 years before *It's a Wonderful Life*. Unemployment remained, a war was coming, but thousands of children had no doubt been made happier and thousands of readers had given money.

Bread and flour, Camp coffee and a twopenny tin of cocoa among the meagre contents of an impoverished Thirties' larder. 'Can't hang up my stocking, mister,' said a child in a depressed area. 'Ain't got one.'

From the **Telegraph**

The first presents in years for the bairns

Friday, December 10, 1937

George has had a pretty rough time in his one-and-a-half years of pinched existence. He "picked up" diphtheria and was very ill in hospital for weeks. He is back home now but, as the doctor told me, "very weak".

When I saw him his thin hand was holding a chunk of firewood, the end of which his father had roughly carved into the shape of a doll's head. It is George's most treasured possession.

There are thousands like George, whose parents find it impossible to spare a penny for a Christmas present. The one gleam of hope is that we may be able to send presents to them.

Cleator Moor, Cumberland, December 24

Tom, five and a half years old, was standing outside the Cleator Moor post office, waiting in the dusk and drizzle for his mother who was buying penny Christmas cards.

Against his jersey Tom clutched with chubby fingers a parcel – a strangely bedraggled and tired looking parcel. Tom's mother told me the history of his present. It had arrived on Wednesday, clearly marked "Not to be opened until December 25" and between then and Christmas Eve it had scarcely left his hands. Unopened, of course.

Tom was told it meant bad luck to cut the string before Christmas morning so he held it – his own parcel, his to show his friends – without having the remotest idea of what it contained, yet deriving three days' delight from keeping this rough brown package near to him.

Haltwhistle, Christmas Day

Off the Main Street lived a mother of four young children, all but the smallest of whom have got toys. I could not set down her words, because the sentences came so fast and incoherently that one could only stand silent and feel ashamed to be the sole, unworthy object of this outburst of gratitude. In effect she said: "It's the first time for years that Christmas has brought anything for my bairns."

Her husband has not worked for nine years. Yes, the presents had arrived the day before. She had been surprised, but decided to keep it a secret from the children. Then Harry, who is eight, came back to say wistfully that other boys and girls, his friends, had had parcels.

So the news was broken, and Harry and his brother and Marjorie, who is seven, awoke their parents at six on Christmas morning to open the parcels and to find a set of conjuring tricks, a knife and a miniature kitchen stove.

INBRIEF

NOVEMBER 20, 1930

On this page every Thursday is presented an abridged version of *Harrods Food News*. It is a shopping guide to provisioning your household, not only with the utmost convenience and economy, but also with the most complete confidence in the Quality of everything that comes to your table.

In ordering by post it is suggested that you mark the list as required, fill in your name and address at foot, and post the complete advertisement to Harrods Ltd, Knightsbridge, London, SW1 (cash being enclosed where sender has no account).

Harrods Motors deliver free in over 1,000 districts, in some districts three and four times daily. Beyond this wide motor radius carriage is paid on food purchases value 20 shillings and over in England and Wales, and 60 shillings and over in Scotland.

Poultry:

English Spring Chickens, each	3/8 to 4/6
Ducks, Oxford per lb	1/3
Fowls, Soup per lb	1/3
Goslings, English per lb	1/0
Livers per lb	2/6
Petits Poussins each	2/3 to 3/0
Pigeons Bordeaux each	2/0, 2/6, 3/0
Pigeons, Wood each	1/3

GERMANY BANS TELEGRAPH

Seized for report of Night of the Long Knives

Goebbels called the Telegraph a 'slop-pail of cowardly falshooods' after it had reported Hitler's purge of the Brownshirts

The July 7, 1934 issue of *The Daily Telegraph* was confiscated in Nazi Germany. It had caused offence to supporters of Hitler, by then German Chancellor, by its comments on the "Night of the Long Knives" when the leadership of Ernst Röhm's Sturm-Abteilung was purged. Hundreds were killed, but little was known in Germany of what went on apart from what Hitler made public later.

"Outside Germany," the *Telegraph* said in its confiscated issue, "opinion on the 'frightfulness' of last Saturday's shootings has undergone a decided change. At first, despite many suspicious circumstances, the tendency was to accept the official account as substantially correct. That was the story of the plot against Hitler among the extreme Left of the Nazis, led by Röhm and the disaffected Storm Troop element in the SA, which was crushed with swift and merciless severity. This was presented as a Purge and a Cleansing, notoriously belated on the moral side, but timely enough on the political, and only to be justified on the doubtful argument of political expediencies.

"Later news, indeed, still leaves a Plot and a Purge, but no one now accepts as adequate Herr Hess's latest description of last Saturday's killings as 'a dozen deserved deaths'. On the contrary, the title of Master-plotters seems unquestionably to have passed to Herr Hitler and General Göring themselves."

"A most damning impression has been made," the *Telegraph* pointed out, "by the refusal of a complete list of the dead." It declared that "unofficially, the list is far over 200" and that Hitler's grim threat "heads will roll in the dust" had been "amply fulfilled".

A few days later the paper reported that the issue in which these remarks appeared had been confiscated, and that "Dr Goebbels the Minister of Propaganda, indulged in a violent attack on the resident foreign correspondents in Germany – naming those of *The Daily Telegraph* in particular, for indulging 'in the worst form of revolver

journalism', for establishing 'lie factories which poison the opinion of the world,' and for emptying 'the slop-pails of cowardly falsehoods' upon those who on June 30 saved Germany and the whole world from a most terrible catastrophe".

"It is safe to say, with a full regard for Dr Goebbels' record," the paper responded, "that the more outrageously he storms against the

Children, with name and address labels tied on, carry their luggage, on the journey of evacuation from London, which was expected to be rapidly devastated by enemy bombing and gas

correspondents of *The Daily Telegraph* in Germany the more surely will he convince their readers that their despatches are a straightforward attempt to set forth the truth as they can ascertain it about the situation in Germany today.

"The German press," the *Telegraph* concluded, "obeys because it must, and the 'discipline' upon which Dr Goebbels congratulated it

On Glasgow Green (right) officials inspect trenches dug to house bomb shelters. 'For the man in the street… no power on earth can protect him from being bombed,' said Stanley Baldwin

SHELTERS AND GAS MASKS

'Gas, more than anything, is likely to lead to panic'

In 1938 plans were made to evacuate more than three million from London. Nothing could protect them from the bombers

In the summer of 1938, even before the Munich crisis of the autumn, British people were expecting high explosives, incendiary bombs and gas to rain down upon cities, London especially, at the very start of a new war.

"I think it is as well for the man in the street to realise that there is no power on earth that can protect him from being bombed," Stanley Baldwin had told the House of Commons in 1932. "Whatever people may tell him, the bomber will always get through."

Since then newsreels from the Abyssinian war and the Spanish Civil War had been seen. The sudden aerial destruction of cities was a commonplace of fiction. Alexander Korda portrayed it convincingly enough in his film *Things to Come* (a version of the H.G. Wells book) in 1936.

Chilling realities were now relayed from a

yesterday is the discipline of the prison-yard. Newspaper correspondents who observe the rules of professional conduct should be welcome wherever Governments have nothing shameful to conceal."

While *The Times* became the leading advocate of appeasement, *The Daily Telegraph* continued its opposition to Nazi belligerence.

Commons debate on June 1, 1938 on air-raid precautions. Some 3.5 million people could, in the Government's view, be evacuated from London in 72 hours.

Sir Samuel Hoare, the Home Secretary, denied that, in considering the danger of high explosive bombs, he had failed to take into account the lessons of the two wars then going on in China and in Spain. A careful analysis had been made of the experiences in Barcelona.

"It was the Government's view that the policy of dispersal was a safer policy than that of concentration of large numbers of the population into certain given spots," the *Telegraph* reported. There should be no action "that would bring to a stand-still the ordinary life of the country". People would, as far as possible, remain in their own houses.

To meet the danger from incendiary bombs there was approval for 100 emergency fire brigade schemes; orders had been placed for 5,000 trailer pumps. But of these only 320 had been delivered, and the orders would not be completed until the end of the year.

"It was necessary," the Home Secretary said, "to make effective preparations against the dangers of gas attack, for it was this more than anything which was likely to lead to panic of the civil population whatever the number of casualties.

"The Home Office took the view, which was supported by experts, that gas masks must be kept in depots if they were to be maintained in proper condition. Steps were being taken to make the depots readily accessible in the areas so that there would be no delays in the event of an emergency." This news might not have had the soothing effect hoped for.

As far as the Palace of Westminster was concerned, the rooms and adjoining corridors on the ground floor facing the Terrace were considered to provide the safest refuge accommodation. "The windows were comparatively small and could be protected by sandbags," MPs were reminded.

Home Office experiments "had evolved a British siren, with an average range of one mile, which was a longer range than seemed to be expected by many foreign countries".

Before the end of June, readers learned that the Dowager Marchioness of Reading, chairman of the Women's Voluntary Services for Air Raid Precautions, would open an intensive course for the training of women instructors.

"Demonstrations," the *Telegraph* reported, "will comprise the bursting of persistent gas bombs, the effects of high explosive bombs on windows before treatment with cellophane and after, the preparation of a refuge room and similar experiments. Several nuns from convents will attend the course."

On September 22, plans were published for providing hospital accommodation for air-raid casualties. In an emergency it was hoped that "most hospitals would be able to clear about 40 per cent of

their beds by sending home those patients who are fit to go". In London 34 hospitals were selected for clearance, with plans for removing "about 3,500 patients by ambulance trains to towns 50 miles or more from London".

"The patients would be taken to railway stations by coaches converted to carry stretchers. These stretchers are held centrally for distribution. Fittings for the coaches have been made, and 300 can be converted into ambulances at 12- to 24-hours' notice."

The next day the Minister of Transport announced a ban on parking or waiting vehicles in 104 streets in central London.

On September 29, readers learned of "a great extension of trench digging for the protection of civilians from air raids all over London. In the Royal parks alone several thousand men were engaged in digging and fixing timber supports to trenches. It is estimated that these trenches in the Royal parks will, when complete, provide

The driver and fireman of a train arriving at Waterloo wear gas masks and tin hats in an air-raid precaution exercise

accommodation for 20,000 people. Large-scale digging is also in progress in Paddington, while many squares in St Marylebone are undergoing a similar transformation. Day and night work, under the direction of the Wandsworth Council, is proceeding on Streatham Common, and Wimbledon has made such progress in its trench digging that the work may be completed by tomorrow."

For the millions with no trench to go to, there were some other opportunities. "Empty buildings in Hendon have been scheduled as shelters for people caught out-of-doors during a raid. Centuries-old tunnels under Greenwich Park and Blackheath are also being examined by ventilation experts for use as possible shelters. 'We do not yet know if the ventilation will be good enough,' said a council official, 'but if it can be made suitable, these tunnels will hold between 20,000 and 30,000 people.'"

On September 28 distribution of gas masks began and on the same day "thousands of people voluntarily left London by road and rail as a precautionary measure".

"An official at Euston said to a representative of *The Daily Telegraph & Morning Post*: 'Most of the people booked to Scotland and Ireland. All lines, however, were busier than usual. At 10am there was a long queue waiting to buy tickets. Complete families with perambulators were among the travellers.'

"At Paddington there was almost a holiday air. Children who had been told that they were going on a holiday clutched teddy bears, mascots and other toys."

In the classified columns of the paper advertisements for properties outside the supposed danger zone appeared: "ABSOLUTE safety – Take a flat outside bombing area, but within 20 mins Oxford Circus, additional advantage bomb-proof shelter – Whitehall Lodge, Pages Lane, Muswell Hill, N10."

Under a cross-heading CRIPPLES SENT AWAY the paper reported "the departure of about 2,500 physically defective pupils – the cripples and heart cases – of 30 special LCC schools. They were taken in coaches and ambulances to St Mary's Camp at Dymchurch in Kent. The children each had food for the day, a change of underwear and a blanket and overcoat. They were told they were going to a holiday camp with school lessons." Other schools deliberated what should be their own best course of action.

At London Zoo arrangements had been made "to kill all poisonous reptiles and insects if an air raid warning is received. In the event of war, venomous snakes will be put in strong metal boxes, which have been placed in readiness in the service passage of the reptile house.

"No other stock will be killed as a precautionary measure. Picked members of the staff, however, have been appointed wardens, and they will shoot any dangerous creature liberated through destruction of cages."

From the Telegraph

Coat the woodwork in the attic with lime wash to prevent it catching fire

September 28, 1938

Action to be taken by every householder to combat gas and the effects of splinters thrown up by bombs.

Prepare your refuge room against the effects of high explosives, gas and incendiary bombs. A dry cellar or basement is best, but any room on any floor, except the top floor, may be used. Paste paper, linen or other material over the windows to prevent glass splinters being blown into the room. Close-mesh wire netting fastened behind the windows will help.

Refuge rooms should be sealed against the entry of gas. Be prepared to block up every crack and crevice in walls, floor and ceilings with putty or pulp made of softened newspapers. Stout paper pasted over key holes, ventilators and window frames will keep out gas. In an emergency the chimney should be stuffed with paper, rags or sacking, and the front of the fireplace sealed with ply-wood if possible.

A piece of wood, padded with felt or cloth, should be nailed to the floor so as to press tightly against the entrance door when it is closed. Smoking in refuge rooms should be strictly forbidden. Provide yourself and the children with something to do – a book to read, games to play.

Clear the loft or attic of any inflammable material. If possible, cover the floor with sheets of iron or asbestos or with two inches of dry sand or dry earth if the floor will bear the weight. It is a good thing to coat the woodwork in the attic or roof space with lime wash to prevent it catching fire. Apply two coats.

See that you have a box or bucket of dry sand or earth, with a long-handled shovel ready to deal with small incendiary bombs. In an emergency, have some buckets or cans of water ready in get-at-able places about the house.

The steel Morrison shelter was intended for use as a table and a safer place to sleep

BRITAIN ALONE: JUNE 1940

Pig clubs and a prohibition of church bells

After Dunkirk, an invasion was expected. The civilian population was asked to rally round, and park railings were sawn down

Despite the godsend of the evacuation of 215,000 British and 120,000 French troops from Dunkirk at the beginning of June 1940, the public mood remained uneasy. Britain had its back to the wall. Although the expected horror of Blitzkrieg and gas had not materialised, the inactivity of the "phoney war" of early 1940 had brought into focus tiresome restrictions. Now invasion was in the air.

A prohibition of the ringing of church bells at home seemed unreasonable to many. "It was officially confirmed yesterday that the ringing of church and chapel bells is forbidden," the Telegraph reported on June 11. "The military authorities have decided that it is essential to use church bells for giving warning of the approach of parachutists or other airborne troops. Only the military will be entitled to ring the bells in future."

"Points which would seem to arise," the paper commented. "are whether the churches are to be kept open day and night and, if so, who is to be responsible for the protection of the building. If churches are locked up at night, are the military or ARP authorities to have the keys or are vergers to be summoned in an emergency?" Moreover, churches were the very buildings with no telephones.

Dorothy L. Sayers, whose Peter Wimsey detective novel The Nine Tailors (1934) turns on the arcane art of change-ringing, pointed out that it was no simple matter to ring a church bell. "To order a completely raw hand to run along and ring a church bell," she said in the Telegraph, "is rather like ordering him to run along and milk a savage and reluctant cow; the net result would be the same except that the bell can kick much harder than the cow."

In Cambridge, when the winder restarted the clock on the tower of Our Lady and the English Martyrs, the mechanism caught up with all the missed quarters and made them chime one after another. "People took to their shelters," Tony Brotchie, the winder, said. "It resulted in the clergy and three policemen climbing up the tower. I had

visions of spending the duration in the cells." The 70-year-old rector of Bolingbroke-with-Hareby, Lincolnshire, actually saw the inside of a cell for 12 days after being prosecuted for ringing his church bells. On appeal his four-weeks' sentence was found to be unlawful, since the regulations had not come into force, and he was released and awarded costs.

Park railings were being eyed up by a body called the Iron and Steel Control, which could require removal of ironwork, notionally for melting down and turning into armaments. "It is estimated that thousands of tons of scrap metal can be made available," the Telegraph reported on June 11. "Railings in London alone would yield between 3,000 and 4,000 tons of metal. More than 1,000 tons would be salvaged from Hyde Park without touching the boundary railings.

"Belisha Beacons are not to be touched for the present," the paper reported on June 29. "Mr Morrison, Minister of Supply, having upheld a ruling of Capt Euan Wallace when Minister of Transport, said that they are more useful saving pedestrian lives than as material for shells.

"A vast quantity of iron is known to lie latent in household railings, but powers of compulsory acquisition may be necessary. Some householders would welcome the abolition of fencing between properties, a common feature of Canadian and American towns."

By the end of June, 1,500 tons of railings had been taken from the Royal parks, including 800 tons from Rotten Row. Few readers would have had the figures at their fingertips to put these amounts in perspective, but in 1937, 3.5 million tons of scrap iron were used in British domestic production. The sacrifice of railings was a mere gesture.

A mood of gloom was reflected in the BBC's Thought for Today, broadcast every morning at five minutes to eight, according to one correspondent to The Daily Telegraph. The presenter's tone was seldom "other than painfully lugubrious. And the counsels he usually has to offer are often uncommonly depressing," wrote A.H. Redfern from West Dulwich. "Why cannot the BBC's presenters give us a heartier and more stimulating 'thought' with which to face the new day's duties and trials? Something more manly – and, if you will, realistic – would make those five minutes worthwhile."

The difficulty of ensuring that identity cards did not get lost exercised another reader. "All women now carry a handbag, containing probably their identification card and latch key," wrote Professor F.A. Cavanagh from King's College, London. "In a sudden alarm this bag may easily be mislaid or snatched. If these essential articles were carried in a strong canvas pocket attached to a waist belt they would be there when required."

Italy declared war on June 10 and some understandable but unpleasant anti-Italian rioting was reported the next day. "In Soho, there were pitched battles between Greeks and Italians and bottles were thrown. In south east and east London, the windows of Italian cafés were broken. Police

Business as usual (right): a milkman makes his way over the London rubble as it is damped down by firemen after a raid in 1940

patrolling in cars prevented trouble from spreading.

"Several people were injured and many arrests made during riots in Edinburgh. Crowds in Port Glasgow looted 15 of 17 Italian-owned shops."

Two days later the *Telegraph* reported that "more than 700 Italians have been detained by Scotland Yard, almost double the number of Germans and Austrians arrested at the outbreak of war.

"During yesterday's round-up many more restaurateurs and waiters were detained in the West End of London. Among them was Signor Italo Sangliacomi, general manager of the Piccadilly Hotel since 1927. For 17 years before that he had charge of the Grill Room." Other respected Italians detained were the Quaglino brothers and Signor Bianchi, head chef at the Café Royal.

One more reason for hating the German enemy was reported on June 13. "All dogs in Germany, numbering three million, are to be killed, under an order issued through the German Press. The official explanation given is that the dogs eat food which might be used for human consumption."

At home a different means of saving food was being put into practice. "Food scraps for pig food are being collected by street sweepers employed by the Westminster City Council. A special compartment is fitted to their hand trucks."

In the country, "parish councils, young farmers' clubs, women's institutes and other rural organisations are co-operating in the Ministry of Agriculture's efforts to establish village pig clubs on a co-operative basis to utilise household waste. It is estimated that if one out of every five allotment holders and rural householders fattened one pig a year, half a million would be available annually."

A phrasebook for German invaders was in the news on June 25. Phrases in the book, which had come into the hands of British military authorities, included: "Are you the Mayor?", "Where is the cash?" and "I confiscate all."

"A whole section," the *Telegraph* reported, "is devoted to questions intended to enable the German troops to find their way about the country. In this case citizens will be assured that 'if you tell the truth you have nothing to fear'."

On June 28, Cardinal Hinsley, Archbishop of Westminster, called Catholics to a week of penance and prayer from July 7. "Some people are now saying: 'Of what use is prayer? Since the Day of National Prayer we have suffered constant reverses. The Day of Prayer for France was ended by her capitulation. I am going to give up praying.'"

He likened the plight of the British to that of the people of Israel facing the Philistines. "They were defeated by the Philistines and in their peril called upon the god of Israel. They brought the Ark of the Covenant from Siloe and made intercession. There followed a gigantic Philistine victory.

"One man only remained serene and undisturbed. The prophet Samuel told them, 'If you turn to the Lord with all your heart, put away the strange gods from among you, Baalim and Astaroth, and prepare your heart unto the Lord and serve Him only, He will deliver you out of the hands of the Philistines.'

"Let us speak plainly. As a nation not only have we not worshipped God but we have served false gods. Social justice, purity of family life, Christian education of youth – all have been widely neglected."

Within a fortnight the RAF took up its role in the decisive Battle of Britain, and from September London sustained the Blitz it had been awaiting.

INBRIEF

MARCH 9, 1940

SUICIDE HAT PROTESTS

Daily Telegraph Reporter

Women disagreed heartily – and traffic experts agreed equally heartily – with the views of Alderman G. H. Barber, an 80-year-old Stoke-on-Trent motorist, on the new "blinker" hats, which he accuses of causing many accidents by unsighting their wearers.

Alderman Barber wants a bylaw prohibiting "blinker" hats and regulating hat angles. He declares that women are giving motorists the blind eye, and says that two women wearing smart hats nearly killed themselves on his radiator.

Here are typical views on fashion "suicide hats" given to me in London, hub of traffic and fashion, yesterday.

Traffic policeman: "I have seen several girls recently stepping off the kerb without seeing on-coming traffic because of the obstruction caused by their hats."

Motoring Association: "These hats completely shut out one side or the other. But we don't see how you could regulate women's fashions by law. They are above the law, though they may land the wearer under a car."

West End hat designer: "I supposed Alderman Barber is referring to those pancake hats worn over one eye. Women don't notice them more than a man notices the brim of his trilby. Now veils and turbans – there I do agree. Veils obstruct vision and turbans deaden hearing."

Woman motorist: "Alderman Barber is talking nonsense. If a woman wants to see on-coming traffic, all she has to do is tilt her head. In a car, she is usually wearing a sports hat."

RATIONING

For supper, fry sandwiches in reconstituted egg

Tea was rationed, coffee wasn't. Bread was rationed after the war. Almost as bad as shortages were some of the cheerful recipes

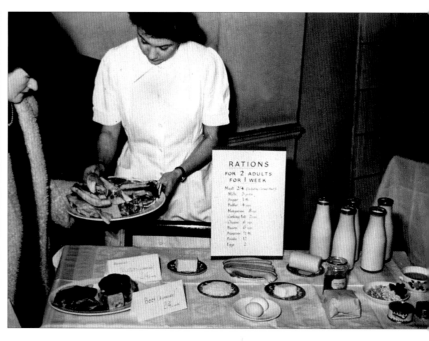

The Food Ministry wanted British housewives to acquire the taste for salted herrings. "Women shopping in the West End yesterday were asking about 'Government' herrings, in view of the scarcity of fresh herrings and kippers," the *Telegraph* reported on June 13, 1940. The former market for salted herrings was the Continent, but now they were seen as a valuable home resource.

The *Telegraph* helpfully suggested a way to make them edible. "Soak in cold water, changing water several times, if necessary for two days. They are best coated with oatmeal, fried and served with potatoes or made into a fish pie, mixed with potato, a little milk and some mustard sauce."

Despite fears of an invasion fleet, that month saw a glut of red mullet "selling at pre-war price, 1s 4d a lb. Crab can be bought for 1s 6d, ready dressed."

Another taste desirable to acquire, but by no means easy for most, was for pickled eggs. Nevertheless, "suggestions that eggs may be dear and scarce have prompted housewives who did not put some down in spring to preserve now", the *Telegraph*'s market correspondent reported in the sunny summer of 1940. "'Eggs are really cheap; they would be another shilling a dozen but for Government control,' I was told. 'They are sold as fast as they arrive, so that women are sure of getting them absolutely fresh for pickling.' The most popular quantity is six dozen, 2s 3d a dozen."

Later, dried eggs became familiar to the rising generation. "Most women realise now what a boon it is to have eggs always at hand in a packet, and to be able to make delicious egg dishes often," said a Food Ministry spokesman in *The Daily Telegraph*. "Here are some suggestions for using them in ways which will be new to many women…

"A 'fresh-flavour' tip for scrambled eggs: have you tried adding a little mustard when making scrambled eggs? Add half a teaspoonful of dry mustard for four eggs.

"Hard-boiled eggs: reconstitute the eggs in the usual way, and pour into well-greased egg cups or moulds – one egg to a mould. Put the moulds into a

saucepan of hot water coming half way up sides of moulds, and simmer gently for 15 minutes, until set. Turn out by running a knife round the edge.

"French fry: dip pieces of bread in well-seasoned reconstituted egg, soak well, and fry with bacon. This is more nourishing than fried bread and uses less fat. Sandwiches can be fried this way too: they make a delightful supper dish.

"Richer milk puddings: add one or two reconstituted eggs to milk puddings, using a mixture of milk and water if milk is short. This improves the flavour and makes a splendid nourishing pudding for children.

"The present allocation of dried eggs is one packet per ration book each four week period."

Rationing had been introduced on January 8, 1940. Meat, bacon, sugar, butter, cheese and tea were rationed by weight. Other foodstuffs, such as canned food and biscuits, were available against "points" – coupons allocated to everyone monthly. Meat remained rationed until June 1954. Indeed, bread was not rationed until after the war (July 1946) and was de-rationed two years later.

If rationing was intended to ensure that poor as well as rich got enough food, there were still luxuries to be had. In the last week of the war, the *Telegraph* reported that "from Norfolk come an increased supply of melons. The smallest of the Norwich Queen variety costs 25s. It is a little larger than an orange. The largest so far delivered is smaller than a football and costs £5.5s." That amount of money would have paid a week's rent on a house.

Newsreels of liberated concentration camps shocked cinemagoers in Britain. In May 1945 the *Telegraph* ran an angry letter from Brigadier General P.M. Davies of Budleigh Salterton: "Our overfed German prisoners should be paraded to see the films made at Buchenwald and Belsen concentration camps to bring home to them the inherent foulness of the German race."

Rations for two adults for a week laid out on a table (top). Rationing was introduced in 1940, but some items were in even shorter supply in the years after the war. In the meantime, public-spirited posters exhorted the replacing of wastefulness with a spirit of self-sacrifice

THE DOODLEBUG AND THE V2

The rockets that arrived in the war's 271st week

It was after D-Day that Germany began to launch the V1 flying-bomb and then the supersonic V2 against civilian England

June 1944 saw the advent of V1 flying-bombs, nicknamed doodlebugs or buzz bombs. Some civilians found it particularly unpleasant to hear the approaching engine, wondering if it would cut out overhead. If it did, there was 15 seconds to seek shelter. Blast damage from the explosion could cause destruction across a 400-yard radius.

On June 18, 1944 the Guards Chapel at Wellington Barracks in Birdcage Walk near Buckingham Palace was hit by a V1, with the death of 119. By the end of the month up to 100 flying-bombs a day were falling on London. Since they came during daylight they could cause high casualties in crowded areas; one that fell in the Aldwych outside Bush House caught workers at lunchtime and at least 48 died. Of the 9,000 V1s launched against England, about 2,000 were shot down or put off course by the RAF and the same number shot down by anti-aircraft fire or caught by barrage balloon networks. In all about 5,500 Londoners were killed by V1s.

From September 1944, Londoners began to suffer the attacks of V2 rockets, which each carried a 2,000lb warhead. The approach of a V2 could not be heard like that of the V1, but the sudden destruction wrought was even more unnerving to many. "The first official announcement that long-range rockets – Germany's secret V2 weapon – have been falling on this country for several weeks was made in the House of Commons to-day by Mr Churchill," the *Telegraph* reported on November 11, 1944. He had warned Parliament in February of the danger of a German rocket assault. So far the casualties and damage had not been heavy.

"Descent from the stratosphere by the rocket is almost as vertical as its ascent," wrote the *Telegraph* military correspondent, Lieutenant-General H.G. Mastin. "As the missile is travelling faster than sound it arrives without warning. The effect of its explosion is localised."

The Daily Telegraph had established a custom of prefacing its leading articles with the number of weeks the war had lasted. By November it had reached "271st Week of War". In the leader underneath it declared that "Mr Churchill was wise to admit that some of these new missiles had arrived, and to describe in general terms their character and results."

German broadcasts had been making alarming claims about the destructive capability of the "V2" weapon. "To those, and they are many who have had no personal experience of the new attempt at terrorism," the *Telegraph* said, "it will be a relief to know that the rocket is on the whole not more formidable than the flying bomb. Its chief disadvantage from our point of view, is that its speed precludes giving any warning to the public of its approach." In conclusion, the paper said: "These weapons have no tactical value."

At least you knew you were still alive if you heard a V2 go off. "When a V-bomb fell in a car park near a cinema in Southern England recently," the *Telegraph* reported that winter, "blowing out all the windows, most of the 400 people in the audience stayed on to watch the performance, which was resumed after a brief interruption."

On November 25, 1944 a V2 hit the Woolworth's in New Cross High Street in south London, killing 160. Because of wartime restrictions, *The Daily Telegraph* reported the incident in this way, on November 27: "Men worked throughout a winter afternoon and night to release people believed trapped after a V-bomb had fallen recently on a multiple shop in Southern England. Fatal casualties were numerous and there were many injured. When the bomb fell, the shop, which occupied the corner site in a main road, was crowded with mothers and children."

Week by week the *Telegraph* reported V2 incidents, but it could not give exact locations or dates. V2 attacks only stopped when the launch-pads were overrun by advancing Allied forces. On March 25, right at the end of the V2 assaults, one hit a tenement at Vallance Road, Stepney, east London, killing 134. Of 40,000 or so civilians in London killed in the war, 2,500 were killed by V2s.

INBRIEF

DECEMBER 3, 1943
By Our Own Representative, Westminster
Mr Bevin, Minister of Labour, announced in the House of Commons today, as foreshadowed in *The Daily Telegraph* on Tuesday, that compulsory recruitment of men for the pits will begin shortly. They will be directed to such work by ballot. The selection will be made from men born on or after January 1, 1918.

There was complete silence in the House when the Minister began his statement, which he read slowly and deliberately, but murmurings broke out when he reached the passage dealing with the method of getting men.

The selection would be made from men who would otherwise be called up for the armed forces and were placed in medical Grade One, or in Grade Two if their disability was foot defects only.

The first V2 to land on London destroyed 11 houses and killed three people at Staveley Road in Chiswick

VE DAY CROWDS

Firemen danced with children round the flames

Bombed sites proved handy spots to light victory bonfires as Londoners attempted to express their feelings after six years of war

A *Telegraph* reporter collected some vivid sights on the eve of VE Day, May 8, 1945 when news of Germany's surrender had been heard on the wireless. "Bonfires burned in the derelict basement of bombed buildings in Soho and Mayfair. With a background of skeleton walls, the crowds danced up and down, waving flags and singing. Nearly all sported conical cardboard hats in red, white and blue.

"An RAF man stood with his back to a cinema in Leicester Square chanting in Arabic. He continued to do so until one of the large gathering of spectators took the airman's hat and started to collect money.

"Public houses sold out of beer rapidly. In the vicinity of Piccadilly Circus there were no houses open. Fireworks exploded every few seconds.

"A banjo player seated himself at the foot of one of Nelson's lions and a score of men and girls danced to his accompaniment. Policemen stood by in small groups. They had an easy time because the revellers kept their merriment within reasonable bounds."

A strangely moving paragraph came in from west London: "Doors were pulled off and windows wrenched from their sockets to start a fire in Rayleigh Road, Hammersmith. The fire brigade was called, but when they arrived the firemen lit a fire on the side of the road and, with the young children, danced around the flames."

It was a puzzle what people could do to express their feelings at the news. That night of May 7 "a procession over a mile long, including students of London University carrying a large flag, marched up and down The Strand. It then went through the Admiralty Arch down the Mall to Buckingham Palace. It was a cosmopolitan crowd with many representatives of the Allied nations present. Flags, rattles and hooters were in abundance."

There was singing and dancing outside the palace and cries of "We want the King". There was no appearance by George VI that night, so the crowd moved off to Piccadilly, making a big bonfire in Haymarket with the help of advertising boards

from outside the Gaumont Cinema. "It was," the *Telegraph* remarked with a shiver, "reminiscent of the 'fire-raising' raids on London of 1940-41."

GERMANY CAPITULATES was the headline in capital letters right across the top of *The Daily Telegraph* the next morning. "This is VE Day," said the report beneath. "After five years and eight months, 'complete and crushing victory' has, in the words of the King, crowned Britain's unrelenting struggle against Nazi Germany."

The King's broadcast was made in simple words undeniably true. "Today we give thanks to God for a great deliverance," he began. "In the darkest hours we knew that the enslaved and isolated peoples of Europe looked to us: their hopes were our hopes; their confidence confirmed our faith. We know that if we failed the last remaining barrier against a worldwide tyranny would have fallen in ruins. But we did not fail. We kept faith with ourselves and with one another. We kept faith and unity with our great Allies.

"We shall have failed," he added, "and the blood of our dearest will have flowed in vain if the victory which they died to win does not lead to a lasting peace, founded on justice and good will."

In Whitehall, Churchill told the crowds: "This is your victory." It was five years to the day since he had become Prime Minister. "History will no doubt decide that Mr Churchill had his faults and made

VE Day: 'Piccadilly Circus was reminiscent of a Venetian carnival, as sober Britons threw off restraint for the biggest night of their lives'

his mistakes," the *Telegraph* said in a leading article. "The fact remains that in its darkest hour the nation felt in its bones that he was the man to lead it and that its feeling has been abundantly justified."

The long years of war, with their incompetencies, shortages, fear, loss, tiredness, strangeness and comradeship, had brought a dawn in which the nation's heroism could be recognised. "The storm of tropical intensity in the early hours which brought an end to the previous night's celebrations cleared by daylight. There was only a slight shower in the morning. Many people, in the tranquillity of Westminster Abbey, bowed in thanksgiving. The pilgrimage to the Unknown Warrior's tomb appeared unending."

At Buckingham Palace, "eight times within 10 hours, in response to the enthusiasm of huge crowds, the King and Queen, Princess Elizabeth and Princess Margaret stepped out on to the balcony." While the crowd was waiting "an Australian soldier climbed the gates of the palace waving a flag and leading the crowd in songs".

"A terrific burst of cheering greeted His Majesty when, at 3.11pm, wearing naval dress and bare-headed, he walked out on to the central balcony, which was draped in gold and scarlet. The King stood for a few seconds alone, waving to the crowd, and then the Queen followed him on to the balcony and stood by his side. Her Majesty, dressed in

powder blue, raised her hand and joined the King in acknowledging the roar of cheers.

"Then the two princesses came out on to the balcony with their parents. Princess Elizabeth bare-headed, in her khaki ATS uniform, stood by the side of the Queen, while Princess Margaret, in blue, stood by her father.

"Mr Churchill's appearance with the Royal family on the balcony of Buckingham Palace at about 5.30pm was the climax of the afternoon's stirring events. The Prime Minister stood between their Majesties and waved his cigar to the crowd and gave the Victory sign.

"In the evening a crowd of 100,000 listened silently to the King's broadcast. They then clamoured for his appearance, and when he again came out on the balcony he was given the greatest ovation of the day." Rattles, whistles, fireworks, "anything that would make noise" was used to greet the floodlighting of the palace, which for so long, with the rest of London, had been blacked out.

"The two princesses, escorted by Guards officers, left the palace after nightfall to mingle with the great crowds outside. Then they appeared again on the balcony with the King and Queen. Their Majesties came on to the balcony once more just before 12.30am. A few minutes later the floodlights were switched off and gradually the crowds dispersed."

Into the night the West End scenes surpassed "even the Armistice of 1918", the *Telegraph* reported. "Piccadilly Circus was reminiscent of a Venetian carnival, as sober Britons threw off restraint for the biggest night of their lives. As long as public houses stayed open, thousands sat on the kerb in The Strand, toasting the victory. Sailors with linked arms marched abreast down the thoroughfares.

"With the coming of dusk, a wilder spirit infected the victory crowd. Crocodiles of dancing soldiers and civilians broke through the mob. Little groups of sailors, soldiers and airmen and their girls formed into crazy, jigging circles.

"More and more fireworks were let off as night drew on. Piccadilly was a tornado of shouting, singing and laughing, interspersed with the noise of rattles, bells, whistles, thunderbolts and rockets.

"A group of British soldiers raced madly into the crowd with a hawker's barrow, some seated on it, until the pressure of the crowd overturned their vehicle. Champagne flowed in abundance. Sailors drank from the bottle in the streets.

"One family party, driving round Hyde Park in a flag-bedecked Governess cart, was followed by a cheery bevy of Wrens astride the roof of a car. A procession up Oxford Street was led by a sailor wearing a top hat, draped with the Union Jack.

"Women brought out their gayest clothes to celebrate Victory night dances. Fashions were disregarded. Every woman, lucky enough to have saved an evening dress from pre-war days, wore it.

"Cheer upon cheer tore the night air as Londoners shouted themselves hoarse. Truly this was a night never to be forgotten."

INBRIEF

MAY 11, 1945

From Frank A. King, St Peter Port, Guernsey

I watched the final surrender this morning of the German garrison in the Channel Islands. As I landed here with the first British soldiers almost indescribable scenes took place. Freedom had come again to the only part of Britain to be occupied by the Nazis.

The 30 British artillery men who took over an island with a garrison of 10,000 Germans, oldish soldiers, went ashore in a German trawler flying the White Ensign.

A police inspector and a sergeant, Guernsey men, were the unofficial reception party on the docks. Both of them were choking back the tears when, speechless, they grasped our hands. The tiny force formed up on the key, fixed bayonets, and marched towards the harbour gates.

Behind those gates was a seething, cheering, crying crowd of men, women and children. Over them the church bells of St Peter Port were clanging tumultuously. Every house had its Union Jack and bunting, saved for this moment through five long, desperate, wearing years. Then the crowd broke through the dock gates.

One second those gunners were marching like Guardsmen. The next they were torn from the ranks, kissed, hugged and cheered. "You have been so long coming." "We have waited so long for you." "British, they're British," the islanders cried.

The joy of these people, who have been eating rabbit skins, getting one and a half pounds of potatoes each week, who had that morning breakfasted on stewed cabbage leaves, was almost heartbreaking.

A DIFFERENT KIND OF PEACE

Churchill is out and Attlee brings in austerity

Britain had voted in 1945 to share fairly the benefits of victory, but all there seemed to be were shortages, rationing and queues

"CHURCHILL RESIGNS: ATTLEE PREMIER. SOCIALISTS GET CLEAR MAJORITY" topped the bank of headlines on the front page of *The Daily Telegraph* on July 27, 1945 after the general election. "The decision of the British people has been recorded in the votes counted today," the defeated Prime Minister said.

"I have, therefore, laid down the charge which was placed upon me in darker times. I regret that I have not been permitted to finish the work against Japan."

The war was not yet over in the East – VJ Day did not come until August 15 – but people were eager to vote for a new kind of peacetime Government. More people than ever – 33 million – were registered to vote, the *Telegraph* pointed out, and more than 25 million had voted. But shortages and Government interference that were put up with in wartime lingered for years longer than most expected.

It was a fixed policy of the *Telegraph* always to refer to the Labour Party as "Socialists", but it was not a title that the new Prime Minister, Clement Attlee, rejected. "We went into this election on a carefully thought-out programme," he said when the results were known. "We have never swerved. We are on the eve of a great advance in the human race. We have no illusions, but we can carry the thing through to success. This is the first time in the history of the country that Labour has ever had a clear majority. It will enable us to implement the policy laid down by the Socialist party."

When Ramsay MacDonald had become the first Labour Prime Minister in 1924, the *Telegraph* had congratulated him on his lack of extremism. "The new Prime Minister has spoken so far in terms of almost flawless propriety and moderation," it said. "Nothing could be less in tune with that spirit of exultation and triumphant fervour which swayed the Socialist mass meeting recently addressed by him in the Albert Hall." But in an industrial climate that led to a general strike in 1926, and which had already produced a railway strike, MacDonald was warned by the the paper that "if he interferes

weakly he will be betraying his trust as Prime Minister; if he interferes strongly, he will be turned upon by all the wild men in the Socialist movement". Twenty-one years later the *Telegraph* still feared those wild men.

"The victory of the Socialist party has come as a severe shock to this country," reported the *Telegraph*'s correspondent in New York in July 1945. "In the United States 'Winnie' is regarded not only as the personification of British courage, tenacity and humour, but as the international symbol of Allied victory. Most people find it almost impossible to understand how Britain could have, as they see it, 'repudiated' him when so much of the war and peace yet remains to be won."

In a leading article, the *Telegraph* judged that "many electors, beset by the domestic problems which are the aftermath of war – scarcity of houses, rationed food and shortages of clothing – cast their votes against existing order without thought of the complete landslide which they have produced."

The great difference between the parties was on nationalisation "the shibboleth, the abracadabra, to which Socialists give a different meaning at every election. In this one it excluded nationalising the land, the oldest nostrum of all; but included coal, fuel industries, iron and steel, inland transport and the Bank of England, under schemes of which not the barest outline has been published, if any yet exists." Nationalised they were, whatever the effects.

Another plank of Labour's programme was the "Welfare State", designed by the coalition Government in the depths of war. A White Paper of 1942 embodied the plan by Sir William Beveridge "to bring the entire adult population men and women of the country into a compulsory, and, in the main, contributory scheme of insurance to

A woman, with her own kind of fashionable hat (top), examines a rack of Utility suits in 1942. By 1949 the New Look (right), with its yards of material, had reached London shops. Post-war life was to be moulded by the Socialism of Clement Attlee (pictured in a rare burst of hilarity), less constrained than that of Ramsay MacDonald

provide against sickness, unemployment, old age, and for families", as the *Telegraph* put it at the time.

But the first thing to hit victorious Britain was austerity. Attlee felt obliged to impose "measures without precedent in peace time" as the *Telegraph* said, to meet a financial crisis. In August 1947 the meat ration was reduced, and the basic petrol ration entirely abolished. "This means an end to motoring for pleasure," the paper explained. "Thousands of owners of new cars will be unable to use them. Dealers will be faced with a widespread cancellation of orders." Petrol rationing continued until 1950.

"Travelling for pleasure abroad, outside the sterling area, or in foreign ships and aircraft, is to be banned after October 1," the *Telegraph* reported in August 1947. Strikes, prohibited in wartime, continued to be illegal until 1951.

At the same time, people were itching to get away from meagre, shabby make-do clothes. The Civilian Clothing Order 1941 had prohibited the use of pleats, turnups, or unnecessary buttons and pockets on clothes bearing the CC41 Utility mark. Fashion designers from Norman Hartnell to Hardy Amies rallied round. In 1943 the Utility mark was extended to furniture, with some success as far as design and soundness of construction went.

It had been no easy matter to combine fashion sense with clothes rationing. The *Telegraph* had tried to help with its series of "Vogue Fashion Service" patterns for dressmaking. Pattern No 9730 in January 1944 was designed to provide a frock of fashionably softer colour that was also "coupon saving" since "sleeves, shoulder yokes and bodice at back may be made out of an old frock; this saves a little more than a yard". A new hat and matching bag for Easter 1944 were promised from an impossibly economical sounding "eighth of a yard of 64-inch wide material".

Not surprisingly there was a reaction after the demands of war were removed. In 1947 came the New Look, which attracted Government disapproval for the amount of material it consumed. But by then the patriotic demands of war were no longer present to attract popular compliance.

In 1949 Harold Wilson, 33-year-old president of the Board of Trade, announced that clothes rationing would end completely. It had been in force since June 1, 1941. But control of prices would continue and the Utility scheme extended. Central Government reserved to itself the fixing of markets. "The end of rationing will not mean more goods for the home market," the *Telegraph* reported. "Export quotas will have to be maintained and will not be reduced to meet any particular shortages in this country."

Things did not improve quickly. Even as late as January 1951 the meat ration was decreased again – to 8d worth a week – because of a trade deadlock with Argentina.

In October 1951, Winston Churchill, aged 76, took to the hustings for the 16th time since 1899, becoming Prime Minister again after an election in which the Conservatives, though gaining slightly fewer votes than Labour, won 321 seats to their 295.

THE FESTIVAL OF BRITAIN

Eight million visitors under the Skylon

Futuristic buildings dominated the South Bank where crowds came to celebrate the best of British – all within the budget, too

In 1951 many were practised in the art of grumbling, and the Festival of Britain was not immune to complaints. But *The Daily Telegraph* started off with a determination to relish the excitement the event engendered.

"At nightfall the Empire's capital sprang to life in a blaze of light," its reporter wrote on May 3. "From the roof of *The Daily Telegraph* building I saw the Skylon, a phosphorescent pencil of light rising from the South Bank site."

The Skylon was the well-contrived name for a 250ft aluminium-plated pencil tapering to a point at each end that seemed to hang in the air without support – in reality kept upright by cables and pylons. The design by Powell and Moya for a vertical feature on the 27-acre Festival site was chosen in a competition that attracted 157 entries from architects. It possessed, in the words of Geoffrey Fisher, the Archbishop of Canterbury, "the supreme merit of serving no useful purpose whatsoever". In years dominated by making do, austerity and utility this was a great virtue.

Gay Scenes by Floodlight was one of the *Telegraph* headlines on May 4. Floodlighting

retained an extravagant air of freedom from ARP restriction. On the night of May 3, 1951 "as if the Skylon's appearance were a signal, buildings that a moment before were sombre silhouettes took on myriad hues. Along the Embankment blues, reds and yellows burst forth in a mass of colour. On the North Bank was Scott's *Discovery*, her masts and rigging ablaze with light. Floodlit landmarks to the east were the Old Bailey and St Paul's. In the west shone Nelson's Column and the Admiralty Arch."

In London the streets were full, in scenes reminiscent of VE Day and VJ Day. "Young and old linked arms and sang and shouted, giving the city a carnival gaiety," the *Telegraph*'s reporter wrote.

It was not just the modernistic Skylon that attracted sightseers. On the other side of the Thames, "extra police controlled a crowd estimated at nearly 10,000 which gathered round the east end of St Paul's Cathedral for a sing-song round a bonfire. The fire was arranged by the Standing Conference of National Voluntary Youth Organisations to celebrate the Festival opening.

"A choir of more than 1,000 boys and girls representing all London youth organisations opened the ceremony by singing a song specially written by Mr Harold Purcell, dedicated to the Festival and called *The Song of the Festival Fires*. Throughout Britain about 100,000 youths had arranged similar ceremonies.

"Many sightseers arrived by Underground trains. As the sing-song continued, the fire was replenished from stacks of wood piled in readiness on a bombed site." Bombed sites were readily available for the next 20 years, some of them to be enterprisingly transformed into car parks.

The Festival of Britain was not just the exhibition on the South Bank. Dozens of exhibitions and arts festivals took place throughout the country. The Land Travelling Exhibition, reflecting British people at play, work and travel, started in Manchester and moved over the next five months to Birmingham and Nottingham.

The Festival had been declared open at St Paul's

The emblem for the Festival (above), chosen in a competition, was designed by Abram Games (1914–96), and incorporated the profile of Britannia, the points of the compass and festive bunting. The remarkable 250ft Skylon, designed by the architects Powell & Moya (right), in shiny aluminium with no utilitarian purpose and no visible means of support, was a great hit with Festival-goers. After the five-month exhibition, it was demolished

From the Telegraph

The extortionate price of the South Bank sandwich

May 5, 1951

Daily Telegraph reporter

The Festival of Britain authorities are inquiring into the high prices charged yesterday by some caterers at the South Bank Exhibition. Visitors were complaining last night that they had paid from 6d to 9d for a cup of coffee and from 1s to 3s each for a sandwich.

At one snack bar I ordered a tongue sandwich and a cup of tea. From my half a crown I received 2d change. The sandwich

was in two halves and was so small that it fitted without pressure into a cigarette carton emptied of its 10 cigarettes.

I decided to have my dessert elsewhere and walked into a snack bar at the other side of the site. There a Royal Navy Petty Officer paid 3s for two glasses of orange squash and four small cream cakes.

Walking from snack bar to snack bar I heard many complaints. Examples of the sandwich prices were: cheese one shilling a round; tomato one shilling; beef 1s 6d; tongue 2s; chicken 2s to 2s 6d; smoked salmon 3s.

In a cafeteria near the Waterloo Bridge entrance, a party of four Welshmen paid 15s 11d for 10 sandwiches, six cakes and four cups of tea. While I was questioning them about the charges people sitting nearby came up to add their complaints.

Cathedral just after noon on May 3 by George VI. Almost half his reign had been dominated by war, and he had less than a year to live. "He summarised the spirit of the Festival in one phrase – 'This is no time for despondency'," the *Telegraph* reported. The Festival, he said, was a "symbol of Britain's abiding courage and vitality". His speech was broadcast to the world.

Reporting on the ceremony at St Paul's, Guy Ramsey, in a bylined report, wrote of a feeling of national and historic unity. "Far away on the South Bank the Festival is spread, and none dare prophesy its failure or success. But that hour of pure emotion and pure beauty, of patriotism untainted by jingo, of loyalty unsmirched by servility, that alone had justified it."

The King and Queen were next day given a view of the exhibition site before its public opening. "Quite simply, without any pomp or pageantry, they toured the South Bank Exhibition. After a 90-minute visit they promised to return in the future for a more extended tour."

"It was a cold, grey morning, with fine rain and cloud and mist that settled on London's river," wrote the *Telegraph* reporter. "The Exhibition seemed to be in a world of its own: a world of cold concrete, icy glass and fantastic contours slashed here and there with colour."

The rain got into the television cables and only five minutes of the Royal tour could be broadcast. "Though engineers worked all night, only one camera was in operation when the programme was due to begin. Bad visibility made the picture dull."

"The Queen wore a powder blue coat, with hat to match. With their Majesties was Princess Margaret, wearing a velvet coat and hat in Garter blue. The tour began at the Dome of Discovery and outside were gathered many of the invited guests, including members of the Government. Mr Churchill and Mr Attlee were both received with cheers.

"In the Home and Gardens Pavilion, the Queen was interested in adjustable furniture for children. 'What a clever idea, and so modern,' she said. 'Unlike so many modern ideas, it is so practicable.'"

The Dome of Discovery, unlike the Festival Hall, was a temporary building; it was the largest dome in the world, with a diameter of 365 feet.

At 2.30pm, the Exhibition was opened to the public. "When the gates closed at 10.30pm the official attendance was given as 20,820." That first weekend, 98,000 people saw the Festival of Britain South Bank Exhibition – 59,214 on Saturday and 38,857 on Sunday, when it opened two hours later.

By the time the exhibition closed on September 30, 8.5 million people had paid to see it. The cost was £10,686,924 – well within the estimate of £11.5 million – and revenue at £2,563,199 slightly exceeded the Government estimate.

That October the Conservatives were voted in. The South Bank exhibition was demolished, as planned, but some saw in this speed a desire to remove a reminder of the Labour Government. Labour was not re-elected until 1964.

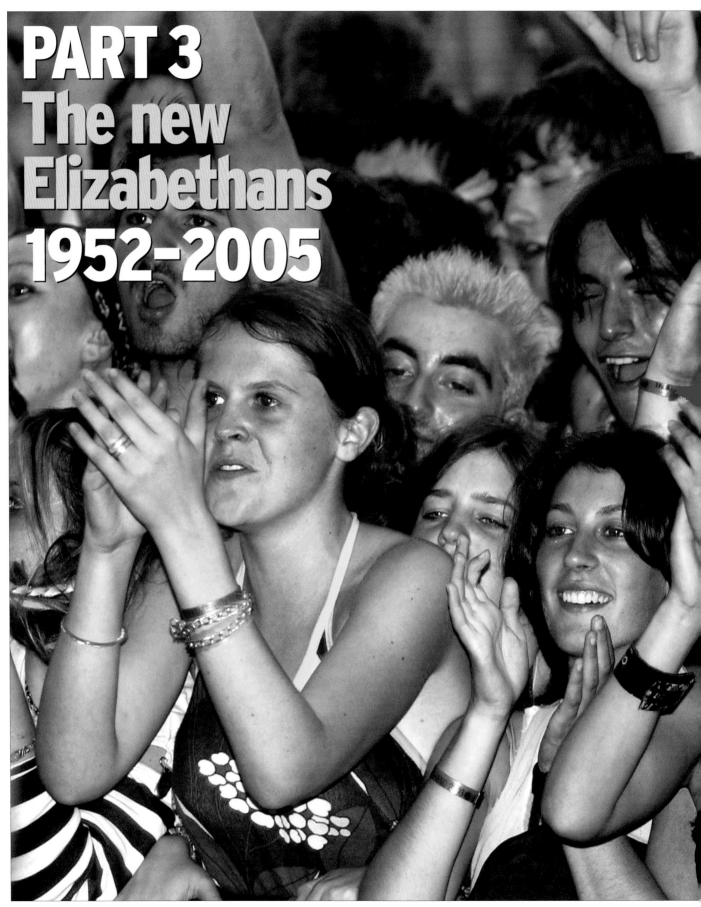

PART 3
The new Elizabethans 1952–2005

Fans at the Reading Festival, 2003. 'The young are devising their own media to express a standard of their own, free of divisions of class or creed,' W.F. Deedes had written optimistically 40 years earlier, when the Beatles confirmed the strength of youth culture

Living with television

From now on, television defined events in the public memory, from the onset of
in establishing the celebrities of the new youth culture. But newspapers continued

WATCHING THE CORONATION

To brave the rain or to cluster round the screen

Nearly half the nation saw on television the ceremonies in the Abbey and the crowds outside catching a glimpse of the Queen

For many, memories of the Coronation are of huddling round a television set. Often it was the first set they had owned or hired. Perhaps theirs was the only one in the street, and neighbours came round to watch. These defined the age: the television and the Queen.

That day, 20 million watched on television; 12 million tuned in on the wireless. Almost 9,000 sat on scaffolding seats in the Abbey. For thousands more the Coronation meant camping out in the streets of London. At home families saw on the dark little screen the strange swaying motion of the Horseguards' plumes each side of the Queen's train as she walked down the nave of t he Abbey, and then the moment the Archbishop of Canterbury holding the crown aloft and settling it on the young Queen's head. For those in the streets it was a glimpse of her as she passed in the gilded coach. To those who were parents she looked very young.

It was the second of June, but "drenching showers driven by a cold wind kept people on the move" the evening before. When the rain stopped that evening thousands converged on the Victoria Memorial outside Buckingham Palace. "Despite the mounted and motor cycle police," the *Telegraph* reported. "they surged across the roads and at times stopped the traffic. When the Queen Mother and Princess

Beatlemania to the destruction of the World Trade Centre, and it supplanted cinema to decide what was news, whether Lady Chatterley or Lady Diana

EMERGENCY EXIT

Margaret left the palace at 7.45pm the crowd was uncontrollable. Thousands of men, women and children forced their way to within touching distance of the Royal car, which could only inch its way forward."

The police would not allow campers immediately outside the palace, but down the Mall "in the cold night, with a temperature of only 45 degrees at 1am, many tried to sleep huddled under rugs and

The decorations put up in the Mall in May 1953 (above) were applauded by the Telegraph. About 20 million watched the Coronation on television; thousands camped out in cold and rain to see the processions

raincoats, while others were sitting patiently waiting for the morning.

"At one spot, waste paper was lit in a brazier. Some of the more enterprising rigged up shelters. They tied blankets to bus stop railings on the kerb-side. Others tied tarpaulins to trees and decorated them with red, white and blue.

"By midnight the pavements all along the route were a solid mass of humanity. People were camping ten deep round the whole of Trafalgar Square, where the procession passes three times. Thousands milled round the Square and buses moved at a crawl. High-spirited youths exploded fireworks at the foot of Nelson's Column."

"Though midnight was zero hour for closing the Square, traffic was still going through and also through Whitehall at 12.15 this morning," the late edition of the Coronation Day *Telegraph* was able to report. "Police began to control Trafalgar Square onlookers at midnight to make room for barriers on the route boundary. People changed their positions in the hope of being immediately behind the barriers. More than 50,000 were there at 4am."

From railway stations, buses and taxis, a constant stream arrived looking for a vantage point. "The Mall had long since been uncomfortably crowded. Spectators were six to ten deep on both sides by early afternoon. Late-comers loaded with blankets and food, struggled from end to end searching hopelessly for somewhere to sleep."

Then "there were cheers as the news spread that Everest had been conquered." This was the Coronation present that Hillary and Tenzing had wrapped up on May 29.

In its "Late news" slot on the front page, the *Telegraph* noted that "when Underground trains started Coronation Day services at 3.00am thousands more people began the journey to central London. London Transport stated at 3.30 that first District Line trains were about three-quarters full. First train from Wimbledon was crowded."

Others had an early start too. "Reveille was at 3.00am for some of the 38,000 Servicemen on Coronation duties today. Others were wakened at four or five o'clock. In their camps in Kensington Gardens, Earls Court, Olympia, and in permanent barracks and the Clapham deep shelter they were roused by loudspeakers. Some men heard bugles, others the shout of 'Wake up!'

"They had a substantial breakfast before setting out on their march to the Coronation route, a distance of 13 miles there and back for the men camping in Kensington. The Army breakfast was: cereal or porridge, fried egg and bacon with bubble and squeak, bread and butter, marmalade, tea or coffee. Rice dishes were served for the Pakistanis and other overseas units who have special food.

"A packed haversack lunch will be delivered by vehicles which will call at food distribution points on the route," the paper said. "It will consist of: cheese spread rolls, spam rolls, bar of chocolate, portion of fruit slab cake, apples, barley sugar."

The *Telegraph* spared a thought for mothers who would be spending much of the day in the Abbey and had to find baby-sitters. "Firms that specialise in this service have been booked up for weeks." Luckily, Viscount and Viscountess Savernake, with a six-month-old son, David, had a solution. "Lady Savernake prefers to look after her baby single-handed, but knows an excellent nanny who will come in when needed." So that was all right.

"Both Lord Savernake and his father, the Earl of Cardigan, are Gold Staff Officers on duty in the Abbey. The Countess of Cardigan will be in the Abbey tomorrow, too, so will her father-in-law, the Marquis of Ailesbury, and the Marchioness. That makes six members of one family in the Abbey. Surely this is a record, apart from the Royal family."

For those outside, the question was what to wear. "Raffia and straw accessories have received a social lift," the *Telegraph* reported encouragingly. "There were many examples at last week's Royal garden party. Large velvet hats were trimmed with raffia, straw handbags, plaited sandals and even raffia embroideries on heavy skirts were seen."

If skirts embroidered with raffia seemed bad, had you seen some of the street decorations? "The decoration of the Embankment leaves much to be desired," the Telegraph said in its Coronation Supplement. "Surely some symbols of Neptune, some majestic water display, could have been attempted." Instead of which all the crowds of schoolchildren saw was "a phalanx of masts in lilac and black, crowned with variations of the helmets of the Household Cavalry".

By contrast "outstanding in interest on the processional route is the Mall. Its feature is the series of overhanging arches in gold and blue, from each of which a coronet is suspended." It was "a simple decoration that serves its purpose well".

And then, when, in its wooden cabinet, the little screen had shrunk into a white dot, and in the streets the footsore had limped back to the Underground, it was time for those steady Servicemen to march back to camp, after hours of little more than spam and cheese spread rolls, to "a hot dinner", typically "lentil soup, roast beef, Yorkshire pudding, roast and boiled potatoes, spring greens, baked rice pudding and fruit salad, bread, tea or coffee." Long live the Queen.

In 1957, Bill Haley (above) and his Comets played in London. Haley looked quite old, but the Telegraph critic found the beat infectious

TEDDY BOYS

Bill Haley and 'Rock Around the Clock'

The cinema, dance halls, records and clothes all identified a new unsquare culture ready to be marketed to youth

They were called "Edwardians" when the *Telegraph* reported their doings in the summer of 1954, but they are better known to social history as Teddy Boys. "One of the main difficulties facing the authorities," the *Telegraph* noted, "is that many youths who favour Edwardian dress are respectable and well behaved." A group of 14 youths and girls on the train from Shoeburyness, Essex, to Fenchurch Street on the previous Saturday night had "smashed electric light bulbs and windows, and pulled the communication chord 10 times", delaying the train and "making some passengers miss their last buses".

Local authorities were invited to discuss with the police how to stamp out hooliganism by such gangs. The Teddy Boys did not go away. When the warm weather returned in 1955 Bath magistrates' court dealt with six youths arrested during Saturday night disturbances at a municipal dance.

The chairman of the bench said to defendants from outside the city: "We don't want people of your type if you are going to behave like this over here." A 23-year-old dock labourer from Bristol was sentenced to six months' for being in possession of a spring clasp-knife, and for assaulting a police sergeant. A youth of 17 from Bath was ordered to be at home by nine o'clock at night for 12 months and fined £15 for carrying a metal chain.

An unnamed 16-year-old Bath boy was fined £5 for carrying a leather belt with a metal buckle. The docker and the 16-year-old were also each fined £5 for stealing a handrail which they tore from the wall of a public convenience.

The film *Rock Around the Clock* hit cinemas in September 1956. Bill Haley sang nine numbers in the film, including *See You Later, Alligator*. The Platters sang *Only You*. It was the complete teen dream, although Bill Haley was by then 31 and looked it. The director, Fred Sears, made 49 films in the nine years before his death in 1957. He was cashing in on the huge hit that the record *Rock Around the Clock* had become after it had been used as the title song for *The Blackboard Jungle* (1955), that remarkable celebration of juvenile delinquency. ("Give me that knife," says Glenn Ford as Mr Dadier the teacher. Vic Morrow as Artie West the gang leader replies: "Here it is. All you got to do is take it. Now, come on. Come on, take it. Come on.")

"Police broke up a crowd of youths and girls who jived yesterday in the aisles of the Davis Theatre, Croydon, while *Rock Around the Clock* was being shown," the *Telegraph* reported on September 10. "At the Gaiety Theatre, Peter Street, Manchester, youths and girls began jiving in the aisles. Youths in the circle grabbed a hose and showered water on people in the stalls. Police restored order."

The film was banned in Blackburn and Preston. "Mr Frank Squires, the Town Clerk of Blackburn, said the ban was 'on the grounds that it contains matter likely to lead to public disorder'. Alderman R.F. Mottershead commented: 'Our police have enough to do without acting as watchdogs outside cinemas.'"

At the Elephant and Castle in south London, a crowd estimated at between 700 and 800 gathered in the street after a showing of the film at the Trocadero cinema. "Many youths and girls were singing and dancing and a gang halted traffic," police said. "Youths banged on the roofs of cars. This went on from nearly 10.40pm to midnight."

In Manchester, police said that after a

'Many youths who favour Edwardian dress (left) are respectable and well behaved,' the Telegraph noted. There was scope for moodiness and hair-oil

showing of the film an unruly mob of 200 youths terrorised pedestrians and obstructed traffic. Three youths and a boy of 15 were fined £2 each. A magistrate said: "It would be better if the police were allowed to deal with you in a way that would give you something to rock and roll about."

On February 6, 1957 Bill Haley and his Comets gave their first show in London, at the Dominion Theatre, Tottenham Court Road. The man from the *Telegraph* was there. "These Comets arm themselves with three loudspeakers, aimed, of course, at the audience. There is the rasping tenor saxophone, the familiar electric guitar and the heavy, infectious unflagging off-beat," wrote the anonymous critic on the front page. "As an added attraction the saxophonist kneels to play and the bass player rides his bass. I believe they break lots of double basses that way.

"Much of rock and roll is played over the old jazz chord sequence of the 12-bar blues. But there the similarity ends, for good jazz it certainly is not. Rather, good fun and, if anything, a caricature of jazz. But there is no more harm in it than there was in the Charleston or the Black Bottom. Any delinquency that has resulted in the past seems to have come from over-dressed young exhibitionists.

"The audience of 3,000 cheered, sang, clapped in time to the music and showed nothing more harmful than healthy enthusiasm. It did not hesitate to voice its disapproval because Haley's appearance lasted little more than half an hour.

"What is its appeal? Two young members of the audience, aged 15 and 16 and both from Hemel Hempstead, Herts, put it this way. 'It's simple and easy to understand. It's got a beat and you can jive to it and sing to it. If you don't like it you are definitely square.' "

From the Telegraph
'Look Back in Anger' – a study in resentful exhibitionism

The hero lashes his wife with a fury often witty and always cruel

May 9, 1956
By Patrick Gibb

John Osborne's *Look Back in Anger*, seen at the Royal Court last night, is the first play to be given by the English Stage Company from a new author. It is a work of some power, uncertainly directed.

The leading character, a man of education living in poverty, would seem to be intended as a full-length study in resentment. Something of a sadist and very much an exhibitionist, he has married above himself, apparently out of spite against middle-class respectability. His wife he lashes with a verbal fury that is often witty and always cruel.

It is not, however, resentment that is personified as much as self-pity, and this causes the sympathy, which the author intends, to be withdrawn. When his wife left him, it seemed she was fortunate. When she returned to him in the end, a broken spirit, were we intended to cheer?

What the hero's predicament was, apart from the hint that he was "born out of his time", I found difficult to decide. He was, perhaps, a character who should have gone to a psychiatrist rather than have come to a dramatist – not at any rate to one writing his first play.

BUYING SANDWICHES

Lots of people rather like the paper these days

Escaping a rocky passage the Telegraph, as a newsy, well written paper, drew readers who found some things worth conserving

After 127 years at the same address in Fleet Street, The Daily Telegraph moved to the Isle of Dogs in 1987, to be followed by other papers. The cartoonist Matt Pritchett (below) played on Max Hastings' reputation for yomping first into Port Stanley during the Falklands War.

Editors (bottom) changed more quickly in the paper's second century

An indicator of social change in the second half of the 20th century was the growing habit, among the sandwich-lunching classes, of *buying* sandwiches instead of bringing them from home. Money was getting easier.

When Elizabeth II was proclaimed Queen, *The Daily Telegraph* cost 2d, twopence. A week's *Telegraphs* cost a shilling. A pound bought five months' papers. It had gone up from a penny-halfpenny in 1951, and the editor, or proprietor, felt obliged to publish a long defensive item on the front page noting, first that the other newspapers were going up a halfpenny too, and secondly that "newsprint is costing British newspapers six times as much as it did in 1939 mainly due to the cancellation through Government action of forward contracts made with Canadian manufacturers". The *Telegraph* sold 1,002,000 copies a day, and could have sold more if the newsprint was available.

'Apparently Max Hastings was the first editor into Docklands'

On the human level there were changes at the beginning of the reign. Its proprietor, Lord Camrose, died in 1954, and Michael Berry, his younger son took over the running of *The Daily Telegraph*, summoning the editor up to the fifth floor at six o'clock each evening. He was created Lord Hartwell in 1968.

Colin Coote, knighted by Macmillan in 1962, stayed editor till he was 70 in 1964. He rewarded Macmillan ill, though unintentionally, by innocently introducing his osteopath, Stephen Ward, to Eugene Ivanov, the Soviet naval attaché. It was a connection that, with the addition of Christine Keeler, made possible the Profumo scandal, a symptom if not the cause of the wilting of Tory rule and the efflorescence of the permissive Sixties.

Sir Colin left the paper with a circulation of 1,319,000. From 1964 to 1974 the popular, donnish Maurice Green edited. The length of editorships had shrunk as the world turned faster. He was followed by W.F. Deedes (1974-86), Max Hastings (1986-95), Charles Moore (1995-2003) and Martin Newland.

Prophecies that newspapers would, before the century was out, be replaced by glowing computer screens proved delusive. Papers grew bigger and bigger, but not without travails. *The Times* was off the streets for the whole of 1979 with strike trouble, and the *Telegraph*'s circulation rose to 1,500,000, the most the presses could manage.

The Berry family suffered from the same union troubles as many other British business managers. *The Times* moved overnight to a fortified site in Wapping. The *Telegraph* committed itself to building new printing works. Money was short and prospects rocky. Conrad Black moved in, invested and took control. In 1987 *The Daily Telegraph* left Fleet Street for the Isle of Dogs, before even the ugly tower blocks of Canary Wharf had been built.

To readers this was of very little interest. They saw their paper changing slowly. The crammed pages, with dog-legs of news reports and columns of pared-down paragraphs, blossomed into layouts with photographs that less seldom looked as if they had been taken at the bottom of the sea. Something was being lost, and yet to compare a copy of the paper from the mid-seventies with one today, is to see more pages of news, features, reviews, sport, business and leisure articles than ever.

Some innovations rapidly gained a timeless quality. Hugh Montgomery-Massingberd was asked to bring the obituaries columns alive, as it were, and succeeded so convincingly that the other newspapers, from the new *Independent* to the *Guardian*, imitated him. And so did his successors in the obituary chair.

The Telegraph had never been Right-wing in Tory terms. Max Hastings liked shooting, but birds, not Reds. Charles Moore liked hunting and country pursuits; he supported the Union of the United Kingdom, and deplored the centralised authoritarianism of the European Union. Three-quarters of the way through his editorship

Colin Coote, 1950–64

Maurice Green, 1964–74

W.F. Deedes, 1974–86

Max Hastings, 1986–95

Charles Moore, 1995–2003

Martin Newland, 2003–

Garland –
after Rembrandt

Nicholas Garland stands alone in the classical tradition of political cartooning. In February 1983 he depicted the Labour Party at a low ebb, with Michael Foot as the anatomist, with, looking on, Tony Benn (top) next to Gerald Kaufman and Roy Hattersley, and below them, from left, Peter Shore, Denis Healey, Eric Heffer and John Silkin.

In 2004 Tony Blair suddenly announced he had had to sleep in the street on his arrival in London; Matt (below) linked this up with the popularity of 'The Lord of the Rings.'

Michael ffolkes illustrated the 'Way of the World' (see extract below) written by Michael Wharton as Peter Simple

"A Free Country" became his watchword, and the newspaper woke up to the fact that it no longer despised people who used the word "gay".

As Michael Wharton, the author of the "Peter Simple" column since 1957, pointed out in his autobiographical volume, *The Missing Will*, the *Telegraph* had, since the Second World War, been written for respectable family people by journalists who were far from respectable and had complicated family circumstances. A notable minority were drunk for a time most days. There was a fearful symmetry in its being the *diplomatic* correspondent who in the King and Keys public house each night would "go critical" after enough whiskies and start to harangue in the most baroque way ("I know you – you've got a blue bottom") any unlucky tourist within range. It was a reversion to the bohemianism of the paper's first 50 years; it was a convention of the times.

In the first decade of the sober 21st century many people, while scarcely aware of the culture of the last generation but one, have grown anxious to grab on to what they can discern as good among things that are disappearing. They are grateful to the last ageing heroes of the Second World War; they showed enthusiasm for the Queen's Golden Jubilee. Sir John Keegan, in his essay on the Queen's reign (page 236), identifies some of the losses and gains.

The Daily Telegraph has shaken itself free from any identification with a dull world that has passed. But, into their eighties, Philip Warner wrote Army obituaries and E.W. Swanton wrote about cricket, because people enjoyed what they wrote. W.F. Deedes continued into his nineties to write leading articles and features for the same reason.

Nicholas Garland, still in his sixties, has been drawing political cartoons in the *Telegraph* since 1966. He is in a class of his own and there is no obvious heir. He has never been doctrinaire, certainly never toed any line set by the *Telegraph*'s own political principles. Since 1988 Matt Pritchett has been drawing front-page pocket cartoons for the paper that are unfailingly sharp, funny and of the moment. Those two cartoonists reflect two sides of the "thing" that gives the *Telegraph* a life of its own. And a lot of people like it.

'And Tony Blair has revealed that for a short while he lived in Middle Earth'

From the Telegraph
Down the leadmine

June 23, 1977
Began work on my *Life of Stephen Spender*. Notes on Spanish Civil War period very wet and almost illegible.

Started to type but when trying to reverse defective spool caught index finger in rusty mechanism and could not release it. Where to get help? Finally Amiel, my pet toad, and, I think, my only real friend, hopped up and began sagaciously gnawing typewriter-ribbon until I got my hand free.

Unfortunately, the poor creature, maddened by hunger, continued eating (I had no heart to stop him) until whole ribbon was devoured. End of work for day. For ever?

Angstometer reading for day: 281.7.
Peter Simple

BEATLES BEDLAM

Pinky and Perky followed by Twist and Shout

It was quite a change of gear from the Royal Variety Performance to a triumphant tour of a hysterical United States

'Veteran reporters said they had never seen anything like this chaotic 20-minute press conference at which photographers and television men fought and scrambled to get pictures," the *Telegraph* correspondent in New York wrote on February 7, 1964. It was the beginning of the Beatles' American tour, which made them global idols with a newspaper image of a different order from that of any other popular singers.

There had been hints of what was to come in the unlikely setting of the Royal Variety Performance in November 1963. Four hundred police had to hold back the crowds. The Queen Mother, then in her sixties, who was meant to be entertained, at the Prince of Wales Theatre, rose to the challenge: "I loved them. They are so young, fresh and vital."

The *Telegraph*'s critic was not quite so sure, except about the audience response. "I have never heard anything approaching the reception," he wrote. "For their *She Loves You* number, the audience were already joining in, clapping the rhythm, but by their fourth song, appropriately called *Twist and Shout*, the general commotion was incredible."

The competition from the evening's other 18 acts was not uniformly strong. There were Max Bygraves and Harry Secombe and, surprisingly, Marlene Dietrich and Pinky and Perky. Worse, Charlie Drake did a sketch that had been seen on television only two nights before, "which does take the edge away", as the *Telegraph* critic put it.

The opening acts proved "hardly more than a warm-up for the Beatles. We have had 'pop' manias before; certainly none has won last night's stupendous applause.

"To a classically minded 'square' seeing them for the first time they were, to begin with, four strange youngsters with below-the-fringe haircuts. Next, one noticed the enthusiasm, the absence of any self-pitying moan, and no suggestive wiggling, the curses of the last 'pop' crop. They are plainly not just entertainers, but a rallying-point for an overspill of teenage high spirits."

That overspill was for export, and "two hours of

'The 1962 Beatles' (above), by Peter Blake, were transformed by the American tour of 1964, with dependable screaming (top) from women and girls elevating them to a higher plane of celebrity

bedlam" engulfed Kennedy International Airport on February 7, 1964, when 5,000 teenagers greeted the Beatles at the beginning of their 10-day tour.

Two days in, when they made their live debut on the Ed Sullivan show, the Columbia Broadcasting System estimated the number of viewers at 30 million. The next day the LP *Introducing the Beatles* was released in the United States.

From then on, the group played catch-as-catch-can with thousands of screaming teenagers inside and outside the venues. An hysterical crowd swarmed around the Pennsylvania railway station chanting "We want the Beatles" when they arrived in New York to play a mid-week show.

When they appeared at the Carnegie Hall, "a frenzied mass of screaming, shouting youths leaped up and down in their seats. The house was packed with an audience of 2,800. But hardly anyone heard what the Beatles sang or said amid the uproar."

And so the tour continued, on a wave of Beatlemania. At Miami Airport "at least 30 students

were cut on the arms and face, none seriously, when they thrust aside police who had linked arms and crashed through two glass doors. Seven thousand jumping teenagers deluged the Beatles with jellybeans when they arrived, and broke windows and chairs."

Back at home an optimistic reaction was available even from some Conservative commentators. "The Beatles were not merely a passing craze, Mr Deedes, Minister without Portfolio, told the City of London Young Conservatives last night," the *Telegraph* reported. " 'They herald a cultural movement among the young which may become part of the history of our time,' he said.

"The young are devising their own media through which to express a standard of their own, free of divisions of class or creed. For they have discerned dimly that in a world of automation, declining craftsmanship and increased leisure something of this kind is essential to restore the human instinct to excel at something."

MODS AND ROCKERS

Sawdust Caesars go to war beside the seaside

Forget the Fab Four, music and clothes became rallying standards for youngsters not averse to a spot of bank holiday bother

Pop culture developed fast, and no sooner had the Beatles fastened themselves on the consciousness of the serious newspaper reader than a new clash of styles materialised that had nothing to do with the Liverpool mop-tops. In 1964 Mods and Rockers adopted tribal styles and went to war.

On the sunny Whitsun bank holiday Monday of May 18, two armies of youths numbering nearly 2,000 surged backwards and forwards across the beach near the Palace Pier, Brighton. Shop windows were broken, cars were damaged. "Children wept as parents hustled them from beach to beach when fighting teenagers hurled milk bottles, deckchairs and stones," reported David

Loshak for *The Daily Telegraph*. "Brighton looked more like a Middle East trouble spot than an English seaside resort." Press photographers were eager to catch shots that would shock respectable readers.

Mods tended to wear lightweight suits with narrow trousers, porkpie hats, and parkas to ride their motor scooters, Lambrettas or Vespas. They liked Ska and the music of The Who, although that group's first hit single, *I Can't Explain*, came out only in 1965. A few took amphetamines. Mod girls wore short hair and eye-shadow. Rockers preferred dirty jeans and leather jackets with studs, and a motor-bike such as a Norton if they could afford one. They listened to Elvis, or John Lee Hooker if they were serious-minded.

"I asked several teenagers why they were in Brighton," David Loshak wrote. "A 15-year-old girl told me: 'Don't know. Just looking for something to happen, I suppose.' Crowds of Mods, several hundred strong, searched the town for anyone wearing a leather jacket, the badge of the very-much-outnumbered Rockers. I was with such a crowd when a Rocker and his girl were sighted.

"A great jeer went up, the couple were roughly jostled and kicked and one youth knocked the boy in the ear and pulled him over on to his back. This incident took place in St James Street, a major thoroughfare. Yet it led to no arrests. There must have been a dozen such incidents for every arrest.

"During the night, thousands of deckchairs had been scattered far and wide, many broken and ripped, some burned to light bonfires on the beaches. Just before noon a strong force of police

A Mod kicks out at a lone Rocker as Whitsun bank holiday trippers in 1964 look on from a shelter at the seaside. 'Brighton looked more like a Middle East trouble spot than an English seaside resort,' said a Telegraph reporter with a certain poetic latitude

began ushering a crowd of about 600 Mods eastwards out of the centre of the town."

Meanwhile at Margate "two youths were stabbed on the sands today and the buffet at the railway station was attacked as violence continues here for the second successive day," reported John Osman. "Following the knifings, thousands of trippers watched police on the seafront search opposing Mods and Rockers."

After violence throughout the Sunday, trouble began early on Monday. At 8am about 200 Mods with a sprinkling of Rockers came in from the beach where many had spent the night, to meet friends arriving on trains from London.

"In the station buffet they smashed three windows and tipped over five tables scattering tea, cakes, crockery and customers. Mrs Lily Stott, 53, manageress, a small, grey-haired woman wearing spectacles, was thrown to the ground by one Mod. Two others dragged her face-down around the floor. They tipped up more tables as chaos developed.

"Mrs Ellen Green, 50, a cleaner, emerged with a broom and started laying about her to assist Mrs Stott. Mrs Green said: 'I caught hold of one girl by the hair and dealt with her.' She chased two youths out through the booking office and held one until police arrived. Most of the Mods, she said, had girls with them and they were showing off to them."

The courts responded quickly. Brighton magistrates heard police evidence that one 18-year-old, from Hackney in east London, brandished a cricket bat on Brighton beach and shouted: "I'm going to get me a Rocker's head. I've never had one yet. This will hurt." He was sentenced to three months' for possessing an offensive weapon.

Dr George Simpson, the chairman of the Margate Bench, described youths who went on the rampage at Margate as "sawdust Caesars". It was not a new coinage (having been applied to Mussolini in the 1930s), but Mods relished the label. They seemed, the magistrate thought, "to find courage like rats by hunting only in packs".

Dr Simpson sentenced a 22-year-old, from Blackheath, south London, the first of 51 in court over disturbances, to three months' imprisonment for using threatening behaviour. "It is unlikely that the air of this town has ever been polluted by hordes of hooligans, male and female, such as we have seen this weekend and of whom you are an example," Dr Simpson told him.

Thirty-nine young men were charged with threatening behaviour; nine with possessing offensive weapons, including a cosh, two knives and parts of deckchairs; and two with causing wilful damage to deckchairs, pictures and plate-glass. Fines ranged from £25 to £75. Four were sent to detention centres.

The *Telegraph* got its stuffiest leader-writer to comment on the events, although he did work up one joke. "Seeing law and order mocked by the callous young," he wrote, "some will say that with more rods there would be fewer mockers."

From the **Telegraph**

Tranquillisers bring an insidious menace to drug addiction

January 21, 1960
By John Prince

"I don't know whether to take a sedative and go to bed or a pep pill and go to a party." This was one dilemma of the Fifties, a decade marked by a sustained, at times almost frantic, search for the perfect pill.

It is common to attribute this malaise to the stress of the times. But, the bomb apart, times were never better materially, at least in the West. The individual Briton is cushioned against most mishaps from before birth to death. The ancient killers such as plague, cholera and diphtheria have been vanquished. But in the mental sphere, it seems, too many people have lost the capacity to resist anxiety or depression. Their one thought is to escape, a dash to doctor or chemist for the latest sedative or tranquilliser.

In the first decade of the National Health Service more than 2,250 million prescriptions were dispensed in England and Wales at a cost of nearly £500 million. Sedatives, hypnotics and pain-relieving drugs accounted for more than 20 per cent of the total and nearly 10 per cent of the cost.

The old drugs such as morphine and aspirin still stand high in reputation and efficacy. Some newer drugs are proving useful and hold out still more promise for the future, especially in the treatment and investigation of mental illness. But present consumption of sedatives and stimulants probably goes far beyond what is really necessary.

After acknowledging that tranquillisers have been of great benefit in mental hospitals, Sir John Charles, Chief Medical Officer of the Ministry of Health, in a recent report, gave warning against indiscriminate consumption, and concluded: "One test of a mature personality is the capacity to face reality and tackle difficult situations with courage and determination. These qualities are ignored if tranquilliser drugs are used too freely."

Much the same conclusion is reached in a review of sedatives, tranquillisers and analgesics by 15 experts in the current issue of the *Practitioner*. Thus Professor E.W. Anderson, of Manchester University, says: "Anxiety is of prime biological value; only when extreme does it hamper living and become a symptom calling for alleviation. The average individual should be encouraged to face his problems without the support of drugs."

The experts point to the limitations of preparation for which great claims have been made, to the unhappy side effects of others, and to the poisoning and death caused by many.

Finally, there is the role played by barbiturates and other drugs in the ever-present danger of the roads. The motorist should know that even a small amount of alcohol in the combination with even a therapeutic dose of barbiturate may cause intoxication.

The disastrous effects of some pep pills and sedatives have occasioned strictures from Parliament and the Bench, and demands that sales be controlled. Drug addiction on traditional lines is a minor problem in Britain, but addiction to some of the newer drugs is causing concern.

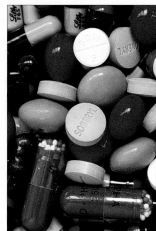

In 1960 it seemed 'consumption of sedatives and stimulants goes far beyond what is necessary'

DYING YOUNG

Marilyn Monroe found dead in bed, aged 36

Only two years after the stunning hit 'Some Like It Hot', the unfathomable blonde star, now in dispute with her studio, died alone

Marilyn Monroe smiles for the camera during the period of her unhappy marriage to Arthur Miller. Her last words were to her housekeeper: 'Goodnight, honey.'

From the first there was conflicting speculation about the shocking death of Marilyn Monroe at the age of 36 in 1962. Her lifeless body was found in bed at her Mexican-style bungalow in Brentwood, a Los Angeles suburb.

"On a bedside table were several medicine bottles, including an empty bottle which had contained the barbiturate Nembutal. She was clutching a telephone receiver," wrote the *Telegraph*'s correspondent in Los Angeles on Sunday August 5.

It was only two years since her stunning performance in *Some Like It Hot*. Fourteen years earlier she had changed her name from Norma Jeane and signed a movie contract; since then she had been divorced from the boy next door, and from Joe DiMaggio, and, in 1961, from Arthur Miller.

"An official of Los Angeles Coroners Office said an early investigation 'indicates suicide', but Miss Monroe's personal doctor, Dr Ralph Greenson, who with Dr Hyman Engleberg discovered the body, disputed this theory. They declared that Miss Monroe was in good spirits yesterday and last night. She said to a friend yesterday afternoon that she was feeling better than for several weeks."

A detective, Sergeant Byron, said that Marilyn Monroe had telephoned Dr Greenson the evening before she died. He had advised her to take a ride to the beach. "Sergeant Byron said that Dr Greenson said the actress called him about 5.15pm. She told him she was having trouble sleeping. Police estimate that she died shortly after she retired to bed at 8pm."

"She said she did not think she would take a ride to the beach, but might take a ride nearby if she couldn't sleep," the sergeant said. Then she went into her room with a cheerful "Goodnight, honey" to Mrs Eunace Murray, her housekeeper.

"The actress had," in the *Telegraph*'s words, "been taking sleeping pills to relieve pains in her head and body which, in spite of numerous tests, doctors had been unable to diagnose.

"Her body was found after Mrs Murray saw a light in her room about midnight. It was still burning at 3am. Mrs Murray knocked on the door, which was locked. There was no answer. The housekeeper telephoned Dr Greenson. After failing to get an answer through the locked door, he called Dr Engleberg. They forced a side window and climbed in to the room."

"Miss Monroe's films earned £70 million at box offices throughout the world," the *Telegraph* added. "She had not been well since she was dismissed in June by 20th Century Fox from the film *Something's Got to Give*. The studio said she was frequently absent from the set. It said it would sue her for

INBRIEF

MAY 7, 1980
The 24-year-old son of the Anglican Bishop of Iran was shot dead in Teheran yesterday. The body of Bahram Dehqani-Tafti, a university lecturer, was found in North Teheran.

In October, gunmen broke into the home of his father, Bishop Hassan Dehqani-Tafti, in Isfahan and fired five shots, which all missed him. He left Iran after the incident.

damages. She claimed her absences were due to illness."

Twelve days later a final report by the Los Angeles Coroner, Theodore Curphey, said that her death was a "probable suicide". The actress had suffered severe fears and frequent depressions, and had been taking sedative drugs to fight insomnia "for years, and she was thus familiar with and experienced in the use of sedative drugs and well aware of their dangers."

The report continued: "In our investigation we have learned that Miss Monroe had often expressed wishes to give up, to withdraw and even to die. On more than one occasion in the past, when disappointed and depressed, she had made a suicide attempt using sedative drugs. On these occasions she had called for help and had been rescued.

"From the information collected about the events of the evening of August 4, it is our opinion that the same pattern was repeated, except for the rescue."

From the **Telegraph**

Britain's most promising poet dies, aged 39

November 10, 1953

Dylan Thomas, the poet, broadcaster and storywriter, who has died in New York, aged 39, was regarded by many as the most promising present-day poet in Britain. His reputation in the United States was as great as in this country.

For a contemporary poet, his sales were regarded by his publishers as exceptional. His *Collected Poems 1934-52* which won him the William Foyle Poetry Prize last January has already sold more than 9,000 copies. Born in Swansea, son of a schoolmaster, his first interest was journalism, but he left it when he found he could not master shorthand.

Edith Sitwell was one of the first to recognise Dylan Thomas's talent. In a review of his second published work, *Twenty Five Poems* in 1936, she wrote: "The work of this very young man [he was then 22] is on a huge scale, both in theme and structurally – his themes are the mystery and holiness of all forms and aspects of life."

In 1940 he published a book of autobiographical sketches, *Portrait of the Artist as a Young Dog. The World I Breathe* appeared in 1940 and *Deaths and Entrances* in 1946.

Since the war he had broadcast often on the Third Programme [*Under Milk Wood* was not broadcast until January 1954, two months after Thomas's death], and had made several successful lecture tours in America. His widow was formerly Miss Caitlin Macnamara. There are two sons and a daughter of the marriage.

AN END TO DEBS, AND HANGING

'They were the last of a lovely, lovely world'

No more debutantes were to be presented at Court, it was decided in 1957, the year in which murderers no longer faced the rope

The decision to abolish debs came in 1957. It was the same year that the Homicide Act abolished hanging for murder, except where it involved theft, shooting, resisting arrest or killing a policeman; a second murder also attracted the death sentence.

In November 1957 the Lord Chamberlain's office announced that the next year's royal presentation parties for debutantes would be the last. The tradition had been that well born young women should "come out" in the London season and be

presented at Court. In future the Queen would hold additional garden parties so that larger numbers might be invited to Buckingham Palace. But even if young women were invited, they would not necessarily meet the Queen, nor would it mean that they had been presented at Court.

It was not that the supply of debs was drying up. "Applications for the debutantes' parties have become so numerous," the *Telegraph* reported, "that if they continued beyond 1958 it would become necessary to hold an extra party. Usually, about 250 debutantes attend the functions compared with between 8,000 and 9,000 at garden parties."

The afternoon presentation party where every debutante made her curtsey to the Queen had been introduced only in 1951. In Victoria's reign there had been what were known as "drawing rooms". In the reign of Edward VII these moved from the afternoon to the evening and were called "evening courts". They continued until the outbreak of war in 1939. The war put paid entirely to the full-dress levées also held at Court. In 1947, presentation parties were resumed, at first outdoors.

Now that presentation was to end, "Does this mean the end of the curtsey?" asked the worried *Telegraph*. "The moment for which finishing schools gave daily lessons – the moment when a nervous 17-year-old stepped out of the queue and was alone before the Queen – will soon be just a memory."

"I'm very, very sad," said Mrs Rennie O'Mahony,

Ninety debutantes in 1949 at the Grosvenor House Hotel, Park Lane, for Queen Charlotte's Birthday ball, a highlight of the season. The custom was to curtsey to the cake

director of one of London's finishing schools. "Maybe presentation parties are an anachronism, too limited for these modern democratic days, but they were the last of a lovely, lovely world."

The provisions made in 1957 for hanging some kinds of murderers came to an end on December 21, 1964, when the House of Commons decided, on a free vote, that hanging would be abolished as a punishment for murder. The principal sponsor of the Bill was Sidney Silverman, a Labour MP. Although it was a private Member's measure, it had the unusual distinction of being fitted into the Government legislative programme.

Sidney Siverman had fought to end hanging, sometimes against resistance from a government of his own party, since 1948. He tried again in 1953, 1955 and 1956 before the limited success of the 1957 Act. "No example in this century of Parliamentary persistence on so big an issue by one private Member comes readily to mind," wrote W.F. Deedes in the *Telegraph* on the day of the 1964 vote.

Reporting the debate of the night on which the vote was taken, the *Telegraph* noted that Mr Silverman suggested "that some members were over-sensitive to what was mistakenly thought to be public opinion". He asked: "Would it be right for a responsible legislator to kill a man he thought he ought not to kill because of some popular pressure? Anyone who did that would be repeating the mistake that Pontius Pilate made 2,000 years ago."

Henry Brooke, the former Conservative Home Secretary, said that "every now and then, it came over me that, while I was having to determine whether a person sentenced to death for capital murder should be hanged or not, other murderers whose crimes were worse than the one I had under consideration at that moment, were not liable to the death sentence."

By the time he came to the end of his term at the Home Office, he had become convinced that the case for retaining the death penalty was no longer strong enough to justify its retention. The right course would be to make it clear beyond all doubt that murder would add materially to the term of imprisonment served for further crimes, he thought.

Brigadier Terence Clarke, a Conservative, opposed abolition. He said that an opinion poll that day had shown that the vast majority of the population was in favour of hanging. He himself was sure that the death penalty was a deterrent. "I don't know what happens to people when they become Home Secretary," he said. "They become so wet they ought to be hanged themselves."

Another Conservative, Thomas Iremonger, said that his private nightmare was that a criminal would use his gun and the widow of the victim would come and say: "If you had not abolished this ultimate sanction, my husband might be alive today."

But just before 11.15pm, MPs voted by 355 to 170 to abolish the death penalty for murder. It was an even bigger victory for the abolitionists than had been predicted.

INBRIEF

JULY 1, 1954

Myxomatosis, the rabbit-killing virus disease, has now taken such a firm hold over a large part of the country that by the end of the summer rabbits may become a rarity in many counties. Already 16 counties are affected.

Reports from Devon, Cornwall, Sussex and Kent state that rabbits are dying in thousands. Some farmers believe that the casualty rate on their land is more than 90 per cent.

The spread would have been even more rapid but for the cold, wet weather, which meant fewer than usual of the blood-sucking insects which carry the disease. Though the Myxomatosis Advisory Committee recommended in a recent report that no attempt should be made to introduce myxomatosis into unaffected areas, some farmers have obtained infected animals and released them on their farms.

An RSPCA inspector said last night that while the Society deprecated spreading the disease artificially it had no power to take legal action. Wild rabbits were not covered by the Protection of Animals Act.

The Ministry of Agriculture said it has no power to stop farmers spreading the disease.

The spectacle of hundreds of rabbits dying near popular walks over the Sussex Downs has disturbed many people. The Society of Sussex Downsmen and the RSPCA have appealed for mercy patrols to exterminate infected animals.

THE FIRST TV ADVERTISEMENT

Commercial breaks and detector vans

Toothpaste paid for independent television but the BBC had to find ways of frightening viewers into buying licences

Just before Christmas in 1956, Charles Hill, the Postmaster General, announced in Parliament that television would be permitted to broadcast between 6pm and 7pm. Until then there had been an hour's shut-down "so that children could be put or sent to bed", as the *Telegraph* phrased it.

"The ITA, in particular, has been anxious to have broadcasts during this period. Outside the London area many viewers prefer to start their evening viewing earlier than 7pm." The thinking behind that last sentence was presumably that outside the metropolis it was more common for tea to be the evening meal, eaten well before seven o'clock. The possiblity of "TV dinners" was not envisaged.

Charles Hill had become Postmaster General the year before, when, on September 22, the momentous decision came into effect of allowing the Independent Television Authority to broadcast in competition with the BBC, and, moreover, to screen advertisements. (The initials ITA appeared on the test card, and that was how the channel was generally referred to, in distinction from the BBC.)

Dr Hill, as he was known, was famous as the "Radio Doctor", giving homely health advice. He was a strong believer in commercial broadcasting and became the chairman of ITA in 1963. From 1967 to 1972 he was chairman of the BBC, an appointment made by Harold Wilson which prompted the comment from Sir Robert Lusty, the acting chairman, that it was like inviting Rommel to take command of the 8th Army on the eve of Alamein.

In 1955 that first ITA broadcast could be picked up only in the London area, being put out jointly by the two London broadcasters, Associated-Rediffusion and the Associated Broadcasting Company. At 7.15 a card appeared on the black-and-white screen: "Opening Night of the Independent Television Service – Channel 9". Then Leslie Mitchell, poached from BBC television, announced, "This is London", as if it were the World Service. Instead of *Lilliburlero*, a fanfare by Charles Williams was heard.

The first advertisement shown was for Gibbs toothpaste. The rest of the evening programmes included bits of drama from John Gielgud and Alec Guinness, a boxing match and, five minutes before closedown at 11pm, the *Epilogue*, a religious talk.

It was "a subdued and dignifed start" in the view of L. Marsland Gander, the *Telegraph*'s Radio Correspondent, already a veteran of television coverage from the 1930s. But in the next paragraph he mentioned that "George Formby was in rollicking form with his ukulele at the May Fair Hotel. He had to shout at noisy people attending a party there: 'Shut up, you lot.' "

But the evening had not become "the hucksters' riot of vulgarity that opponents of commercial television had predicted," he judged. Gander was unconvinced by the advertisements. "Three announcements followed one another in about two minutes, so rapidly that though watching intensely I found they made little impact." Perhaps he had not taken account of the force of repetition.

Gander also found that advertisements popped up confusingly, as in the middle of that night's boxing match. "At one point the commentator was just exclaiming 'now the boy's nose is bleeding too' when a seal balancing a glass of stout waddled across the screen and a zoo keeper was heard crying: 'My goodness'." The product was Guinness, of course.

Changed values came, Gander suggested, in the Independent Television News bulletin presented by Chris Chataway. "He included the un-BBC-like item of a brief account of the Jack Spot trial." Spot was a gangster involved in a shooting. If the BBC hadn't reported the trial, the *Telegraph* certainly had.

Many could not receive ITA because they did not have the right aerial or because their sets were not capable of tuning in to the signal. BBC radio launched a splendid spoiler by killing Grace Archer in a stable fire at Ambridge.

Any who watched only commercial television were still obliged to buy licences to receive both radio and television. In 1957, the Post Office, which collected the licence money, launched a campaign to frighten the licenceless. It was the advent of "detector vans". Six were sent roving round the country. "These, it is claimed can detect where TV sets are working," said a *Telegraph* news report sceptically. "When one appears in a locality there is usually a rush to buy licences."

In addition, "a poster featuring the three wise monkeys who see, hear and speak no evil has been distributed to 25,000 post offices throughout the country. With Simeon illustrations it says: 'To £ook, or £isten. Buy a £icence'. It also carries a reminder that a separate £1 licence is necessary for wireless sets in cars."

Protesters in Bradford set fire to a copy of Salman Rushdie's novel (below) 'To give in to pressure to stop the distribution of a book on the very day the book is burned invokes horrific images of censorship,' said the Telegraph

BURNING RUSHDIE'S BOOK

Bradford protest sets fire to 'The Satanic Verses'

British Muslims denounced as blasphemous a prizewinning novel, and then Ayatollah Khomeini condemned its author to death

Local Muslims burnt copies of Salman Rushdie's novel *The Satanic Verses* in the square outside Bradford town hall in January 1989. The year before, the book had won the Whitbread literary prize. A rally of 1,000 Muslims gathered in Bradford on January 15, claiming the book was blasphemous, and the newspapers, including *The Daily Telegraph*, ran

photographs of it being burnt. Then two branches of W.H Smith in Bradford withdrew the novel from sale.

Liberal sensibilities were left in something of a quandary. *Bienpensants* were careful to defend Muslim minorities in British cities, who were often the target of racial prejudice. But book-burning had an atavistic power of repulsion for the liberal-minded.

"To give in to pressure to stop the distribution of a book on the very day the book is burned invokes horrific images of censorship," the *Telegraph* quoted Mr Bill Buford, the editor of the literary magazine *Granta*, as saying. "It is at the heart of the whole issue of free expression."

"Mr Rushdie's work explores religion and revelation from a secular viewpoint," the *Telegraph* explained, "and contains portrayals of figures and incidents clearly based on the Koran." It had been banned in India and Saudi Arabia.

W.H. Smith's retail marketing director denied that the company had bowed to pressure from Bradford's 50,000-strong Muslim community. "We had some discussions with the police in Bradford who were concerned about a possible outbreak of public disorder," he said. "We have not given in to pressure. We have supported the author in the way we should have done."

Salman Rushdie soon needed all the support he could get, for a month later came news that he had been sentenced to death in a judgment or *fatwa* delivered by the Ayatollah Khomeini, the *de facto* ruler of Iran.

In 1989 very few British people had much knowledge of the difference between Sunni and Shia Muslims, even though the Islamic revolution in Iran had been accomplished because of that nation's long identification with Shi'ism. And it was the first time that many British readers learned that there was such a thing as a *fatwa*.

Khomeini said: "I informed the proud Muslim people of the world that the author of *The Satanic Verses*, a book which is against Islam, the Prophet and the Koran, and all those involved in its publication who were aware of its content, are sentenced to death."

If Muslims were killed carrying out this order to execute Mr Rushdie and his collaborators, they would be considered martyrs, Khomeini said. Mr Rushdie was believed by neighbours in Islington to have gone into hiding with his wife.

The next day, Iran was reported to have offered a reward of $3million to any non-Iranian who carried out the "execution order". Several thousand demonstrators gathered outside the British Embassy in Teheran shouting and throwing stones.

Mr Rushdie hid, and later paid for police protection out of his own pocket. Little by little he re-emerged into literary society, at first in private parties, then at friendly book launches, and at last joining ordinary theatre audiences. He went on writing books, but none gained the fame of *The Satanic Verses*.

LADY CHATTERLEY'S SECRET

What the couple in Lawrence's novel were up to

A jury read it and, with the help of expert witnesses, found it not to be obscene. Then John Sparrow revealed its true contents

D.H. Lawrence had seen 'Lady Chatterley's Lover' confiscated as obscene on its first publication. Now, three decades after his death, its status was re-examined under a new obscenity law. 'The curtain is never drawn,' said the prosecuting counsel. 'One follows them not only into the bedroom but into bed and one remains with them there.'

The Lady Chatterley trial in 1960 was theatre from the first. Before the curtain went up *The Daily Telegraph* reported that "over 100 applications have been received for seats in the famous oak-panelled No.1 court" at the Old Bailey.

The jury had to decide whether *Lady Chatterley's Lover* was obscene or not. At 10.30am on October 20, the nine middle-aged jurymen and three women picked up copies of the book from the court and went to a "special room" to read it. Leather was the decorative theme. "Four leather easy chairs were moved in yesterday and put by the fireplace," the *Telegraph* reported. "Along the side walls are leathered-covered settles."

The oak-panelled room, 40ft by 20ft, with a red Axminster carpet, also contained a huge oak table covered with red leather, around which stood 12 red leather-backed chairs. Two telephones in the room could be used by the jurors to summon refreshments while they got through the 317 pages.

D.H. Lawrence had written the novel in 1927 and it had then been published on the Continent, but now it was printed in full for the popular market at three shillings and sixpence by the defendants, Penguin Books Ltd.

The prosecution was brought under the Obscene Publications Act, passed the year before. It was the second prosecution under the new Act, the first being over *The Ladies' Directory*, which contained names and addresses of prostitutes.

At the beginning of the Lady Chatterley trial, the prosecuting counsel, Mr Mervyn Griffiths-Jones, asked a question that was to become renowned, though it is often erroneously attributed to the judge, Mr Justice Byrne. Would the jury approve of their young sons and young daughters reading the novel? "Is it," Griffiths-Jones asked, "a book you would even wish your wife or your servants to read?"

Griffiths-Jones explained that the new Act stipulated that a book was "deemed to be obscene if its effect, taken as a whole, is such as to tend to deprave and corrupt persons", but there would be no criminal offence "if it is proved that publication of the article in question is justified as being for the public good on the grounds that it is in the interest of science, literature, art or learning or of other objects of general concern".

The jury should consider "the passages of sexual intercourse. There are, I think, described in all 13 during the course of this book. You will see that they are described in the greatest detail, save perhaps for the first.

"You may think that this book, if its description had been confined to the first occasion on which sexual intercourse is described, not only would cause little complaint or less complaint but be a much better book than it is. But 12 of these, certainly, are described in great detail, leaving nothing to the imagination. The curtain is never drawn.

"One follows them not only into the bedroom but into bed and one remains with them there. That is not strictly accurate, because one starts in my lady's boudoir: one goes to a hut in the forest with a blanket laid down. We see them doing it again in the undergrowth in the forest amongst the shrubbery, and not only in the undergrowth, again in the forest, in the pouring rain, both of them stark naked and dripping with raindrops. One sees them in the keeper's cottage, first in the evening on the hearth rug. Then we have to wait until dawn to see them doing it again in bed. Finally we move the site to Bloomsbury, and we have it all over again in an attic in a boarding house."

Referring to some of the words in the book, the prosecution said that no doubt they would be said to be "good old Anglo-Saxon four-letter words". One word "appeared 30 times, and another 14 and others 13, six, four and three times." The *Telegraph* did not say which word was which.

Mr Gerald Gardiner, defending, claimed that the book had literary merit, which reflected the views of the author. As a puritanical moralist, he suggested, Lawrence disapproved of casual sex, of sex for experiment, of sex without love, of promiscuous sex.

Over the ensuing days a rich procession of the great and the good declared that the book was not obscene. "I think Lawrence tried to portray this relation as in a real sense an act of Holy Communion, said Dr John Robinson, the Bishop of Woolwich, who was to cause a stir in 1963 with a book of his own, of quite a different stripe, called *Honest to God*.

Asked by the defence, "Is this is a book which, in your view, Christians ought to read?" He replied: "Yes, I think it is…. Clearly Lawrence did not have a Christian valuation of sex, and the kind of sexual relations depicted in the book are not those that are necessarily of the kind I should regard as ideal. But what Lawrence is trying to do, I think, is to portray the sex relation as something sacred."

Dame Rebecca West said: "The Baronet and his impotence is a symbol of the impotent culture of his time. The love affair with the gamekeeper was a

calling for a return of the soul to the more intense life that he felt people in a different culture, such as a culture based on religious faith."

But Lawrence, she added, "also had a great defect which impairs this book. He had absolutely no sense of humour, and a lot of the sentences in this book are to my view ludicrous. All the same, it is a book of undoubted literary merit."

Richard Hoggart, the author of *The Uses of Literacy* and Senior Lecturer in English Literature at Leicester University, described *Lady Chatterley's Lover* as "probably one of the 20 best novels we have had written in Britain in the last 30 years". Asked if it was a proper book for the young people in his care to read, Mr Hoggart said he would tell them to ask their parents first. "I would not take it on my own responsibility."

Richard Hoggart's evidence continued next day. Asked whether he thought four-letter words in the book were genuine and necessary, he said: "Fifty yards from this court this morning, I heard a man say —— three times as I passed him. He was talking to himself, and he said, '—— her, —— her, —— her.' He must have been angry."

Mr Mervyn Griffith-Jones, cross-examining: "You described this book as a highly virtuous if not puritanical one. That is your genuine and considered view?"

Mr Hoggart: "Yes."

Mr Griffith-Jones: "I think I have lived my life under a misapprehension of the meaning of the word puritanical. Will you help me?"

Mr Hoggart: "Yes I will. Many people do live their lives under a misapprehension of the meaning of the word puritanical. For a long time, the word puritanical has pretended to mean somebody who is against anything which is pleasurable, particularly sex, but the proper meaning of it to an historian is somebody who belongs to the tradition of British Puritanism. And the main weight of that is an intense sense of responsibility for one's conscience. In that sense, the book is puritanical."

Mr Griffith-Jones: "I am obliged for the lecture on it."

E.M. Forster, at 81 a grand old man of English letters, gave his address as "King's College, Cambridge" and admitted that he had written "a number of well-known novels". "I knew Lawrence quite well," he said, "and kept in touch with him." Forster was of the opinion that *Lady Chatterley's Lover* had a very high literary merit.

Roy Jenkins, Labour MP for Stechford, said he was the author of a number of books. Asked if *Lady Chatterley's Lover* was literature, he said, "Yes. It most certainly is."

Ann Scott-James, the journalist and broadcaster, said she wrote mainly on children, education and family and marriage topics. She was the mother of a girl of nine and a boy of 14. Mr Griffith-Jones asked her: "Do not think I am intending to be rude, but evidence as to the literary merit of this book is confined to experts. Do you claim any particular qualifications to be a literary expert?" "I do yes, of a

John Robinson, the Bishop of Woolwich, told the court: 'What Lawrence is trying to do, I think, is to portray the sex relation as something sacred'

Norman St John-Stevas said: 'I have no hesitation in saying that every Catholic priest would profit by reading this book'

Richard Hoggart, the author of 'The Uses of Literacy', described Lawrence's book as 'a highly virtuous if not puritanical one'

popular kind," she replied. "I was a classical scholar at Oxford."

On November 1 the court heard from Norman St John-Stevas, who was described as a Roman Catholic barrister, an MA of both Oxford and Cambridge, a doctor of philosophy and science who had studied moral theology, and the author of the book *Obscenity and the Law*. "I have no hesitation in saying that every Catholic priest and every Catholic moralist would profit by reading this book," he said

That afternoon, Mr Griffith-Jones had the chance for a tussle with the Rev Donald Alexander Tytler, director of religious education in the Birmingham diocese, who said that "by reading it, young people will be helped to grow up as mature and responsible people."

Mr Griffith-Jones: Is there anything in *Lady Chatterley's Lover* which suggests marriage is sacred and inviolable?

— It is a novel, it is not a tract.

— Never mind whether it is a novel or a tract, is there anything in this book which suggests marriage is sacred and inviolable?

— There is a great deal to suggest that between man and woman marriage is sacred.

— Is there anything in this book which suggests marriage is sacred and inviolable?

— I think it is taken for granted.

— Let us see. Mellors, the gamekeeper, did not regard marriage as sacred and inviolable?

— He was much attracted by Lady Chatterley.

— Of course he is. Everybody who commits adultery is very much attracted by the man or woman with whom they commit adultery. Just answer my question, please. There is nothing in Mellors's history which suggests he regards marriage as sacred and inviolable?

— That might well be.

— And not only was he committing adultery but he was committing adultery with someone else who was herself committing adultery?

— Yes.

— There was nothing in the book to indicate that Lady Chatterley regarded marriage as sacred and inviolable?

— That is a fair assumption.

The last of the 35 witnesses for the defence was the youngest, Miss Bernadine Wall, aged 21. She said she was educated at a convent. Mr Gardiner asked her: "Did you know the four-letter words?" "Yes," she replied.

In his summing up the following day, Mr Justice Byrne told the jury that they would not "exercise the question of taste or the functions of a censor. But you will decide whether it has been proved beyond reasonable doubt that this book is obscene."

The judge continued: "To deprave means to make morally bad, to corrupt morally, and to corrupt means to destroy morally the purity or chastity, to debase, to defile. You will observe that there is no intent to deprave or corrupt necessary to be proved.

"You must not select a passage here and a passage

there and say that you think that is obscene. You must take the book as a whole."

Recalling that a witness had said the book spoke of the nature of proper marriage, the judge observed: "There was a very proper marriage in this book, Lady Chatterley and her lawful husband. Another relationship which, it is suggested, became a permanent relationship, was the relationship between Lady Chatterley and the gamekeeper, but there is nothing in the book to indicate that there was ever a marriage or ever would be. Lady Chatterley's husband had said he would not divorce her and the gamekeeper had a wife also.

"This is a Christian country and right throughout Christianity there has been lawful marriage, even if it was only contracted before a registrar. When you read the book, were you capable of understanding what the author's view was on marriage?"

The judge recalled that the Bishop of Woolwich had said sex was something sacred as an act of Holy Communion. Looking at the jury, the judge asked: "Where are we getting?"

Referring to evidence by Mr St John-Stevas, the judge said: "You may perhaps think that it was a little presumptuous for him to say that every Catholic priest would profit by reading it, but at any rate, he is entitled to express his opinion and he has expressed it. It is for you to say what you think of it."

On November 2 the jury decided *Lady Chatterley's Lover* was not obscene. Penguin Books arranged "immediate distribution of 200,000 copies". Also ready for distribution were "gaily-coloured posters saying 'Lady Chatterley acquitted'."

After the hearing, one male juror, a toolmaker, commented: "I was not embarrassed by the book. I found some of the passages rather dull and I was

Once 'Lady Chatterley' had been acquitted, Penguin arranged for the immediate distribution of 200,000 copies. Men far outnumbered women in the queues to buy

certainly not uneasy about reading it in the same room with the women." The jurors left in four taxis provided by Penguin Books.

The Daily Telegraph reported that George Lawrence, 88, the novelist's surviving brother, denounced the verdict. "I don't think this book is fit for young people. These books that introduce a lot of sex I don't like. I had more than one argument with him but I did not manage to persuade him."

Mr Ernest Lawrence, a Nottingham dentist and nephew of the author, said: "I don't feel it is suitable for adolescents. My father was pretty disgusted at the time David wrote the book. It shook all the family and they had strong words about it."

When copies were put on sale on November 10 all 200,000 copies sold out. "I searched from Fleet Street to Charing Cross Road and called at more than 20 shops before I could obtain a copy," the *Telegraph* reporter wrote. "They were being sold at the rate of one every two or three seconds. In queues men far outnumbered women. 'Women seem to be more reticent,' said an assistant."

After Penguin had been cleared of obscenity, a close reading of the novel by a man qualified to judge, John Sparrow, the Warden of All Souls College, Oxford, revealed what no witness had mentioned in court: that Mellors indulges in a spot of anal intercourse with Lady Chatterley.

Sparrow's essay, *Regina v Penguin Books Ltd: an Undisclosed Element in the Case*, appeared in the February 1962 number of the intellectual periodical *Encounter*. "The Warden of All Souls argues that the book is permeated with a glorification of unnatural as well as natural practices," wrote Kenneth Rose in his renowned Albany column, in the January 21 issue of *The Sunday Telegraph*. "He furthermore maintains that had the prosecution not failed to make this clear during the case at the Old Bailey, they would probably have succeeded in having the book banned."

Sparrow put the experts – "clergymen, professors and lecturers in literature" – in an even more ludicrous light than that in which, to many observers, they had already appeared. Where, asked Sparrow, did this leave the Bishop's judgment that Lawrence represented the sexual act as "in a real sense something sacred", or the declaration by an academic that his descriptions were never "perverted"?

After Sparrow's scholarly exposition of incidents in the novel, there could be no doubt what Mellors had been up to, nor how much Lawrence esteemed the practice. Unlike homosexual activity, which, if performed by men, in those years still attracted a penalty of two years' imprisonment, the crime of *penetratio per anum* made the parties, even if husband and wife, never mind gamekeeper and lady, liable to imprisonment for life. Few prosecutions for heterosexual buggery were instigated in 1960, but, criminal liabilities apart, in that year no ordinary jury of 12 men and women would have rejoiced in reading a novel knowing that it detailed such things. Sparrow was convinced that he had exposed Regina v Penguin Books Ltd as "humbug".

'Don't die of ignorance' was the refrain of a television advertising campaign in 1986. The National Anti-Vivisection Society (above, right) had its own take on the Aids crisis

FROM THE PILL TO AIDS

A Sixties sexual revolution and an Eighties crisis

'Oral family control pills', as the Telegraph called them, changed behaviour. It had to change again urgently two decades later

I n Philip Larkin's memorable lines, sexual intercourse began between the end of the Chatterley ban and the Beatles' first LP. Something that made all the difference was the availability of the contraceptive pill from January 1961. Before the end of the year they were being prescribed on the National Health Service.

"Oral family control pills for sale," was the quaintly phrased headline in *The Daily Telegraph* for January 31. "They are claimed to be effective and safe, and can be obtained only on a doctor's prescription," wrote the reporter, John Prince.

The Pill, as it was soon to become known, had been undergoing trials with the help of hundreds of married women volunteers in Birmingham and Slough. The trials were sponsored by the Family Planning Association. The British pill had the trade name Conovid and was being sent out to more than 20,000 family doctors by the manufacturers. "A

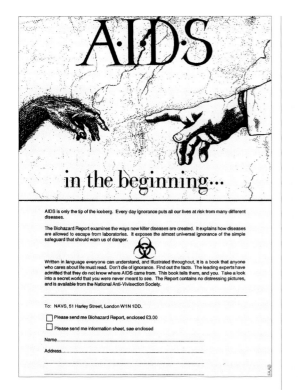

AIDS is only the tip of the iceberg. Every day ignorance puts all our lives at risk from many different diseases.

The Biohazard Report examines the ways new killer diseases are created. It explains how diseases are allowed to escape from laboratories. It exposes the almost universal ignorance of the simple safeguard that should warn us of danger.

Written in language everyone can understand, and illustrated throughout, it is a book that anyone who cares about life must read. Don't die of ignorance. Find out the facts. The leading experts have admitted that they do not know where AIDS came from. This book tells them, and you. Take a look into a secret world that you were never meant to see. The Report contains no distressing pictures, and is available from the National Anti-Vivisection Society.

To: NAVS, 51 Harley Street, London W1N 1DD.

☐ Please send me Biohazard Report, enclosed £3.00

☐ Please send me information sheet, sae enclosed

Name..

Address..
....
....

month's supply would cost 23s 3d." In 1961 an agricultural labourer earned about £8 6s 8d a week.

"Doctors are not yet sure about the long-term effects of these hormone substances," the *Telegraph* noted. "Some believe that a chemical compound will eventually prove more satisfactory."

The news that birth control pills were to be available under the NHS was announced in the Commons by Enoch Powell, the Minister of Health. When asked if, on account of the cost, he "would publish careful instructions as to when they could be used", Powell replied: "It is not for me to indicate to doctors when they should decide for medical reasons to prescribe for their patients."

With the coming of the Pill, condoms began to seem old-fashioned. In 1986 they made a sudden comeback. Advertisements for contraceptives were not allowed on television, but this ban was lifted when a new emergency appeared. Aids prompted both independent television and the BBC, which in those days did not show advertisements even for its own products, to screen advertisements described in the press as "explicit".

A 45-second advertisement was broadcast in December. It showed a young man and woman in bed. A voice-over asked: "Who are you sleeping with tonight? Who did you sleep with last night? Who slept with her last night?" The commentary said: "It's not just gays that can get Aids. Don't die of ignorance. Read the Aids leaflet now."

The anti-Aids advertising campaign was to cost £20 million, the *Telegraph* reported. "Leaflets warning of the risks of Aids will be put through every letterbox in 23 million households," it said.

"In the future," the leaflet said, "sleeping around is quite simply risking your life." In any case, by then Philip Larkin had been dead for a year.

From the Telegraph

Thirteen nudes in the musical 'Hair' bid the Lord Chamberlain goodbye

September 28, 1968

Just one day after the Lord Chamberlain's censorship powers were removed, 13 members of the cast of *Hair*, the American tribal musical, stood up and faced the audience naked for 30 seconds at the Shaftesbury Theatre last night.

We had been told that, as in America, the scene would take place in very dim lighting and would pass almost unnoticed. Even in Row N, the 12th row from the front of the stalls, there was nothing dim about the lighting, which last night illuminated nine women and four men. The scene went off without apparent embarrassment either to the performers or the audience.

Advance bookings stand at £40,000.

W.A. Darlington, who is retiring after 48 years as dramatic critic of 'The Daily Telegraph' reviews 'Hair' in his last notice for the newspaper.

Last night at the Shaftesbury, in the middle of the first act of *Hair* somebody – I think one of the performers, who were running about all over the place – handed me a yellow paper on which was printed a cabalistic design in red.

This, when more closely examined in the light of the interval, proved to bear the words: "Be-in, Be-in, Be-in. Yip, Yip, Yip, Yip, Yip, Yip, Yip."

Well, if that was intended as advice I needed it, for I have seldom been more out of anything as I was of this production. Obviously I am the wrong age for it and possibly the wrong nationality. For this is the youth of America expressing itself in very American terms.

To me the evening was a bore. It was noisy, it was ugly, and quite desperately unfunny. As for the much-discussed nudes, there were some bare looking skins at one point in the shadows at the back of the stage, but if that's all it amounts to, some people are going to be disappointed. The piece had what is usually called a mixed reception – cheers and boos.

Since I find it personally uninviting, let me at least try to weigh up the reason for the cheers. The company have enormous vitality and a great sense of rhythm, and their concerted dancing carries them along very effectively. This, added to their infantile desire to flout established standards, may earn them a success. But I doubt it.

When the cast removed their clothes it 'went off without apparent embarrassment'

Macmillan at the controls of an Austin Seven boosting export earnings

From the Telegraph

Macmillan's 'never had it so good' remark takes last place in report

July 22, 1957

Mr Macmillan, speaking at Bedford on Saturday, said that the credit squeeze, though unpopular, was still necessary to restrict spending. "We shall continue it as long as necessary."

The Prime Minister was addressing 1,500 people on Bedford Town's football ground at a meeting to commemorate 25 years unbroken service by Mr Lennox-Boyd, the Colonial secretary and MP for Mid-Bedfordshire. Britain's general economic prospects were good, he declared.

Balance of payment prospects were favourable. We look like earning a really worthwhile surplus this year because our exports were holding up well. In the first half-year they had risen by six per cent and to North America by seven-and-a-half per cent.

Invisible earnings, from shipping and oil particularly, were doing well. Gold and dollar reserves rose in the first half of this year by £88 million. A large part of the increased production of main industries, steel, coal, cars, was going to export.

"Indeed, let us be frank about it. Most of our people have never had it so good. Go around the country – go to the industrial towns, go to the farms – and you will see a state of prosperity such as we have never had in my lifetime, or indeed ever in the history of this country."

VASSALL SPYING SCANDAL

'An ideal victim of Russian intelligence'

John Vassall lived far above his income as an Admiralty clerk, thanks to Russian money. But he continued to be trusted

The Vassall affair made spicy reading in 1962. It had the thrill of Russian espionage, homosexuality (still a criminal offence), louche living, a British political scandal involving a minister, and finally the jailing of journalists who refused to reveal their sources.

John Vassall himself was sentenced to 18 years as "a treacherous tool of the Russians". He was a clerk in the Admiralty, blackmailed into passing secrets to the Soviet Union. A year after he had been posted to Moscow, a Polish man with whom he had become friendly invited him to join some friends at dinner at a restaurant near the Bolshoi Theatre. Vassall was "plied with very strong brandy" and afterwards he was, in the phraseology of *The Daily Telegraph* "induced to remove his clothes like other members of the party, and certain sexual practices occurred".

Photographs had been taken of him by the KGB on that occasion, and on March 19, 1955, the night of the St Patrick's Ball at the American Club, the trap was sprung. Introduced to a stranger, a KGB man posing as an ordinary soldier, he was taken back to a flat. As Vassall put it later: "There was nothing faked about his love-making. Suddenly the light went out. Somehow I knew it was not a power failure. I was suddenly cold and terrified. I started to shiver."

Two Soviet secret policemen entered the flat, and told the naked clerk that he was guilty of an offence which was taken very seriously in Russia. At that moment Vassall considered suicide and made a dash for the window, but he was hauled back. So began a long process of threats and promises that led him more firmly into the clutches of the Soviet spy apparatus.

A few months after his treachery began, Vassall's Foreign Office departmental report remained favourable: "A pleasant young man of first-class appearance and manners. Never ruffled. Always helpful. His moral standards are of the highest."

Lord Parker, the Lord Chief Justice who sentenced Vassall, accepted that when he first

At his flat, Vassall was able to show police after his arrest a concealed compartment in a bookcase given him by a Russian known as Nikolai, which contained 140 undeveloped films of photographed secret documents

started spying in Moscow it was under pressure, but emphasised that when he returned to England he could have made a clean breast of the matter, and left his Government work. Instead, Vassall got deeper into difficulties.

He more than doubled his £688 a year salary with Russian money, so that in London he was able to pay for a flat in the then fashionable Dolphin Square in Pimlico, the rent for which was £500 a year, and to buy antique furniture and smart suits. Vassall tried to distract his guilty conscience by travel, taking holidays over the next few years in Capri, New York, Florence, Brussels, Vienna, Geneva, Cairo, the south of France and Spain, all on a clerk's salary.

He visited Rome, and was delighted to see the Pope, holding fast on to the idea that, whatever he had done, he was still a Roman Catholic. (He had been

received into the Church in 1953.) But he felt unable to go to Confession for seven years, until after his arrest.

In 1956, Vassall had access to Naval secrets in London, and passed information to a Russian agent known as Gregory, who paid him sums varying from £50 to £200, made up in little bundles of £5 notes. Vassall would extract documents from a file at the office, take them home with him in a briefcase, photograph them and returned them the next day. His controllers gave him a Minox miniature camera.

"When he was arrested," the *Telegraph* reported after his conviction, "he had 20 expensive, immaculate suits in his wardrobe. He furnished his Dolphin Square flat with the antiques he loved: a £400 Queen Anne wardrobe, a £300 cupboard, a £150 Persian carpet. All were paid for in cash." Unknown to him, MI5 men had burgled his flat and found incriminating documents.

On September 12, 1962 Vassall was approached by two men in macintoshes. They were Special Branch officers. "I think I know what you are after," he told them as he stood by their car beside the statue of Captain Cook behind the Admiralty building in the Mall. They took him to Scotland Yard where, with the help of tea and sandwiches, his long interrogation began. Even then he wondered if he might be able to persuade the security services to allow him to start a new life abroad.

At his flat, he showed police a concealed compartment in a bookcase given him by a Russian known as Nikolai, which contained 140 undeveloped film exposures.

During the trial Lord Parker said: "What worries me is how comes it that a man whose real salary is something under £700 gets access to top secret documents?" The Attorney-General said: "He was a clerical officer, and he only got access because he was a personal assistant and worked in the same room as the person who was the actual head of the section."

Quite a bit was made of Vassall's homosexuality, even by his defence counsel, Jeremy Hutchinson QC, who told the court that Vassall was "an untough man and one who could be described as unadult. He had a weakness and that is that, within him, he is a latent homosexual, which brings in its train inner turmoil and suffering."

"Arrogance and an uncontrollable passion for gracious living ruined William John Vassall," was the *Daily Telegraph*'s version of it. "He had a problem that led finally to the loss of any integrity he ever had and made him an ideal victim of the Russian intelligence organisation. He was a homosexual.

"Vassall was not frail, but throughout his life he was basically afraid of getting hurt. And he took this handicap with him to Monmouth public school. Because of loneliness he was almost glad to go into the Royal Air Force."

"Before Christmas 1960," the paper added, "he suffered a severe blow. His mother, whom he worshipped, died. He turned to his daily help, Mrs Doris Murray, 50. Within a short time he had created a 'mother image' out of her. Whenever he was abroad, he sent her a card or a long, descriptive letter. He took her to West End restaurants, and told her to use the flat whenever he was away."

Within hours of Vassall's conviction, Harold Macmillan, the Prime Minister, announced the appointment of a committee of inquiry. There was an urgent need to limit the damage done by an exchange of letters over a five-year period with Thomas Galbraith, who was Civil Lord of the Admiralty when Vassall was employed as a clerk in his office. The most recent letter had been sent only five months earlier. They were surprisingly informal, and there was plenty of rumour and speculation.

"There was no hint of imputation against Mr Galbraith's personal character," the *Telegraph* reported. "But the existence of the correspondence was regarded by the Opposition as evidence of a social relationship unusual between a Minister and a minor official employed in his department."

Twenty-two letters or messages from Galbraith to Vassall, and two from Mrs Galbraith, were immediately published by the Government in the unusual form of a White Paper.

"Perhaps, as there is this secret Defence estimate paper, you should bring it up this weekend," Galbraith wrote from Scotland in August 1958. In the same letter he said: "You can assume my signature on the Honours List. I have no objection."

In 1957 Galbraith had expressed in a letter his gratitude for having his office tidied, and for advice on its decoration. "My room at the Admiralty is in a filthy state and I am most grateful to you for having taken steps to have it improved," he wrote. "In addition, could you clear the drawers in the two tables? There are the dregs of years in them and they should be empty.

"If possible, too, I think we should start the ball rolling to get some decent pictures. I believe Greenwich have a store. Try to find out about this. And what about curtains? It is extremely dreary in winter."

In February 1963 the Vassall tribunal trawled the clubs of Soho and the West End frequented by homosexuals. Although Vassall was familiar with Soho, his nickname among those who knew him well being "Vera", the tribunal met a blank wall. No one at the Music Box said they knew him, or at the Rockingham Club. The secretary of the Alibi Club told the tribunal that it was not known as a place where members of the Admiralty visited. The secretary of the Leo Club, Panton Street, said it did have two members associated with the Admiralty, but not Vassall; about 25 per cent of its members were women.

The tribunal found nothing improper about Vassall's relations with Galbraith. Vassall himself claimed to have slept with two other Conservative MPs, and it is not difficult to think of candidates,

but this need not have posed any further security lapse.

The Vassall affair had a sequel that seemed to confirm that the Government resented the role of the press in the affair. In February 1963 two reporters who refused to reveal their sources to the tribunal were sent to jail. Brendan Mulholland, aged 29, of *The Daily Mail*, was sentenced to six months' for contempt of court, and Reginald Foster, of *The Daily Sketch*, to three months'. Another journalist who refused to name his sources, Ian Waller, the political correspondent of *The Sunday Telegraph*, counted himself lucky to escape jail.

Mulholland refused to name his sources for three statements: that a girl typist at the Admiralty had decided that no £15-a-week clerk like Vassall could possibly live as he did honestly; that Vassall's colleagues at the Admiralty knew him as "Auntie"; and that sponsorship by two officials had enabled Vassall to avoid the strictest part of the Admiralty's security vetting. Mulholland told the court: "I am being asked to do something which is morally wrong."

In a *Daily Sketch* report by Foster, one sentence read: "Why did the spy-catchers fail to notice Vassall, who sometimes wore women's clothes on West End trips?" In sentencing Foster, the judge said there was no doubt that he had refused to answer the tribunal's question as to his source. But the judge had to consider whether the question was relevant and necessary for the tribunal's purposes. Although the shop where Vassall had bought such clothes had since been ascertained, the question which concerned the tribunal was Vassall's notoriety – the extent to which his habits were notorious. This question was, in the judge's view, relevant and necessary. Foster had refused to answer it, and an offence was thereby committed.

Vassall himself served 10 years of his jail sentence. He found some solace in tending a little flower garden. In Maidstone Jail, he was much taken by Frank "The Axeman" Mitchell. "He was a colossal figure and arrived in white T-shirt and smart slacks, with a chest expander under one arm and a record player under the other," he remembered. "I could see he was somebody exciting and I was terribly curious to see how he ticked."

On his release, Vassall spent some time in a monastery writing a book, *Vassall* (1975), naturally a self-serving account. He changed his name to John Phillips and found a job as a clerk at the British Records Association, an organisation representing archivists, near Smithfield. He travelled each day, unrecognised, by Underground from his flat in St John's Wood. A picture of Churchill hung over his mantelpiece and he often went to Lord's to watch cricket.

The prosecution at Vassall's trial summed up his downfall by saying: "He was entrapped by his lust, and thereafter cash kept him crooked." Vassall's own verdict on his life was: "Well, I've done the best with the body and mind that I was given." John Vassall died in 1996, aged 72.

INBRIEF

SEPTEMBER 30, 1978

By John Weeks, Crime Staff
The Bulgarian defector Georgi Markov was murdered with an impregnated alloy ball less than the size of a pinhead which was injected into his thigh, possibly by the tip of an umbrella, Scotland Yard revealed yesterday.

The ball, measuring 68 thousandths of an inch in diameter, had two holes 16 thousandths of an inch drilled into it containing the substance which killed 49-year-old Mr Markov. He died in St James's Hospital, Balham, 18 days ago.

Scotland Yard, investigating one of the most bizarre murders in its history, said it would be "months rather than weeks" before tests by scientists at the Government germ warfare centre at Porton Down were able to say what the substance was. [It turned out to be ricin.]

An identical ball was surgically removed from the back of another Bulgarian defector, Vladimir Kostov, in Paris last Tuesday, the Yard revealed. Mr Kostov was jabbed in the back outside the Arc de Triomphe Metro station on August 26, but recovered after 12 days in a French hospital.

Mr Gilbert Kelland, Assistant Commissioner (Crime) at the Yard was asked yesterday who may have been responsible for the attack. He replied: "The world is the field in this case." Mr Markov, an author and regular broadcaster on the BBC's external services and on Radio 3 Europe, was standing at a bus stop on the south side of Waterloo Bridge on September 7 between 1.30pm and 2.15pm waiting to catch a bus back to Bush House where he worked. He later complained he had been jabbed with an umbrella and showed a colleague a small mark on the back of his thigh. [*Georgi Markov was later found to have been murdered by the KGB acting on behalf of the communist regime ruling Bulgaria.*]

Michael Foot (with stick) in the forefront of the Aldermaston march to London which reversed the route of the first march in 1958, re-using its original banner, with its small CND symbols

BAN THE BOMB

CND march puts Aldermaston on the map

Easter 1958 saw the first march to the Atomic Weapons Research Establishment, and its badge proved a powerful symbol

The Campaign for Nuclear Disarmament's new banners got their first outing at Easter 1958. The symbol they bore became one of the most powerful in the last four decades of 20th-century Britain. Marchers walked the 56 miles from London to Aldermaston in Berkshire over the four days of the Easter holiday carrying banners and placards with

the CND badge. (The word "logo" was not then in general use, although as an abbreviation for the printers' term "logotype" it had been employed in advertising since the late 1930s.)

"The organisers of the Easter anti-hydrogen-bomb march claimed there were 12,000 people at the final meeting near the gates of the Atomic Weapons Research Establishment, Aldermaston, yesterday," reported *The Daily Telegraph* on April 8.

Five hundred cardboard "lollipop" banners had been made for the marchers, half of them with the CND symbol in white on black, symbolising death, for Good Friday and Holy Saturday. The other half, for use on Easter Sunday and Monday, were white on green, for life.

The symbol itself had been designed earlier that year by Gerald Holtom, a member of the organisers of the march, the Direct Action Committee against Nuclear War. It incorporated the naval semaphore symbols for N and D, standing for Nuclear Disarmament.

Holtom, who died in 1985, explained that he designed the symbol while in a mood of despair. "I drew myself the representation of an individual in despair, with palms outstretched outwards and downwards, in the manner of Goya's peasant before the firing squad." If he meant Goya's *The Third of*

May, the man before the firing squad has his hands held up. The origins of the symbol remain stubbornly controverted despite Holtom's clear evidence. The same symbol, only the other way up, appeared on the cover of a novel called *The Notch in the Stick* by Leslie Moore, published in 1912. The symbol used within the circle of the CND badge is also the rune representing the sound "k" in the Anglo-Saxon version of the runic alphabet. It seems likely that both these facts are coincidence.

In a leading article after the first Aldermaston march, *The Daily Telegraph* admitted that the marchers were patently sincere, but accused them of basing their arguments on misconceptions, among them the belief that "Communists can be swayed by Messianic gestures of renunciation". None of the demonstrators had considered that "the action which they demand invites the very disaster from which they shrink".

On the same day as its Aldermaston report, the Telegraph carried a headline: SOCIALIST CALLS TO KEEP H-BOMBS. It was still the paper's policy to use the word "Socialist" to refer to members of the Labour Party. Labour was deeply divided over nuclear arms at the time. The news report under the headline concerned a pamphlet published by John Strachey, who had been Labour's Secretary of State for War in the Attlee Government, in 1950–51.

The very title "Secretary of State for War" was soon to become a victim of modern political presentation. It was changed, by the Conservatives, in 1964, when Peter Thorneycroft became the Secretary of State for Defence. The Secretaryship for War had been invented in 1855, with the appointment of Lord Panmure, the man who sent official despatches to the newly-born *Daily Telegraph* from the Crimea. Before this, the Secretary of State for War also had responsibility for the Colonies.

In his pamphlet of 1958 Strachey wrote: "Much as every sane man and woman detests the H-bomb, the British people are perfectly well aware that Britain cannot and must not scrap her own nuclear deterrent unless and until the other nations scrap theirs."

A subsidiary headline on the *Telegraph*'s report

From the Telegraph
Russian tanks put down the Hungarian uprising

October 27, 1956

The following eye-witness despatch by Gordon Shepherd, *Daily Telegraph* Special Correspondent, from Hungary's isolated capital was brought out yesterday by an Austrian refugee who carried it across the frontier for safe transmission to London.

Budapest, Friday

Russian T34 tanks and "loyal" Hungarian troops were still fighting in the streets of this shattered and sealed-off capital today to crush the great Budapest uprising. To judge from the fading scale of gunfire over the past 18 hours since my arrival here, the last defiant flickers of organised resistance are now being extinguished.

As this is being written, my hotel window is vibrating with the noise of tanks rumbling along the Danube embankment towards the southern end of the town. Heavy gunfire comes across the misty river from Csepel, where a pitched battle has been going on all night.

This is no mere revolt of a disgruntled party junta. It is no mere demonstration which has got out of hand due to trigger-happy citizens. It is an outright civil war in which the 90 per cent of Hungary's anti-Communists have struggled to express their hatred for the regime and its Russian protectors.

The number of dead and dying is impossible to estimate. One doctor assessed it for me at more than 3,000 killed and seriously wounded. But he was judging only from the state of the Budapest hospitals. Every ward of these, he said, has been crammed since Wednesday with injured, lying sometimes two in a bed and one on the floor space between.

I drove slowly through the centre of the city soon after dawn

today. Tanks blocked the main Danube bridges and covered all principal cross roads. Burnt-out lorries and cars lay on their sides in the street.

Broken glass glistened on the pavements and the smashed cable wires of the tram system trailed on the ground. From some blackened doors came that acrid war-time smell of debris mingled with spent gunfire and corpses. It was last in the air of Budapest in 1944. On that occasion, the Russian troops came as "liberators".

In an attempt to disguise the detested Soviet presence, Hungarian flags have been hung on many Russian tanks. The rebels seem to have only one clear way of identifying themselves. This is to fly Communist flags with the hammer and sickle slashed away to leave a ragged hole in the middle.

It seems fair to say that in some cases the Soviet troops appeared reluctant to carry out their unpleasant job. Yet, in other cases, their hastiness or their wilful brutality have caused needless slaughter.

One of the worst massacres of the last three days happened when Russian tanks opened fire without any clear reason on a crowd of passive and unarmed people in the Parliament Square yesterday. The total dead here alone is put at over 100. Women and children were among the dozens mown down.

This is the most impossible thing to convey out of the tragic Budapest scene yet the most important: the choking hate of the ordinary people against their present masters, and the Russians who protect them.

A dozen or more times driving around Budapest my car has been hemmed in by passers-by, shouting in English, German or Hungarian: "For God's sake, tell the truth about these massacres," and "Do they know in the West what these Russians are doing?"

It was only by describing myself as anything but a journalist that I got through to the capital. The most effective description was "delegate". This worked where "diplomat" failed. Two colleagues and I were the only foreign correspondents to get into Budapest by any route since the fighting began.

From rune to logo – the development of the CND symbol. The device on the novel 'The Notch in the Stick', 1912 (top), resembles, upside down, the design (centre) made four decades later by Gerald Holtom, which incorporated the semaphore letters N and D, standing for Nuclear Disarmament. It was produced in black on white for lapel badges, in white on black for Good Friday placards and in white on green for Easter. Later versions (bottom) adopted a bolder outline

said: "Mr Gaitskell approves Strachey pamphlet". Hugh Gaitskell, the Labour leader in opposition, was resisting Left-wing attempts in his party to commit itself to unilateral nuclear disarmament. He thought it would destroy the party.

Two years later Gaitskell made an impassioned speech at the Labour Party Conference, which had just voted for a unilateral policy against the wishes of its leadership. "It is not in dispute," he said, "that the vast majority of Labour Members of Parliament are utterly opposed to unilateralism and neutralism. So what do you expect them to do? Change their minds overnight?

"There are some of us, Mr Chairman, who will fight, fight and fight again to bring back sanity and honesty and dignity, so that our party, with its great past, may retain its glory and greatness."

Gaitskell died in 1963 and Harold Wilson became party leader. He had been a cabinet minister aged only 31 under Attlee, and was regarded as on the Left of the party. But unilateralism did not appear in the party manifesto in 1964, and Labour was

elected to power, though with a majority of only five.

Unilateralism was again adopted as official Labour policy in the early 1980s, when the party reached its electoral nadir under the leadership of Michael Foot. A founder of CND, he had seen crowds of 60,000 people join a rally in Trafalgar Square at the end of the march (this time from Aldermaston) in 1960. But, despite the Cuban Missile crisis of October 1962, which had convinced many that the world might end at any moment, the Aldermaston march of 1963 attracted much reduced support, and CND decided it should be the last. Michael Foot stepped down from the Executive Committee.

The march was revived in 1972, from Trafalgar Square to Aldermaston again, with 3,000 greeting the marchers at the end of their 56-mile journey. In 2004 the march was revived once again, but only 1,000 people turned up in Trafalgar Square to see off 400 marchers. "I know it's Good Friday," commented Damon Albarn of the group Blur, "but people could give a little bit of thought. It's not even raining."

Buildings in Budapest were reduced to ruins by Soviet tanks in just a few days in October 1956

From the Telegraph

Will Harold Wilson still take Mary breakfast in bed at Number 10?

October 17, 1964

By Alice Hope (the day after Harold Wilson became Prime Minister)

From a semi-detached to No.10 Downing Street. It's a long way to travel but cool, calm Mrs Mary Wilson seems to be taking it all in her stride.

In any case she won't have to worry about her curtains or her carpets not fitting, or her furniture being inadequate when she moves into No.10. All the furnishings in the Prime Minister's home were well taken care of when Mr Raymond Erith, the architect, did his mammoth job of reconstructing and refurnishing recently.

In fact, the private rooms of No.10 are not as grand as you might expect. True there are nine bedrooms, a study, bathrooms, and reception rooms all stretching over the top of the neighbouring houses.

The boys, Robin 20 now at Balliol, and Giles 16, who is at University College School, Hampstead, will be able to pick and choose both bedrooms and music rooms – Robin has a collection of instruments, including a harmonium, recorder and balalaika.

At No.10 Mrs Wilson will undoubtedly appreciate the kitchens. There are two, one big kitchen downstairs which is used for official entertaining, when a chef is called in, and the family kitchen next to the private dining room in the flat upstairs. This is full of mod cons and up-to-date arrangements with stainless steel, shining work surfaces and brand new cooking stoves.

The new Prime Minister is not fussy about his food but he watches his weight and his favourite meal is said to be cold roast beef, jacket baked potatoes and salad. Sunday mornings have always been special in the Wilson household – Mr Wilson takes his wife her breakfast in bed. Will he have time to do the same now?

Mary Wilson the poet at home with one of her volumes

SOLIDARITY

The strikers who cracked open the Soviet bloc

The people of Poland united against their Soviet-imposed government, inspired by the election in 1978 of a Polish pope

Pope John Paul II kissed the ground of his native Poland on June 2, 1979. It was a visit that the Communist government and its Soviet sponsors feared. They were right to do so. The Church in Poland was immensely popular, and it provided the vehicle for virtually universal opposition to a regime that ruled only through the power of the secret police.

In the summer of 1980, strikes at the Lenin Shipyards in Gdansk brought to prominence a workers' movement called Solidarnosc – Solidarity. Solidarity was a concept often mentioned in the Pope's addresses on the subject of human dignity. It meant action based on the common dignity of mankind, the reverse of a socialistic totalitarianism. Through Solidarity's non-violent action, the Polish government was forced to agree to a free trade union movement – a thing unheard of in the Soviet bloc.

Emblematic of the movement was the Solidarnosc logo designed in 1980 by Jerzy Janiszewski. It featured on flags and banners, alone or with the Polish eagle or with the anchor of hope, or with the image of the Virgin of Czestochowa.

From August 1980 onwards, *The Daily Telegraph* followed developments closely. The shipyard strikes made front-page news even before the name of the strike-leader Lech Walesa became internationally familiar. On August 17 thousands of striking workers attended an open-air Mass at the end of which a large cross made by shipyard carpenters was blessed by the presiding priest. It commemorated strikers shot at the shipyard in 1970.

In a leading article that was published on August 19, *The Daily Telegraph* cautioned against any action that would provoke a Russian invasion, which "could not be effectively countered by anything short of starting world war three". The paper hoped instead for "a non-violent development leading to at least some increases in industrial democracy in Poland".

That is what happened in the short term. But the struggle was by no means easy. In October that

In 1980 strikers at the Lenin shipyard at Gdansk fixed to the railings a cross (commemorating workers shot in 1970) and a photograph of the Pope. The Solidarnosc logo proved a potent symbol of the free trade union movement, led by Lech Walesa, (right, chaired by fellow strikers) even when it was declared illegal and streets protests suppressed (above, Gdansk) with teargas and force of arms

same year Solidarity called a general strike lasting for just one hour. "The strike was a complete success," Lech Walesa told the *Telegraph*. "We showed that we know how to start a strike and how to end a strike."

But in December, with the President of East Germany calling for the Soviet Union to save "socialist" Poland, an invasion seemed likely. It became known only years later that the Pope had written a letter (in diplomatic French) to President Leonid Brezhnev invoking the Helsinki Final Act of 1975 by which the Soviet Union had recognised Poland's sovereignty. The letter also spoke of the nation's "moral reconstruction based on the conscious engagement, in solidarity, of all the forces of the entire society".

On December 13, 1981 a Polish military takeover saw Solidarity's leadership arrested and the movement sent underground. Even during the "state of emergency" that made Solidarity illegal, its logo decorated pencils and mugs and headed *samizdat* publications. When the Pope succeeded in making another visit in June 1983, he was followed by crowds chanting "Solidarnosc!".

On September 12, 1989 Tadeusz Mazowiecki, one of the Solidarity leaders imprisoned in 1981, became the first non-Communist Prime Minister of an Eastern European country. On the night of November 9 to 10, 1989 the Berlin Wall fell to cheers from both sides.

TRISTAN DA CUNHA

An entire island evacuated to an unfamiliar world

When lava poured over their remote island, Tristanians found refuge in England. After a few months they decided to return home

T he 268 people of Tristan de Cunha were evacuated in 1961 when the island turned into an erupting volcano. "Glowing lava bubbled down the steep slopes of the island, a mountain peak rising 6,760ft out of the South Atlantic," reported *The Daily Telegraph* on October 11.

"Since August the island, known as the world's loneliest, had been shaken by earth tremors of increasing intensity. Huge cracks opened up in the ground. Then the earth began to heave and bulge. Red-hot lava streamed out of the cracks, threatening to engulf the stone and thatch cottages. Huge fiery bubbles appeared. Sulphurous smoke hung over the island."

When the cracks opened, the islanders left their settlement and went to an area called "the potato patches", and then by fishing boats to Nightingale Island, 18 miles away. After a cold, wet, shelterless night they were taken off by a Dutch liner and sailed 1,700 miles to Cape Town.

They had lost all their possessions and all their

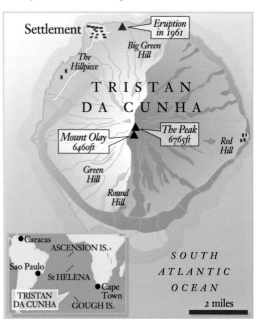

INBRIEF

MAY 31, 1963

The Peerage Bill, which enables hereditary peers to renounce their titles for life and stand for election as commoners, was published yesterday. With the Opposition ready to give it a fair wind, there is every likelihood that it will be passed by the beginning of August.

Mr Wedgwood Benn, who has campaigned incessantly for a change in the law ever since the death of his father, Viscount Stansgate, expects to be re-adopted as prospective Labour candidate for Bristol SE. His election is practically certain. "On the day Parliament is dissolved I shall deliver my instrument of disclaimer," Mr Benn said last night.

animals had to be left behind. "About 380 head of cattle, 800 sheep, 50 donkeys and about 100 cats and dogs are fending for themselves," the *Telegraph* reported.

The islanders were used to a hard life. They were an extraordinary community, and, beyond their remoteness, their character was rather difficult for the British press to do justice to. The remoteness was no myth. If Cape Town to the east was far, it was further, 2,120 miles, to Uruguay in the west. There were some connections with that other remote Atlantic island, St Helena, Napoleon's last prison, but that was 1,400 miles away.

Most of the island is inaccessible from the sea, with cliffs rising to 1,900ft. Above the cliffs a plateau, called "the base", stretches towards the central steep cinder slopes of the peak. Hazardous ravines, known as gultches, cut into the base and run down to the sea.

The sole village, known simply as "the settlement" is on a coastal strip between 100 and 200ft above the sea on the north-west, about five miles long and up to three-quarters of a mile wide. The only road leads to the potato patches, which are vital to survival, along with fishing.

There were seven surnames on the patriarchally run island, Glass, Swain, Rogers, Green, Hagan,

and volcanic dust still lie over Tristan," reported M.T. Scott, the Master of the rock-lobster ship *Tristania*, by radio. "At the present rate the rock-lobster factory will be overwhelmed by lava and rubble very soon." Captain Scott had been dealing with the islanders for 13 years, as part of their crawfish export business.

"For the moment we have abandoned plans to salvage any property on the island," Captain Scott said. "No one was hurt during the evacuation and the islanders have taken four of their flimsy long boats with them. But they have lost everything else.

"Our first warning was on Monday while we were off the big beach at Tristan. We were told from the shore to watch a certain hill which was cracking. After six hours it rose to about 30 feet with the ground cracking around it. The islanders were moved to the potato patches. At two o'clock on Tuesday morning we observed a volcanic blaze near the abandoned settlements. On approaching at daylight we saw that the volcano had developed where the ground had risen the day before. We decided to evacuate the inhabitants.

The captain of the Dutch ship taking the Tristanians to Cape Town said: "They are quite happy and there are no casualties." The people had sobbed openly as they took a last look at Tristan.

After a fortnight in Cape Town, the islanders were brought to England, arriving on November 3, 1961. They stayed at a disused army camp at Redhill, Surrey, for a few months. The climate at home never falls below 36F, and they had little resistance to some germs in England. Three elderly islanders soon died of pneumonia, and many suffered from chest infections. Next year they were settled at Calshot Camp, a former RAF station near Southampton, and found jobs in local factories.

There were difficulties. They were shocked to find unattended groceries were stolen. One elderly man was beaten up by a Teddy Boy. They were pestered by Jehovah's Witnesses and, worse, by scientists. Daniel Schreier, who has written most knowledgeably about the Tristanians, was told they felt they were treated like animals, as objects of study. Someone suggested they should be sent to the Falkland Islands. One MP proposed that their own island should now be used as a nuclear weapon test-site.

A survey of Tristan da Cunha later that year found that 25 arable acres were covered by lava, which had also destroyed the canning factory. But the settlement had been spared by 100 yards.

The refugees voted overwhelmingly to return. Only five decided to stay in England. After the terribly cold English winter of 1962–3, they returned in two parties, in April and November. It was hard work to begin again. Seed potatoes brought back were full of worm and failed. But the canning factory was rebuilt and even electric light introduced to houses. In 2001 a hurricane destroyed the only pub, the little hospital and several houses. But the islanders stayed on, and they remain intact as a community.

Repetto and Lavarello. Three of these derived from shipwrecked mariners. Island fortunes varied in the 19th century, declining as whaling failed. For 10 years from 1909 not a single mail ship called. Money was introduced only in 1942. Ox carts were the transport.

Missionaries had been defeated by the life, more than one becoming depressed and recommending the evacuation of the island. But the people would not go. They were least impressed by the Rev Harold Wilde who ministered there from 1934 to 1940. He read all mail he could lay his hands on, rationed food and put up a pillory to punish sinners and offenders. Many islanders converted to Catholicism, which a pair of sisters had introduced in 1908.

The great improvement in prosperity of the islanders before the volcano erupted was with the building of a canning factory for rock-lobsters or "crawfish". Though there was no higher education, nor was there crime in the ordinary sense. It was a healthy life, and many lived to great ages. From the time of the Second World War onwards there was permanent radio contact with the "outside world".

Two days after the Tristanians were taken off the endangered island, the *Telegraph* gave the first eyewitness account of the eruption. "Heavy smoke

The anxious faces and assorted clothing of the refugees from Tristan da Cunha on the rescue ship in the Atlantic in 1961. At first they were taken to the nearest mainland, 1,700 miles away at Cape Town, South Africa

A BIT OF A HURRICANE

The great storm that blew down 15 million trees

The worst storm since 1703 took England by surprise, disrupted transport and the City, and transformed the landscape

A car lies crushed beneath a fallen plane tree on the morning after the storm. The wind that hit the trees met resistance from foliage which had not yet fallen for the winter

A great storm, the worst since 1703, ripped across southern England in the early hours of October 16, 1987. The experience for Londoners and those in the trail of the strongest winds was astonishing. That night saddled the television weather forecaster Michael Fish with a slightly undeserved reputation of making a blunder. "A lady has rung in to ask if there is going to be a hurricane tonight... There is not," he told viewers.

The Beaufort Wind Scale classifies as hurricanes winds over 75mph; but the Saffir-Simpson Hurricane Scale provides for five levels of hurricane, the strongest for winds above 155mph. The storm of 1987 produced gusts of 110mph. Some 15 million trees were uprooted, partly because they had not lost their leaves for the winter, and so presented more resistance to the blast. Avenues were felled sideways, or like dominoes, according to their orientation. Hundreds of acres of woods were flattened and became impassable for years.

"More trees were destroyed and disfigured in the south by the night of hurricane-force winds than were killed in a decade by Dutch elm disease," reported Charles Clover in *The Daily Telegraph*. At Kew Gardens a third of the trees that had stood for 100 years were down.

"Railway lines and thousands of roads were blocked by fallen trees and debris," reported Colin Randall, "With train services into London halted and few Underground routes operating, long queues waited at bus stops, but many bus services were withdrawn because of blocked routes." Londoners walked to work over pavements strewn with branches and green leaves from plane trees.

The London Fire Brigade answered a record 6,000 calls in 24 hours. Electricity supplies to much of the South East were shut down to save the National Grid from collapse. "With computers and some telephone exchanges out of action because of the power failure, the Stock Exchange had to suspend dealing for a time." For the City it was the calm before the storm, for on October 19 came "Black Monday", in London and New York, where percentage losses exceeded those in the 1929 crash.

From the Telegraph

Dutch elm disease kills 6,500,000 trees

October 9, 1974

Dutch elm disease could wipe out all the mature elms in London's Royal Parks by the end of next year, Baroness Birk, Parliamentary Under Secretary of State, Department of the Environment, said yesterday. So far this year 856 elm trees have been killed in Hampton Court and Bushy Park; 132 in Hyde Park; 121 in Regent's park; 70 in Kensington Gardens.

October 31, 1975

The destruction caused by Dutch elm disease on Britain's pastoral landscape is underlined in a Forestry Commission report on the spread of the infection, published yesterday.

More than a quarter – six-and-a-half million – of all elm trees in the South have been killed, the survey says, and there are signs that, helped by the hot summer, the more virulent strain of the disease is spreading northwards.

Steps being considered included more rapid clearance of infected elms and a closer preventative watch in areas which have escaped. So far this year 1.9 million trees have been infected in Southern England.

From the Telegraph

Heavenly ire discounted as lightning strikes and York Minster burns

July 10, 1984

By Guy Rais

A bolt of lightning was blamed last night for starting a fire which devastated the south transept of York Minster early yesterday, causing damage estimated at more than £1 million.

Suggestions of "Divine intervention" connected with the controversy over the consecration at the Minster last week of the new Bishop of Durham, the Rt Rev David Jenkins [notorious for his remarks on traditional beliefs], were dismissed as "ridiculous" by the Archbishop of York, Dr Habgood.

And the Archbishop of Canterbury, Dr Runcie, who is in York for the General Synod, said individuals should be very cautious about claiming Divine intervention. He thought it "miraculous" that the damage was confined to the south transept which "would rise again".

The money to rebuild the transept will come from the Church of England's own insurance company as the Minster is insured for several million pounds.

The Minster's consultant architect, Mr Charles Brown, said the south transept gable would have to be removed and replaced, and the famous Rose Window dismantled. "It will probably take two years before the restoration work is complete," he said. "Our first priority will be to put a roof over the transept and that will take six or seven months, but we hope to have a temporary structure in place within weeks."

He said the building was "fully protected" against lightning.

Dr Bernard Feilden, a former surveyor of fabric at the Minster, added: "Lightning is very unpredictable. The Minster is fully equipped with fire detectors but these wouldn't have been given a chance to work properly owing to the speed of the flames."

The fire started at about 2.30am during an electrical storm over the city.

Firemen from a wide area went to the scene after the alarm was raised by schoolchildren from a nearby youth hostel. The children said they saw "huge orange flashes" coming straight down to the ground.

Flames were shooting through the roof of the south transept when the first fire crews arrived. As molten lead poured down, water was sprayed over the Minster's entire roof to stop the blaze spreading to the 200ft central tower.

Inside the cathedral, clergymen who live nearby rescued most of the valuable treasures and relics before the heat became too intense.

Flames shot through the roof of the south transept and molten lead poured down

FOOT AND MOUTH

Plumes of smoke from burning pyres of cattle

Reaction to the foot and mouth epidemic of 2001 showed little had been learnt from outbreaks over the previous century

When it was clear that the epidemic of foot and mouth that broke out in October 1967 was likely to be the worst known, starlings were blamed. The original site of infection had been among pigs near Oswestry, but when new outbreaks were found in far-away counties, an unnamed veterinary officer was reported to have said that starlings could have brought the disease from the continent. Whenever the veterinary officer had gone to deal with sick animals, the birds were close by.

"A Ministry of Agriculture departmental committee, under Sir Ernest Gowers," said *The Daily Telegraph*, "reported some years ago on foot and mouth disease that the case against the starling as a spreader of the disease was formidable, but not proved."

Before the epidemic that began in 1967 could be contained, 433,987 animals had to be slaughtered. But when the disease returned in 2001, despite developments in scientific knowledge, the number killed was more than six million.

The nation's attitude to cattle disease had been formed by the epidemic of rinderpest that lasted from 1865 to 1867. It derived from a cargo of cattle from the Baltic and was ended only by the hurried passing of an Act that provided for inspection, compulsory slaughter and compensation.

A hundred years later, on November 22, 1967, the *Telegraph*'s agricultural correspondent, W.D. Thomas, wrote that "the number of animals slaughtered in the foot and mouth epidemic passed the 134,000 mark yesterday. The previous highest total was 128,000 in 1923."

Mr Fred Peart, the Minister of Agriculture, asked farmers to keep as many animals as possible under cover, to have all animals examined at least once a day, and to keep people and vehicles off their farms.

When another epidemic of foot and mouth had broken out in 1951, readers were assured that the meat ration would not be affected, because 70 per cent of the animals slaughtered in measures to combat the disease would be made available for consumption. "These are animals which have not

been in close contact with infected beasts," it was said.

In the 1967 epidemic there were fears that meat rationing might have to be re-introduced, 13 years after it had belatedly ended in the postwar recovery. Instead the price of the "weekend joint" went up by between 6d and 10d a lb.

In a letter to the *Telegraph* during the epidemic of 1967, George Ridley of the badly hit Eaton Estate, Chester, suggested one reason why the Government had been slow to take a grip on the epidemic. "Perhaps the prime reason behind political apathy," he wrote, "is the fact that the farming community do not represent a substantial proportion of the voting power."

The same reason was put forward in 2001, when the elections was delayed by a month, from May to June, yet the ruling Labour party found its majority unaffected by the agricultural disaster.

The policy used throughout was that used against rinderpest in the 1860s: slaughter and burning, and then precautionary slaughter of cattle near to

A motor-car is sprayed with disinfectant at Cockernach Farm, Barkway, Hertfordshire, during a foot and mouth outbreak in 1933. Much the same strategy of isolation and slaughter was used to limit the epidemic in 2001, while the pyres of dead cattle (right) burnt day and night

In the first week 2,000 livestock were slaughtered and a ban on livestock movements imposed. With the discovery of the disease in Devon, cattle traders were criticised for the movement and mixture of stock. Also blamed was the distance that animals had to be taken for slaughter in new, bigger abattoirs.

Royal parks were shut to protect deer herds. The huge "Liberty and Livelihood" march planned for late February in London was cancelled. This demonstration had attracted support from widespread antipathy to the Labour Government's plans to make hunting illegal, and its other signs of not understanding rural life.

After a month, farmers were loudly criticising the Government for reacting too slowly. Tim Yeo, the shadow agriculture minister, called for the Army to be used. Tourism suffered badly. Even when the Government declared that the country was "open for business", much was obviously closed.

After five weeks, the backlog of dead livestock waiting to be burnt or buried had risen to 80,000. A vast site, like an opencast mine, was prepared for burials at Great Orton, Cumbria. In April the Army was called in, as the number of beasts slaughtered or awaiting slaughter passed a million. On May 3, the Prime Minister, Tony Blair, said that the epidemic was effectively beaten, although millions more animals were to be killed before it petered out.

That summer arrangements were made "for the slaughter and destruction of about one million healthy lambs which escaped the epidemic," the *Telegraph* reported. "The operation will cost the taxpayer £10 million." The lambs could not be sold because of export restrictions.

The Daily Telegraph had taken a prominent role in exposing the bungles, scandals and human tragedies of the epidemic, partly through the energies of its agriculture editor, David Brown. In August he died of a sudden illness.

That August saw a return of foot and mouth, and worse was feared if it was a wet autumn. But on September 11 attention was drawn away from agricultural concerns by the destruction of the World Trade Centre in New York.

INBRIEF

FEBRUARY 18, 1972

More power restrictions will be introduced on Wednesday whether or not the miners' strike is settled, Mr Davis, Trade and Industry Secretary, announced in the Commons yesterday.

Details of the economies – the final stage before a near total blackout – have not been settled, but all of the electricity industry's 18 million customers will be hit.

Consumers face longer and more frequent blackouts. Manufacturing industry faces being reduced to a one-day week or forced to close, laying off about eight million workers. Yesterday the Department of Employment reported that 1.5 million workers had been laid off so far.

A total shutdown could follow within three or four days if the strike continued, Mr Davis said after his Commons statement. By the following weekend stocks at 142 coal-fired power stations would have been exhausted.

outbreaks. Inoculation was objected to on scientific grounds, and was said to be an enemy of future meat exports.

At the end of the 2001 epidemic, Robert Uhlig, then the paper's farming correspondent, wrote: "From February to September 30, when the 2,030th and last foot and mouth outbreak was detected, more than six million animals were slaughtered and burnt on funeral pyres across the countryside."

It was the daily sight of burning piles of cattle on television, and the endless revelations in the press that thousands of sheep and cattle were waiting far too long for slaughter, that made the epidemic so depressing to the nation.

The first signs of the 2001 epidemic had appeared in February when the disease was spotted in an abattoir in Essex. A few days later it was found at a pig farm at Heddon-on-the-Wall, Northumberland. There was to be much loose talk among Government officials about infection coming from Chinese restaurants or illegally imported meat.

On the historic day in 1954 Bannister stands between Brasher (left) and Chataway, who both ran with him in the record-breaking mile

From the Telegraph

Roger Bannister runs a mile in under four minutes

May 7, 1954

Daily Telegraph Reporter

Roger Bannister, 25, British one-mile record holder, yesterday became the first man to run a mile in under four minutes. On the Iffley Road ground, Oxford, he covered the distance in 3 minutes, 59.4 seconds, a world record that officials said was certain to be ratified by the International Athletics Federation.

He made his successful attempt in a match between the Amateur Athletic Association and Oxford University in conditions which were not perfect. Blustery weather, which might have caused postponement of the attempt, eased about an hour before the race. There was a 15mph cross wind during the run. The fastest time for the mile previously recorded was 4 minutes, 1.4 seconds by Gundar Haedd, the Swede, in 1945.

Bannister, tall and fair haired, is a student at St Mary's Hospital, London, and a former president of the Oxford University Athletic Club. In the race with Bannister were C.J. Chataway, of Oxford; C.W. Brasher, Olympic steeplechaser; W.T. Hulatt, Northern Counties Champion; and two Oxford runners, G.F. Dole and A.D. Gordon.

Just over two hours after making the new record, Bannister was seen by television viewers in the BBC programme *Sports View*. Bannister said that the main problem was the weather: "Like the cricketers, we have been pretty upset this week and we were worried about the very strong wind, which certainly was going to slow us down."

At the Oxford Union last night, a member from the floor of the house proposed, amid cheers, that the debate be adjourned for 3 minutes, 59.4 seconds to mark Bannister's achievement.

Unattainable as Everest

By Michael Melford

There seems to be something entirely fitting in the accomplishment of this fabulous feat, for so long as elusive and seemingly unattainable as Everest, by an Oxford man at Iffley Road. For Oxford had had a unique influence on the history of mile running and indeed athletics generally.

Exeter College, Oxford – Bannister's own college – has almost certainly the oldest athletics club in the world. The AAA was founded at a meeting in the Randolph Hotel.

In the spring of 1947 after months of frost, snow and flood, there had been no sport at Oxford or Cambridge, and little was known of current form when the two teams came to the White City for the University Sports.

It was the moment for surprises and the biggest came in the mile when the Oxford third string drew away at the beginning of the back straight and won in a manner which must have set alight the imagination of the dullest spectator. It was the start of Roger Bannister's great career, the career of an athlete of singular determination and intelligence. He was just 18.

From the Telegraph

Devon Loch falls yards from winning the Grand National

March 24, 1956

By Hotspur (The Daily Telegraph's racing correspondent, who had the previous day written that Devon Loch, the 10-year-old owned by Queen Elizabeth, the Queen Mother and ridden by Dick Francis, had "the best credentials to win" the Grand National)

With 55 yards to go and the Grand National at his mercy Devon Loch clear of all opponents, stumbled, skidded, tried to keep his legs and stopped at Aintree on Saturday. It was, I think, the saddest and most dramatic event I have ever seen on a racecourse.

Captain Peter Cazalet, Devon Loch's trainer, who watched the race, said yesterday: "The horse just slipped from behind. No blame at all can be attached to anyone. It is quite untrue to say that Devon Loch was a spent horse. He was finishing very strongly. It was a most incredible thing and it happens once in a million...."

Among questions being asked are: Was Devon Loch frightened by the cheers coming from the stand for a royal victory. Did the reflection from the water jump nearby put it off its stride? Could water from that jump have seeped through onto the course to cause the horse to lose its footing?

It is unlikely that anyone will ever really know exactly what happened to Devon Loch. It was all over in a matter of seconds and occurred on the run-in from the last fence to the winning post, exactly opposite the water jump.

Some held that Devon Loch might have run into a patch of false-going. I do not think so. My impression was that the horse was in pain. One of the racecourse vets who examined Devon Loch immediately after the race thought he might have had a sudden attack of cramp.

Another felt his behaviour might have been due to a small blood clot in a hind leg. The latter condition is known to cause paralysing pain and would explain the fact that Devon Loch appeared for a few moments to have no strength in his hind legs.

I can think of only two other National incidents of a comparable nature. One was in 1936 when Cazalet's great friend, the late Lord Mildmay, appeared to have the race won on Davy Jones, two fences from home when the reins broke and the horse ran out; the other when Reavey took the wrong course from the last fence on Zahia in 1948. There is no doubt, however, that Devon Loch was the unluckiest loser in the 120-year history of the race....

I shall long remember the picture of the Queen Mother, as ESB [ridden by D.V. Dick, who had stridden on past Devon Loch to win the race] was being led triumphantly in, going quietly towards the racecourse stables with a smile on her face, to see if her horse was all right.

A few minutes later, after the vets had examined Devon Loch, the Queen and the Queen Mother were congratulating Mr and Mrs Leonard Carver, the owners of ESB, his rider, D.V. Dick, and his trainer, Fred Rimmell, on their victory. It was just as if nothing untoward had happened.

Dick Francis almost loses his seat as Devon Loch stumbles, is overtaken by ESB, and falls with all four legs out. He recovered after the race

Getting over the Sixties

The abolition of shillings and pence somehow set a seal on the innovations of the
settled into decrepitude. By the time of the Queen's Golden Jubilee people were able

DECIMALISATION

Out go shillings and pence and in comes the p

Jettisoning the ancient system of £sd was
disorientating. It symbolised the separation
of the Sixties from the decades to come

James Callaghan surprised the nation on
March 1, 1966 when he announced in his
Budget as Chancellor of the Exchequer that
Britain was to adopt a decimal currency in
February 1971, preparations for which
would begin immediately.

Like the Channel Tunnel, it was no new idea. In
1849 the first florin had been minted, a coin worth
two shillings, a 10th of a pound, as a step towards
decimalisation. But it never seemed to be the right
time to go through with the scheme.

Anthony Trollope in *The Eustace Diamonds* (1871),
has the fictional Chancellor working feverishly
to prepare the ground in Parliament for the
five-farthing penny. The idea there would be to
have 100 pence in 10 shillings, instead of 120, but
with each penny made up of five farthings –
provisionally given the name "quints" by the
fictional politicians – instead of four. Of course it
would be a slightly loose fit, since ordinarily there
were 480 farthings in 10 shillings, not the 500 that
Trollope's Mr Palliser wanted. It was not, though,
such a Procrustean bed as the real-life arrangments
in the 1970s that made a new penny worth so much
more than old pennies.

In Mr Callaghan's scheme the pound was to be
divided into 100 pence, instead of the immemorial
240. Therefore one new penny would be worth 2.4

old pence – no easy equivalent for the purposes of
ready mental arithmetic.

As older readers know, in the existing system of
£sd (pounds, shillings and pence), 12 pennies made a
shilling and 20 shillings made a pound. The pound
was represented by the £, l for *librum*, the shilling
by s for *solidus*, and the penny by d for *denarius*. The
s and d went after the figure. So £1 3s 4d was one
pound three and fourpence. Everyone who spent or
gained money knew that 6s 8d was a third of a
pound; 3s 4d a sixth of a pound; 2s 6d (half a crown,
which had its own coin) was an eighth of a pound.

In 1966 the decision had not been made whether
to call one-hundredth of a pound a "penny" or a
"cent". Eventually the penny was chosen,
represented by p instead of d. This was to give rise
to the unexpected and, to some, annoying
neologism "pee", as in "25p". In the meantime the
Government announced the setting up of a Decimal
Currency Board to organise the "historic change".

And it was an historic change, even if the process
seemed trivial. Decimalisation was a watershed, a
symbol of Sixties revolution and reform, the last
target of a decade that had brought the Pill,
legalised abortion and homosexuality, the abolition
of the stage censor and the introduction of
comprehensive education. It brought Britain
notionally closer to Europe.

It was supposed to make it easier to calculate bills
in shops, although its introduction coincided with
improvements to automatic tills that would end in
the triumph of the supermarket bar-code reader,
which would ensure in future that no check-out
girl would be required or able to add up the cost of
groceries either mentally or in pencil on the back
of a paper bag. Customers soon lost the knack, too.

In 1967 the Decimal Currency Bill was published
and the Government stood firm on retaining the
£1 instead of 10s as the unit to come into force in
1971. A Gallup Poll at the time showed that the
10-shilling unit was favoured by the public.
"Ministers are privately making it clear," the
Telegraph reported, "that they do not intend to
budge from their decision, however persuasive the
arguments for 100 new pennies to 10s." For all that,
the next step came in 1969 with the issuing of the
50p coin in October to replace the 10-shilling note.

INBRIEF

FEBRUARY 16, 1971

A four-point guide for anyone
worried today about decimals:
1 – Multiply shillings by five to
show the decimal amount,
i.e. 5s X 5 = 25p.
2 – There are only three new
coins. When you get them in
change put them away until you
get home. You can learn the
values later.
3 – All shops will accept
threepenny bits and pennies
providing they add up to 6d.
Many will still be trading in £sd
prices.
4 – To reckon in shillings and
pence try halving them, i.e. 4s 2d
(42 halved = 21p). This is only a
rough conversion but it works to
the nearest halfpenny.

decade before. So, as cheap flights struggled against cartels, nationalised railways to put some of the losses and gains into perspective

How much change in new money when you buy a tin of ham with a 10-shilling note? Two shoppers obligingly ponder the conversion tables for the cameras on D (for Decimal) Day, 1971

The first 50p coin was large, and with its seven sides brought complaints that it made holes in pockets. It was later reduced in size, and in general the new coins were much smaller than the old.

In April 1970, a new Labour Chancellor, Roy Jenkins, announced a change of mind by the Government over the fate of the sixpence. "One could not exclude the possibility that the Decimal Currency Board might be mistaken," the *Telegraph* had him saying in an announcement that seemed almost heretical in opposing the "unanimous and strong advice" of the board, which wanted the sixpence abolished when the new money came in. Mr Jenkins gave it a stay of execution for at least two years, until February 1973. The coin – pretty and small by pre-decimal standards – would of course be worth two-and-a-half new pence: a quarter of 10p, a useful, but not a decimal, division.

In a leading article that applauded the Chancellor's decision, the *Telegraph* said: "It is going to create a lot of red faces at the Decimal Currency Board, which counted on the rapid disappearance of the sixpence after decimal day and wished to encourage the process. So much the worse for the Board. What the Government has had to admit is that the

public's instinct is a truer guide than the Board's expertise."

When D-Day came – D for "decimal" – Britain was overcome by a sort of Dunkirk spirit. "In the great majority of shops, large or small," the *Telegraph* reported, "there was nothing but helpfulness and goodwill."

"Selfridges was among the big stores which had it cut and dried, with remarkable efficiency," wrote Gerda Paul on February 16. "The store accepted only decimal currency and had installed not only 15 money-changing counters, but also a patrolling team of 'Miss Decimals' in white, polo-necked sweaters and midis over hot-pants, to help with the facts." Hot pants were the exciting successors to the miniskirt, although it is hard to understand how they would be discernible during ordinary shop duties under the more demure midi.

"The big MacFisheries supermarket in Kensington High Street priced all its goods in new pence," the paper found. "But there were understanding smiles for the woman who wanted a 'shilling-sized kipper'."

"In the little shops, the will was there – even if the new cash registers were not. I found a tobacconist who charged me 27p for a packet of cigarettes, and rang up 5s 3d on his till." The exact equivalent of 27p was five shillings and 4.8 old pence. But it was to be suspected that the shopkeeper had rounded up his decimal price to 27p in the first place, when it might have been rounded down by 0.6d to 26p. The inflation that accelerated in the 1970s was soon to become connected in the public mind with the price increases imposed at the time of decimalisation.

"There is a queue for new tills," the tobacconist explained, "and we will not get one for a fortnight. But I want to go along with things. I have written out all my price tickets in the new money, but I have to convert back again to put the money in the till."

"The biggest row was, understandably, in the branches of Boots the Chemists, which are not yet 'converted'," the *Telegraph* reported. "I heard a woman arguing: 'I have been trying to get rid of all these pennies and 3d bits, and I do not see why I should get them all back from you.'"

GOODBYE ADLESTROP

Terrible crashes, then Beeching wields his axe

Railways seemed to have a poor future after nationalisation in 1948. But there was an outcry when 2,000 stations were to close

D r Beeching's axe chopped off the branch lines of the British railway system in 1963. By then rural railways had become part of what it meant to be British, particularly English. Edward Thomas's poem *Adlestrop* embodied this feeling: "*The steam hissed. Someone cleared his throat./ No one left and no one came/ On the bare platform.*"

Adlestrop station was closed in 1966, one of the 2,128 condemned by Beeching. They included the station the Queen used when she went to Balmoral each summer (Ballater, closed in February 1966).

Richard Beeching, Dick to his friends, was universally referred to as Dr Beeching, for he had a doctorate from Imperial College, London. A physicist and engineer, he was 47 when appointed chairman of the British Railways Board in 1961. After attempting to carry through his reforms, in an uncertain political climate, he resigned in 1965, slightly hurt, and went back to ICI, the chemicals company. He died in 1985.

On both branch lines and suburban routes the trains were slow and often late and always unprofitable. The railways were hardly out of the slough of the Second World War when the companies that ran them were nationalised in 1948. Although rail remained far safer than road transport the 1950s saw some terrible train crashes. Five years after the word "Harrow" established itself as a shorthand reference to the crash that killed 112 in 1952, "Lewisham", with 90 deaths, joined it in 1957.

It was dim morning when the crash at Harrow and Wealdstone took place; the memory of it would be associated with grainy newspaper photographs and arc lights amid the sooty gloom. *The Daily Telegraph* for October 9, 1952 reported: "The 8.15pm sleeper express from Perth to Euston, travelling the two-mile straight at nearly 70mph and 95 minutes late, smashed into the rear coaches of the 7.31 rush-hour local train from Tring to Euston in which were about 600 passengers. Then the 8.00am businessmen's express from Euston to Manchester, travelling at 45mph, hit the wrecked engine and coaches thrown in its path. The two 120-ton

An express going at 70mph ploughed into a commuter train at Harrow and Wealdstone on

October 8, 1952. Then an express smashed into the wreckage. A hundred and twelve people died. There were many moving tales of heroism that day

engines of the Manchester express sliced through the carriages, plunged 50ft across the platform and, rearing up, overturned on the parallel Bakerloo line."

Harrow was the worst British train disaster for 37 years. "It was estimated that about 1,000 people were in the three trains. Many of the compartments had people standing.

"Carriages split open by the force of the impact were spread-eagled over the tracks. Into this chaos of wheels, wood, steel, glass and hissing steam ran the Manchester-bound train. The coaches detached from the two locomotives, climbed on top of the other two trains, already a mass of dead and injured.

"Among the first on the scene were local doctors Dr M.E. Winters and Dr F. O'Sullivan. They worked among the wreckage for four-and-a-half hours. Dr Winters said: 'In one compartment of the Manchester-bound train we found three people alive and four dead. There did not seem to be anything else there but a pile of dust. As we turned to go away, someone called that the dust was moving. We went back, dug about and found a little old lady of about 75. She walked out, quite calm and uninjured and asked for her little dog. Everywhere there were people with terrible injuries who refused morphia, saying there were people who needed it more.'

"The scene on the wrecked station resembled a major war-time bomb incident. Constantly during the night salvage men had to be treated for injuries to their hands, and many suffered from exhaustion. A 70-year-old grandmother, Mrs Elizabeth Wells, of Wealdstone, was still working at the scene after midnight, having been there nearly 15 hours. She was accompanied by her 15-year-old granddaughter, Dorothy, a Red Cross cadet."

In a leading article the paper commented: "There is something particularly heartrending about a railway accident, perhaps because it is so sudden and unexpected. Not without reason in this country, we take the safety of a railway train for granted. We travel cheerfully, leaving behind us countless words unsaid, countless tasks undone, confident that we can do them later 'at the other end'."

Five years later, in fog, at 6.20pm, after dark on that December 4, two trains crashed under a railway fly-over bridge 200 yards on the Lewisham side of St John's station. It was the rush-hour.

"A fast steam train, bound from Cannon Street to Ramsgate, ran into the back of a stationary electric train," the Telegraph reported. "A carriage, forced upwards by the impact, hit the bridge as a third train was about to pass over it. The bridge collapsed onto wrecked coaches underneath.

"People in the train approaching the bridge were saved by the driver who saw the structure collapsing. All the trains were crowded with City and West End workers and Christmas shoppers. In the two which crashed, said a British Railways spokesman late last night, were at least 2,000 people. The work of extricating the dead was stopped shortly after 2.30 this morning."

After the crash "firemen worked to release steam from the engine. The hissing of the steam mingled with the screams of a woman who lay trapped in the wreckage. People who ran to the scene helped the injured down ladders and across make-shift causeways to the ambulances.

"In the guard's van of one of the trains lay the bodies of the guard and one other man. The van hung over at a dangerous angle, threatening houses below. Policemen ushered helpers away as firemen worked to free the bodies. In the tiny back yard of one of the houses a woman held up a tray holding five steaming cups of tea. 'Here you are, mates, cups of tea for you,' she shouted in a Cockney voice.

" 'You'd better watch it, ma,' shouted back a fireman. 'The carriage may fall over on you.' Unperturbed, she held up the tray until someone took it from her. Beside her a cockerel, wakened by the floodlights, crowed.

"In the alleys and passageways near the crash, the dead and injured lay waiting for ambulances. Among scenes as terrible as those many of them remembered from the war, the occupants of the houses worked quietly and without fuss. Among them were many who on other days might have been derisively labelled as Teddy Boys.

"The worst scenes were under the iron fly-over bridge. The dead hung from the wreckage inextricably until the bridge could be jacked-up."

Every now and then a body was brought out covered with a blanket on a stretcher. Occasionally," wrote the unnamed Daily Telegraph reporter, "I heard the rescuers call, 'Here's one still alive.' "

Such disasters were as old as railways (see page 88), but safety measures constantly improved. The worst casualty total had been in 1915 with a triple collision that left 227 dead at Quintinshill, Dumfriesshire. But still people generally connected railways in their minds with daily routine and interesting travel, not with the horrors most never saw. Thus it was that for all but the most hard-boiled, Beeching's cuts seemed a kind of vandalism.

Beeching intended to do away with a quarter of the railway system. There would be no passenger services in Scotland north of Inverness or in most of the West Country. Fares would rise, although he expected rail jobs to be cut by about 70,000. In the year the Telegraph was founded, there were 98,000 railway employees; in 1873 there were 275,000. The peak came in the First World War with 650,000 (56,000 of them women), and by 1948, the year of nationalisation, numbers had fallen to 629,000. Thereafter the fall was dramatic, to 251,000 by 1970 and 116,000 by 1994.

Towns threatened by the Beeching axe feared unemployment, too. "Whitby Hotel and Catering Association is to start a campaign to keep at least one of the three lines to the town open," the Telegraph reported. The town had 23 per cent unemployment already. It succeeded in keeping a railway line.

If Beeching's plan had been fully adopted, the Isle of Wight would have been left with no railways. "Mr James Shaw, chairman of Oakham Urban Council,

INBRIEF

MAY 6, 1980
BBC AND ITV SWITCH TO FINAL SCENES
By Robin Stringer, Television Staff
Millions of viewers were able to see live last night the end to the Iranian Embassy siege as both BBC and ITV interrupted scheduled programmes to give live coverage.

Such coverage is almost unprecedented. The siege itself is, of course, unique. Neither of the two previous London sieges, Balcombe Street and Spaghetti House, ranked for this sort of treatment.

Live coverage began last night at about 7.30. The BBC showed the fire and emergence of the hostages on both its channels, cutting into the World Snooker Championships on BBC2 and a John Wayne film on BBC1. ITV postponed its feature film, Detour to Terror to take in the action.

Some viewers were so riveted by the events that they were surprised when after about half an hour, both television companies reverted to normal programmes. Later programmes were interrupted for news flashes.

said it would fight the plans to close all Rutland's eight stations 'to the last straw'." It, too, won a reprieve, although the name of the county of Rutland disappeared for many years with unpopular reorganisations in 1974.

The station nearest the country house of Harold Macmillan, the Prime Minister, at Horsted Keynes, would shut. "But he will be little affected," the *Telegraph* noted. "He normally travels between his home, Birch Grove, and London by road." That was despite free travel afforded him as a director of the former Great Western Railway.

"Many just happen to like railway, and not road, transport," the *Telegraph* noted in a leading article. "But the real fear is of a possible lack of any sort of public transport." The fear was to prove no delusion.

For the time being there seemed no limit to the destruction. Just before Dr Beeching's report, the Euston Arch (or propylaeum), the 70ft Doric structure that had stood outside the station since 1837, was demolished even though it did not stand in the way of the uninspired redevelopment of the station behind it.

The even more extraordinary St Pancras station and gothic hotel very nearly went the same way. But on November 3, 1967 the *Telegraph* reported its reprieve. "Mr Greenwood, Minister of Housing and Local Government, announced that it had been placed on the list of buildings of 'special architectural or historic interest'.

"Many experts regard the station as a unique example of the architecture of the 1860s. Professor Nikolaus Pevsner, chairman of the Victorian Society, last night welcomed the news as a victory for the preservationists.

"A railways spokesman said last night that the listing would not interfere with plans. 'We intend to re-develop the whole area and release St Pancras for other purposes,' he said. In the *Daily Telegraph* magazine last year, John Betjeman said it was 'horrible' to contemplate St Pancras being destroyed and replaced by another 'new slab'."

Freddie Laker (above) challenged the cartel of the big airlines by providing cheap flights across the Atlantic. Richard Beeching (below) produced a report, 'The Reshaping of British Railways', that made economic sense of the run-down railway network of the time but enraged thousands whose local stations were to close

CHEAP FLIGHTS

Laker's Skytrain beats the cartel over the Atlantic

A scrap-dealer's son showed how a no-frills service could cut fares. The big airlines crushed him, but the seed had been sown

The dream of cheap, long-distance air travel was interrupted on February 5, 1982 when Laker Airways went into receivership. "As Sir Freddie walked the floor at his Gatwick headquarters 'in a state of misery'," Air Commodore G.S. Cooper, the *Telegraph*'s air correspondent, reported next day, "passengers were turned away from Laker planes."

Sir Freddie Laker's trans-Atlantic "Skytrain" had been operating since 1977. His idea had been a no-frills service to America for £32.50 when the regular fare was £200 – five times the cost in real terms at the beginning of the 21st century. But "hurt by competition from Laker, the big airlines turned to attack him by lowering prices to his levels".

Barbara Conway of the City staff wrote: "To many, including the Prime Minister, the classic rags-to-riches story of Laker's success was a prime example of British private enterprise.

"The birth of Laker Airways went back to 1948 when the ambitious Freddie, once the bottom of his class at school in Canterbury, and the son of a scrap dealer and a char woman, was 26 and a few months into his very first business. It was an aircraft spare parts company based on his entire capital of £240.

"A Scottish banker, Bobby Sanderson, invested in Laker's idea of buying a dozen converted Halifax Bombers just before the 1948 Berlin Airlift. Laker planes were responsible for nearly 12 per cent of the food and fuel airlifted to Berlin in nearly 13 months.

"Laker then went into the scrap-metal business, using Army surplus planes. In 1965 Laker Airways was born. In 1970, Laker saw the chance to enter the trans-Atlantic market. But he ran into opposition from aviation authorities as well as the scheduled carriers. Eventually, in 1977, Skytrain won the right to take off and proved an immediate success." Laker was knighted in 1988.

A recession put pressure on his business and "dollar borrowing became a desperate burden as exchange rates fell and interest rates rose".

Richard Branson's Virgin Atlantic later followed Laker's lead. Cheap fares were also to transform British habits in visiting continental Europe.

SOHO NIGHTS

The end of a long-running tragi-comedy

In the decade following Francis Bacon's death a very strange species disappeared from a bohemian enclave in London

The end of the 20th century was a *fin de siècle* indeed for a generation of drunken, bohemian, creative figures who lived out their tragi-comic lives in Soho. They gave an interest to the obituaries page of *The Daily Telegraph* different from the stirring stories of a passing generation of war heroes.

Obituaries had become an eagerly read genre thanks to Hugh Montgomery-Massingberd who, as obituaries editor of *The Daily Telegraph* from 1986 to 1994, made them a truthful, slightly theatrical but humane record of people's lives; other newspapers and his successors at the *Telegraph* followed his cue.

A rich crop of Soho fruit fell into the obituaries lap in the decade from 1992, when Francis Bacon died. Some thought him the greatest painter of the century. Unlike his one-time friend Lucian Freud, he frequented Soho to the end, drinking at the Colony Room Club especially on bank holidays when people with more conventional lives tended not to be around.

It would be a mistake to think Bacon the centre of a circle. Soho society was a three-dimensional net, not a series of solar systems. If it was bohemian, its bohemia was very different from that sampled by George Augustus Sala or Clement Scott in the 19th century. Soho in the second half of the 20th century was, to its most committed denizens, home.

It might have been a voracious jungle had it not been for a compensating readiness to accept anyone without preconditions. It was prevented from sinking into darkness and mere squalor by the comic effect of a constant procession of strange people, all thoroughly familiar to each other. As situation comedy it left television outclassed.

The dynamic was strong. Of the following dozen who died in the decade after 1992, some are well known, but each knew the others; some did not like some: Francis Bacon (died 1992), Isabel Rawsthorne (died 1992), David Wright (died 1994), Ian Board (died 1994), Michael Andrews (died 1995), Mick Tobin (died 1997), Jeffrey Bernard (died 1997), Daniel Farson (died 1997), Henrietta Moraes (died 1999), Bruce Bernard (died 2000), Marsh Dunbar

(died 2001), and Graham Mason (died 2002). Bacon himself, a hilarious conversationalist, was dangerous at the same time. The rules of the game in Soho allowed not merely obscene but deadly abuse. Some was levelled at bores to drive them away. "In the Fifties everyone was extremely rude to one another," as Henrietta Moraes put it.

One night in the Gargoyle club, a man who was the current infatuation of the writer and photographer Daniel Farson butted in on Bacon's conversation. Farson apologised to Bacon, only to be met by: "It's too bad that we should be bored to death by your friend and have to pay for his drinks, but now you have the nerve to come over as well, when you're not invited." But next day, Bacon bought Farson champagne in the Colony Room Club: "If you can't be rude to your friends, who can you be rude to?" Bacon had an unusual verbal delivery – camp Mayfair cockney, slightly strangulated and swooping; it could be unnerving.

An interesting angle on Bacon came from John Edwards, his friend of 30 years, whom Mick Brown took the trouble to interview for *The Daily Telegraph* in 2002. Edwards died the next year.

No matter what time he had been drinking until the night before, Edwards said, Bacon would get up between six and seven o'clock and start painting. That would be in his studio in South Kensington. On the floor were piles of paint-encrusted papers and photographs, on the tables jars full of ruined brushes. "The first time I saw it," Edwards recalled, "I said to Francis: how can you work in here? But he said it was how he liked it."

At nine, Bacon would telephone Edwards who would join him in the studio, where Bacon would fry eggs. Bacon liked only egg white, Edwards only the yolk. Edwards was the only person allowed to watch him at work. When Bacon discovered that Edwards had never learned to read or write, he said to him: "God, that must be marvellous."

" 'I think,' says Edwards, 'he felt very free with me, because I was a bit different from most people he knew. I wasn't asking him about his painting or anything like that. I asked him once: what do you see in me? And he laughed and said: you're not boring like most people.' "

Someone who wrote often on Bacon was Daniel Farson (1927–1997). Farson's memoir of him had an apparently silly title: *The Gilded Gutter Life of Francis Bacon*. But the dustjacket showed a telegram to him from Bacon suggesting just that title if he ever wrote his biography. That was before they quarrelled.

"He was a talented television journalist, writer and photographer," began Farson's own obituary in the *Telegraph*. "He was also a nightmare drunk.

"From middle age Farson was a fat man – the solid kind rather than sagging jelly. He never lost his hair, which was fair; in old age he presumably dyed it. In London he dressed in a suit with sleeves cut long to cover the tattoo of a fish on the back of one hand that he had had done in the merchant navy. He was brave even when sober.

"To meet Farson at nine in the evening in the

Henrietta Moraes in the early 1960s, in one of a series of photographs taken by John Deakin for Francis Bacon, one of whose nude potraits of her, painted in 1963, is now displayed at the Galerie Beyeler, Basle. She was annoyed to find a little later that Deakin had been selling copies of the photographs to sailors for ten shillings

Colony Room Club was to see a transformation that any actor in *Dr Jekyll and Mr Hyde* would think strained credibility. Within minutes, fuelled by a series of large gins scarcely diluted by tonic, polite talks about his great uncle Bram Stoker would turn into a rant of increasing volume and decreasing intelligibility: 'I loathe you, I can't stand you,' he would roar, gargling in his podgy throat. 'You're so clever, so patronising.' Sometimes Ian Board, the club's proprietor, would chase him down the steep, dark stairs, belabouring him with an umbrella.

"Often, the morning after, Farson would appear with a cut face, from a fall, a fight with a rent boy or some forgotten tussle with a policeman. But he would return immediately to the alcoholic fray.

"In later years he lived in moderate peace in Devon, writing books. Every now and then, he would make increasingly suicidal raids on London, getting drunk earlier and earlier. He would miss his train back to Devon, and perhaps return home three days late.

"He was barred from several hotels for trivial offences such as being found with his trousers round his ankles in the corridor. One quiet afternoon in the Coach and Horses an angry rent boy (aged about 30) came into the pub and tried to shame Farson into paying him for his services. Farson was shameless: 'But you didn't bloody do anything,' he shouted back. 'And I bought all the drinks.' "

By the 1980s three places in Soho where conversation could be found were the Coach and Horses, under its rude but bashful landlord Norman Balon; the York Minster (the "French pub"), run by Gaston Berlemont, confidant and unofficial banker; and the Colony Room Club, founded by Muriel Belcher, whose style may be judged from the fact that her customary term of endearment was "c—ty".

She died in 1979, and her barman Ian Board took over the Colony. He was the reason why many, including Bruce Bernard, a good judge, no longer went there. Brandy drove him to spectacular fits of rage. It was not only Farson he pursued from the club; he would sometimes launch into a tirade against Francis Bacon, with a parting yell down the stairwell: "You're no use. You can't f—ing paint."

If a monster, and there was no doubt about that, he was tremendously funny. As a deflator of pretentiousness, he should have been hired out. "Perched on a stool by the door, clad in tasteless leisurewear, his eyes protected by sunglasses, Ida (as he was known to closer friends) would trade coarse badinage with members," said the *Telegraph* obituary on his death in 1994, on Muriel Belcher's birthday.

"Board was an heroic smoker and drinker – he would breakfast on brandy, and once consumed a bottle of *crème de menthe* at a sitting. And if his drinking destroyed his youthful good looks it also shaped and nourished his bulbous nose."

He suffered much for his drunken art. Broken limbs might be occasional but difficulty in eating was daily – perhaps a pilchard pulled from the tin at midnight. Shaking morning sickness would be followed by a restorative "Vera Vomit", as he personified the exercise. Often he would wake in the morning to find himself on two cushions on the tarmac-like carpet of the cigarette-smoked Colony, having been too drunk to bother getting home.

A drinker who remained in control was Bruce Bernard (1928–2000), an art historian really, whose most conventional job was as picture editor of the *Sunday Times Magazine* in its heyday. "He fell into Soho's intoxicating milieu as a teenager," said his obituary in the *Telegraph*. "He remained true to some of its more demanding values all his life. He was never to own a house, he seemed indifferent to the clothes he wore. Sometimes he had debts and no money. Soho's democratic mix of painters, writers, publishers, gangsters and women determined the course of his life."

It was he who retrieved John Deakin's surviving photographs from beneath his bed after his death. Some of these, cracked and dog-eared, were shown at the V&A in 1984. His own photographs and books were admired. He would have published a perceptive book on Francis Bacon had not Bacon suddenly refused permission to reproduce copyright material, destroying the project. He did publish a telling essay on Lucian Freud in a large book of his paintings. Freud made two oil portraits of him.

His younger brother Jeffrey died before him, a few days after the Princess of Wales in 1997. His "Low Life" column in *The Spectator* was a running commentary on his physical decay and a sharply observed picture of his habitat. He had much charm and a tenacious long-term memory.

Of the three remarkable brothers the eldest, Oliver, the poet, survived them both. A typical entry in his diary for 1946 read: "Went to Bianchi's for spaghetti. Met Harry Diamond on the way to the Duke. Bruce was there, so were the Schnorrer and the Fine Doll. Robert MacBryde and Nelson and I went to Tony's. A brawl started over Dinora's alleged insulting some awful tart (who had got three years for slashing someone) and who screamed filth, undressed, tore down the lapels of Bruce's overcoat, pulled my hair and tried to get at Dinora again. Her girl friend picked up a knife which Bruce tore away from her." The night ended with five of them sleeping on someone's floor. That was still a pattern of life in Soho in the 1980s before the enclave changed and the survivors departed.

"Graham Mason, the journalist who has died aged 59, was in the 1980s the drunkest man in the Coach and Horses," said his *Telegraph* obituary in 2002. "His claim to a title in bibulous misbehaviour was staked against stiff competition.

"Mason was a fearsome sight at his most drunkenly irascible. Seated at the bar, his thin shanks wrapped around the legs of a high stool, he would swivel his reptilian stare round behind him to any unfortunate stranger hoping to be served, and snap: 'Who the f— are you?' Sometimes this prompted a reaction, and once, a powerful blow to the head sent Mason flying, with his stool, across the carpet. Painfully clawing himself upright, he set the stool in its place, reseated himself and, twisting his head round again, croaked: 'Don't you ever do that again.'

"Unlike his friend Jeffrey Bernard, Graham Mason did not make himself the hero of his own tragedy. His speciality was the extreme. In one drinking binge he went for nine days without food. At the height of his consumption, before he was frightened by epileptic fits into cutting back, he was managing two bottles of vodka a day. His face became in his own description that of a 'rotten choirboy'. At lunchtime he would walk through the door of the

Coach and Horses still trembling with hangover, his nose and ears blue whatever the weather. On one cold day he complained of the *noise* that the snow made as it landed on his balding head.

"Mason had a gift for contriving nicknames. A failed actress who rode a bicycle and was addicted to tittle-tattle became 'The Village Postmistress'. Gordon Smith, a stage-door keeper of fussy temperament, was 'Granny Gordon'.

"In a couple of hours one evening in February 1988 Mason had loud altercations with John Hurt ('You're just a bad actor'); with a law writer nicknamed The Red Baron, who was later murdered ('You know I don't like you. Go away and leave me alone'); and with Jeffrey Bernard (who stood up and shook him by the lapels). Michael Heath often featured Mason in his strip-cartoon "The Regulars". In one episode he is shown apologising for being so rude the night before: 'I'm sorry. You see, I was sober.'

"Amid the violence of Soho arguments he became a friend of Elizabeth Smart, the Canadian author of *By Grand Central Station I Sat Down and Wept*, a book about her lover George Barker, the poet, who became another friend. The poet John Heath-Stubbs, before he lost his sight, also took a shine to him.

"He defended John Deakin, the photographer, against the charge, put about by Daniel Farson, of being cruel to everyone. 'The only man John Deakin was unkind to was David Archer,' Mason asserted. David Archer, who ran a bookshop at a loss, was the man Deakin lived with.

"Mason's own closest friendship was with Marsh Dunbar, the widow of an admired art director at *The Economist*. He lodged with her at first in a fine house in Canonbury Square, Islington, where she was bringing up three sons. She had herself fallen into Soho after the War, knowing everyone. Though enthusiastically heterosexual, she lived with Mason until her death.

"In the days before licensing liberalisation, he resorted in the afternoon when pubs were closed to drinking clubs such as the Kismet, a damp basement with a smell that wits identified as 'failure'; it was known as The Iron Lung, and Death in the Afternoon. But his favourite resort remained the Colony.

"His successful career as a foreign correspondent ended one day when he was found asleep under his desk at ITN, drunk. It was something of a low point. A fire at the flat in Berwick Street, Soho, that he was then sharing with Marsh Dunbar sent them, fleeing bills, to a run-down council tower-block on the Isle of Dogs.

"Graham Mason cooked Mediterranean food well, liked Piero della Francesca and Fidelio, choral evensong on the Third Programme and fireworks. After Marsh Dunbar's death in 2001, with almost all his friends dead, he sat imprisoned by emphysema in his flat, with a cylinder of oxygen by his armchair and bottles of white wine by his elbow, looking out over the Thames, still very angry."

INBRIEF

DECEMBER 17, 1988
POISON OUTBREAK IS 'WORST EVER'
By David Fletcher, Health Services Correspondent
Mrs Edwina Currie resigned yesterday as junior Health Minister as the Government announced that it would be introducing a multi-million pound scheme to buy up surplus eggs to avert bankruptcies in the poultry industry devastated by her remark that most egg production was infected with salmonella.

But Mrs Currie was right to say that egg production in Britain is infected with salmonella, Dr Richard Lacey, Professor of Clinical Biology at Leeds University, said yesterday. He said the country was experiencing the worst-ever outbreak of salmonella.

"Mrs Currie has been made a scapegoat by the egg producers, by the Ministry of Agriculture and by all those trying to find someone to blame. It won't work because it does not solve the problem – the salmonella is still there."

He said salmonella was present in the internal organs of chickens and in their feed and the infection found its way into some eggs. "We have got to sample all the flocks to see how many are infected and slaughter those that are. Then we have to sterilise the hen-huts and sterilise their feed to make sure the disease is not recycled.

"There are 300 cases reported each week and most of these will be from eggs. We know there is a very large amount of under-reporting of cases, so the real number of people involved is about 3,000 cases a week. That means 150,000 people a year are getting salmonella food poisoning from eggs."

CHANGES IN A REIGN

The Queen who helped us over the dead years

In 2003, the historian Sir John Keegan, the Telegraph's defence editor, pinpointed some of the losses and gains of half a century

How has Britain changed in the 50 years since the Queen came to the throne? Has the Queen herself changed? The questions are not unconnected. Deny it though anti-monarchists do, the personality of the Queen permeates British life. A fascinating discovery of a social survey some years ago was that many of her subjects have recurrent dreams about meeting the Queen and holding conversations with her.

In their waking hours, of course, the British recognise that such encounters are fantasies. The Queen does not hold intimate conversations with her subjects, perhaps with no one at all except her husband. It is part of the royal mystique that the sovereign is intimate with no one outside her immediate family. This sovereign is notable for her reserve. The British do not like her any the less for that. Rather the contrary. Reserve, if obviously accompanied by integrity and the ethic of public duty, continues to be a quality that the British admire. The Queen qualifies on all those counts. She personifies the sort of human being the nation still thinks is ideally British – upright, moral, impartial, fair, patriotic, public-spirited.

It is true that the Queen is rich, immeasurably richer than almost any of her subjects, absolutely detached from the day-to-day financial concerns that afflict the rest of us and surrounded by the trappings of huge wealth – castles, carriages, footmen, Old Masters. On the other hand, she does not seem to care. If detached from financial anxiety, she is equally detached from the habits of the international monied class. She does not go to the south of France, or go shopping, or go skiing. She does not give parties, except as a public duty. She notoriously does not spend money on clothes.

If asked how the Queen enjoys herself, most of her subjects, after a little thought, would say she puts on her wellies and takes the dogs for a walk. It is true that she likes going to the races. Millions of her subjects also like going to the races and even more of them know elderly, grey-haired ladies who like nothing better than taking the dogs for a walk.

Dream of her as they may, while the British do not know the Queen in any corporeal sense, they all know women like her. They are women, on the whole, whom they admire as grandmothers, heads of families, animal-lovers, members of the WI or the Townswomen's Guild, school governors, parish councillors. They are a bit stuffy, worry about what they read in the papers and perhaps think Britain was a better place when they started out in life.

Yet does the Queen think that the Britain of 1952 was a better place – or, more pertinently, should she? The memories of those who grew up with her – I was born eight years later than she, in 1934 – are likely to be mixed. Materially, the Britain of the time of her father's death and her coronation remains, in my mind, a dreary place. London, my home city, was still terribly knocked about by the Luftwaffe. There were huge areas of bomb damage and a universal absence of paint. Everything looked run-down, including the people. Rationing was still in force. In my first term as an Oxford undergraduate – a member of a very privileged and tiny minority – I had to take scraps of butter to hall for breakfast. I remember pasty faces in bus queues, drab clothes.

As the product of a single-sex school, I was looking forward to meeting girls at Oxford. Those on parade at my first lecture seemed the product of a practical joke – shapeless skirts, even more shapeless tops, rag-doll haircuts. "The aim," said Maureen Cleave, later a very glamorous *Evening Standard* journalist, "was to look 35. That was what our mothers wanted." Fifty-five, I would have said. I did not have a girlfriend during my Oxford years.

On the other hand, spiritually there was hope in the air. Whatever one's political inclination – like most undergraduates of that time, I thought belonging to a political club boring, even stupid – there was general approval of the Attlee

In 1952 at the beginning of the Queen's reign 'everything looked run-down, including the people. Rationing was still in force.' For some it was a tray at the first Lyons Teashop, at Piccadilly (right), which opened in 1953. For others it was a choice from the menu and the carving trolley at the Café Royal (below)

Two undergraduates take it easy in a punt on the River Cherwell after traditional May morning festivities in 1952. Oxford undergraduates of the 1950s, an undoubted elite, 'approved of almost every element of the Attlee programme'

government's programme. Attlee's second Labour administration had been defeated at the polls, but the return of Churchill aroused little enthusiasm, the prospect of Eden's succession even less.

The Oxford undergraduates of the 1950s, with their Cambridge contemporaries an undoubted national elite, formed a tiny proportion of the school-leaving population but approved of almost every element of the Attlee programme: full employment, of course; the National Health Service, emphatically so; social welfare; social housing; equal educational opportunity for all able to pass the tests (most of us were at Oxford thanks to that criterion); above all, the idea of equal opportunity in every walk of life.

Like many of the generation of the Queen's accession, I look back on the 1950s as a golden age of hope and good feeling. Yet I suspect I see it through rose-tinted spectacles. The degree of snobbery would be intolerable today. Because of National Service, which obliged all fit young males to serve, usually in the Army, the ideal of universal patriotic duty was strong.

The divisions between those judged suitable to be

trained as officers and those judged not was equally strong also. It persisted into the university years. Worse, those who had been accepted into the smart regiments – Guards, Cavalry – brought with them an aura of exclusiveness. Everyone in my college knew where National Service had placed their fellow undergraduates in the pecking order, which was as much social as military. It was reinforced by school backgrounds. Oxford and Cambridge in the 1950s were largely grammar-school universities, far less "elitist" than today. Socially, however, the public schools still dominated.

What was true of the small stage was true of the world beyond. Society remained divided into officers and other ranks, with the difference that the Armed Forces were not as admired as they are today. Almost everyone had served, including the women of the war years, but there was no desire to perpetuate the "them and us" of service life. On the contrary, "us" wanted what they believed they had fought for: a fairer, better-paid, more secure way of life. Attlee had made the foundations: free hospitals and visits to the doctor, employment in industries – coal, steel, transport – owned by the state, a cushion against unemployment, the beginnings of comprehensive welfare.

Yet there was a paradox. The Attlee government, in its way, was officer class. Welfare came from on high, dispensed as if by Lord Bountiful. Despite the population of Old Labour by genuine proletarians, Ernie Bevin foremost, the Attlee government's ethos derived from his own – public school, officer class. In a sense, it was colonial, its urge being that of the late imperial class to introduce a subject people to the benefits of enlightened administration.

That was not surprising since many of the Labour leaders had a background in imperial service. They knew the leaders of the Empire's independence movements, and were committed to granting them freedom, India first. The less evolved colonies could wait; Attlee's government was as strongly paternalist abroad as it was unconsciously at home. Yet there was little opposition to its policies of decolonisation. As Kipling had suspected, popular imperialism had shallow roots and, when the time came to say farewell to palm and pine, there were few regrets.

In this the Queen differed from her subjects, as she continues to do. Never empress of India, she became head of the Commonwealth with great enthusiasm, travelled in it widely and grew closely acquainted with its leaders, who deeply appreciated her attention. The British remained indifferent, believing that the imperial episode was over. They scarcely noticed the beginnings of immigration from the ex-empire. When they did, they displayed a remarkable impassivity. In 1952 Britain was a completely white country, with no non-Christian minorities, apart from the Jews. Its good-natured acceptance of several million cultural outsiders is one of the most remarkable features of its post-war life.

The British had much else to think about, particularly what Whitehall chose to discuss as "decline" – in international standing and in relative prosperity. Attlee's government had continued the dissipation of national wealth begun during the war, had borrowed from America and had also unleashed expectations, particularly for investment in social programmes, that it could not sustain.

Neither could any of its successor governments. Election after election returned parliaments – Labour and Conservative alternately – that did not know what to do. The period 1955 to 1979 must be reckoned one of the worst in Britain's political life, characterised by Cabinet ineffectuality and the intrusion into public affairs of unelected powers, particularly the large unions of the unskilled.

The dead years are today better remembered than the post-war time of hope, though the two periods are intrinsically connected. Much happened that was important, particularly the waging of the Cold War, but foreign policy, except through CND, impinged little on public consciousness. Cultural change did, the permissiveness of the 1960s decisively altering behaviour and outlook for good and ill. It deeply undermined the "officers" and "others" basis of society, to Britain's benefit, but it also weakened the stability of family life and the

solidarity of old communities, first disturbed by the upheaval and destruction of the war.

It also set in train the movement of public admiration from one sort of icon to another, from those supplied by traditional hierarchy – the Royal Family foremost – to those supplied by defiance of convention. The Beatles, superficially unconventional, were the first such celebrities, subsequently to be replaced with bewildering frequency by an insatiable media appetite for sensation, decreasingly arresting.

Yet beneath the pall of the dead years, the public life of the nation survived. Exasperation became the strongest mood, expressed eventually in the election of a government that at last did seem to know what to do. In a little over 10 years, Margaret Thatcher found ways both to pay for the cherished public programmes of 1945–51, largely by forcing denationalised industries back into profit, and to compel the unions that fed on them to behave themselves. It was an extraordinary exercise both of political intelligence and political will.

It is today not much appreciated. Blairism is a strange reversion, imputing to the Tory years immediately preceding it the inegalitarian faults that Attlee largely cured. Social exclusiveness was real in the 1940s, as was lack of opportunity. Both have almost disappeared in my lifetime. Mediocre comprehensives are palaces of learning compared with the secondary moderns of 50 years ago. Hospitals – I am a survivor of old-style long-stay healthcare – are five-star hotels. As far as life in general is concerned, my generation would say that today anybody can achieve anything, if they are prepared to try.

Many are prepared to try and do achieve. Something, however, has been lost. My long illness in youth exposed me to an unusual experience for a member of the middle class – immersion for three years in a completely working-class environment. Most of my fellow patients in the orthopaedic hospital where I spent 1947–50 were young former servicemen from inner London, the Elephant, the Borough, the Old Kent Road. Many had contracted orthopaedic TB, rather fewer had survived polio. It is an index of how life has changed that polio has disappeared and orthopaedic TB is scarcely seen. Indeed, the open-air hospital in which we were treated has been knocked down as redundant and the site is occupied by a private housing estate.

All that is absolutely to the good. Yet I look back to those three years with considerable nostalgia. The spirit of my fellow patients was admirable. They would not have known what "dependency" meant and would have despised it if they did. Wracked with ghastly disabilities as they were, their one thought was to get better so that they could return to work. They looked forward, literally, to standing on their own feet again. They did not expect state support nor seek it. Moreover, they had standards and values.

There was a curious respect for education, though few had any, and a habit of good manners. Because

Jamaican immigrants arrive at Victoria Station in May 1956. 'Britain's good-natured acceptance of several million cultural outsiders is one of the most remarkable features of its post-war life'

Mrs Thurtell, a cleaner, scrubs the entrance to Boots all-night chemist's at Piccadilly Circus in 1953. 'Social exclusiveness was real in the 1940s, as was lack of opportunity. Both have almost disappeared'

we were nursed by young unmarried women, public opinion on the ward banned both bad language and sexual innuendo. Anyone who broke the rules was denounced as "ignorant", the ultimate condemnation.

That self reliance and highly moral working-class culture has been undermined in my lifetime by an artificial culture, propagated by a new university-educated class, of welfare entitlement and "social inclusion". Social inclusion forbids overt disapproval of much behaviour by which my fellow patients would have been outraged and tolerates habits of selfishness and fecklessness alien to their outlook.

It is fostered, of course, by the modern media which, by a hypocritical combination of denunciation and celebration, relentlessly propagate bad behaviour, particularly by portraying it on television. Indeed there is a curious community of interest between many media people and others in the so-called caring professions, based on their exposure during education and training to believe in the "unfairness" of the "system", an outlook that has come to be called political correctness.

It says a great deal for the fundamental common sense of the British that so many of them retain a healthy scepticism about political correctness. One reason why the Queen seems to grow in popularity, as her reception during her tour of her kingdom demonstrates, is that there is nothing politically correct about her. In one sense, political correctness is simply politeness, tolerance and kindness, and those qualities the Queen has in abundance. For the

sillier side of political correctness, the refusal to distinguish between good and evil or truth and falsehood, she patently has no time at all. She is a deeply devout Christian, and there is steel in her character. Given the chance, exercised by her sweet-natured and utterly upright father during the Second World War, to exert moral leadership, who can doubt that she would take it?

Indeed she has already done so. A principal weakness of Blairism is that, while the Prime Minister exemplifies in his personal life the Christian beliefs, particularly about the sanctity of marriage, which he is known to hold, he lacks the confidence to state his creed in plain language. The Queen does not. Indeed, her Christmas broadcasts become evermore explicit expressions of the Christian message. Her award of the Order of Merit to Cardinal Hume just before his death, beside giving joy to her Catholic subjects, also indicated her recognition of the importance of simple goodness in human beings.

Can she go further? As she has travelled around Britain these past months, she must have noticed how decrepit many of our towns still look, 60 years after the war. The Queen is not notable as a leader of taste but she has greatly beautified Buckingham Palace by building a new gallery for the public. Perhaps in her declining years she will inaugurate a new era of royal architectural patronage. Most of Europe's heritage is owed to monarchs. What a conclusion to her reign the undertaking of a new heritage townscape would be.

INBRIEF

OCTOBER 9, 1965

GPO 'SYMBOL OF OUR PRIDE' Britain's tallest building, the Post Office tower in London, was officially opened yesterday by the Prime Minister. It would be, he said, a new symbol of pride in the country's scientific and technological achievements.

He went up nearly to the top of the 620ft structure to see the view. Although the public restaurant from which he looked at London in the fog is not due to be completed until next March, it was revolving at two revolutions an hour, as it will do for diners.

Mr Wedgwood Benn, Post-Master General, said at the ceremony that the tower, lean, practical and futuristic, epitomised the technical and architectural skill of the new age. "This new, bigger Big Ben captures the spirit of our time, dwarfing monuments of earlier days."

THE STUFF OF FAIRYTALES

The Princess of Wales as a truly tragic heroine

The description of Diana on her wedding day as 'a perfect princess and future queen' proved an increasingly poignant irony

Charles and Diana with Prince William, born in June 1982. 'Beyond anything,' the Telegraph thought, 'her children are the lasting good she has left behind'

The wedding day of the Prince of Wales and Lady Diana Spencer, on July 29, 1981, was crowded with hostages to fortune. In retrospect the dramatic irony was extraordinary. The bride, so the *Telegraph* reporter remarked next day in his news piece, "by broad and affectionate acclaim, makes a perfect princess and future queen".

The couple were married in St Paul's between "the rich pageantry of the carriage processions" through the sunshine. The crowds were "delighted most when Prince and Princess of Wales obliged with a kiss on the balcony of Buckingham Palace". Even "the black youth of Brixton demonstrated its affection for the monarchy with a special 'peace dance', on the front line of recent vicious rioting".

In sum, "all these things, relayed by television to 700 million people, made a magical spectacle which, in the words of the Archbishop of Canterbury, Dr Runcie, was the 'stuff of which fairytales are made'." Seldom could a sermon have contained such unwittingly doom-laden words.

"The Spencer family has through the centuries fought for King and Country," said the Princess's ailing father, Earl Spencer. "Diana will be vowing to help her country for the rest of her life. She will be following in the traditions of her ancestors, and she will have at her side the man she loves."

On December 8, 1992 their separation was announced. "There were gasps of disbelief from MPs," reported the *Telegraph*, "when Mr Major [the Prime Minister] said that 'there was no reason why the Princess of Wales should not be crowned Queen in due course'."

Argument on the question was to prove pointless. On July 12, 1996, after months of legal negotiation, they were divorced. "Despite the obvious sadness of a divorce," Lambeth Palace said, "the Archbishop of Canterbury, Dr George Carey, hopes this settlement will help ease the burden of past problems and enable all concerned to find renewed life and hope for the future." It was a vain hope.

Diana, Princess of Wales, as she was now styled, died with her lover Dodi Fayed in a motor accident in Paris on August 31, 1997. As with Kennedy's assassination, everyone remembers where they were when they heard the news. Her death did not stop waves of ever more baroque revelations flooding the press.

"In the 16 years left to her after her marriage to the heir to the throne, her story changed from one of a fairytale princess into that of a woman who felt a captive of circumstances and made increasingly desperate attempts to escape unhappiness," the *Telegraph* obituary judged on the day after her death, before an epidemic of mourning broke out.

"Diana, Princess of Wales had been driven by a tragic flaw into yet another love affair, which ended, not through her fault, but through the cruel visitation of nemesis, in her death. If she had been made unhappy by her marriage, she had found nothing to replace it; if she found fault with the way of life of the Royal Family, her own life was often taken up with trivia. In her good causes, yes, she discovered values with a sure foundation. Among all the culs-de-sac, her charity and, beyond anything, her children are the lasting good she has left behind."

From the **Telegraph**

A.N. Wilson on Plum Tart, Edna the Cruel and other prelates

June 17, 2003

The Bishop Elect of Reading, the Rev Jeffrey John, has attracted a lot of notice, particularly in this newspaper. The reason is that he has been brave enough to admit that he is a homosexual. He lives with his friend, but tells us that he will in future be celibate.

I was asked recently whether I had been at the Oxford theological college St Stephen's House at the same time as he was.

As it happens, I think I'm a bit older than Dr John. In the mists of time, I remember meeting him, and I think he was chaplain of Magdalen College, Oxford. He asked me to give a talk to the undergraduates, and I seem to recollect a fairly earnest evening discussing religion and literature. He is certainly not the wild gay revolutionary depicted in the media.

St Stephen's House is a High Church theological college in Oxford. I lasted only a year. At the end of this period, it had become clear to me that, fascinated as I was (and still am) by theology and religion, I did not have sufficient faith to be a priest and I did not have a vocation.

Every now and then, however, I come across one of my fellow-collegians, now a priest.

At Staggers (as St Stephen's was known), they gave most of the students "names in religion". This meant that the young men called one another by girls' names. Young homosexuals of my acquaintance aren't camp in this way any more. That whole Colony Room, Francis Bacon tradition of calling one another a silly bitch has rather gone out, to be replaced by earnestness of one kind or another.

I never found out whether I had a "name in religion". When I went to the college, I was a married man. I was treated with great tolerance, but I think it might have been thought to be bad form to call me Alice Wilson or Anthea Wilson.

I left and, in the subsequent 30 years, I have led what has been in many ways a selfish and silly life. The others – Tawdry Audrey, Bobo, Maud, Pearl – have been devotedly unselfish, good people, who have given their whole lives to Christ and to the service of those less fortunate than themselves.

Not long ago, I went to a town in the North to give a reading in a bookshop. At the end, a priest came up to speak to me. It was Plum Tart. Such a pretty, clever boy 30 years ago. Ever since, he has given his learned, pious good life to the service of the Church.

As often happens when I meet one of my fellow-collegians, I momentarily forget his real name. One finds oneself going into a room and meeting an archdeacon, and becoming completely tongue-tied. One can hardly say: "Hello, Gladys." All one can remember, when seeing the portly, distinguished form of some Anglican cleric, is an evening that began with Solemn Benediction and clouds of incense, followed by a boozy dinner, followed, probably, by disco dancing in a gay club.

St Stephen's House when I was there was a Firbankian madhouse. The principal, a saintly man called Norah, made the fatal mistake of allowing the students to make their confessions to him. If you confess your sins to a priest, he is bound to secrecy. He cannot act upon what he has heard.

Poor Norah, a celibate mystic, was therefore aware of the fact that, among his little flock of 45 young men, there were some very disturbed souls, and a few who needed to kick their heels before settling down to a life of complete self-abnegation.

Norah was sacked – and ended her life as a parish priest in Eastbourne. David Hope, now Archbishop of York, was brought in to sort the place out, and by then I had fled and become a schoolmaster.

Medical students are especially raucous, drunken, randy people because, at a shockingly young age, they are being confronted with life and death. So, too, are trainee priests.

When, last year in the northern bookshop, I had parted from Plum Tart, I went out, and like Peter in the Gospels, I wept bitterly.

My life had been supposedly a success. I had written books, and newspaper articles. I had made, by the standards of an Anglican clergyman, lots of money. As I had grown older, my bisexuality had disappeared and I had become wholly heterosexual and agnostic.

Maybe my friend Colin Haycraft was right to say that religion is for women and for queers. When I look back on my years as a Staggers Bag (a student at St Stephen's) with Bobo, Plum Tart, Tawdry Audrey and the rest, I think of a time that was, first, hilariously funny and second, deeply serious. Apart from the handful of psychopaths, saddoes who kept being arrested in public lavatories, and so on, they were in fact an extraordinarily dedicated group of men.

I have lost my religion – their religion – but I do not feel that this is a good thing. I am aware that the spiritual life of England is most alive in its national church, and that the best priests in that Church are people who, for a few silly but highly amusing years of their youth, were known as Pearl and Gladys and Edna the Cruel (that was the nickname for David Hope).

These are men who have been prepared to devote their whole lives to working in poor parishes, visiting the sick, the housebound, the lonely, the prisoners and the captives. They believe in, and live, the Gospel of Christ. They think that God became a poor man to carry our sins. Many of them, but not all, carry with them the strange burden of being homosexual.

Apparently, we are still not grown-up enough in England to believe that this is rather marvellous. I wept after meeting Plum Tart, because I thought, and think, that his life has been so much more useful, so much better in every way than my own. I am sure the same is true of the Bishop Elect of Reading, and of many of these characters who are so regularly held up for ridicule in this newspaper.

If I were as brave or as unselfish as they are, I should be proud of myself.

A MIRACLE

The woman who was cured by Mother Teresa

Mick Brown journeyed to a simple Indian village to ask Monika Besra about her inexplicable healing by a reputed saint

As if to reflect the spirit of simplicity and self-denial in which she led her life, the tomb of Mother Teresa is strikingly austere. It stands at one end of a large and otherwise empty room on the ground floor of the Mother House – the small convent of her order, the Missionaries of Charity (MoC), where she lived for almost 50 years until her death in 1997. A bulking concrete rectangle, the tomb is surmounted by a small statue of the Madonna and Child, the words "Peace Be With You" picked out in blossoms and seeds across its surface. Nearby stands a large hardboard cutout of Christ on the cross, hung with a plaque which reads "I thirst". Around the wall, in the artless manner of schoolwork displayed in a classroom, is a history in words and pictures, chronicling Mother Teresa's life from her childhood in Skopje, in what is now Macedonia, to her death in Calcutta at the age of 87.

The Mother House, a bleak, grey, pockmarked building, stands on a noisy and congested road in the centre of Calcutta, flanked by scrap-metal workshops and wreathed in traffic fumes. The constant stream of people who come to kneel at the tomb are obliged to focus their prayers amid the constant thunder of traffic passing by the window outside.

It was here, in June 1999, that Monika Besra, an illiterate tribal woman from West Bengal, came to pray. Besra had a particular reason for visiting Mother Teresa's tomb. Nine months earlier she had been suffering from an enlarged tumour which threatened to kill her. After prayers from two sisters of the Missionaries of Charity, the tumour vanished. Besra, it was said, owed her life to a miracle.

In normal circumstances – if this can be said to be a normal circumstance – Besra's recovery would have been an occasion for private rejoicing, contemplation and nothing more. Yet it has come to assume a monumental importance for millions of Roman Catholics around the world. In October, in high ceremony at the Vatican, the Pope will beatify Mother Teresa, declaring her as "a blessed"; it is the first step towards the late nun being admitted to the pantheon of Catholic saints – as Saint Teresa of

Monika Besra (right) photographed by Raghu Rai in 2003, after her cure. 'I had taken lots of medicines,' she said, 'but I was not cured. But when the Sisters prayed, in the morning the tumour was not there.'

Calcutta. Since 1999 an assortment of committees and tribunals have been carefully sifting the evidence of Mother Teresa's life to see whether it conforms to the standards of "heroic Christian virtue" necessary for her to be declared a saint. Central to that process has been the requirement to prove that she has been responsible for at least one "intercessory" miracle since her death. The healing of Monika Besra, it is claimed, is that miracle.

Born Agnes Gonxha Bojaxhiu in Skopje to Albanian parents, Mother Teresa made her decision to become a nun at the age of 18. She joined the Loreto Sisters and travelled to Calcutta, where she taught in a convent school. In 1948, answering what she described as a "call by God", she founded the Missionaries of Charity in two rooms in a Calcutta side street, its purpose to minister to "the poorest of the poor". Since then, the order has grown to some 600 missions in 130 countries. It runs orphanages, clinics, homes and refuges for the dying, the sick, the handicapped and the insane. As head of the order, Mother Teresa became a figure on the global stage, and, for many, a byword for selfless service to others – an exemplar of the saintly life.

But in the latter stages of her life she also became an increasingly controversial figure. She was accused of currying favour with the rich and powerful, of exaggerating the good works of her organisation, of being less an angel of mercy than a fundamentalist Catholic evangelist.

She was regarded with particular ambivalence in Calcutta, the city with which she became synonymous. The state funeral accorded her on her death in 1997, and the tens of thousands of people – most of them poor and dispossessed – who queued to pay their respects, were measures of the esteem in which she was held by the highest and the lowest. Yet immediately afterwards, Calcutta's English-language daily newspaper, the *Telegraph*, which had supported her unstintingly throughout her life, gave vent to a simmering resentment, arguing that Calcutta "had little reason to be grateful" to Mother Teresa, and that it was she who owed a debt to the city. "It was the misery of Calcutta that built up and sustained her reputation... No other city in the world would offer up its poor and its dying to be stepping-stones in a relentless ascent to sainthood."

Mother Teresa's beatification will be the fastest in the history of the Catholic Church. Under canon law laid down since the Middle Ages, five years must pass between a candidate's death and the start of the beatification procedure. But such was the clamour for Mother Teresa's recognition that in 1999 – just two years after her death – the Pope waived the five-year rule. With this move he was said to be underlining the belief of many in the Church who regarded Mother Teresa as a saint in her own lifetime.

Her cause is also said to be particularly close to the Pope's own heart, her stern adherence to conservative Catholic values chiming closely with his own views. The beatification ceremony will coincide with the 25th anniversary of his own

election as Pope, and he is said to have expressed a wish for her to be canonised before he dies.

Beatification, the first stage of the canonisation process, is really a formal permission for the individual to be venerated locally, in the church with which they were associated – in Mother Teresa's case, Calcutta. Canonisation makes this veneration "universal and obligatory"; it is a way of the Church saying that here is a person who should be revered because they are believed to be next to God.

The making of saints dates from the early days of Christianity, when the faithful prayed at the tombs of the Christian martyrs for their divine intercession. In the Middle Ages the worship, and making, of saints was entirely local; it required only a dozen or so people to supplicate their bishop for a person to be canonised. Popular fervour and the laxity of bishops in examining the supposed virtues and miracles of candidates led to a proliferation of questionable canonisations. This resulted in the Church instituting a more formal procedure through its general councils. By the 17th century it had been brought entirely under the control of the Pope.

Nowadays, saint-making is a process of tortuous complexity and thoroughness. Firstly, a representative from the local diocese must apply to Rome for permission to begin the beatification gathered by the postulator, or proposer, of the Cause, to demonstrate that the candidate has led a life embodying the Christian virtues of humility, simplicity and service to others. It must also be demonstrated that they have performed at least one miracle by divine intercession since their death. The Vatican describes a miracle as an intervention of God that goes above and beyond the laws of nature – usually a cure which is deemed to be "scientifically inexplicable". (A second miracle is required after beatification before the person can be canonised.)

This body of evidence, or *positio*, is then passed to the Vatican and the Pro Causis Sanctorum, or Congregation for the Causes of the Saints (made up of nine theologians), which since 1558 has examined the cases of would-be canonisations. A separate medical committee evaluates the evidence for the claimed miracle. Only after these bodies have ruled on the evidence does the Pope "pray to God for guidance" and give his final approval.

The time period between beatification and canonisation depends on when an alleged miracle appears. In the case of Padre Pio, the Capuchin monk who died in 1968 and was canonised in 2001, it took only two years. But there are thousands of candidates who have been beatified over the centuries who have never gone on to be canonised – at least not yet.

The present Pope has demonstrated a remarkable enthusiasm for making saints. Since his election in 1975 he has created 473 saints (from the 12th-century Latvian Meinardo to Josemaría Escrivá who died in 1975) and 1,310 "blesseds" – more than all his 20th-century predecessors put together, leading to the Vatican being dubbed "the Saint factory". This enthusiasm seems to be underpinned as much by

AUGUST 30, 1967
PROVOKING VIOLENCE
Walter Farr, Diplomatic Staff
The attack by Chinese diplomats on police and bystanders in front of the Chinese Mission in London yesterday was described by the Foreign Office last night as a deliberate attempt by China to provoke violence.

A Foreign Office statement issued on the orders of Mr Brown, Foreign Secretary, said the Chinese diplomats provoked "today's deplorable incident" in order to try to justify the action which the Chinese have taken against the British Mission in Peking.

In the Peking attack, the British Mission was burnt, the home of Mr Hopson, the Chargé d'Affaires, looted and members of the Mission were beaten up.

A boy carrying a baby begging in Calcutta

pragmatism as piety. With the Catholic Church in crisis, the Pope has been eager to promote good examples of the holy life, and to bolster wavering faith by canonising figures from countries where saints have traditionally been thin on the ground.

But he has incurred criticism not only for the number of candidates, but also for some of his choices, notably the founder of the controversial Catholic organisation Opus Dei, Escrivá – who, until Mother Teresa, held the record for the fastest beatification in history, 17 years after his death – and the 19th-century Pope Pius IX, who was declared a "blessed" in September 2000, an event described by the Catholic newspaper the *Tablet* as "a beatification too far".

The proposer of the Mother Teresa Cause is a 46-year-old Canadian priest, Father Brian Kolodiejchuk. He first met Mother Teresa in Rome in 1977, when his sister was entering the novitiate for the Missionaries of Charity. "After the ceremony, Mother said, 'I want to pin a cross on you, too.' She invited me to join the Brothers (the male order of the MoC), so I did." He went on to found a priest branch of the MoC in the Bronx, New York, before being asked by the Diocese of Calcutta to act as proposer for Mother Teresa's Cause. In 1999 he took up residence in Calcutta and began the task of assembling evidence.

During the next two years he interviewed 113 witnesses from all over the world (more than double the number usually questioned for a beatification: "We didn't want to just do minimalist," he explains). They included people who had worked with Mother Teresa all her life; church and civic leaders; patients from her homes; Hindus, Muslims, her long-standing next-door neighbour. Thirty-three were from the Missionaries of Charity. Each was asked to reply to a list of 263 questions about her life, and the evidence was then divided into three basic sections: a biography; a section on "Reputation of Holiness"; and an evaluation of her adherence to the Virtues. The Virtues are considered one by one: faith, hope and charity; prudence, justice, courage, temperance and humility; along with the three vows of the religious life, chastity, poverty and obedience.

"The person has to be heroic in all these virtues," says Father Kolodiejchuk. "It's not enough to be good in one and average in the others. And one of the signs is that a person can combine and live by virtues that seem to be contrary – courage and meekness, for example."

Under Vatican rules, Father Kolodiejchuk was obliged to seek evidence from those antagonistic to Mother Teresa. Among the "hostile witnesses" was the journalist and broadcaster Christopher Hitchens, who in his 1995 book and television film *The Missionary Position* famously attacked Mother Teresa as a hypocrite who had no compunction about accepting "dirty money" from the likes of the Haitian dictator Papa Doc Duvalier and the financier Charles Keating, and who allowed a cult of celebrity to accrue around herself which she did little to dispel. Hitchens gave evidence to the

Archdiocese in Washington, DC, where he lives.

"We didn't have to prove that she was perfect or never made a mistake," says Father Kolodiejchuk. "If there was anything in the evidence to suggest she was not of heroic virtue, we certainly would have presented it. But at the same time we had to decide what she really did, because sometimes the criticisms were not based on the truth."

None the less, if he had failed to present a case for beatification, he admitted, "we'd have had a lot of explaining to do".

In August 2001, 35,000 pages of evidence, in 76 documents, was submitted to Rome for consideration by the Congregation for the Causes of the Saints. Then, last September, they delivered their verdict. It was unanimous. Only one final hurdle remained for the beatification: the evidence for an intercessory miracle.

Early in 1999, Sister Nirmala, Mother Teresa's successor as the head of the MoC, had circulated a letter to all the order's homes and offices asking for any reported cases of "divine intercession" on the part of Mother Teresa. In April 1999, news of a miracle duly appeared. Monika Besra, a 30-year-old tribal woman and the mother of five children, had been a patient in an MoC home in the town of Patiram, West Bengal, suffering from a large ovarian tumour.

On September 5, 1998, the first anniversary of Mother Teresa's death, two sisters at the home had reportedly placed on the tumour a medallion which had touched the body of Mother Teresa, and offered prayers for Besra's life. Eight hours later, the tumour had vanished. It was this story that Father Kolodiejchuk presented as evidence of divine intercession, and which was ratified as a miracle by the Pope last December.

I had read accounts of the miracle of Monika Besra. Inevitably, it was shrouded in controversy. The Indian press, rationalist by disposition, had proved particularly hostile. Doctors who had treated her were quoted as saying there was a medical explanation. There were allegations that Besra, an illiterate and simple woman, had been swayed by the Church to say her cure was a miracle. Even her husband, Seiku, a farmer, was said to believe her cure was due to medical, rather than miraculous, intervention.

Besra lives some 200 miles north of Calcutta, near to the town of Malda. Before setting out to meet her, I went to see the former Archbishop of Calcutta, Henry D'Souza. It had been his responsibility to make the first formal application to Rome seeking permission to begin the beatification process, and to oversee the procedure to its conclusion. Since Mother Teresa's death, he told me, Father Kolodiejchuk had received almost 900 reports of "graces and favours" attributed to Mother Teresa.

Most were answered prayers for good fortune in a new job or a school exam. Some were cures that could have been psychosomatic or coincidental – somebody with back pain praying to a picture of

INBRIEF

FEBRUARY 19, 1976
Iceland is expected to announce today that it has decided to break off diplomatic relations with Britain because of the cod war over the 200-mile fishing limit claimed by Reykjavik. Off Iceland yesterday the 920-ton gunboat Thor crashed into the side of the frigate Lowestoft, 2,380 tons. The Ministry of Defence accused the gunboat of "deliberately and without warning" ramming the frigate.

The Common Market Commission is to propose that the EEC should establish a joint 200-mile fishing limit. Each EEC nation would have a 12-mile coastal zone open only to its own fishermen.

Monika Besra: care from Mother Teresa's nuns

Mother Teresa and, the next morning, finding the pain had gone.

They finally settled on three putative miracles. One concerned a sister of the MoC in India who was paralysed from the waist down after a hernia operation. Two days after Mother Teresa's death, a friend of the nun had prayed before Mother Teresa's body and touched it with a piece of white cloth. This cloth was pinned to the paralysed body of the nun, and she was cured. The second concerned an eight-year-old girl in Palestine who was suffering from bone cancer, and who was said to have recovered after Mother Teresa appeared in her dreams and declared, "Child, you are cured."

Then there was Monika Besra. It was her case, Archbishop D'Souza said, that best fulfilled the necessary criteria: that the cure was organic and immediate; that it could not be explained by natural causes, and was irreversible; and that it took place through the intercession of Mother Teresa. The close proximity of the miracle to Calcutta seemed particularly convenient. Was this mere chance, I wondered, or perhaps Divine Providence – God making matters easier? I intended the question half in jest, but Archbishop D'Souza considered it seriously. "It could happen. Divine Providence works in so many ways. There must have been some particular plan of God in it, because this lady, Monika Besra, was by no means a Catholic or in any way connected with Mother Teresa or the Church. Whether Mother worked the miracle to give us a little local colour is a factor. But then somebody could say it seems too convenient; that we're trying to make a story out of it. But that is not the case. This is authentic."

In fact, the miracle of Monika Besra proved not to be so convenient after all. It took me the best part of 19 hours to reach the small village in West Bengal where she lives. The overnight train from Calcutta arrived in Malda at dawn. I hired a taxi and headed north, the Bengal countryside unfolding in a patchwork of fields and rice paddies. At a roadside stall we stopped to ask for directions. Besra's fame had evidently spread throughout the district – I needed only to mention her name for a man to step forward and point the way. Of course he had heard of the miracle, he said, and he believed it. Why? I asked. "Because it was in the newspapers. It must be true."

We turned off the main road, passing down an avenue of eucalyptus trees, then through a hamlet of mud huts, their walls painted white and yellow, and daubed with political slogans and the sickle and wheatsheaf – the symbol of the Communist party of India. The road became a track, and at last we reached Besra's village. Her husband, Seiku, a small man wrapped in a blue *dhoti*, was squatting outside their house in the shade. Monika, he explained, was not at home; she was at her sister's house, preparing for a family wedding. He would take us there, but first he had to wash. He led the way into their home – four low mud-built dwellings, with roofs of sloping tiles, enclosing an open courtyard. In the centre of the yard, under a thatched roof, was a cooking area, clay pots on a sill, a collection of stainless-steel pans drying in the sun. Four families lived here, Seiku explained, his own and his three brothers'.

Outside, I was approached by a villager. He wore a crucifix around his neck. I asked him, was Christianity the prevailing belief in the village? Some were Christian, he said; in the next village there were Muslims, but here most people prayed to Morol. Morol? He led the way to a small shrine, a rough pyramid of black clay, its flat top daubed with *kum kum*, red paste. The shrine, he explained, had been built by the headman, the Morol; it was here that villagers prayed to ward off evil. He, too, had prayed to Morol since childhood. "But then I lost my belief. I thought there was no saviour through Morol. That is why I converted."

Seiku emerged from his home and we got in the car. He pulled a small Mother Teresa medallion from his shirt and began to chant. It appeared he had not disowned the miracle after all. He is praying to Mother that the journey goes well, my interpreter said. "Since his wife was cured he prays any time and anywhere to Mother. He says that if he does not do this then evil will happen to him and everything will be destroyed – his family, his happiness and everything."

Buoyed by this utilitarian approach to faith, we passed out of the village, leaving behind the shrine to Morol, and pressed deeper into the countryside. Grey clouds were banking in the sky and now the first drops of rain began to fall on the windscreen. After an hour's drive we came to a tiny hamlet of neat, mud houses with thatched and corrugated iron roofs. Dressed in a vivid orange sari, Monika Besra came out of one of the houses. She was unusually tall for a tribal woman, graceful and composed, with an air of palpable serenity about her.

A crowd had gathered. Apparently unembarrassed by the attention, Besra led the way to the house of her sister Kanchan – almost identical to Besra's own. We sat on a camp-bed, under the eaves of a roof, the rain drumming above our heads. A hen pecked its way across the yard, trailed by a brood of chicks. I felt as if I had entered the Middle Ages, a universe away from the complexities of theological debate and Papal deliberation. Besra began to tell her story, speaking in a quiet, unhurried fashion, leaving no detail unmentioned.

In 1997, she said, she had fallen ill with fever, headache and vomiting. She had been given medicine, but it hadn't worked. She had visited doctors, been referred to hospitals, and diagnosed as suffering from TB meningitis. Treatment had been spasmodic, dependent on what her husband could afford. In May 1998, she was admitted to the MoC home in Patiram. It didn't cost anything. "The days were passing by," Besra said. "I was getting iller and iller." Until that point, she had never heard of Mother Teresa. By now she was experiencing acute pains in her stomach, and a swelling was beginning to appear. "I was almost senseless with the pain."

Besra's medical notes record that on May 30 she

INBRIEF

DECEMBER 22, 1965
RANDOM DRINK TEST FOR DRIVERS
John Langley, Daily Telegraph Motoring Correspondent
Mobile police will have powers to carry out random roadside checks with new breath-testing equipment to detect drivers who have been drinking, under the Government's forthcoming Road Safety Bill.
The Bill will prescribe an alcohol concentration of 80 milligrams per 100 millilitres of blood as the level above which it will be an offence to drive. Motorists stopped in the roadside checks will be asked to breathe into a rubber mouthpiece through a tube of chemicals into a plastic bag. If a colour change in the tube (from yellow to green) indicates that blood-alcohol is "over the line" the driver will have to go to a police station for a blood or urine test. Penalties for exceeding the 80mg level will be similar to the existing punishments for drunken driving.
Sir Edward Wayne, representing the BMA, said it was impossible to give precise figures of the amount of drink needed to give an 80mg blood-alcohol level. It could be achieved by about four or five single whiskies or two to two-and-a-half pints of beer, taken rapidly. In social drinking, such as in a public house or at a dinner, it would be nearer eight whiskies or four pints of beer.
I tried one of the breath testers about two hours after having four half-pints of bitter and a sandwich and got a reading of around 30mg.

was taken by sisters of the MoC to Balurghat District Hospital, where she was admitted to the TB ward. She was discharged after one week. On June 11 she was readmitted to the emergency ward of the same hospital, under the care of Dr Tarun Biswas. Confirming the diagnosis of TB meningitis, he gave her a referral letter to two Calcutta hospitals. On June 15 she was discharged, with medication, and returned to the MoC home at Patiram. But over the next six weeks her condition continued to deteriorate.

"The headache and the fever subsided, but the tumour was getting bigger. It was getting so big, I looked as if I was five or six months pregnant. I couldn't stand up straight. I could not eat. I was vomiting everything – even water and medicine, everything. Like this the days were passing."

On August 6 she was once again taken to Balurghat hospital where she was examined by a gynaecologist, Dr Ranjan Mustaphi. In his notes, under provisional diagnosis he wrote: "Ovarian tumour? Pregnancy?" He recommended an ultrasound, which was performed two days later. This revealed a large cystic lesion in the lower abdomen and pelvis, suggestive of an ovarian cyst.

On August 31 Besra was examined by Dr Gautam Mukherjee at the North Bengal Medical College Hospital. He noted that she had been taking anti-TB drugs since June, and that the ovarian tumour was "a lump of about 24 weeks' [pregnancy] size". He described her general condition as "poor". It was decided to perform a laparotomy (to open the abdomen and investigate the cyst) but not for another three months. Besra's condition, it seemed, was too precarious for her to undergo even this straightforward procedure. "The doctors said I may not survive if I was administered anaesthetic at this time. I was told to go back to the Patiram home and come again after building myself up." She returned to Patiram, she said, expecting to die.

September 5 was the first anniversary of Mother Teresa's death. The day was observed by constant prayers in the chapel. At 8am Besra was asked by the Sisters if she would be joining the prayers. "At first I thought I was so ill and weak that I couldn't, but then I thought, no, I will go. Two attendants helped me to the chapel. And as soon as I entered I felt a beam of light coming out of the photograph of Mother. It came out from that photograph and into my heart. I became nervous. I became hot and I didn't feel well. I told the attendants to let me sit so I could rest, but I did not tell them what had happened." Eventually, she returned to her bed. "I was feeling different. I felt my mind had changed."

At 5pm two sisters of the order, Sister Ann Sevika and Sister M. Bartholomea, the Sister Superior, came to her bedside. "They said they wanted to tie a medallion with Mother's blessing around my waist. They did this with a black cord, and then they prayed, and I began to feel better. The sisters didn't know what had happened to me in the chapel; they just prayed over me because it was the anniversary of Mother's death."

Sister M. Bartholomea gave her own account of this moment to the inquiry. "We laid our hands on [Monika's] stomach... I prayed silently in my heart: 'Mother, today is your death anniversary. You love all the people in our homes. Now Monika is sick, so please heal her.' Then we prayed out loud nine Memorares, because Mother loved this prayer very much. I looked at Monika's face. It was looking relaxed and she was sleeping. We kept silence for a while and moved out to the convent."

"Until then I couldn't sleep because of the pain," Besra told me. "But that night I fell straight asleep. At around one o'clock I got up. I felt like I had to go to the toilet. And I found that the tumour was not there. It had been so big and so painful and it was absolutely not there.

"Holding the wall, I went to the loo. I came back and slept for a while. Then, again I woke up. I woke up Samira, the patient in the next bed. I told her what had happened in the chapel in the morning. I asked her, should I tell the Sisters about what has happened or not. Samira said it would be better to tell them in the morning. So that's what I did."

Besra paused. The rain had stopped. I noticed that she was wearing a small medallion around her neck. Was this the one that the Sisters had placed over the tumour, I asked. No, she replied. She had worn that one around her neck, but then the chain wore thin and she lost the medallion in a pond. This was another one. She shrugged.

Did she believe that she had received a miracle from Mother? She nodded. "I had taken lots of

Mother Teresa being driven to a meeting. Years earlier she had heard Christ saying to her: 'You did not die for souls. That is why you don't care what happens to them. You are afraid that you will lose your vocation.' She then founded her Missionaries of Charity to work with the poorest of the poor

medicines but I was not cured. But when the Sisters prayed, in the morning the tumour was not there. Then my belief grew towards Mother, that she had done this." And why did she think Mother chose her for this miracle? She paused, for so long that I thought she had not understood the question. At last she replied, "I cannot answer that."

Listening to Besra, I felt as if I was a witness to something strange and extraordinary. I had no doubt the story she told me was the truth. But was it a miracle? Her case quickly became a delicate political issue.

In support of Mother Teresa's Cause, Father Kolodiejchuk solicited copies of Besra's medical reports and statements from doctors involved in her treatment, and from other medical experts. She had been treated by government doctors. The state government of West Bengal is Communist. For doctors to be seen to be endorsing "miracles" was not necessarily a wise move.

"The problem emerged when it suddenly came out that [Besra's story] was accepted by the Pope as a miracle," Archbishop D'Souza told me. "Then the doctors were all asked, did you certify a miracle? How do you certify a miracle? And they all said, we didn't certify it as a miracle; we don't believe in God, we don't believe in miracles."

I telephoned Dr Biswas, who had prescribed Besra with drugs for TB meningitis in June 1998. Besra, he said, might claim that her cure was the result of a miracle. "But in our opinion it was due to the treatment of the tuberculosis, not miraculous belief."

But a tumour was diagnosed by ultrasound. Could TB cause such a tumour? "It may."

And could any treatment for TB lead to the disappearance of such a tumour in eight hours? "It is impossible."

So was he saying Besra was lying? "She is lying. We think this. It is not possible to believe in miracles."

However, Besra's description of the tumour's sudden disappearance is further borne out by Samira Tudu (her bedside neighbour), Martha Handsa (a helper) and Sister M. Rosamina, all of whom testified that they had seen her looking perfectly well on the morning of September 6, had felt her stomach, and could find no sign of a lump or tumour.

Sister Ann Sevika, who had prayed over Besra, told me how she, too, found her in good health the next morning. "That day, all the patients were talking, saying Monika is all right! I went to see her and she no more had great pain or sickness. Then I checked her stomach and it was normal, not hard like before, and there was no lump, there."

When I contacted Dr Mustaphi, who had initially diagnosed an ovarian tumour, he told me that he now thought the origin of the mass was tuberculosis. "So most probably it was a tubercular mass, or pelvic mass that responded to anti-tubercular drugs."

Four weeks after the "miracle", Besra was taken back to see Dr Mustaphi. He told her it was no longer necessary for her to have a laparotomy. He next saw her in May 1999, when an ultrasound revealed no sign of the tumour. Three months later, in August 1999, Besra was examined once more, at the Woodland Hospital in Calcutta, by a consultant surgeon and neurologist, Dr Mohan Seal. He confirmed that the tumour had totally vanished. After studying her case notes, Dr Seal testified that he could offer no medical explanation for her cure. "To say this is a miracle is technically difficult for us [as doctors]," he told me. "But I will say that to the best of my knowledge as a doctor this case is inexplicable, and I stand by that."

The final verdict – at least for the purposes of beatification – fell to the medical committee of the Congregation for the Causes for the Saints. This committee, made up of five doctors, has been chaired for the past 20 years by Professor Raffaele Cortesini, the head of surgery and transplantation at Rome University Medical School. In that time Cortesini has investigated more than 700 purported miracles, some 300 of which he has ruled as authentic, including innumerable tumours and recovery from brain death. The case of Monika Besra, he told me, was among the most convincing he had ever seen. After examining the medical records and witness statements, Cortesini concluded that Besra's case fulfilled all the conditions of the inexplicable: "suddenness, completeness and long-term stability".

"The patient was very critical," he said. "If the doctors couldn't even perform a laparotomy she must have been in a very bad state. In real terms,

INBRIEF

SEPTEMBER 7, 1966

Frank Taylor, Daily Telegraph staff correspondent, Cape Town
Dr Hendrik Verwoerd, South African Prime Minister and chief architect of the Apartheid policy, was assassinated by a white man seven minutes after taking his seat in the House of Assembly this afternoon.

He was stabbed four times in the chest by a Parliamentary messenger. Dr Verwoerd, who became Prime Minister in 1958 and survived a previous attempt on his life in 1960, was given heart stimulant injections, heart massage and the kiss of life.

The Prime Minister, a brown blanket over his body, was wheeled from the debating chamber on a stretcher. MPs and parliamentary officials seized the assassin, identified as Demetrio Tsafendas.

According to those MPs nearest to the Prime Minister when he was stabbed, Tsafendas did not utter a single word as he pulled a long stiletto from his belt, whipped off the sheath and plunged the blade into Dr Verwoerd.

Colleagues said Tsafendas had frequently declared that the present South African government was "doing too much for the coloureds and nothing for the poor whites".

A prostitute in Calcutta - on the street, uncared for

she was sent back to the Mother Teresa home to die. And yet she recovered."

The exact nature of the tumour – whether it was an ovarian cyst, carcinoma or a tubercular lesion – was not an issue, Professor Cortesini told me. Without a surgical specimen it would be impossible to draw a firm conclusion about the diagnosis. The central point of the case was the sudden and complete recovery.

Anti-tubercular drugs, he said, could not account for the sudden disappearance of the tumour in the time-frame described. And, "If the cyst had burst, the abdomen would have been filled with fluid; she would have developed peritonitis and a very adverse reaction. But the abdomen was not full of fluid. The mass disappeared overnight. She was completely cured. This was the crucial point." So was Cortesini convinced it was a miracle? "Surely. In all my life I have studied so many cases. When you have all the criteria fulfilled then you are sure."

While the healing of Monika Besra might make a compelling case for the "scientifically inexplicable", to believe it was a miracle requires the one thing that shaped the entire course of Mother Teresa's life: faith.

Among the documents considered by Father Kolodiejchuk were previously unseen letters written by Mother Teresa to priests who acted as her spiritual confessors, in which she described four mystical visions which she claimed to have had between September 1946 and October 1947, immediately prior to founding the Missionaries of Charity. In these letters she spoke of a dialogue that she claimed to have had with Christ, in which He instructed her to leave the Loreto convent in Calcutta where she was teaching children, and found her own order to serve the poor.

When Mother Teresa asked why she could not remain "a perfect sister of Loreto", Christ apparently reproached her. "Is your generosity grown cold. Am I a second to you? You did not die for souls. That is why you don't care what happens to them. Your heart was never drowned in sorrow as was my mother's. We both gave up all for souls – and you? You are afraid that you will lose your vocation, you will become secular, you will be wanting in perseverance." A year later she founded the MoC.

This vision of a suffering Christ was to become the backbone of Mother Teresa's mission. To minister to the sick and dying, she believed, was to minister to Christ on the cross. And to do this it was necessary oneself to live as "the poorest of the poor"; she insisted that her nuns own nothing more than three saris, a spoon and a dish, and follow lives of the utmost austerity.

But this identification with the pain of Christ led some to wonder, in the words of the religious writer Clifford Longley, "whether Mother Teresa wasn't just a little bit too much in love with the suffering of the poor, for their, or her, own good." "Her principle was that it was good for people to suffer," says Aroup Chatterjee, a Calcutta-born GP who wrote *The Final Verdict*, a book critical of Mother

Teresa, and who also gave evidence to the tribunal for the Cause. "There's a famous comment that a woman once said to her, 'Mother Teresa, I'm in great pain', and she replied, 'Jesus is kissing you', in great delight. What is not so often reported is that the woman replied, 'Tell Jesus to stop kissing me.'"

Archbishop D'Souza hotly disputes this interpretation of Mother Teresa's calling. "She certainly did not think that pain itself is good. But she did believe that if you had not accepted pain in your life, then you had not begun to work as a Missionary of Charity. She always said that she worried that the sisters would become social workers, doing things for the social needs of people. She said, I want you to do it because you see Christ in that person, and you will not be able to do that unless you first see Christ in your own pain and life."

Much of the criticism levelled against Mother Teresa arose from her dogmatic theological conservatism – a fanaticism, according to her sternest critics – which kept her organisation trapped in its role of ministering to the poor without ever addressing or challenging the causes of poverty, and which fuelled her adamant opposition to birth control in a society struggling against the compound problems of overpopulation.

But whatever the criticisms of Mother Teresa's work, they seem to pale into insignificance when you step through the door of Nirmal Hriday, the Home for the Destitute and Dying in Calcutta. As the first home she founded in Calcutta, Nirmal Hriday has a symbolic importance in the mythology of Mother Teresa. I had been here before, five years ago, but memory had not prepared me for the emotional assault the home brings. It comprises two wards, for men and women; large, gloomy rooms with whitewashed walls and hard stone floors. Both are filled with rows of metal beds, each one numbered and each one occupied. The criterion for admission is destitution; many of the patients are suffering from TB, malaria, malnutrition or simple yet potentially fatal neglect. These are people nobody else wants.

Not everybody comes here to die: some are fed, cared for and then go back to the streets – often to return again and again. But many never leave. When I arrived at 8.30am the first body was being loaded into an ambulance. Nuns and young volunteers moved among the beds; one man was being carefully shaved; another, too weak to move, was being washed in his bed. A young English volunteer – a gap-year student – spoon-fed a pathetically emaciated figure, then tenderly lifted him in his arms to carry him to the lavatory.

Nothing has changed here since Mother Teresa's death. "Mother is still here," Sister Georgina, the Sister Superior, told me. "We believe that." And here, at least, there is no question about her sanctity. "For us, and for thousands, Mother was a saint when she was alive," said Sister Georgina. "She was reflecting God's love. What else is a Saint?"

In a way, Nirmal Hriday seems to embody all the contradictions in Mother Teresa's life. The medical

INBRIEF

FEBRUARY 16, 1976
The Tate Gallery refused to disclose last night how much it had paid for a pile of 125 fire bricks which had twice been displayed as a work of modern art. The bricks are locked away in a storeroom.

Carl Andre, the American artist responsible, calls them low sculpture. He first created the design in 1965 in America where he put them on sale for about £4,000. No one bought them but in 1972 officials of the Tate saw a photograph of the bricks and offered to buy them.

By this time the sculptor had sold the bricks back to the yard from which he had bought them and the yard had closed down. But Mr Andre bought another 120 bricks, crated them up and sent them to the Tate with assembly instructions.

Sir Norman Reid, Director of the Tate, said last night: "We consider it a work of art. It has been on show twice but we are strictly limited on space so it has to take its turn. The situation will be improved when we get our new building opened next year." The Tate Gallery receives a grant of £500,000 a year from public funds.

Two children who live at a railway station

treatment is no more than adequate, the conditions spartan. In the laundry room nuns and volunteers trampled sheets in a trough of disinfected water, as if they were treading grapes. When I asked Sister Georgina whether a washing-machine wouldn't be more efficient, she replied that washing by hand "made the sheets cleaner", but finally allowed that "Mother believed washing-machines were for rich people". And yet despite all this – perhaps because of it – the Home for the Dying is a profoundly inspiring place.

At one point I noticed a nun pause over a man lying in bed, his breathing becoming ever fainter. He was little more than skin and bone. He was clearly about to die. She summoned two other sisters. One kneeled at his head, tenderly cooling his brow with a damp cloth; the second knelt at his side, holding his hand; the third dipped her finger in a cup of milk and gently moistened his lips. They began to pray. A priest appeared and read the last rites. Two more volunteers stopped their work and joined the group in prayers. It seemed irrelevant whether the man was Hindu, Christian or Muslim; whether the prayers were appropriate or not. On the streets, he would most likely have died alone, unnoticed. Here, he died with six people comforting him. Nothing else seemed to matter.

One of the criticisms levelled against Mother Teresa was that she was always more interested in conversion than in care (although it was not a charge ever voiced by those in her homes). In the wake of her remarkable recovery, Monika Besra was baptised as a Christian (although her husband was not). "I was not Christian before," she told me. "But I thought Mother has done this to me, and after returning home I would take Christianity and obey Mother as next to God." Indian newspapers, I said, had suggested that she had come under pressure from the Missionaries of Charity. "They have said this?" She shook her head. "Nobody can tell me what to believe, or stop me."

Sitting with Besra in her sister's village home, I was struck by a single thought. No matter what Mother Teresa's reputation for saintliness, the fact of her beatification ultimately rested on just one thing; the miracle of Monika Besra. This simple, illiterate tribal woman had, in a sense, become the most important person in the entire procedure. On her rested the entire weight of the Cause. I tried to formulate these thoughts as a question. Did she understand her importance in Mother Teresa's beatification? Did she even understand what beatification meant? She did not understand the question. Before her illness she had never heard of Mother Teresa, never heard of the Pope, never heard of Rome, never left the small area around her village where she had lived all her life. She knew nothing of all this. She knew only that she had been ill and now she was cured. That, she said, is why she came to Calcutta in June 1999.

Mother Teresa was beatified by Pope John Paul II on October 19, 2003.

NOT THE END OF THE WORLD

After the dot-com bubble and the Millennium Bug

Aeroplanes did not fall out of the sky when 2000 dawned. But, while terror and war throve, a new myth dominated the cinemas

In 1999 some people used to speak of "Y2K", meaning the year 2000. This was annoying; they had probably picked up K, meaning "thousand", from advertising-speak for salary levels. Some people also said things like: "No way you'll get me on a plane with that Millennium Bug on the loose," as *The Daily Telegraph* reported at the beginning of 1999.

Things turned out better than expected. Most people stopped saying "Y2K" and "No way", and the Millennium Bug did not bring aeroplanes raining from the skies or fill the streets with Hogmanay rioters battling to force their way into off-licences closed by the mysterious force of a computer malfunction.

"As much as £400 billion was spent around the world to eradicate the date-related computer glitch," reported Robert Uhlig, the *Telegraph*'s technology correspondent, on January 1, 2000. "But early indications from the Far East were that the Millennium Bug did not trigger an electronic meltdown as some experts had predicted." Traffic lights continued working, money remained in bank accounts. The Bug was a Boojum.

Something that did not go away in the new Millennium was the mobile phone. "From this week, having a mobile phone became the norm," the paper reported on July 8, 2000. "There are now 30.6 million mobile subscribers. That's more than one in two of the country's total population."

The machines caused much annoyance in public places, particularly trains, where commuter silence was constantly breached by loud announcements from mobile-users that they were on the train. Mobile phones rang, with a variety of ring-tones, in churches and concert halls, at funerals and plays. Young people began to spend more on new ring-tones than on pop-music singles. Soon the rumour got about that the signals from mobile phones caused brain damage; this merely confirmed half-formed suspicions.

Gordon Brown, the Chancellor of the Exchequer, made mobile telephone companies look less than brainy when they competed to pay him huge amounts of money. "The auction of next generation mobile phone licences smashed through the £20 billion level yesterday," reported George Trefgarne in April 2000, "as telephone companies continued their frenzied battle to win one of the five franchises." The auction was creating an embarrassment of riches for Mr Brown. "I am not going to say before the money comes in what should be done with it," he said.

The irony was that early versions of new generation mobiles did not work. Advertisements promised much joy from something new called "WAP" – wireless application protocol. Customers would be able to get the internet on their mobile phones. But it was too slow and kept crashing. The mobile phone companies, having bid so much for franchises, found their finances in a mess.

The stock market followed their downward trend, helped by the bursting of the dot-com bubble. Somehow, when shares were doing well in any case, people had formed the idea that shares connected with internet ventures would keep on going up even when the companies that issued the shares were making losses with no indication of future profit. In March 2000 the Nasdaq index reached its high point of 5048.62, more than double its nominal value the year before.

There was something wrong. "Eeh-oh," as the Teletubbies might have said. The Teletubbies in their time proved more reliable than telecoms. "Which is your favourite – Tinky Winky, Dipsy, Laa Laa or Po?" asked Serena Allott in the *Telegraph* in August 1997. By then everyone was supposed to know, even though "these big-bottomed, bright-coloured, babyish creatures with televisions in their tummies were designed to entertain the under-fours".

The Teletubbies were controversial, despite their anodyne adventures. One objection was that they did not talk properly. "Eeh-ho is a sound frequently used by babies," said a speech therapist who helped write the scripts.

Then the Teletubbies became cult viewing for students and teenagers who got up in the morning in time to catch their programmes. "*Melody Maker*, *The Face* and *Loaded* ran tributes to the show, DJs mixed Teletubby voices into club hits, Teletubby T-shirts (adult-sized) were rushed into production," the *Telegraph* reported, as if the children's cuddlies were more dangerous than the clubbers' drug ecstasy.

After the Millennium, after September 11, 2001, after Big Brother on television, and daily images of torture in Iraq, it became harder to worry about the controversial status of the Teletubbies.

There was though a discernably new spirit abroad in the first years of the century, years which had no collective name as the Nineties had had. "Seven years ago, an obscure New Zealand film-maker named Peter Jackson was given $300 million to make J.R.R. Tolkien's *Lord of the Rings* trilogy," wrote John Hiscock in the *Telegraph* in December 2003. "With a cast of mainly unknown actors, he

'I'm just ringing to say my test is going brilliantly'

LAST GOLDEN EAGLE IN ENGLAND

'Where R U? I'm feeling really * * * * * !'

'We call him The Dome; he's very expensive and we can't get rid of him'

More than half the country had a mobile phone by 2000. Their use by drivers was banned in 2003, by which year the Millennium Dome stood empty

filmed all three stories over a 15-month period. The first two – *The Fellowship of the Ring* and *The Two Towers* – both earned $1 billion or so each. The final chapter, *The Return of the King*, opening worldwide on December 17, is expected to enjoy even greater box-office success, and is tipped for the best picture Oscar."

It got it, and scooped 10 other Oscars. So it was that the film that dominated the Oscars in 2004 was not an old-style Hollywood number, or anything arty, even less something sexy.

Someone who had been quick to spot the change of public taste was the Anglo-Saxonist Tom Shippey, the author of the provocatively titled *J.R.R. Tolkien: Author of the Century*, published in 2000. Writing in *The Daily Telegraph* at the beginning of 2002 he described the trilogy of *Middle Earth* as "a myth of the woods and the stars; we are lost, bewildered in the woods, and look up at the heavenly stars. Death, a dominant theme in the myth, is the divide between earth and heaven.

"Leaving the world, even for Heaven, is not a perfect solution for Tolkien, or for his characters, or for us. We'd rather stay here, most of us, make this world a better one, re-establish England's green and pleasant land as the Shire. But we can't. Death prevents us, and the passage of time, and the shifts of power and politics.

"Tolkien speaks to that sense of loss and rather surprisingly he speaks not just to English people, but to people across the world. His images are universal, his myth is timeless. Up there are the stars, unaffected but unreachable; down here the wanderers, lost in shadow." At the same time "the one thing definitely wrong is giving up, losing hope".

The Millennium was not the end of the world. The Millennium Dome remained as a monument to the sillier aspects of modern life; the ruins of the World Trade Centre to the more wicked. Yet it was a world where it was no surprise when readers of *The Daily Telegraph* sent in a million pounds at Christmas time to send cows to African villages and Marie Curie nurses to help people dying of cancer.

Six decades on from his work to send toys for the children of the poor in the 1930s, William Deedes was manning the telephones to take the numbers of credit cards, which hadn't been invented when he began his fundraising work for good causes.

It was a strange outcome of the desire of an opinionated Colonel in 1855 to do something about the Crimean war by founding a newspaper.

'We're just running things until a peaceful and smooth transfer of power can be arranged'

'Who did you torture in the war, daddy?'

'Eh oh'

In 1997, the Teletubbies (left), divided the nation. In 2004 (top) Lord Black left the Telegraph, from Iraq came evidence of brutality, and the BBC sought a Director-General

Index

Picture credits

COVER Front, top, left to right: Topham, (detail) Bridgeman Art Library, Corbis, Hulton Archive/Getty Images, Tim Graham. Bottom, left to right: Teletubbies© and ™1996 Ragdoll Ltd, Licensed by BBC Worldwide Ltd, Hulton Archive/Getty Images, Mary Evans Picture Library, Hulton Archive/Getty Images, Corbis. Back, top, left to right: Camera Press/Jane Bown, Rex Features, Hulton Archive/Getty Images, a/c. Bottom, left to right: Hulton Archive/Getty Images, Corbis, Art Archive, Hulton Archive/Getty Images, Ian Jones. Inset: Tom Stockill.

P4 Hulton Archive/Getty Images. P6 Daily Telegraph. P7 Eddie Mulholland. P8 Tom Stockill. P10/11 (detail) The Royal Collection ©2004, Her Majesty Queen Elizabeth II. P12/13 Mary Evans Picture Library. P14 *Punch*. P17 ©Museum of London. P18–19 *Punch*. P20 Topham. P21 Hulton Archive/Getty Images. P22 Mary Evans Picture Library. P23 National Army Museum. P24/5 (detail) The Royal Collection ©2004, Her Majesty Queen Elizabeth II. P26/7 (detail) Bridgeman Art Library. P28 Royal Photographic Society Collection at the National Museum of Photography, Film and Television. P29 Hulton Archive/Getty Images. P30 Corbis. P31 top Courtesy of Stephen Halliday, *The Great Stink of London*, bottom (detail) Bridgeman Art Library. P32 Corbis. P33 Hulton Archive/Getty Images. P34–P35 DT. P36 top DT, middle Hulton Archive/ Getty Images, bottom DT. P37 DT. P38–39 Christopher Howse. P41 © Museum of London. P44 top CH, bottom The Salvation Army International Heritage Centre. P45 Mary Evans Picture Library. P47 (detail) Corbis. P49 Mary Evans Picture Library. P52 top ©Museum of London, bottom Art Archive. P53 Mary Evans Picture Library. P54 Corbis. P56 Hulton Archive/Getty Images. P58 a/c. P59 Reuters/Adlan Khasanov. P60 Mary Evans Picture Library. P61 Hulton Archive/Getty Images. P62 CH. P64 National Museum of Photography, Film and Television/ Science and Society Picture Library. P66 DT. P68 Hulton Archive/Getty Images. P69 Courtesy of Madame Tussauds. P72/3 Hulton Archive/Getty Images. P74 V+A Images/ Victoria and Albert Museum. P75 Heritage Image Partnership. P76 The Royal Borough of Kensington and Chelsea Libraries and Arts Service. P77 Ian Jones. P78 top Courtesy of the Royal Naval Museum, bottom Topham. P81 Bridgeman Art Library. P85 ©Museum of London. P87 Library of Congress, Prints and Photographs Division LC-USZC4-7134. P88/9 The Art Archive/ Russell Coates Art Gallery/Eileen Tweedy. P90 top Mary Evans Picture Library, bottom Hulton Archive/Getty Images. P91 CH. P92 top West Sussex

Solution to the first *Daily Telegraph* crossword, which appears on page 131

Record Office, bottom Corbis. P94 North Road Cycling Club. P95 Mary Evans Picture Library. P96/7 (detail) Bridgeman Art Library. P99 top Hulton Archive/Getty Images, bottom a/c. P100 CH. P103 top Hulton Archive/Getty Images, bottom CH. P104-105 CH. P106 (detail) Bridgeman Art Library. P107 Hulton Archive/Getty Images. P108 Mary Evans Picture Library. P108/9 National Museum of Photography, Film and Television/Science and Society Picture Library. P109 (detail) Mary Evans Picture Library. P110 top Topham, bottom a/c. P113 Hulton Archive/Getty Images. P116 CH. P117 Hulton Archive/Getty Images. P118 The Robert Opie Collection. P119 Hulton Archive/ Getty Images. P120/1 The National Portrait Gallery, London. P122 Peter Newark's Pictures. P123 top and bottom Mary Evans Picture Library. P124 -125 Hulton Archive/ Getty Images. P127 Mary Evans Picture Library. P128/9 DT. P130 DT. P131 DT. P132/3 Corbis. P133 DT. P134 Courtesy of BT Archives. P135 Corbis. P136/7 Hulton Archive/Getty Images. P138 Hulton Archive/ Getty Images. P139 Hulton Archive/Getty Images. P143 Rex Features. P145 top Topham, bottom a/c. P146 CH. P147 left Corbis, right AP. P148 Department of Manuscripts and Special Collections, University of Nottingham. P149 Westminster Cathedral Chronicle. P151 top DT, bottom Crown Copyright reproduced courtesy of Historic Scotland. P152/3 Hulton Archive/Getty Images. P154 Corbis. P155 Hulton Archive/Getty Images. P157 Bridgeman Art Library. P158 a/c. P159 Hulton Archive/ Getty Images. P160 Charlotte Cory. P161 top Corbis, bottom DT. P162 Hulton Archive/ Getty Images. P162/3 Norfolk County Library. P163 By permission of the Imperial war Museum, London. P164 Corbis. P165 DT. P166–172 Hulton Archive/Getty Images. P174/5 Taken from *The World at War* a/c. P175 Centre Press Agency. P176–179 Hulton Archive/Getty Images. P180 top Hulton Archive/Getty Images, middle/bottom The Advertising Archive Ltd. P181 Chiswick Library. P182/3 Corbis. P184 top Hulton

Archive/Getty Images, middle Corbis, bottom Topham. P185 Hulton Archive/Getty Images. P188/9 Steve Gillet. P190 top Hulton Archive/Getty Images, inset Corbis, bottom Topham. P191 Hulton Archive/Getty Images. P192 Corbis. P193 top Ian Cook (a/c), bottom DT. P194 DT, Ian Jones (Moore), Abbie Trayler-Smith (Newland). P195 Garland, Matt, ffolkes cartoons DT, P196 Peter Blake 2004, All Rights Reserved, DACS. P196/7 Hulton Archive/Getty Images. P197 Corbis. P198 Reproduced with the kind permission of the Royal Pavilion, Libraries and Museums (Brighton and Hove). P199 Adam Hart-Davis/Science Photo Library. P200 Corbis. P201–203 Hulton Archive/Getty Images. P204 Azadour Guzelian. P205 DT. P206 top Hulton Archive/Getty Images, middle/bottom DT. P207 Hulton Archive/Getty Images. P208 The Advertising Archive Ltd. P209 top The Advertising Archive Ltd, bottom Hulton Archive/Getty Images. P210 DT. P211–213 Hulton Archive/Getty Images. P215 Corbis. P216–217 top Hulton Archive/Getty Images, left Hulton Archive/Getty Images, top middle Rex Features, bottom middle Corbis. P218 illustration: Susanna Hickling. P218/9 Hulton Archive/Getty Images. P220 Hulton Archive/ Getty Images. P221 top Hulton Archive/Getty Images, bottom Topham. P222/3 Hulton Archive/Getty Images. P223 AP. P224 Popperfoto. P225 top Hulton Archive/Getty Images, bottom BBC Pictures/Devon Loch. P227 Popperfoto. P228/9 Hulton Archive/Getty Images. P231 Hulton Archive/Getty Images. P233 Estate of Daniel Farson. P234 Estate of Francis Bacon 2004, All Rights Reserved, DACS. P236 Hulton Archive/Getty Images. P237 top Hulton Archive/Getty Images, bottom Corbis. P238 Hulton Archive/Getty Images. P239 Hulton Archive/Getty Images. P240 Tim Graham. P241 Philip Hollis. P243 Magnum/Raghu Rai. P244–215 Abbie Trayler-Smith. P247 Magnum/Raghu Rai. P248–249 Abbie Trayler-Smith. P251 Teletubbies© and ™1996 Ragdoll Ltd, Licensed by BBC Worldwide Ltd.

a/c–awaiting claim
CH–Christopher Howse
DT–Daily Telegraph

P144 The despatch for *The Daily Telegraph* by Rudyard Kipling is reprinted by permission of A.P. Watt Ltd on behalf of the National Trust for Places of Historic Interest or Natural Beauty

The Daily Telegraph
Editorial Projects Director: George Darby
Creative Director: Clive Crook
Designer: Mark Hickling
Editorial Assistant and Picture
Co-ordinator: Lucy Verey
Additional picture research:
Suzanne Hodgart, Abi Patton
Production: Bill Owen, Roger Williams,
John Barton, Liza Millett